Ever since Adam and Eve
The evolution of human sexuality

MALCOLM POTTS trained originally as a physician and subsequently specialised in the control of human fertility and reproduction. He was the first Medical Director of the International Planned Parenthood Federation in London, England, before moving to North Carolina, America, to become President and Chief Executive Officer of the organisation Family Health International, where he pioneered some of the first efforts to slow the spread of AIDS in Africa. Always closely involved in teaching and research, he has co-written or co-edited 12 books including *An Atlas of Human Contraception* (1995), *Natural Human Fertility* (1988) and *Textbook of Contraceptive Practice* (1984). He is currently Bixby Professor in the School of Public Health at the University of California at Berkeley.

ROGER SHORT qualified as a veterinarian before embarking on a career in research and teaching that has encompassed many aspects of human and animal reproduction. Currently Wexler Professorial Fellow in the Royal Women's Hospital at the University of Melbourne, he previously established the British Medical Research Council's Unit of Reproductive Biology in Edinburgh and was its Director for 10 years before taking up a personal Chair in Reproductive Biology at Monash University in Melbourne, Australia, for 13 years. He has also been involved in the World Health Organization's Human Reproduction and AIDS prevention progammes. He is co-editor of the multivolume work *Reproduction in Mammals*, first published during the 1970s.

The authors have been friends for most of their professional lives. Both travel widely in the course of their work and between them they have visited over 100 countries around the world. The richness and diversity of the patterns of human reproduction that they have encountered have provided them with endless fascination and have been the inspiration behind this book.

Why do people have sex? Why are some people unfaithful? Why do some parents harm their children? And how different are humans from other animals? Eminent scientists Malcolm Potts and Roger Short view the broad panorama of human sexual and reproductive behaviour to reveal an inextricable mixture of nature and nurture – a combination of innate actions that have evolved over the millennia to adapt us to a nomadic, hunter–gatherer lifestyle, overlain by more recent cultural constraints imposed by civilization. For each of life's milestones – love, marriage, sexual intercourse, pregnancy, birth, puberty, parenting, menopause and death – they describe the biology behind our actions and consider how pressures imposed by various historical and contemporary cultures have further influenced our behaviour. By looking back at the past they attempt to make sense of the present, to see how and why these cultural modifications arose, how they have contributed to the richness of human sexual behaviour, and how our biological and cultural inheritance can help us to develop a more rational approach to the problems that now beset us – declining reproductive health and excessive population growth.

Ever since Adam and Eve

The evolution of human sexuality

Malcolm Potts and Roger Short

CAMBRIDGE
UNIVERSITY PRESS

PUBLISHED BY THE PRESS SYNDICATE OF THE UNIVERSITY OF CAMBRIDGE
The Pitt Building, Trumpington Street, Cambridge, United Kingdom

CAMBRIDGE UNIVERSITY PRESS
The Edinburgh Building, Cambridge CB2 2RU, UK. http://www.cup.cam.ac.uk
40 West 20th Street, New York, NY 10011-4211, USA. http://www.cup.org
10 Stamford Road, Oakleigh, Melbourne 3166, Australia

First published 1999

Printed in the United Kingdom at the University Press, Cambridge

Typeset in 10/13pt Linotype Sabon and ITC Franklin Gothic
in QuarkXPress 3.32 [HOBDEN GRAPHICS]

A catalogue record for this book is available from the British Library

Library of Congress Cataloguing in Publication data
Potts, Malcolm.
Ever since Adam and Eve:the evolution of human sexuality/
Malcolm Potts and Roger Short.
p. cm.
Includes bibliographical references and index.
ISBN 0 521 47042 0
1. Sex customs – History. 2. Sex – History. I. Short, R. V.
(Roger Valentine), 1930– . II. Title.
HQ12.P68 1999
306.7'09 – dc21 98 – 45618 CIP

ISBN 0 521 470420 hardback
ISBN 0 521 644046 paperback

To Aristotle, who first opened the door on the Western scientific understanding of human sexuality.

CONTENTS

PREFACE

We have been friends for over 40 years, one of us a physician and the other a veterinarian, with a shared interest in animal and human reproduction. Being biologists at heart, we have attempted to understand the human condition by looking at our species through the mirror of Darwinian evolution. We have also found this to be immensely helpful in our personal lives when confronted with love, marriage, parenthood, divorce and bereavement. Both of us have travelled widely in developed and developing countries, and we have found the richness and diversity of human sexual behaviour sometimes comic, often tragic, but always endlessly fascinating.

This book had its beginnings over 15 years ago when a Canadian television producer, Gail Singer, suggested that we try to write down some of our ideas. The first draft was written on a paper napkin in a restaurant in North Carolina. We benefitted greatly in those early years from the inputs of Winfield Best, and some of his ideas have survived into the final version. The book really began to take shape when the three of us were able to spend an unforgettable month working on it full time whilst guests of the Rockefeller Foundation at Villa Serbelloni, Bellagio, on Lake Como in northern Italy, and the Fikes Foundation provided us with some invaluable financial support.

After a brief flirtation with an American–British television consortium, which came to nothing but helped us focus our ideas, the two of us decided to start again and write the final version. Our aim throughout has been to look at human reproduction not under the high power of a microscope but rather through the wrong end of a telescope, so that we might see ourselves and the world around us in broader perspective.

Many people have helped us over the years, but we would particularly like to thank Lynne Hepburn, Kim Hayes, Yvonne Prevo and Megan Dumbar, who helped to type and retype innumerable versions of the manuscript. Many people generously donated photographs, including Dr Frans de Waal, Professors David Morley and Colin Morley, Mr Peter Stirling, Dr Kurt Benirschke, Professor L. Malcolm, Professor David Chivers and

Professor Marilyn Renfree. Dr Edward Stim of Yokohama, Japan, Professor William Potts of Caton, Lancaster, England, and Dr Martha Campbell of San Mateo, California, America, were tireless and meticulous commentators and critics of many aspects of the book. But pulling it all together, and checking and cross-checking all the details has been a task of Herculean proportions for Dr Maria Murphy and Mrs Sandi Irvine at Cambridge University Press, and we have been most grateful to Dr Alan Crowden for his constant support. Any infelicities remaining are our responsibility.

Finally, we would like to point to the special role played by our wives, Dr Martha Campbell, Professor Marilyn Renfree and the late Marcia Potts, who have done their best to help us to close the gap separating the perspectives of men and woman on the subject of sexuality. Inevitably we have written a male's eye view, but we hope it has been tempered with some female common sense.

M. Potts and R.V. Short

ACKNOWLEDGEMENTS

The authors are extremely grateful to the many art galleries, museums, picture collections and individuals who have given permission to reproduce paintings, photographs and engravings. These are credited beside the individual illustrations in the text.

Thanks are also due to the following publishers and individuals for permission to reproduced quoted material:

Charles Scribner's Sons: extracts from *The High Valley* by Kenneth E. Read.

Clarendon Press: extract from *The Journal and Letters of Fanny Burney*, vol. VI, ed. J. Hemlow.

Fourth Estate: extract from *The Diving Bell and the Butterfly* by J.-D. Bauby, tr. Jeremy Leggatt.

Kelly Stewart, extract from 'A gorilla gives birth', 1982.

National Committee for Gibran: extracts from *The Prophet* by Kahil Gibran.

Random House UK Ltd: extract from *Facing Mount Kenya, The Traditional Life of the Gikuuyu* by Jomo Kenyatta.

Sterling Lord Literistic, Inc.: extracts from *Demonic Males: Apes and the Origins of Human Violence* by Richard Wrangham and Dale Peterson.

Syracuse University Press: extract from *Khul Khaal: Five Egyptian Women Tell their Stories* by Nayra Atiya.

The Independent on Sunday: extract from 'Eating the placenta' by Sarah Lonsdale.

The Indonesian Times: extract of an article by Tahmina Ahmad.

University of Utah Press/School of American Research: extract from *Florentine Codex: General History of the Things of New Spain* by Fr Bernadino de Sahagun, tr. A. O. Anderson and C. E. Ribble.

W. W. Norton & Company: 'may I feel said he' is reprinted from COMPLETE POEMS 1904–1962, by E. E. Cummings, edited by George J. Firmage, by permission of W. W. Norton & Company. Copyright © 1991 by the Trustees for the E. E. Cummings Trust and George James Firmage.

INTRODUCTION

'If I were to give an award for the single best idea anyone has ever had, I'd give it to Darwin, ahead of Newton and Einstein and everyone else. In a single stroke, the idea of evolution by natural selection unifies the realm of life, meaning, and purpose with the realm of space and time, cause and effect, mechanism and physical laws. But it is not just a wonderful scientific idea. It is a dangerous idea.'
Daniel C. Dennett, *Darwin's Dangerous Idea,* 1995

Many people have sex in mind a great deal of the time. It is the mainspring of our existence and the very centre of our being. It is our unseen guide along all the walks of our lives. It is the triumph of life over death, and offers our genes the promise of immortality. Sex controls our relations inside and outside our families. It accounts for many of our murders, all of our rapes, and possibly most of our wars. Our bodies and our behaviour are the product of Darwinian evolution driven by a ruthless competition to reproduce.

Poets, ancient and modern, have tried to describe our sexual passions, lawyers to define them, and priests to control them. In our private lives, sex can bring great companionship, or utter loneliness. It can open a window to heaven or a trap door to hell. No wonder our sexual desire is the most feared of our emotions, and hence the most repressed. But as scientists we want above all to understand our passions and to explain them. In this book we look at the milestones in life's cycle: falling in love, marriage, sexual intercourse, conception, pregnancy, birth, puberty, parenting, divorce, menopause and death. Of each we ask: what are the biological foundations underlying our behaviour? How have various historical and contemporary cultures built on these foundations? What new insights can be gained into current problems, both to help the individual and for the community at large? We will argue that our behaviour is an inextricable mixture of nature and nurture. The facts do not support exclusive biological determinism, which would say that our fate is unalterably spelt out in our genes, or exclusive cultural determinism, which would maintain that there is little or nothing in our behaviour that our culture cannot change.

Our genes build our brains, our hormones colour our behaviour and our culture moulds these behaviours in an infinite variety of ways. Sex inspires our art, nourishes our literature and even transforms the very words it touches. Six hundred years ago, Geoffrey Chaucer used the verb swive for intercourse – 'Thus swived was this Carpenteris wyf.' In the seventeenth century the first vernacular version of the Bible called the book of Genesis, with some aptness, the book of Swiving. Today 'swive' has become the mechanical 'swivel'. Conversely, bland words can become sexually tainted: 'fuck' is merely the Norse word 'to push'. Innocent words can be misunderstood. Nineteenth century puritanical Americans could not bring themselves to call a male chicken a cock, so they called it a rooster, and while the British saw nothing wrong with the word cockroach, Americans prudishly abbreviated it to roach. Sex even invades our nursery rhymes. Grimm's story of the maiden who spins flax into gold is derived from an earlier, more earthy story where the maiden sits on a phallic stick, which in turn becomes an elf-like man call Rumpelstiltskin – rumpled skin on a stilt.

Since our tribal beginnings our music has taken sex for its theme. The hymns we sing in church take their name from the songs sung at ancient marriage ceremonies and hymn and hymen have the same linguistic root. Sexual overtones lurk in strange places. In a Roman court of law, a witness placed his hand on his testicles when he took an oath, so he 'testified'. The Bible recounts how, when the patriarch Abraham was dying, he called 'his eldest servant of his house... [and said to him] "Put, I pray thee, thy hand under my thigh: And I will make thee swear by the Lord, the God of heaven, and the God of the earth"' (Genesis 24:2–3). This is the coy way the King James' translation of the Bible describes the servant putting his hand on Abraham's testicles as a symbol of the truth. Indeed, the Bible is divided into the Old and New Testaments of gonadal truth.

Sex can be difficult and painful as well as joyous. It can bring ecstasy or confusion; it can be the culmination of love, or the destroyer of hope. But sometimes we create sexual conflicts where none should exist, and the history of ideas is replete with examples of where mild perturbations of thought have fed on themselves until they became destructive ideologies. The Early Fathers of the Christian Church and mediaeval thinkers made a terrible misinterpretation of natural creation. 'A beautiful woman,' wrote the thirteenth century theologian Bromyard, 'is a temple built over a sewer'.

Yet, for most people sex and love between a man and a woman are magical and mysterious, a compulsive engine of desire and at times an uncontrollable emotion. We seek our own sexual fulfillment, but we may hurt others and ourselves in the process. Rather sensibly, the Greeks did not have one word for love but two: *eros* for the passions of sexual love and *agape* for the non-sexual attachment we feel towards a fellow human being. *Eros* and *agape*, the Greek myths teach, can often be in conflict. And the Greeks also recognized same-sex love – a biological conundrum, but also a powerful reality.

Today, after thousands of years of religious proscription and centuries of psychological searching, we are at last beginning to reach a broad-based

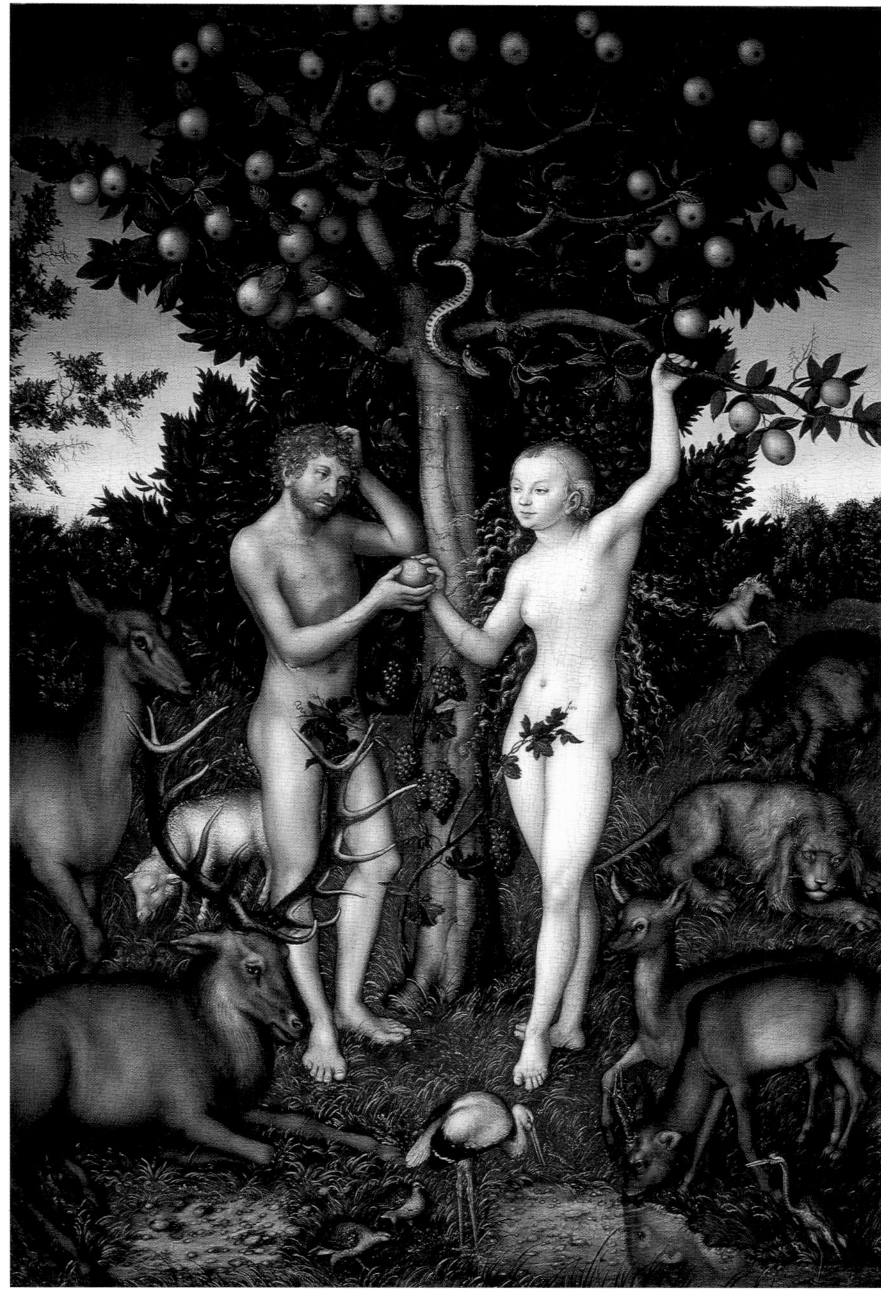

[Courtauld Institute Galleries.]

Adam and Eve, **Lucas Cranach the Elder, 1526.** Cranach the Elder's beautiful painting shows the serpent persuading Eve to tempt Adam with an apple, the fruit of the Tree of Knowledge. Saint Paul thought that this was Adam and Eve's transgression, the Original Sin, that brought death to the whole of humankind, and so baptism was necessary for the remission of this original sin. The serpent in the tree is no allegorical accident, as snakes are attracted to fruiting trees, knowing that it is a good place to catch birds and other animals. The grapes depict the fruit of their concealed loins, and a single stork waits patiently for the outcome. A stag and hind (*left*) and roebuck and doe (*right*) serve to accentuate the differences between the sexes.

Cranach also depicts an umbilicus on Eve. This problem was taken up in the nineteenth century by Philip Henry Gosse, a fundamentalist English preacher and Fellow of the Royal Society. In his book *Omphalos: An Attempt to Untie the Geological Knot*, published two years before Darwin's *The Origin of Species*, he argued that God created belly buttons in the Garden of Eden and fossil fish on the tops of mountains in order to test and fool humankind.

biological comprehension of our sexuality, thanks to a new evolutionary understanding of the selective forces that have made us what we are. We can now look at ourselves as part of, rather than standing apart from, the Animal Kingdom. Unfortunately, yesterday's myths often persist as strongly held beliefs, which are sometimes in head-on conflict with the new explanations that science provides.

An explosion of knowledge is occurring in the understanding of the evolution of sexuality, especially in the field of primate behaviour. Modern biology is providing increasingly convincing explanations of why men and women must make compromises if they are to enjoy a happy marriage. Explanations derived from biological evolution are being explored for the origin of language and to explain the human propensity for war. Biology can give a woman a child after the menopause, and help the fertile to limit the size of their families. It can provide new perspectives on teenage sexuality, or on cruelty to children. The revolution in our understanding of human sexuality is more profound and far reaching than many people realize.

We hope to show that there is little in the natural world that cannot be explained by biological evolution. Evolution accounts for, and is relevant to, all aspects of human anatomy, physiology and behaviour. Where the detective work comes in is in trying to decide which path we followed in the evolution of such complex behaviours as love, language, patriotism and parenting. Often, more than one scenario can be suggested. We must always remember that, even when certain evolutionary steps appear plausible, it does not necessarily mean things happened that way.

If we are to be captains of our souls and masters of our fates, we need an accurate chart of the waters in which we sail. Biological evolution is a powerful tool for examining our behaviour – in a way it is the ultimate tool – but its very power makes it difficult to use. Mistakes and misinterpretations are inevitable. Some could be dangerously misleading. Caution, caveats and humility are needed. But excitement, ingenuity and bold intellectual experiment are also in order. Our aim is not to say, 'This is necessarily the way we travelled to reach our present position in life'. We will assert, repeatedly and unequivocally, 'The vehicle that brought us here was Darwinian evolution'.

If we are to complete the civilization of sex and meet the great contemporary challenges in managing our daily lives, and our global ecology, then the mythology and superstition of the past must be laid aside, although with reverence and understanding, for without that background we would not have been able to reach our present insights.

1 BEGINNINGS

'And, since you know you cannot see yourself
So well as by reflection, I, your glass,
Will modestly discover to yourself
That of yourself which you yet know not of.'
William Shakespeare, *Julius Caesar* (Act I, Scene II)

The Ape and the Skull, **Reinhold, 1892.** This statuette, on display in the Zoology Department in the University of Edinburgh, Scotland, is one of a small number of bronze castings made. The pedestal is inscribed with the words 'eritis sicut deus' [you will both be like God], a modification of the words of the serpent to Eve (Genesis 3:5). An identical statue is on Lenin's desk in the Kremlin in Moscow; Lenin was a great admirer of Charles Darwin.

[Department of Zoology, University of Edinburgh.]

Charles Darwin convinced most thinking people that we have evolved by natural selection from other primates. But so keen have we been to distance ourselves from the animals that we have sought, in the words of the Bible, 'to have dominion over them'. We hunt them, shoot them, farm them, eat them and sometimes exploit our relationship with them to conduct medical research. Yet we have been remarkably slow to realize that the behaviour of these same primates may help us to understand ourselves. We have been incredibly reluctant to take an analytical look at the one thing we have been consistently curious about over the millennia – sex and love.

Darwin's great work *The Origin of Species by Means of Natural Selection, or the Preservation of Favoured Races in the Struggle for Life*, published in 1859, saw evolution as a dynamic process made possible by natural selection and the survival of the fittest. Darwin also realized that mere survival was not enough; unless the favoured few were fertile, and capable of passing on their characteristics to succeeding generations, natural selection could have no long term value. Thus Darwin came to appreciate that reproductive success was the key to the origin of species. At a stroke he ended millennia of poetic speculation and philosophical reasoning about the meaning of life. Nature judges us by our reproductive success, so that it is not surprising, as Sigmund Freud emphasized fifty years later, that every aspect of our being is touched in some way by sex.

Evolution has created the amazing diversity of living things that surrounds us, and it has also tailored our body and our behaviour to ensure that we have the maximum chance of reproducing and passing on our genes to the next generation. One look at a chimpanzee or gorilla tells us that we have many physical characteristics in common with them. But the very idea that we may also have the same basic behavioural drives as our great ape cousins is much more disturbing, even distasteful. Today, more Americans believe in extra-terrestrial visitors than in evolution.

Prompted by Thomas Robert Malthus' *An Essay on the Principles of Population* (1798), Darwin saw the significance of the fact that plants and animals tend to produce more offspring than normally survive to the next generation. He therefore proposed that it was only those individuals best adapted to the rigours of their environment that would be most likely to survive and pass on their genes. This simple concept has been the single most important insight in the history of biology, and no observation has ever been made in natural history to challenge Darwin's basic thesis, although a great deal has been discovered to reinforce his great vision. Darwin had to guess at the machinery of inheritance, while today we understand the structure of DNA and the way in which this amazing molecule carries and replicates genetic information.

Before Darwin, almost all educated people believed in a divine creator and in humankind's unique separation from all other animals. In 1828, the theologian William Paley argued that the very wonder and complexity of creation was proof of the existence of God, just as finding a watch on the ground is evidence of the existence of a watchmaker. In our time the Oxford zoologist Richard Dawkins has turned this metaphor around, calling evolution the 'Blind Watchmaker'. We are an improbable accident, but one that took billions of years to occur. Over the vastness of the geological time scale we have separated from our cousins the great apes relatively recently, a mere four to seven million years ago.

Malthus, Darwin and Mendel

Robert Malthus was a shy young bachelor don in Cambridge in 1798, when he published his famous pamphlet *An Essay on the Principle of Population...* (see p. 286). He pointed out that, if unchecked, the human population would continue to increase geometrically in an exponential manner, and would soon outstrip the world's ability to feed it. He predicted that the population would always expand to the limits of subsistence, so that it would ultimately be held in check by famine, war and pestilence. The only way he could see of averting this deteriorating situation was by late marriage and sexual restraint before marriage. Malthus died on 23 December 1834.

Charles Darwin read Malthus' *Essay* for the first time on 28 September 1838. It made a deep impact, for it provided Darwin with the missing link in his chain of thought: the overproduction of individuals could be compensated for by selective mortality of the least fit. Darwin eventually published *The Origin of Species* in 1859.

Darwin's works were purchased by Gregor Mendel, a monk living in the monastery of Brno in Czechoslovakia. He was studying the hybridization of plants, particularly the garden pea, in an effort to understand the basic principles of heredity. He did not publish his results until 1866, and Darwin was unaware of them. But it was Mendel's discovery of the particulate units of inheritance, or genes, that provided an understanding of the mechanism by which the benefits of natural selection, operating on the parents, could be transmitted to their offspring.

Mendel's work was published in an obscure journal, and remained unknown until three European botanists obtained independent confirmatory evidence of his findings in 1900, only to discover that Mendel had trodden the path thirty-four years earlier.

The primal hermaphrodite? A Greek bust (AD 100 – 200) showing the faces of the gods Dionysos and Silenus. The Greeks believed that the first human was half male, half female, and was cleaved by the gods into the two separate sexes.

Predictably, *The Origin of the Species* raised a heated debate in its time that still flashes into flame even today. In 1996 the Tennessee State Legislature narrowly defeated a bill to ban the teaching of evolution in that state. The nineteenth century debate over human evolution was fought largely by anatomists and anthropologists in their search for the so-called 'missing link' between us and our presumed anthropoid ancestors. The most exciting application of evolutionary theory in the second half of the twentieth century may well have been its application to the study of animal behaviour, and the lessons it has taught us about human behaviour. Human evolution is no longer an academic discussion about our origins; it helps to explain our pillow talk and our daily lives, and gives some intimation of our ultimate fate as a species. By explaining where we come from, Darwin also helped to explain who we are.

Creation myths

Human beings have always been concerned with life's entrances and exits, whether it be at the level of the birth or death of the individual, or the origin and destiny of our species. We have struggled long and hard to attain our present level of understanding, which is neither universally accepted nor anything like complete. Genesis, the first book of the Bible, begins with an account of the Creation of the Earth, followed by the creation of Eve from the primordial Adam in the Garden of Eden. Although we are all conversant with the idea that Eve was formed from Adam's rib, this appears to be due to a mistranslation of the early Hebrew text, where the word used for rib was *zela*. However, a more appropriate translation of *zela* would be 'side', as in the side of a mountain. Thus it seems likely that the true intent of the Old Testament was to describe the primordial Adam as a gynandromorph, male down one side of the body and female down the other. God cleaved the two apart and, since there was one male for every female, this accounted for the Church's belief in monogamous marriage. The Christian marriage ceremony itself was seen as a symbolic indissoluble reunion of these two halves, and hence the statement in the marriage service that 'those whom God hath joined together, let no man put asunder'.

The ancient Greeks believed human beings were originally hermaphrodites with four hands and four feet and two faces looking in opposite directions. Such individuals were so strong and mighty that they represented a threat to the gods, so Zeus decided to enfeeble them by cutting them in half, but immediately the two halves embraced one another. 'Each of us when separated', wrote Plato in the *Symposium*, 'having one side only like a flat

Creation of Adam, **Michelangelo, 1510.** Michelangelo, in this famous painting on the ceiling of the Sistine Chapel in the Vatican, depicts an umbilicus on Adam, and there is a veiled hint of one on God as well. At a time when people believed in the literal truth of the Bible, this could have been interpreted as heresy.

[Vatican Museums and Galleries / The Bridgeman Art Library.]

fish, is but the tally-half of a man, and he is always looking for the other half'. That the other half could even be of the same sex was the Greeks' explanation for homosexuality.

All societies had their creation myths, but they did not completely satisfy enquiring minds. Aristotle was the first to take the giant step of trying to understand human beings, and in particular human reproduction, by looking systematically at other animals. His books on the *History of Animals* and the *Generation of Animals* are amazing for their breadth of knowledge and factual accuracy. Aristotle was born in about 384 BC at Stagira in Thrace, and died in Athens in the year 322 BC. His most productive years were spent at the Academy in Athens, where he was a pupil of Plato and subsequently tutor to the young Alexander the Great. Aristotle concluded that the human embryo was produced by the 'seed' of the male, which was merely nurtured by the 'soil' or menstrual blood, which did not contribute materially to the embryo itself. Likewise Aeschylus, the Greek playwright, in *Orestes* said; 'The so-called offspring is not produced by the mother. She is no more than nurse, as it were, of the newly conceived fetus. It is the male who is the author of its being.' When Moses exhorted the Israelites to take revenge on the heathen Midianites (Numbers 31:17–18) he ordered,

> *Now therefore kill every male among the little ones, and kill every woman that hath known man by lying with him.*
> *But all the women children, that have not known a man by lying with him, keep alive for yourselves.*

It all made sense in a society that saw the woman as contributing nothing material to the next generation, merely serving as an incubator to facilitate the development of the male's seed into an egg, embryo and fetus.

The search for understanding

What shaped the embryo? How did it grow and develop? Aristotle postulated a life force or soul which both formed and gave life to the embryo. 'What the male contributes to generation is the form and the efficient cause, while the

Wind eggs

Aristotle believed that all eggs were products of conception, formed by coagulation of the seed of the male within the womb. How was it then that hens which had never associated with the cockerel could still lay eggs? Aristotle got around the difficulty by calling them 'wind eggs', observing that 'wind eggs are called by some zephyr eggs, because at spring-time henbirds are observed to inhale the breezes'. Did Aristotle really imagine that a puff of wind into the vagina could coagulate into an egg? He was concerned about the state of ensoulment of these eggs and concluded that, since wind eggs could go bad, they must have participated in life and therefore they must at least possess a vegetative soul.

Two thousand years later, William Harvey, the discoverer of the circulation of the blood, also got into difficulties over wind eggs. His wife kept a tame parrot for many years, to which she was quite devoted; it is almost the only thing that Harvey has to say about his wife. Such was the bird's excellence in singing and talking that it was naturally assumed to be a male. When it died, Harvey performed an autopsy and found an egg in the uterus. He concluded that the hapless bird expired because it was 'corrupt for want of a male'.

Harvey's patron, King James I of England kept a menagerie, where there was a cassowary that had been sent to him from Java by Prince Maurice of Orange. The bird was thought to be a male, until one day an egg was found in its cage. Harvey dissected this and pronounced it to be a 'wind egg'. He therefore predicted that the bird would soon die in similar circumstances to his wife's parrot. It did, and on autopsy it did indeed have a decomposing egg in its uterus. No wonder he became a fervent believer in Aristotelian concepts.

But wind eggs still have some surprises, even to this day. Virgin chickens and turkeys do indeed occasionally lay unfertilized 'wind eggs' that undergo spontaneous parthenogenetic development leading to hatching and the eventual production of a few adult, fertile, male offspring with a full complement of chromosomes – a truly immaculate conception, and living proof that fertilization cannot be regarded as the moment when life begins. It is interesting that the Catholic Congregation for the Doctrine of the Faith decreed in 1987 that a new individual comes into existence at the time of union of male and female pronuclei to create the zygote – an interesting example of how sophisticated scientific concepts are beginning to inform religion.

[The National Gallery, London.]

***Cupid Complaining to Venus*, Lucas Cranach the Elder, *ca.* 1530.** In this painting, Cranach the Elder discreetly depicts the dilemma of Saint Augustine's original sin, sexual intercourse. Bees are stinging Cupid as he steals a piece of honeycomb, and he complains to Venus, his mother. The inscription reads 'As Cupid was stealing honey from the hive, a bee stung the thief on the finger. So we seek transitory and dangerous pleasures which we must mix with sadness and which bring us pain'.

female contributes the material,' wrote Aristotle. He believed that all forms of life were derived from eggs, formed by coagulation of the male's semen within the female. Since a hen's egg left on the table would eventually putrefy, it must once have been living matter, and so he thought that all eggs must be endowed with a Vegetative Soul that gave form to the developing embryo. Animals he postulated also had a Sensitive Soul, since he reasoned that there could be no movement without sensation. The onset of 'quickening', when the mother first becomes aware of fetal movements, was regarded as synonymous with the second stage of ensoulment. Finally came the Rational Soul, a concept Aristotle admitted was the most difficult of all to discuss. The Rational Soul conveyed the ability to reason and to think, attributes which, until recently, all philosophers regarded as uniquely human; all other animals merely possessed imagination. Thus the Rational Soul was regarded as Divine, separating us from all other animals. It was thought to enter the body from without. Aristotle did not even hazard a guess as to when in development this might be.

Aristotle's interpretation of reproduction had long lasting and far reaching consequences for Western culture that persist today. In the thirteenth century, Saint Thomas Aquinas accepted these Aristotelian concepts about the timing of prenatal body and soul development in their entirety, concluding that 'in the generation of man, first comes the living thing, then the animal, and finally the man'. Thus the early Catholic Church raised fewer moral objections to abortion than to infanticide, and even counselled against baptizing a baby too early lest it had not acquired its Rational Soul. Then in 1588 Pope Sixtus V attempted for the first time to outlaw abortion, equating the killing of even an inanimate, unformed embryo with murder. However, his ideas were immediately overruled by his successor, Pope Gregory XIV in 1591, who reverted to the concept that the fetus had to be '*formatus et animatus*' (formed and animated) before abortion could be equated with murder. It was not until 1869 that Pope Pius IX declared abortion at all stages of pregnancy to be a sin punishable by excommunication. Since Aristotle taught that male semen was a pure essence capable of striking life into formless retained menstrual blood and perfecting the work of generation, the early Fathers of the Church held that to waste the semen outside the body was an abomination. Therefore, male withdrawal from the vagina before ejaculation (coitus interruptus) for contraceptive reasons was strongly condemned – and in some quarters still is.

Not surprisingly, the myths and legends we have built up about human sex and reproduction continue to influence our moral judgements. By the time of the flowering of Muslim theology, the role of the ovaries in

The Homunculus

Spermatozoa were first seen by the Dutchman, Anthony van Leeuwenhoek, in 1678. (He thought they were parasites invading semen and called them spermatozoa – animals in the semen.) The mammalian egg is much larger than the sperm, but still microscopic and difficult to find, and it was not seen until 1827, by the German microscopist Karl von Baer. Mammalian fertilization was not described until 1875 by the Belgian Edouard van Beneden.

Speculation therefore ran rife in the eighteenth century. There were Ovists, who in line with Rueff's drawings in the sixteenth century, thought that the new individual was solely derived from an egg made by the female, although they wrongly imagined that the large graffian follicle (a fluid-filled sac surrounding the egg) represented the egg itself. There were Animalculists, who thought that the preformed individual might exist in the head of each spermatozoon, as depicted in this drawing by Hartsoeker of a human sperm. Laurence Sterne gives a whimsical account of the homunculus in his jerky, idiosyncratic, impertinent book *The Life and Opinions Tristam Shandy* (1760).

> *The minutest philosophers, who, by the by, have the most enlarged understandings (their souls being inversely as their inquiries) show us incontestably, that the HOMUNCULUS is created by the same hand, – engender'd in the same course of nature, endowed with the same locomotive powers and faculties with us – That he consists, as we do, of skin, hair, fat, flesh, veins, arteries, ligaments, nerves, cartilages, bones, marrows, brains, genitals, humours and articulations; – is a Being of as much activity – and in all senses of the word, as much as truly our fellow creature as my Lord Chancellor of England. – He may be benefited, he may be injured, – he may obtain redress; – in a word he has all the claims and rights of humanity.*

Sterne was making an eighteenth century in-joke but not everyone laughed and the idea of a little man curled up in the heads of every sperm helped to persuade some theologians that fully formed human life was present from the very beginning of pregnancy. Some even asked whether Adam's sperm had little men inside little men, like a set of Russian dolls, for all the generations that were to follow? It is the homunculus which convinced theologians that 'human life' could be present from the beginning of pregnancy, and this view was the ancestor of today's Right-to-Life movement, which seeks to accord full adult rights to the embryo from the moment of its conception.

The true scientific story is more subtle and it is still unfolding. Recently, we have come to understand how the DNA of the spermatozoon and the egg come together after fertilization in a process known as syngamy. The paternal and maternal sets of DNA are initially 'imprinted' (coded) with their sex of origin, so that the male's nuclear DNA preferentially makes the placental membranes, and the female's makes the embryo.

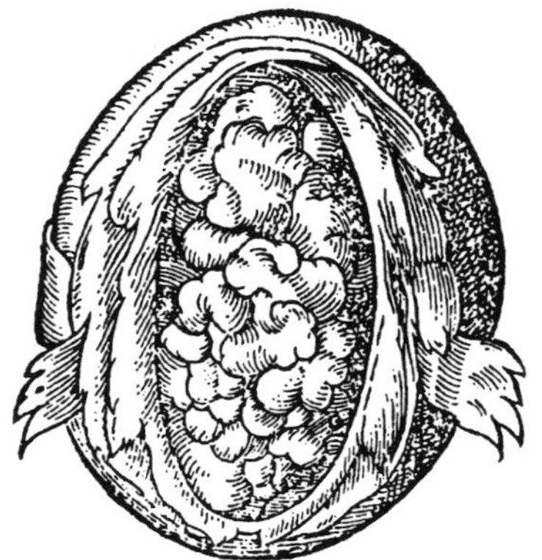

Rueff, 1554

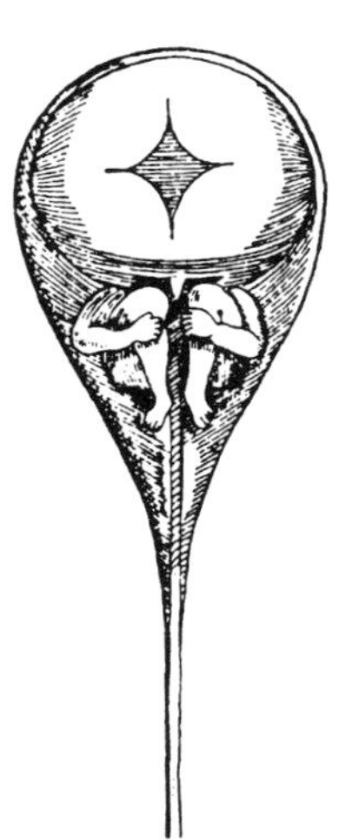

Hartsoeker, 1694

reproduction was beginning to be recognized. The sayings of the Holy Prophet Mohammed recorded in the Hadíth include a verse saying God 'created both the semen of the man and the semen of the woman. The Man's semen is thick and forms bones and tendons. The woman's semen is fine and forms the flesh and blood'. Once it was recognized that women also contributed something to the make-up of the embryo, then male semen was seen to be incomplete on its own, so it did not matter if it was lost by masturbation, or male withdrawal. Thus modern Islam finds artificial contraception morally permissible, while the Vatican still condemns all forms of modern family planning.

The origins of reproductive science

The study of reproduction has usually lagged behind that of other bodily systems, not because it is less important but because it is technically more difficult and emotionally more challenging to ask the right questions and accept unexpected answers. For one thing, reproduction is discontinuous and for another there is great physiological variation between animals, particularly in relation to the early stages of pregnancy. The English physician William Harvey, famous for his discovery of the circulation of blood in 1628, ran into both these problems when he turned his scientific skills to the study of mammalian reproduction. Towards the end of his life in 1651, he published his great work *De Generatione Animalium*, in which he set out to discover by observation and experiment, both with hen's eggs and with deer, precisely how reproduction came about. Relying on Aristotle, he was looking for a large egg-like structure in the deer's uterus at rutting time in the autumn, and so he failed to recognize the early conceptus, which in deer grows from an invisible speck to a thin ribbon of tissue that attaches to the walls of the uterus long before the embryo proper can be seen with the naked eye. Harvey was baffled; in despair he was forced to conclude that 'The foetus doth neither proceed from the seed of male and female emitted in coition, not yet from any commixture of that seed (as the Physitians will have it) nor yet out of the Menstruous blood, as Aristotle conceits.'

In contrast to the ancient lineage of our ideas about the form and function of the reproductive organs, the study of the complexities of reproductive behaviour developed much later, and from a very different source. In the Middle Ages, falconry and hunting were the sport of kings, and a courtier's standing depended in part on the skill of his huntsmen in providing a good day's hunting for the ruling monarch. This meant that the huntsman had to be a skilled observer of the behaviour of his quarry. Huntsmen became our first

Human sexual intercourse. 'I display to men the origin of their existence', wrote Leonardo da Vinci on this magnificent drawing (*Coition of Hemsected Man and Woman*), made in 1492. The fact that he was a homosexual may be why he added the comment 'The act of coition and the members that serve it are so ugly that, if it were not for the beauty of the faces and liberation of the spirit, the species would lose its humanity'.

Following Aristotelian tradition, it was believed that the spinal cord, not the testis, was the source of semen – both are white and creamy, and the idea that the ejaculate came from various parts of the body and was transmitted to the penis by spinal nerves is faithfully depicted by Leonardo. This multifocal origin for semen was also used to explain why an orgasm appears to involve the whole body.

Aristotle also drew a duct connecting the uterus to the nipple. This was because he believed that milk was made from menstrual blood, since women who were lactating did not menstruate – the phenomenon we now call lactational amenorrhoea.

naturalists. By the sixteenth century, accurate accounts of the sexual behaviour of the beasts of the chase, including deer, wild boar, badgers, otters, foxes and hares began to appear. The mediaeval huntsmen knew venison was at its best when the stag was in 'pride of grease' immediately prior to the rut. For those seeking an assured supply of venison throughout the year, some of the seasonal changes in carcass quality could be avoided by castration of the stag to produce a 'havier'.

The era of European colonization introduced the Western world to a whole range of strange new animals. The colonial hunter, of military rather than scientific upbringing, regarded it as his duty to conquer these savage herds of brute beasts with the bullet, sending their skulls and skins back as trophies for his home or, when guilt began to assail him, as specimens to fill the new museums of natural history. The big game hunter relied on the skills of the local natives to bring him within range of his quarry, but he seldom thought to question them about their intimate knowledge of the animal's behaviour. He rarely paused to watch the animal himself before squeezing the trigger and obliterating it forever. Skeletons and skins we can preserve, but behaviour, that finely tuned interaction between the animal and its environment crafted by millions of years of evolution, departs on death.

In the laboratories of the nineteenth century, physiologists began to experiment by removing and transplanting various glands. A. A. Berthold grafted testicles from a young cock into a castrated bird. It was the first true endocrine experiment and the growth of the comb, so characteristic of the male bird, was duly restored. By the end of the nineteenth century, Charles-Édouard Brown-Séquard, the doyen of European physiologists, went a step further and began, at the age of 72, to inject himself with an extract of guinea pig testicles. He claimed he felt twenty years younger. The *méthode séquardienne* was taken up by older men eager to rekindle the splendid vigour of youth and restore hair to balding heads. A little later Eugene Steinach of Vienna began promoting vasectomy to salvage lost youth. He claimed 'the general rejuvenating effect has been sufficiently observed both in animals and man to remove any doubt about it'.

Sexual selection

Darwin understood with great clarity that the sexual behaviour in the mind of the animal was as important to evolution as the plumbing of its reproductive system. But it is easier to measure a skull than it is to record behaviour and the range of scientific observations on animal behaviour that Darwin had to look at was limited, especially in primates. In April 1847 an American missionary,

T. S. Savage was unexpectedly detained on the Gaboon River in West Africa while *en route* home and he stayed with a resident clergyman. His host, the Rev. J. L. Wilson showed him the skull of a large primate he had obtained from the natives, and this was how the Western world first became aware of the existence of the gorilla. Savage persuaded Wilson to ask the natives to collect additional specimens and to act as interpreter while he questioned them about the animal's behaviour. Neither man had ever seen a gorilla, alive or dead; they handled only the bones. The natives, however, accurately observed that 'one adult male is seen in a band; but when the young males grow up, a contest takes place for the mastery, and the stronger by killing or driving out the other, establishes himself as the head of the community.' The scientific paper Savage wrote with J. Wyman, then Professor of Anatomy at Harvard University, provided Charles Darwin with some key information.

Pondering the ways in which natural selection ultimately might lead to reproductive success, Darwin developed the concept of sexual selection in *The Descent of Man, and Selection in Relation to Sex* (1871). In it, Darwin makes several references to Savage and Wyman's account of gorilla behaviour. He realized that the degree of sexual selection is greatly influenced by the mating system. In a monogamous mating system, in which one male pairs

Darwin's voyage of discovery

Charles Darwin set off on a voyage around the world on the 240 ton *HMS Beagle* in 1831. A generation later, in 1859 he published *The Origin of Species*. During the clash between Darwin's supporter Thomas Henry Huxley and his opponent Bishop Samuel Wilberforce during the 1861 British Association Meeting in Oxford, Wilberforce asked whether Darwin was descended from an ape on his grandmother's or his grandfather's side – hence the cartoon. Huxley countered, '"If the question is put to me, would I rather have a miserable ape for a grandfather or a man highly endowed by nature and possessed of great means of influence, and yet who employs those faculties and that influence for the mere purpose of inducing ridicule into a grave scientific discussion – I unhesitatingly affirm my preference for the ape." Whereupon there was unextinguishable laughter among the people.'

[*The London Sketch Book*, 1874 / Mary Evans Picture Library.]

with one female for life, as in gibbons or marmoset monkeys, the competition between the males for access to the females would be equal to, and counterbalanced by, the competition between females for access to males. In polygynous mating systems, on the other hand, where one male mates with several different females, as does the gorilla or the lion, the competition between males for access to females would be enhanced, leading to the exaggerated development of weapons of offence and defence used in inter-male aggressive encounters.

It was, and still is, difficult to accept that Darwin's logic applies to human beings as well as to stags and gorillas. To Aristotle and the early Fathers of the Christian Church, human beings appeared to be separated from all other animals by an unbridgeable chasm. God, after all, had given Adam and Eve 'dominion over the fish of the sea, and over the fowl of the air and over every other living thing that moveth upon the earth' (Genesis 1:28). All creation myths derive their authority by claiming to describe the action of the gods, and most also seek to define and explain moral behaviour in the context of the origin of the world in which we live. Evolution is a history of biological consequences, not a story of forward planning to a logical design. Given time and the tiny incremental steps making up evolution, the end result often looks remarkably well designed; but, as we will see, biology also has its compromises and its flaws.

Science, unlike mythology, carries no hidden moral messages. Science does not tell us what is good and what is bad, only how, by observation and experiment, we understand how things came to be the way they are. Although misappropriated as a false foundation for 'social Darwinism', evolution is neutral on which social structures to accept and which to reject. To make value judgements we must use the brain evolution has bequeathed to us. Nevertheless it is far nicer to imagine that we are close to the angels rather than descended from the monkeys, and the idea that we can learn more about human sexuality and social organization by studying apes in the jungle than we can by reading the scriptures still remains a difficult idea for many people to accept.

Throughout the twentieth century an increasingly persuasive body of knowledge and a valuable set of methodologies were developed to study behaviour in other animals, particularly by ornithologists. The work came to be known as ethology, from the Greek *ethos*, meaning 'character'. The term was attached to animal behaviour by the French zoologist Isidore Geoffroy Saint-Hilaire in the same year that Darwin published *The Origin of Species*, 1859. But, for well over a century after Savage and Wyman, biologists were privy to scant additional information on the behaviour of primates in the

[Frans de Waal.]

Pygmy chimpanzees (bonobos) copulating. Bonobos are found only in the Democratic Republic of Congo (formerly Zaïre) and have become separated from the main chimpanzee population by great river systems. In contrast to other chimpanzees, male and female bonobos regularly mate in the ventro-ventral, 'missionary', position like humans, and are the only other primate to do so. Like us, they also seem to use sex for pleasure, frequently copulating over much of the female's menstrual cycle, and not just around the time of ovulation. Females sometimes indulge in ventro-ventral copulation with other females, masturbating to orgasm, although they remain strongly heterosexual.

wild. The subspecies of chimpanzee called the pygmy chimpanzee or bonobo was not even recognized until 1928.

Anyone who studies primate behaviour must be prepared to spend thousands of hours in patient observation. Imagine how long a chimpanzee studying human sexuality would have to watch before seeing a marriage, a seduction or a rape. The few troops of apes and monkeys left in today's crowded world necessarily live in remote areas, not yet touched by the greed and destructiveness of humankind. Ethology is surely a labour of Hercules and it must often be conducted in extreme physical discomfort, pestered by biting insects, in self-imposed exile from humanity and the comforts of civilization. Occasionally the work is life threatening, as witness the kidnapping of some of Jane Goodall's researchers studying chimpanzees in Tanzania, or the murder of Dian Fossey in Rwanda. It is interesting that it was men such as Thomas Henry Huxley who studied evolutionary anatomy so assiduously in the nineteenth century, while it has been women, such as Jane Goodall, Biruté Galdikas, Sarah Hdry, Caroline Tutin, Dian Fossey and Kelly Stewart, who have taken the lead in observing primate behaviour in the twentieth century. Poignantly, it is only now that we are obtaining the most interesting and useful information, at a time when the natural environment of nearly every primate species is being destroyed. Orangutans have lost 80 per cent of their forest habitat in a mere twenty years.

[The Associated Press Ltd.]

Smiling submission. The sociable or submissive primate often grins and bears its teeth – humans and chimpanzees alike. Chimpanzees, like humans, also greet one another by touching hands. Women of the Fulah tribe in Africa greet strangers by presenting their buttocks whilst bowing deeply, just like some monkeys do. When General MacArthur entered Tokyo after the defeat of Japan in 1945, his officers thought the Japanese troops who turned their backs on his procession were showing vulgar disrespect. But, knowing their culture better, MacArthur recognized that they were acknowledging defeat and humiliation.

Perspectives

Just as the dualism between body and soul, so imprinted in our Western way of thought, has no basis in biology, neither does the distinction between human beings and animals. Yet we seek constantly to distance ourselves even from our closest living relatives, the chimpanzee and gorilla. Any attempt to describe their behaviour in human terms is dismissed as anthropomorphic; to call another human being an ape is taken as an insult, although the study of our DNA shows that human beings and chimpanzees are more closely related to one another than are chimpanzees and gorillas. We want to regard all animals as 'lower' forms of life, more 'primitive' than ourselves, or 'less highly evolved', as if becoming human were the ultimate goal of all species, the pinnacle of achievement for life on Earth. It was Alexander Pope in the eighteenth century who stated that 'the proper study of mankind is man'; the facts of human evolution now invite the rejoinder, 'But what can we know of man, if only man we know?'

Scientific anthropology began in the nineteenth century, and at first human societies were seen as a ladder ascending from primitive savages at the bottom to Victorian English gentlemen at the top. Twentieth century observers have taken the ladder apart and placed many of the rungs at the same level. One human society is not necessarily 'better' or 'worse' than another, for they have taken the same basic elements biological evolution has

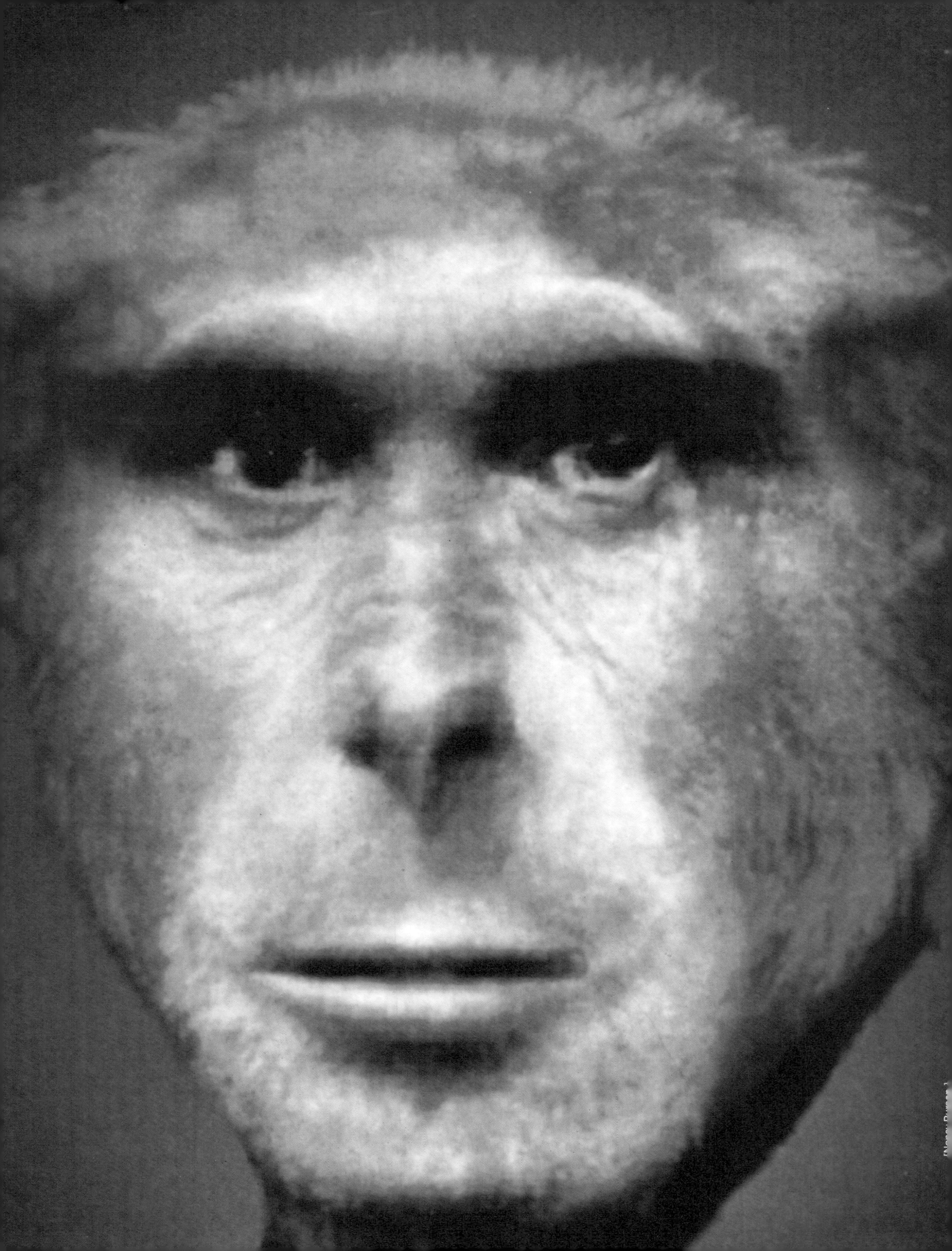

A 'manzee' (*opposite*). This is a computer-generated portrait of a simulated hybrid between a human and a chimpanzee, with each species contributing 50 per cent to the final display. Chimpanzees are our closest living relatives, having split off from the hominid line of evolution about seven million years ago. Although chimpanzees and gorillas have forty-eight chromosomes, compared to our forty-six, we have over 98 per cent of our DNA in common with them, and it is highly probable that they would hybridize with humans, although the progeny might be sterile, like mules. Some attempts have reputedly been made in the past to artificially inseminate female chimpanzees with human semen, but no pregnancies resulted. How would today's ethical committees react to such a proposal? And how would society react to any such offspring?

given them and fitted them together in different ways. By looking at other societies we can often understand our own more fully. At the same time, we can never be totally objective observers of our fellow human beings. What we see is always coloured by who we are and what we expect to see. Margaret Mead's book *Coming of Age in Samoa* (1928) has been immensely influential in the West, partly because she gave her readers something they wanted to hear. Reanalysis of her work shows she interviewed only fifty young women, spent all of three months in the field, had a poor grasp of the language and misunderstood part of what she saw.

As two people who have visited over 100 countries between them, and literally spent years in other cultures, the authors are aware of the problem of verifying observations and the dangers of generalizing from small samples. Some of the examples used come from previous centuries and report contact with people whose way of life has now disappeared, or has been seriously altered. Just as scientists are beginning to ask exciting questions about apes as they near extinction, so we are only now beginning to ask some of the right questions about the last preliterate societies at the very moment that they are being homogenized into bra-wearing, alcohol-consuming, shack-living, fringe communities.

While many traditional societies are changing irrevocably in our frenetic world, we have also succeeded in posing some novel problems for ourselves. In times past, an individual was almost always born into a clan or tribe with a stable culture that provided many expectations while imposing few choices. Today, a jumble of lifestyles exist side by side, especially in large urban areas: some people are monogamous, some are not; some have premarital sex, some do not; some are heterosexual and some are homosexual. The modern Western woman, in particular, is tugged and bruised by a changing world with many choices.

From the perspective of evolution we are a very 'new' species, barely 100 000 years old. But we can do something that no other animal can do. We can accumulate knowledge, and transmit it by means of the spoken and the written word to succeeding generations. This has given us immense power. It has enabled us to dominate and control our environment, so that we have freed ourselves from the chains and shackles of Nature that hold all other species in check. Already in our short existence we have overrun the Earth and we are causing the extinction of a great many species at an accelerating rate. Already there is a gulf separating the lifestyle of the affluent few who have the good fortune to live in the developed world from that of the millions of poor in the developing world. There are simply not enough resources to enable everybody to live as well as we do, and yet we would never contemplate our own de-development in order to improve the lot of the underprivileged. We are too self-interested to behave like that.

So we are left with a grim prospect. Ironically, our superior intellect has made us a suicidal success. We should all shudder a little at the fact that, to date, the world's astronomers can find no evidence of any other intelligent life forms within the universe. There are billions of suns that could be orbited by planets on which life might evolve. Astronomers estimate there could be 1000 to 10000 civilizations close enough to beam out radio messages. But if, as seems likely, the same processes of competition occur on such planets as they do on Earth, then perhaps any species intelligent enough to make radios also destroys itself in a relatively short time. Is the lifespan of a species inversely proportional to its degree of intellectual development? We may live in a silent universe for a very good reason: intelligent creatures produced by competitive evolution end up destroying themselves pretty quickly. The world will survive, and other forms of life will move in to occupy the niche we once occupied, but we could yet prove to be one of the shortest-lived species ever known.

It is our hope that, if we can escape from some of the sexual superstitions that have surrounded us in the past, we will begin to understand ourselves and the world we live in a little better. To do this we must be prepared to learn from other cultures and from biology. We must stop distancing ourselves from other animals, particularly our fellow primates. It is quite possible that, if we chose to, we could successfully interbreed with chimpanzees or gorillas. That surely would be the acid test of our relationship. The experiment could be performed quite simply in any one of a number of laboratories. Chimpanzee semen can easily be obtained from any zoo since, unlike gorillas, chimpanzees in captivity masturbate frequently. The semen immediately coagulates on ejaculation to form a plug that can be retrieved from the floor of the cage. This subsequently liquefies to release entrapped spermatozoa. Human eggs are not difficult to obtain. Women entering *in vitro* fertilization programmes (*in vitro* means literally 'in glass', i.e. fertilization outside the body) for the treatment of infertility are frequently given fertility drugs which yield more than enough eggs for their own immediate needs. Such women might consent to donate some of their surplus eggs for research. It would then be a simple matter of adding the chimpanzee sperm to the human eggs in the laboratory to see whether fertilization and cleavage took place.

If one believes in an insurmountable barrier separating humans and animals, such an experiment would be the ultimate blasphemy, but others might regard such a laboratory experiment as ethically acceptable, provided that the conceptus was not transferred back into the uterus of a woman or chimpanzee to undergo further development. Some might condone the insemination of a chimpanzee with human semen, while drawing the line at the insemination of a woman with chimpanzee semen. There might even be those who would wish to raise any resulting 'manzees' to adulthood, in order to study their intellectual and linguistic ability and their potential fertility.

Everyone will want to step off this train of thought at some point along the line, and it is interesting to analyse our reasons. When we explore such possibilities for hybridization between ourselves and chimpanzees, even if only in the course of a 'thought experiment', the concepts acquired during thousands of years of cultural history are brought up short by observable facts. If fertilization failed to take place, many people would heave a sigh of relief. If it occurred, our treasured wall of separateness from other animals would be finally and irrevocably shattered. At the same time our sense of pity for other creatures would be increased. Perhaps we are especially challenged by the idea of fertilizing the human egg with chimpanzee sperm because, intuitively, we know that a child developed from such a union would be a living challenge to the concept of a divine and uniquely human soul.

2 THE POLYGYNOUS PRIMATE

'I think I may fairly make two postulata. First, that food is necessary to the existence of man. Secondly, that the passion between the sexes is necessary and will remain nearly in its present state.'
Thomas Robert Malthus, *An Essay on the Principle of Population as it Affects the Future Improvement of Society*, 1798

The author William James told the story of Mrs Amos Pinchot, who in a dream thought she had discovered the meaning of life. Sleepily she wrote down what she believed to be a profound poetic statement. Fully awake, she saw she had merely written:

Hogamus, higamous
Man is polygamous
Higamus, hogamous
Woman monogamous.

Yet, in a way, Mrs Pinchot was closer to the discoveries of modern biology than perhaps she realized. Men do appear to be intrinsically polygamous animals struggling to accommodate the woman's need for monogamous support. Marriage, divorce, battered wives, romance and boredom in sexual relationships, the gay lifestyle and what Sir Walter Raleigh long ago called the 'sunshine mixed with rain' of love, can all be seen in new ways through the insights of evolutionary biology.

Mating patterns

Think back to your last visit to a zoo. Mammals can be divided into two distinct groups. There are those where the two sexes are markedly different and those where males and females are practically indistinguishable. The large-bodied, shaggy-maned lion, all head and shoulders, looking indeed the King of the Beasts, is very different from his elegantly proportioned, sleek, svelte queen. The great, antlered, bull-necked, roaring, stinking stag in rut, eyes crazed by lust, is so very different from his shy, demure, chaste hind that you could be forgiven for thinking they were two different species. Amongst the apes there is the vast male orangutan, with odd face and close-set eyes, a Buddha-like caricature of a beast, so apart in appearance from his agile, arboreal lady love. The male chimpanzee, although not much bigger than the

[David Chivers.]

The gibbon, a monogamous ape. The male and female gibbon are almost identical in size and shape, apart from the obvious signs of the male's scrotum and the female's breasts when she is lactating. They live in the forest canopy of Southeast Asia and feeding on fruits, and there is usually an abundance of food available. So the female has much to gain by having the male as her permanent consort. Since the male is not in continuous competition with other males for access to females, there is no selection pressure for him to develop greater muscular strength or weapons of offence, such as large canine teeth. Copulation is also a relatively rare event, since it takes place only when the female is in oestrus; oestrus is suppressed during pregnancy and lactation. His testes are therefore relatively small. Neither sex has needed to develop organs of sexual display, like a large penis or swollen female genitalia or breasts, since they do not need to advertise their sexuality to others. Recent observations, however, also demonstrate that even gibbons can be 'unfaithful' and males may end up living with 'step-children'.

female and facially similar to her, may provide a glimpse of his large canine teeth. His great swollen scrotum reflects his zoological name *Pan* – the Greek god of fertility. The female chimpanzee, so human in her facial appearance, causes nannies and parents to pull their children away hurriedly when she stands up to reveal her red tumescent posterior. Then there is the male gorilla, King Kong in person, most human and hence most intimidating, lord of all the primates, exuding the primal musky smell of masculinity, but with virtually invisible genitalia in spite of that, and with apparent total indifference to the presence of his flat-chested female companion. All these species, like most mammals, are polygynous, one male having several mates. Polygynous males are consistently larger than the females of the same species because they must compete with other males for access to the females: scientifically, they are said to be sexually dimorphic.

How different are the truly monogamous animals, such as the airborne gibbons, swinging in great arcs from branch to branch, rejoicing in their agility but totally concealing their sexuality unless you happen to catch a fleeting glimpse of their very modest genitals. With relatively abundant food in the forest canopy, monogamy is the female's preferred mating strategy and there is no selection pressure for the male to be any larger than the female. The male, after all, is merely a vehicle to carry the testes around. The diminu-

[Ballerina © Jane Mont / PAL, Muscleman © Tom Duffy / Allsport.]

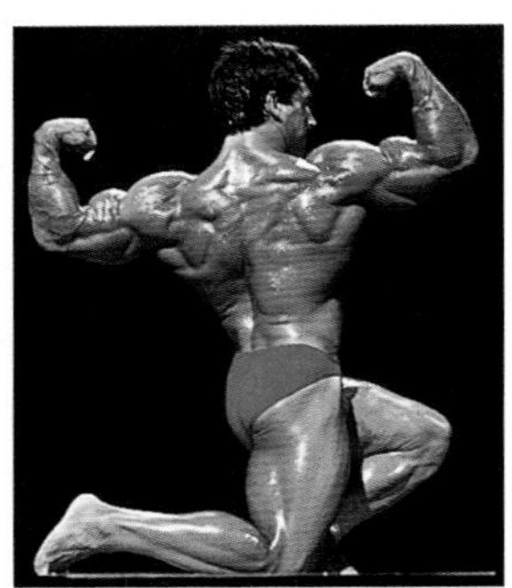

Extremes of human sexual dimorphism. The bodybuilder and the ballerina are both at the peak of their physical fitness. The bodybuilder may use anabolic steroids to increase his muscle mass – and probably his aggression – although they will also cause testicular shrinkage and sterility. The ballerina is likely to have quiescent ovaries and an absence of menstruation as a result of her exercise régime, and the general absence of body fat means that neither her breasts nor her buttocks are pronounced.

tive, chattering marmoset monkeys from the forests of South America, where the male and the female take turns in carrying their twin babies, show a true equality of the sexes in both size and behaviour.

How do humans fit into this scheme? After looking at other animals, pause to look in the mirror and reflect on your own kind. Imagine a cage containing a man and a woman, stripped of their cultural acquisitions, naked and unadorned. The man stands out; not only is he usually heavier, taller and stronger than his mate, but he has a shaggy beard, maybe a bald pate, a large floppy, flaccid penis and a dangling pendulous scrotum, weighed down by a middling sized pair of testicles. The woman, larger of breast, broad hipped, rounded of buttock, is finer boned, less muscular than her consort and instantly attractive to most male onlookers. On average, men are 15 to 20 per cent heavier than women and also physically stronger. Human beings are not as dramatically different in size as, say, gorillas, but we are unambiguously sexually dimorphic.

Biology, however, does not merely make static comparisons; it has developed behavioural explanations for these enigmatic anatomical variations on the theme of sexuality. The anatomical differences between the sexes we see in different animal species are all ultimately related to the mating system, and a biologist would predict that human beings should be polygynous. But we have codified and complicated mating with the notion of marriage, a socially sanctioned event that links families and transfers property. While many cultures sanction polygyny and many people of both sexes have more than one sexual partner in a lifetime, the majority of today's world live in societies that subscribe to the ideal of monogamous marriage. How can we explain this apparent paradox in both biological and cultural terms?

An asymmetrical investment

Who chooses this mating system? Male anthropologists of the past, like the late Lord Zuckerman, championed the Master Male Concept. But today, thanks to the fieldwork of female anthropologists, such as Jane Goodall, who have studied the behaviour of apes and monkeys in their natural habitats in the wild, there is growing support for the alternative concept, that of the Subtle Female who determines the mating strategy for the species. Perhaps the male is not so dominant after all.

Evolution always chooses the strategy most likely to lead to the greatest number of offspring surviving to the next generation, and for this reason the

***Lovers in the Park*, François Boucher.** The woman's reproductive needs and the man's polygamous strategy are caught by the eighteenth century artist François Boucher. Romantically, the man places flowers in the hair of his lover while she rests trustingly on his thigh. Their dalliance is interrupted by a flower-seller tripping lightly behind the girl: instantly, the man's eyes meet the eyes of the new arrival, flashing the possibility of man's alternative reproductive agenda. Even the dog appears alarmed, but the man's lover sees nothing.

[The Putnam Foundation, Timken Museum of Art, San Diego.]

Where musth and rut doth corrupt

'When a bull elephant is in musth he must', to quote the late J. H. (Elephant Bill) Williams. Musth has been recognized for centuries in Asiatic elephants; it is a time when the animal becomes extremely aggressive to man and beast, and captive males will kill their mahout (keeper) if given half a chance. The temporal gland, situated on the side of the face between the eye and ear, swells up and begins to exude a strong-smelling secretion down the side of the face; the penis hangs out from the prepuce, and constantly dribbles urine; the surrounding countryside is permeated by a most mighty odour of elephant – once smelt, never to be forgotten. In such a state, the bull is quite uncontrollable, and has to be chained by all four legs to stout neighbouring trees, which must be out of his reach or he will destroy them.

[J. Poole.]

A fight to the death? Two mature African elephant bulls, who both happened to be in musth at the same time, fighting in Amboseli National Park, Kenya.

Although musth appears to be a more-or-less annual event, its relation to male sexual activity has always been something of a mystery. Males in musth have staggeringly high levels of the male sex hormone testosterone in their blood – presumably the cause of their increased aggressive activity. Bulls that are not in musth have far lower levels of testosterone; they are the ones used in captive breeding programmes, and there seems to be nothing wrong with their libido and fertility.

Joyce Poole, working in the Amboseli National Park in Kenya, has provided us with the first vivid accounts of musth in free-ranging wild elephants. It occurs only in fully mature males when they reach the age of about 30, although bulls, like boys, go through puberty at about the age of 12. The older the bull the longer he is likely to remain in musth, and an animal in his prime in his late forties may be in musth for three to four months each year. When in musth, the bull becomes dominant to all non-musth bulls, even though they may be older and bigger than him. He is constantly on the search for any cow coming into heat, and he appears to be able to detect her from far off by her long-range infrasonic vocalizations. Although non-musth bulls will mate with an oestrous cow, when the musth bull arrives, he has exclusive rights to any cow. Bulls in musth seem to avoid others in the same state – although on the rare occasions when they do meet, there may be a fight that results in the death of one or other of the protagonists. Since different bulls come into musth at different times of the year, this minimizes the chances of these life-threatening intermale encounters.

As far as the elephant is concerned, musth ensures that every bull will have his day, once he has reached the years of discretion, and every cow will not want for suitors during the brief one to two days of oestrus every few years.

Unlike the equatorial elephant, animals living in temperate latitudes have to time their births, and hence their matings, with precision, so that the young are born at the most favourable time of the year, when food is plentiful. The need for tight synchronization of mating has produced a different reproductive strategy – the rut. This is a characteristic, for example, of most wild species of sheep, goats and deer. Once again the males become extremely aggressive, driven by their testes, which pour out large amounts of testosterone during the rutting period.

Although all stags rut together, unlike the staggered musth of elephants, only the older stags of 5 years or more are sufficiently well grown to hold hinds and fight off intruders. Younger animals will have to bide their time and, as in elephants, many years may elapse between male puberty and the first successful copulation, whereas all the females will conceive at puberty. Rutting appears to be a veritable cascade of sexual emotions; the roaring of the stags hastens the onset of oestrus in the hinds, which further inflames the passion of the stags, culminating in a few brief days of frenzied orgasmic activity.

Fortunately or unfortunately for men, depending on your point of view, our lack of seasonal breeding and more monogamous lifestyle has meant that we are immune to the passions of musth and rut.

[United Distillers and Vintners / The Bridgeman Art Library.]

***Monarch of the Glen*, Edwin Landseer, 1851.** Landseer, the renowned nineteenth century painter of animals, was captivated, like his Victorian patrons, by the romance of red deer rutting in the Scottish Highlands, and this memorable painting shows a fine 12-pointed stag (a 'Royal') at rutting time in October. The animal is 'in pride of greace', having fattened on the summer grazings in preparation for a month-long fast during the rut. His neck muscles are greatly hypertrophied under the influence of testosterone, since they will be the driving force for his hard horn antlers (grown anew each year) in many a contest with rival stags over a harem of hinds.

In the seasonally polygamous society of red deer, copulation is confined largely to the month of October. Although the female may have little choice over which stag wins the right to hold the harem and mate with her, it is in the female's interest to rut and conceive in October, so that her calf will be born in early June. This will be late enough that there is sufficient food available to support her lactation, and yet soon enough that her calf will be sufficiently well grown to survive the coming winter. Fortunately for the hinds, the stags live apart from them for eleven months of the year, thereby minimizing the competition for food at times of the year when the hind needs it most, during late pregnancy and lactation.

two sexes can have very different reproductive agendas. Because female mammals have to cope with the considerable energetic demands of pregnancy, lactation, and child rearing to puberty, they have a much greater energy investment in reproduction than the male. Food availability tends to be the limiting resource for all living things, so the female mammal in particular must develop a strategy to maximize her food supply if she is to reproduce successfully. If food is in short supply, it may therefore pay her to share a male with other females; after all, you only need him around now and then so that you can get pregnant, and for the rest of the time he is just another mouth to feed. So most mammals, especially the larger ones, have opted for polygyny, where several females share the male between them for the purpose of mating. It is only when the food supply is abundant that the female may choose to have a male as her constant consort in a monogamous relationship: the disadvantages of competition for food are outweighed by the benefits of shared care of the young and defence of the home range.

When it comes to women, who are pregnant for nine months, may breastfeed for two to three years, and then are the primary caregivers until puberty or beyond, the gulf between the investment each sex makes in passing its genes to the next generation widens to gigantic proportions. By limiting

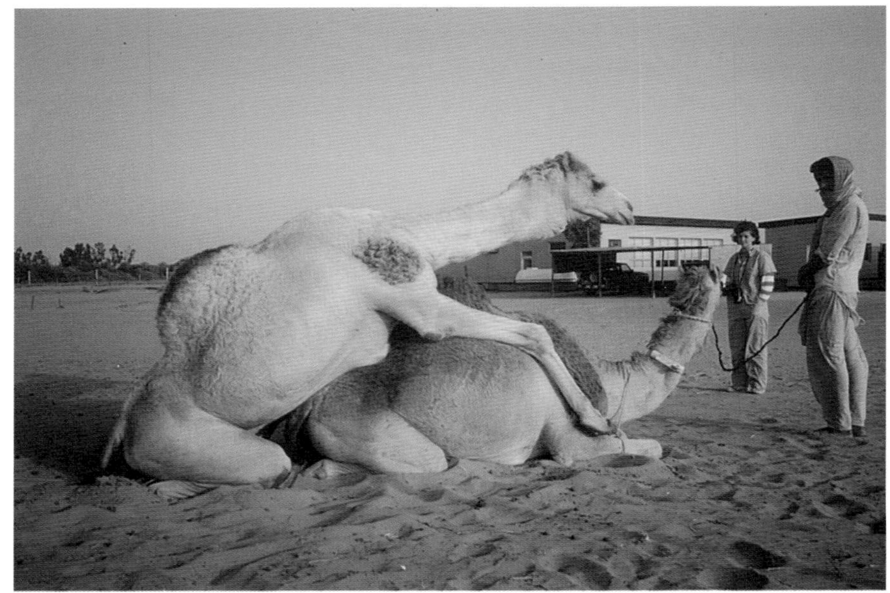

Copulating camels. These dromedary camels will spend up to an hour *in copulo*, although the Sphinx-like expression on the female's face gives no indication when in this long drawn out process the male ejaculates. We know that it is the act of copulation that induces the female to ovulate and, by monopolizing her in this way, the male may be ensuring that it is only his sperm that will fertilize the egg he has caused to be shed.

Aristotle was fascinated by camels. He classified them as a separate group of mammals because the males are retromingent – they urinate backwards. The penis has to turn through 180° on erection in order to enter the vagina. He also recorded how female camels were ovariectomized when used in warfare. This was probably because a non-pregnant female will sit down at the sight of a male. So if you went to war on a non-pregnant female camel, you were likely to get killed. How the Arabs were able to perform this major surgical operation on female camels, history does not relate, and there is no record of the operation being performed on female camels in the present day.

lactation to females, evolution has let male mammals off the hook: the different investment of the two sexes in the next generation is so great that in the vast majority of mammalian species, the male impregnates as many females as he can but makes no contribution whatsoever to the welfare of his offspring. Until the modern age, nearly all women married and bore children, but even the most fecund women could not bear many children in a fertile lifetime. Biologically, a man can father more children than one woman can bear. At most, an individual woman may release up to 450 eggs in her lifetime, of which only a tiny proportion are ever likely to be fertilized. By contrast a man makes 150 million new sperm every day throughout his life and releases enough genetic information in a single ejaculation to repopulate half the USA. As men compete for access to a fixed number of females, their reproductive achievement is more variable than that of females: a significant number of men never father children, while a small number have a very large number of children.

Charles Darwin was the first to understand the role of sex in evolution. In *The Descent of Man* (1871) he wrote:

> *Sexual Selection depends upon the success of certain individuals over others of the same sex, in relation to the propagation of the species;*

whilst Natural Selection depends on the success of both sexes, at all ages, in relation to the general conditions of life. The sexual struggle is of two kinds; in the one it is between the individuals of the same sex, generally the males, in order to drive away or kill their rivals, the females remaining passive; while in the other the struggle is likewise between the individuals of the same sex, in order to excite or charm those of the opposite sex, generally the females, which no longer remain passive, but select the more agreeable partners.

In a polygynous mating system, one male mates with several different females. Such males usually tend to be heavier, larger, stronger and better equipped than females, with offensive weapons such as canine teeth, claws, horns, spurs or antlers: consider the huge strength of the male gorilla or the large canine teeth of the male chimpanzee, used to compete against other males for access to females. Again, as Darwin wrote:

[The Master and Fellows of Trinity College Cambridge.]

Bluff King Hal. King Henry VIII founded Trinity College, Cambridge, and his portrait by Eworth (after Holbein) hangs above the Master and Fellows in the dining hall there. His courtly garb includes a distinctive codpiece, to conceal yet emphasize his genitalia. In the twentieth century, the singer Elton John revived the fashion of codpieces, wearing one with lights that flashed when he hit a particular note on his guitar. And it was Elvis Presley, Elvis the Pelvis, who drew attention to the erotic appeal of the male's pelvic region in general.

It is certain that amongst all animals there is a struggle between the males for possession of the females. This fact is so notorious that it would be superfluous to give instances. Hence, the females have the opportunity of selecting one out of several males.

In monogamous mating systems, where the competition between males for access to the females is counterbalanced by the females' ability to select the most attractive males, there is little or no sexual dimorphism. In both polygyny and monogamy, it is the female that usually sets the pace in mammalian reproduction, even when the outcome may seem to place her in an inferior position. Yet, as we will see later, in a world complicated by economics, politics, religion and the law, which have become predominantly male preserves, the innate reproductive agenda of the female has often become subordinate to that of men.

The obsession

Human beings understand that sex leads to pregnancy, and it is just possible that other big-brained animals such as chimpanzees or elephants also have this insight. For all other animals we can safely assume that evolution has built in a drive to copulate. But once we accept that human beings evolved from less intelligent animals with a stand-alone sex drive not consciously related to pregnancy, then it would seem redundant for evolution to have added any other innate behavioural mechanism to drive copulation. The fantasies and sexual dreams of men and women are almost exclusively about intercourse, not about pregnancy, childbirth and breastfeeding. The sex drive is so strong it has become an end in itself, and the male obsession with ejaculation and with the female body is often bewildering to women.

Very little is known about how the genetic code contained in our DNA is translated into the neuronal circuits that drive behaviour. It is self-evident that we have evolved to be highly flexible in our behaviour. Our ability to learn means we can modify our behaviour to fit the world around us. In this book we have used the word predisposition, first suggested by E. O. Wilson of Harvard University to describe innate behaviours, such as male aggressiveness. But such predispositions are often highly malleable and a tendency to assertiveness could, in one environment, motivate a man to shoot his rival, while in another the same predisposition might motivate him to buy his girlfriend flowers.

For most of history, the sex drive has perpetuated our genes. The predisposition for sexual satisfaction is one of the most focused of human behaviours, yet once human beings discovered that sex led to pregnancy they also began to try to separate one from the other by using contraceptives or inducing abortions. In our modern, complex, contraceptive-using societies we are having fewer children, but not less sex.

Secret infertile sex

In one sense, we are a mammal that has gone one step too far in the investment we make in the next generation. Our most remarkable feature is the expansion of our brains relative to those of other apes. This in turn has produced an extremely helpless human baby that requires many years to grow and programme its big brain. The length and scale of human investment in the next generation exceeds that of all other species, and the investment required to bring a human child to maturity appears to have crossed the threshold of what a female can do by herself. The solitary adult male orangutan may never ever see his children; adult male chimpanzees or baboons defend a territory and are tolerant of youngsters, but they play no role in their upbringing; the children of the huge silverback gorilla may look to him for guidance in the presence of danger, but little else. Among human beings a new set of behaviours needed to evolve to ensure that the adult male shared in the direct care and sustenance of his children. Evolution is a notorious improviser: scales evolved into the complexity of feathers, and the joints of a reptile's jaw became a mechanism for amplifying sound in the mammalian ear. Where

He Man. This warrior of the Karamojong tribe in northern Uganda has managed to elongate his penis to an extraordinary degree, probably by tying weights on it, so that it has to be tied up in a knot when not in use.

Humans have the most conspicuous flaccid penis, and the largest erect penis of any primate, so we can only assume that it must have evolved as an organ of sexual display. But to whom? Because we conceal the male genitalia in public in almost all human societies, the human penis is unlikely to have evolved for intermale display. Since sexual intercourse is a very private affair, maybe the penis evolved to make the man more attractive to his partner. A larger penis might also have allowed the couple to indulge in a wider variety of copulatory positions, thus making intercourse more pleasurable.

The penis, even when not erect, appears to be the most taboo aspect of our sexuality. The English Law Lords recently met to consider the offence of Indecent Exposure in this new era of sexual equality in all things. They concluded that it must remain a male-only offence, because the female has nothing indecent to expose.

did evolution find the cohesive force to bond males to females so that they could share in parenting? One answer is infertile sex.

With a long gestation and two to three years of lactation, early hominid females would have been fertile for only a few days every three or four years. A male gorilla, with his harem of three or four females, may have to wait a year or more before one of them is sexually receptive and allows him to mate. If the same pattern existed in the early hominids as they moved towards monogamy, or even serial monogamy, then intercourse might have occurred only at three to four yearly intervals. Instead, at some point in the evolution of human sexuality, changes occurred permitting frequent, infertile sex that could bond the two parents in the task of bringing big-brained, slow-developing children to maturity. The ability to have sex for pleasure, not just for procreation, means we became one of the sexiest of mammals, or as Aristotle put it, the most salacious. It was probably also this sexual bonding that made early hominids seek to copulate in private and avoid displaying the genitalia in public. We may be a sexy ape but we are also a bashful one.

Globally, the World Health Organization estimates that around 100 million acts of human sexual intercourse take place each day; but there are fewer than one million conceptions. In other words 99 per cent of sexual encounters are infertile. In order for evolution to build a sexual bond to unite

Madam will you walk? Sex is the cement of chimpanzee social structure, necessary for harmonious male co-existence, and it makes sense for the female to advertise where she is in her sexual cycle to all comers. This is achieved by pronounced reddening and swelling, of up to 60 cubic inches (1000 cubic centimetres) or more, of the vulva at the time of ovulation, as seen here. The male has also developed a large penis and testes. The penis is invisible when flaccid, concealed within the prepuce beneath the skin of the belly, but when erect its red colour is conspicuous and is used, as here, to signal to the oestrous female. Perhaps the chimpanzee's thin penis is necessary for penetration of the female's tumescent genitalia.

It is common for infant chimpanzees to be present when adults mate and indeed, they sometimes appear to try to stop their mother having sex – has evolution told them it is not in their interest to have a sibling too soon? Males may clutch at one another's penises during moments of anxiety or excitement and they masturbate frequently in captivity.

the parents, certain anatomical and physiological changes had to evolve. The female had to conceal ovulation, and she had to be prepared to accept male sexual advances at any time in the menstrual cycle. The woman's anatomy, physiology and behaviour is such that neither she nor her partner knows which sexual act is going to result in fertilization and the beginning of a new life. We celebrate our birthday but can only make a rough guess as to our conception day. While human beings use frequent sex to bond the man and woman in the hard work of parenting, chimpanzees use frequent infertile sex to achieve very different social relationships.

There are two species of chimpanzee, the familiar zoo or circus animal with the scientific name *Pan troglodytes*, found in both East and West Africa, and the much rarer bonobo or pygmy chimpanzee, *Pan paniscus*, which is confined to a small area south of the Zaïre River in central Africa. (Bonobos may have diverged from *Pan troglodytes* after the last Ice Age, when the pattern of forests in Africa changed.) *Pan troglodytes* overlaps with gorillas in some parts of its range in Africa, for example the rain forest of Gabon. In this situation, chimpanzees concentrate on eating fruits and gorillas on eating leaves; but where bonobos live there are no gorillas, and so *Pan paniscus* eats both fruits and leaves. Bonobos are more slender than other chimpanzees, their ability to walk upright is excellent, and unlike other chimps they play and swim in water and they have an awful lot of sex; even the infants join in the fun! Observation suggests that female bonobos may have over 3000 episodes of sexual intercourse before their first pregnancy and around 2500 over the rest of their fertile life. Unlike other chimpanzees, in both the wild and in zoos, bonobos often have sex in the missionary position with the female lying on her back, so that the two partners can look into each other's eyes. They appear to enjoy the moment, but like *Pan troglodytes*, bonobos remain a promiscuous species, with no lasting bonds between individuals of the opposite sex. The male has a more prominent penis than *Pan troglodytes* and the female a relatively larger clitoris. Bonobos engage in what can only be called deep French kissing, putting their tongues in each other's mouths.

Primate penises. These drawings, not to scale, illustrate the bizarre appearance of the penis in a range of primate species. It is difficult to imagine why there should be such a spectacular array of different shapes and designs.

One feature that distinguishes the human penis from that of other primates is the absence of a bone, or 'os penis'. In some species, such as the chimpanzee, this bone is particularly well developed, whereas in the gorilla it is vestigial. An os penis is also found in many other groups of mammal species, and its function may be to maintain an erection and hence prolong sexual coupling after orgasm and penile detumescence. It has been suggested that the spines on the penis of species such as dogs and cats may be devices to help to remove the coagulated semen or copulatory plug of any other male who might previously have mated with the female.

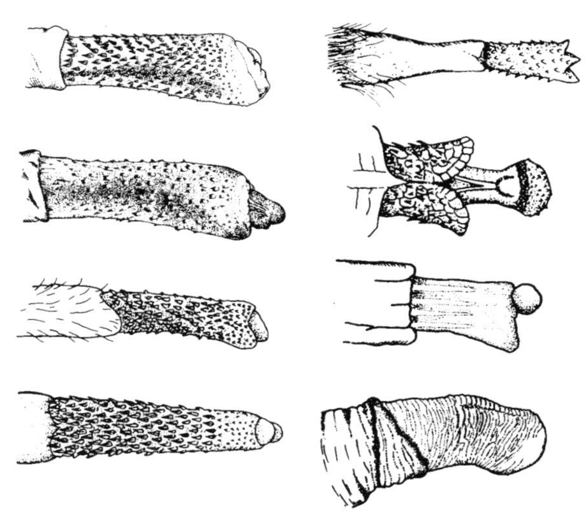

[A. Dixson © *Journal of Zoology*.]

Same-sex activity is common. Males masturbate other males and provide oral sex, and females give one another pleasure by rubbing their genitals together until they reach orgasm. This homo-erotic activity, however, in no way interferes with heterosexual intercourse. In human terms, bonobos could be described as bisexual. Female bonobos, like women, engage in sex not just when they are ovulating, but during a much greater proportion of the menstrual cycle. The vulval swelling advertising ovulation in *Pan troglodytes* is still present, but it is not as prominent in adults, and it is much less conspicuous in young bonobos.

Studies of their DNA suggest that *Pan paniscus* and *Pan troglodytes* have been separate species for two to three million years. They are anatomically similar, yet have different sexual behaviours. In the past seven million years since *Homo sapiens* shared a common ancestor with chimpanzees, several different patterns of sexual behaviour could have evolved and some perhaps have become extinct. Sexual bonding can be an exceedingly important part of primate behaviour, but it can be used in different ways. *Pan paniscus* uses sex to reduce tension. Their solution to any problematic situation is to have sex. If they find a tree full of ripe fruit where competition is likely to arise, they have sex. If they meet a foreign troop of bonobos, they have sex. It is interesting that neither bonobos nor *Pan troglodytes* use sex to build any type of lasting bond between males and females. That evolutionary trick is purely human. As we will see in Chapter 13, same-sex activities in female bonobos appear to build long lasting social bonds between females. Heterosexual activity in *Homo sapiens* builds long-term bonds between males and females. But by using sexual pleasure as a bond to involve men in the care of their children, evolution has chosen a potentially explosive device. Sexual jealously, as has been noted earlier, is a universal human predisposition. Whereas bonobos use infertile sex to lower tension, the infertile sex we practice often raises tensions. In order to avoid humans being in a perpetual state of rut, it seems to have been necessary to evolve a second set of behaviours that conceal the external reproductive organs of adults in public and that make sexual intercourse a secret act conducted well away from the rest of the clan. It would have been extremely difficult to live in close-knit social bands if all adults were continuously interested in sex but were also sexually jealous. The life of the troop would be forever disrupted, and both men and women would be fighting constantly if sex partnerships were both visible and likely to change.

Most societies accept nudity in children before puberty: absence of body hair, absence of breast buds or a small penis make little children innocently acceptable. But once puberty begins, even societies that go almost naked either cover up the pubic area, or adopt other behaviours to hide their nakedness. Many parents will remember how young boys and girls resent even their parents seeing them naked in the bath or the shower as puberty begins. The natives of Tierra del Fuego, whom Darwin saw on the voyage of *HMS Beagle*, lived without clothes in the windswept, icy environment of Cape Horn, but women still remembered to cross their legs and cover their vulvas when they sat down. Hollywood and the Hawaiian tourist board have made the grass skirt seductive, but its real purpose was to conceal. We will probably never know whether clothes were used first for protection, thermo-regulation, or for sexual concealment. What is certain is that clothes and other bodily decorations can be used to allow sexual interest to simmer without boiling over.

Once the sex organs began to be covered up, it followed that the sex act itself needed to take place in private. Sex involving more than two people is commoner in fantasies than in reality: it happens, but not often. Men in traditionally polygamous societies, such as the East African Kikuyu, respect the privacy of each of their wives, and the husband has intercourse with only one wife at a time. In all parts of the world, young couples studiously avoid sexual advances to one another anywhere near their parents, and parents have sex away from the children, or wait until they are asleep – or think they are asleep. As people grow richer they build houses with separate bedrooms for parents and children. One of the reasons for the popularity of Church Sunday Schools in the nineteenth century was that families often had to accommodate the youngest child in the parents' bedroom, and sending children off to Bible Class on Sunday afternoon was the only chance working class parents had for sexual games. Above all, couples want to keep out of sight and hearing of other adults when they make love. Sexual shyness, delicacy, modesty, a dislike of pornography, and expressions of prudery, inhibition and sexual squeamishness may all be expressions of a recent evolutionary need for men and women to bond together by using frequent infertile sex, without at the same time destabilizing the rest of society. The wonder of biological evolution is in the accidental ingenuity of its many and varied solutions for the survival of the species. In the case of human beings, this accidental ingenuity has used to bond couples the same mechanism that causes offspring to be born. Thus the offspring will survive to reproduce themselves. As we will see in Chapter 4, the predisposition for frequent, infertile sexual relations has been coloured and edited in a rich variety of ways by different cultures.

The male agenda

Men are more likely than women to seek multiple partners; they usually mate with women who are younger than they are, and the older the man when he makes a second marriage the greater the average age difference is likely to be. In 1989, in Nova Esperanca, Brazil, the local court registered Joaquin Cesario, who reported he was 112 years old, as the legal father of a child born

The size of the human penis

'Big men, big cock, small men, all cock', or so the saying goes. The size of the penis is the source of many ribald jokes. Everybody is familiar with the apocryphal story of the American-made condoms that were exported to Japan, where they were found to fall off. The *Kama Sutra*, that third century AD Sanskrit treatise on Indian sexual practices, first translated into English at the end of the last century by the renowned explorer Sir Richard Burton, vividly describes how men should be divided into three classes – hares, bulls and horses – according to the size of their *lingam*. Women should likewise by classified by the depth of their *yoni*, into deer, mares or elephants. It was thought that there were only three equal unions possible between men and women of comparable dimensions, hare with deer, bull with mare, and horse with elephant. If an equal union could not be arranged, then it was preferable for the man to seek a higher union with a woman of smaller dimensions.

Unfortunately, the precision of scientific measurement has shattered these picturesque concepts. In the 1940s Lieutenant William Schonfield of the USA carried out one of the most detailed studies on a population of 1500 normal white boys and men in the New York area, representing many different nationalities. He concluded, like others before him, that the size of the penis was in no way related to the general body build. Realizing that the flaccid penis could vary greatly in size depending on factors such as the room temperature, he confined his measurements to estimates of the length of the fully erect penis, having first established that the length of the flaccid penis at full stretch is practically identical to that of the erect penis. His measurements revealed a rapid elongation of the penis during puberty, starting as early as 12 years of age, and reaching adult size by the age of 17. The mean adult length was 5.9 inches (15 centimetres), with 90 per cent of penises being over 4.3 inches (11 centimetres) and 5 per cent less than 2.2 inches (5.5 centimetres). We are indebted to a group of prostitutes in a Japanese brothel for publishing in a popular magazine the erect measurement of their clientele. The results, based on 2319 observations, showed a mean length of 5.4 inches (13.75 centimetres); only six men failed to achieve 3.5 inches (9 centimetres), and only one attained a record value of 7.9 inches (20 centimetres). Within the limits of experimental error, there would appear to be no significant difference between the two populations. Contrast this with the mighty male gorilla, weighing an estimated 550 lbs (250 kilograms), whose erect penis measures a mere 1.2 inches (3 centimetres).

to a 27 year old woman. Even allowing for exaggeration, Joaquin's case demonstrates that male fertility is ended only by death.

In practically all societies, men compete for power, wealth and status. It is a drive that is so universal, and has become such an end in itself, that many people would not relate it to sexual behaviour. Yet from a biological point of view, the predisposition for influence, substance and prestige are all merely expressions of a male positioning himself to acquire women with whom to mate. Even in hunter–gatherer societies with few material goods, successful hunters and socially charismatic men have more sexual partners and father more children. This is true where the women enjoy some degree of sexual autonomy, as among the Ache of Paraguay, and where sex often involves coercion, as among the Yanomamo of Venezuela. Kim Hill and Magdalena Hurtado of the University of New Mexico found that Ache men share any game animals they hunt with meticulous equality among all members of the tribe; yet the women know which men bring home most meat. Some successful hunters fathered as many as fifteen children, while other men had

[Anthony Bannister.]

San Bushmen of the Kalahari in the making. A woman pauses to gather berries from a brandybush. Her 3 year old son rests on her shoulders, and she carries her young baby. Having children too closely spaced together is a severe handicap in this nomadic hunter–gatherer lifestyle. The contraceptive effect of prolonged breast-feeding normally keeps births spaced about four years apart, so that there is never more than one child that needs to be carried constantly. Note that there is no man in sight – he is away hunting.

none at all. Napoleon Chagnon of the University of Chicago, who has made a life-long study of the Yanomamo, notorious for their propensity for warfare, observed that warriors who have killed other men have three times as many children as men not honored as warriors, and he traced the lineage of one such man who had 14 children, 143 grandchildren and 335 great-grandchildren.

Anthropologist Laura Betzig has written:

> *As men have the potential to father many more children than women can mother, they should have been selected to compete for both the number and quality of their mates. An important part of this mate competition will involve contests over resources their wives will need to raise children.*

Sexual deception is common. About one in five Western men and one in ten women admit being unfaithful during marriage. The deceived partner of either sex often feels great pain at being betrayed. But it is important to note that, from a biological perspective, male adultery and female cuckoldry represent somewhat different reproductive strategies. A man may attempt to make a woman pregnant with no intention of supporting any child he fathers. The mother carries the burden of pregnancy all alone and the child is likely to suffer as a result. When a woman cuckolds a man, she typically attempts to conceive a child by a man who is not her husband and to deceive her regular sex partner into thinking the child is his. The child does not suffer, but the husband makes an investment in bringing up a child that does not carry his genes, and in biological terms that is a waste of effort. The woman who carries the child of an adulterous relationship but without any support from the father may be cross with herself; the man who is cuckolded by his wife has reason to be angry with his wife.

The female burden

The human mother must deliver a baby with an enormous, but still growing, brain. The child must be carried around until it can walk. Following birth, the mother must pour out unprecedented amounts of energy in the form of milk. Brain tissue itself, at any age and in both sexes, burns up a great deal of energy, even when the body is at rest. The mother in particular, with her own big brain, and also carrying a growing child nourished from her own breasts, needs extra help. As we moved away from our ape-like ancestors we adopted a more easy to digest, nutritious diet, including eating more meat.

(Gorillas are pot-bellied because they eat leaves and need a huge rumbling intestine to digest a food source that is low in calories and difficult to digest.) As in other apes, mechanisms evolved to ensure that human births are spaced three to four years apart because otherwise the mother could not lead the nomadic life of a hunter–gather; she could not carry two babies-in-arms everywhere. Above all, the enormous demands of child rearing meant that it was more and more advantageous to have a man who was bonded to the woman and would help to feed, shelter and protect his mate and her offspring. Children born to partnerships involving the regular attention of a male were more likely to survive in the struggle for existence.

In a way, though, in bonding to one man a woman surrenders some of the choice she previously enjoyed. Therefore, it becomes to her advantage and

The difference between a man and a woman

The female is softer in disposition, is more mischievous, less simple, more impulsive, and more attentive to the nurture of the young; the male, on the other hand, is more spirited, more savage, more simple and less cunning. The traces of these characteristics are more or less visible everywhere, but they are especially visible where character is the more developed, and most of all in man.

The fact is, the nature of man is the most rounded off and complete, and consequently in man the qualities above referred to are found most clearly. Hence woman is more compassionate than man, more easily moved to tears, at the same time is more jealous, more querulous, more apt to scold and to strike. She is, furthermore, more prone to despondency and less hopeful than man, more void of shame, more false of speech, more deceptive, and of more retentive memory. She is also more wakeful, more shrinking, more difficult to rouse to action, and requires a smaller quantity of nutriment.

Aristotle, *History of Animals*, Book IX, *ca.* 350 BC

Woman, owing to her maternal instincts, displays those qualities towards her infants in an eminent degree; therefore it is likely that she would often extend them towards her fellow-creatures. Man is the rival of other men; he delights in competition, and this leads to ambition which passes too easily into selfishness. These latter qualities seem to be his natural and unfortunate birthright. It is generally admitted that with woman the powers of intuition, of rapid perception, and perhaps of imitation, are more strongly marked than in man.

The chief distinction in the intellectual powers of the two sexes is shown by man's attaining to a higher eminence, in whatever he takes up, than can woman – whether requiring deep thought, reason, or imagination, or merely the use of senses and hands. If two lists were made of the most eminent men and women in poetry, painting, sculpture, music (inclusive both of composition and performance), history, science, and philosophy, with half-a-dozen names under each subject, the two lists would not bear comparison.

Charles Darwin, *The Descent of Man and Selection in Relation to Sex*, 1871

A woman can, if she strives against her temperament and natural physical structure, carry out with some success all the duties assigned to man by nature, but no man can make himself bear and rear children.

S. Abdul A'la Maududi, *Purdah and the Status of Women in Islam*, 1939 increases the chances that her children will survive if she evolves behaviours that make her much more cautious than the male when selecting a mate. The predisposition to be cautious may be partially unconscious but it is usually there, especially as the woman matures and if she already has children. Hard choices may need to be made and paradoxes resolved. In some circumstances it may pay to share a male with considerable wealth and status with one or more other females, rather than entering into a strictly monogamous relationship with a powerless man. Within a relationship, whether it is exclusively with one man, or involves sharing a man with other females, the same desire for consistent, long-term support will be found, the same need for some degree of physical closeness and a genuine sharing in the hard task of bringing up a family. In competing for wealth and power, men, like male chimpanzees, make coalitions: an enemy one year can become an ally the next. Men may spend more time with their buddies in the sports team or the pub. Women tend to make fewer, but longer-lasting human relationships, and when it comes to potential aggression they may simply side step the issue by avoiding each other.

Mating strategies

Some principles of the male and female mating strategies spring directly from the unequal investment males and females make in reproduction, and they are common to all mammals. How they are implemented varies. At one extreme, lumbering bull elephant seals or antlered stags will fight their rivals with brute force and the females, it seems, may have relatively little choice other than to submit to the biggest and the strongest male. At the other end of the spectrum are the dolphins, many primates and human beings, where the males usually get their own way without physical conflict, and females exercise a great deal of direct choice.

Chimpanzees live in mixed-sex groups, usually of ten to twenty adults and, unlike most other species except human beings, it is the group of males, often sons of the same mother, who form the backbone of chimpanzee society, the females migrating to another troop after puberty. Chimpanzees have intense social relationships with a strong and continued need for reassurance expressed by physical touching, grooming, embraces and kissing. Chimpanzees scream, hoot and grunt greetings and messages, point when they want to draw one another's attention to something, shake sticks at one another and throw stones, and they can be literally sick with fear. Adult males make alliances to gain status within the troop.

[Christine Drea.]

The hyaena. This drawing of a spotted hyaena, *Crocuta crocuta*, shows a fetus in the uterus and the long birth canal opening at the end of the clitoris. The clitoris is indistinguishable from the male's penis, and the female even has a 'scrotum' although devoid of testicles. Internally she has normal ovaries and a uterus. During copulation, the males' penis must somehow become invaginated into the end of the female's clitoris, although it is very difficult to see exactly what happens. Birth is even more remarkable, because the young have to be delivered through the female's clitoris which becomes greatly distended and torn in the process. Two-thirds of the firstborn pups die during delivery.

This male mimicry is achieved by the female passing large amounts of male sex hormones to the fetuses during pregnancy. Not only does this masculinize all the female offspring, but it also makes them extremely aggressive, so that at birth the young have a full set of canine teeth. They begin to fight amongst themselves and kill one another within minutes of birth. There are few survivors.

Hyaenas have the reputation of being cowards and scavengers, whereas in fact they are more successful hunters than lions. Is it the male hormones that make the females such powerful hunters? Does the female need to be larger and stronger than the male to defend herself and her cubs against his predatory inclinations? Why should this be the only species of hyaena to show this remakable adaptation? Hopefully current research on this truly remarkable animal will provide some of the answers.

Observing chimpanzees moving through a forest is difficult. Jane Goodall's studies in Tanzania had been in progress for many years before she saw them make and use tools, or kill other animals and eat meat. Watching animals in zoos permits some behaviours to be followed more readily, but does the zoo environment modify behaviour? A chimpanzee cannot choose to leave the troop, and chimpanzees, like people in prison, may be more violent in a zoo than they would be in the wild. In the case of a chimpanzee troop in Arnhem Zoo in the Netherlands, observed by Frans de Waal, one literally murderous attack occurred. The dominant male called Luit was locked in a cage at night with a coalition of two rival males. His competitors attacked Luit, who

> *had many deep gashes on his head, flanks, back, around his anus, and in the scrotum. His feet in particular were badly injured (from one foot a toe was missing, from the other foot several toes). He also had sustained bites in his hands (several nails were missing). The most gruesome discovery was that he had lost both his testicles ... contrary to our expectation [the scrotal sac] had* not *been ripped wide open. Instead, there were a number of relatively small holes. It was unclear how the testicles had come out.*
>
> *Luit died the same day.*

When not pregnant or breastfeeding, females have a menstrual cycle that lasts thirty-seven or thirty-eight days, and for a week in advance of ovulation they advertise the impending event by a huge red swelling of the labia. During these fertile days a female may mate with any or many of the males in the troop – a regular chimpanzee 'gang bang'. At first sight, there appears to be relatively little sexual competition between the males, but a closer look suggests a well orchestrated pattern of dominance and restraint. In one troop kept under close scientific observation, one out of six mature males enjoyed nearly half of the 400 recorded copulations. Chimpanzee troops are not democracies. In de Waal's words, male chimpanzees live in a 'hierarchical world with replaceable coalition partners and a single permanent goal: power. [While] females, in contrast, live in a horizontal world of social connections'.

The behaviour of dolphins is an interesting example of parallel evolution, which occurs when two unrelated species evolve a similar anatomy or behaviour because they face similar sets of problems. (The classic example is the wing of a bird and that of a bat.) In many ways dolphins and chimpanzees are hugely different: one eats fish, has lost its fingers, has no hind limbs, uses its ears for echolocation under water and never comes ashore even to breed; the other eats fruits, lives, sleeps and gives birth in trees, has five fingers, an opposable thumb and powerful legs, and acute, stereoscopic vision. But in the battle between the sexes, chimpanzees and dolphins have evolved some similarities in mating strategies.

Although there are still gaps in our knowledge of dolphin social life, Randall Webb in Sarasota, Florida, Richard Connor in Shark Bay, Western Australia, and Rachel Smolker of Anne Arbor University in Michigan, USA, have been able to follow schools of dolphins, in different parts of the world, for a decade or more. Like chimpanzees (and people), dolphins live in noisy, interactive social groups of males, females and children, a structure which is relatively rare among mammals. Schools of dolphins may number hundreds of animals. Swimming together protects the animals against predators, improves fishing performance, and encourages complex social and sexual interactions. Males cooperate to 'herd' females away from their swimming partners. Two or more males will execute a well choreographed aquatic ballet of somersaults, bellyflops and high leaps in perfect synchrony. If the female remains unimpressed by this display of talent, then they will bite her or slap her with their tails. One group of males will recruit the help of another in a complex game of social chess that involves remembering past favours and thinking ahead. Females, for their part, are intelligently aware of male strategies and attempt to turn them around for their own purposes.

Dolphins and chimpanzees can put on an amusing show in an aquarium or a zoo, but their diverting performance is more cunning than it appears at first. In a limited but genuine way, these two species with brains almost as large as our own are politicians: they substitute duplicity and cunning for physical violence and they wait for opportunities rather than seek quick solutions. Under certain circumstances both can be ruthless and vicious: friendly, funny Flipper, like Pan the chimpanzee, will kill for sex. What about human beings?

Homicide

A chimpanzee gathering data on human sociology, even in a city as violent as Miami, Florida (350 murders per million citizens per year), would have to be very patient or extremely lucky to see a murder. Conversely, when homicides do occur then drama and accuracy of documentation throws useful light on our behaviour as primates and on the very guile that is the successful alternative to male/male violence. The criminal justice system demonstrates that men are more aggressive than women, and the data are strong and consistent across all cultures and for all historical periods for which records are available. Martin Daly and Margo Wilson from the University of Toronto have analysed records of murder in Canada and other countries to test evolutionary hypotheses. They found that in thirty sets of criminology statistics male/male murders outnumbered female/female by a ratio of 10:1. The more detailed the analysis, the stronger the effect. In Daly and Wilson's Canadian sample there were 2965 murders where one male killed another and only 175 cases of female/female murder; however, half of the latter were where mothers killed their daughters (itself a rare event). When same-sex murders were classified so that the parties' ages were within ten years of one another, then there were 1519 male/male homicides and only 39 female/female – a ratio of 39:1. Women are more likely to be first offenders than men. The most plausible explanation for these marked differences is that they are an expression of our biological predispositions, albeit modified by the local social environment. We are not, after all, so different from other polygynous animals.

The largest group of murders are aptly described as the outcome of trivial altercations between young men, often resulting from a minor insult, curse or pushing, and commonly involve acquaintances. Murders of this type rarely hit the headlines but they are more frequent than, for example, a killing during a robbery. Violence and murder are most common among those who have least to lose: they occur in that group of young men who are furthest removed from the rich and powerful. In the 1960s, following President Kennedy's assassination, the US government established a National Commission on the Causes and Prevention of Violence. The thirteen volume report concluded 'Ostensible reasons for disagreements are usually trivial, indicating many homicides are spontaneous acts of passion, not products of a single determination to kill.' According to Daly and Wilson, a Dallas detective noted:

> *Murders result from little arguments over nothing at all. Tempers flare. A fight starts, and somebody gets stabbed or shot. I've worked on cases where the principals had been arguing over a 10 cent record on a juke box, or over a one dollar gambling debt from a dice game.*

What is really happening? Are some men of an intrinsically violent irrational disposition? The 'trivial altercation' may be more likely to turn from a fist fight into homicide if men can draw a sword, or if they have a gun or knife in the belt, but murder has always happened. Indeed in the thirteenth century the murder rate in England was twenty times higher than it is today, and in Miami in the 1920s it was almost three times as high as in 1980. Competitive, polygynous men, who find themselves at the bottom of the social pile, have a particular need to establish their place in the world, to be ready to reinforce their posturing with violence. Women are less competitive: if she is willing to lower her sights sufficiently and if she is very eager to have a child, then any woman can find a man to inseminate her. Not all men, however, can find women who will agree to have intercourse with them. The high rate of male/male homicide contrasts strongly with the much lower rate of female/female violence leading to death. In genuinely monogamous species, such as marmoset monkeys and gibbons, females are as hostile to one other as males, and it is reasonable to speculate that if we had evolved to be genuinely monogamous then probably the ratio of male to female homicides would have been close to unity.

Polygyny

If there are no constraints on either sex, and each has multiple partners, this is referred to as promiscuity. Chimpanzee society is promiscuous. In a polygamous mating systems, one sex has more than one sexual partner of the opposite sex. We can distinguish between two types of polygamy: polygyny where one male has several females; and the much rarer variant, polyandry, where one female has several males. Seventy per cent of all human cultures that have been investigated allow polygyny, whereas polyandry is confined to one or two societies – one of them in Tibet. Despite the fact that most cultures permit polygyny, numerically most people in the contemporary world now live in societies where laws and traditions support monogamy. Even so, all human societies permit men greater sexual freedom than women. Polygyny is of obvious advantage to a successful male, who is able to father many offspring if he can maintain access to several different mates. In preliterate societies, however, and therefore throughout most of the time human beings have been on Earth, when food was scarce or disease common, then polygyny was often also to the female's advantage. On average, the wife in a polygynous union has fewer children than a woman in a monogamous partnership and she can expect less help with bringing up the children she does have, unless her mate is exceptionally wealthy. Nevertheless, polygyny can still be to a woman's long term biological advantage if the alternative is a relationship with a male with few or no resources to share. Where marriage rules are rigid and strictly enforced, as in some socially and economically highly stratified societies, then sometimes a small (often genetically related) élite controls a disproportionate share of the total resources. They may make polygynous matches that are cruelly restrictive for women and may also leave many other males in society without a chance of marriage.

King Solomon is said to have 'had seven hundred wives, princesses, and three hundred concubines' (1 Kings 11:3). The Bible does not record Solomon's progeny, but the Pharaoh Ramses II (1279–1213 BC) was credited with 186 children by numerous concubines, many secondary wives and one Great Royal Wife. King Louis XIV of France had seventeen children divided between his queen, mistresses and paramours. Augustus the Strong, elector of Saxony and king of Poland, acknowledged having 354 bastard offspring. Morlay Ismail the Bloodthirsty, king of Morocco in the early eighteenth century, had 500 concubines and acknowledged 888 children. He reinforced his position of wealth and authority with great personal violence: concubines who gossiped among themselves had all their teeth extracted and Ismail the Bloodthirsty used to divert his guests by ordering his executioner to behead slaves for no reason. 'I have sixty-seven children. You shall educate them, and as many wives, likewise, as may wish to learn English' said His Majesty Maha Mongkut, king of Siam, to Anna Harriette Leonowens as he engaged her as his children's governess in 1862. Her experiences in the Royal harem became the basis of the musical *The King and I*. In Anna's original words the king 'is not merely enthroned, he is enshrined. To the nobility he is omnipotence, and to the rabble mystery'. Each night at 9 o'clock he retired to his domestic apartments and 'named the women whose presence he particularly desired, in addition to those whose turn it was to "wait" that night'.

Bartell interviewed Americans who were involved in group marriages in the 1960s, where several men and women share each other's sexual favours, and relationships disintegrate spontaneously and rapidly. The experimental or 'swinging' marriages of the 1960s soon gave up group sex, and children were always identified with particular parents. A few ideologically driven groups agreed to rotate sexual partners according to strict rules, but only in a joyless, mechanical way. It is plain that human beings, unlike chimpanzees, are not predisposed to be promiscuous even when they have the freedom and think it might be a good idea.

Polygyny can be a stable mating pattern when some men have above-average wealth or power. An interesting example is that of Joseph Smith and his relatives, who founded and ran the Church of the Latter-day Saints. Smith claimed that in 1827 he had discovered the Book of Mormon inscribed on gold plates in New York State. The Mormons are renowned for maintaining excellent family records. Steven Faux and Harold Miller of Brigham Emery University have analysed Mormon genealogies from an evolutionary perspective. Joseph Smith began in secret as he put it, to 'teach' polygyny to selected Church faithful in 1837. The practice was publicly acknowledged in 1852 and ended in 1906. Polygynous marriages were always closely regulated and a man did not so much choose to take multiple wives, as to follow Church instruction. By 1880 fewer than one in ten males in Utah was a polygamist and most of those only had two wives, but among the twenty-nine founding members of the Church hierarchy, ten had multiple wives and on average they had five wives and seventeen children. Polygyny was only for the élite and the nepotists: among this prolific group of ten men, eight were blood relatives of Smith. Throughout the nineteenth century Smith's relatives had an average of 24.2 children, while his non-relative polygamists in the hierarchy had 11.4. Brigham Young, Smith's successor, had fifty-three wives who bore him fifty-seven children. The Mormon religion, it seems, was not written on gold plates buried in a muddy field, but transcribed from the genes of Joseph Smith and Brigham Young. Religion had been given a reproductive goal and Brigham Young taught that God's glory resided 'in the number of his posterity'.

Hogamus higamous

Our behaviour is balanced on a knife's edge. Female mammals put more energy into reproduction than males and therefore most mammals, including most primates, are polygynous and males play no direct role as parents. *Homo sapiens* is different. We have united two very different reproductive agendas by some clever sexual strategies, and have ended up combining extreme sexiness with a huge and rich variety of cultural arrangements and behavioural practices without parallel in the animal kingdom. It is this powerful combination of culture and biology that dominates our thoughts, our advertising hoardings, our music, our literature – and drives forward the major part of our lives. Behind it all are two very different animals with very different reproductive agendas: the male and the female of our species.

From an evolutionary perspective, if we were truly monogamous, then men and women would be of similar size and shape. Men should not have beards, or women breasts that develop at puberty. Men should have small penises and tiny testicles. But the fact is that men and women are physically very dissimilar, and not only are men 15 to 20 per cent taller and heavier, but they are also physically stronger than women. It is also worth noting that women usually choose to marry men who are taller than themselves, thus perpetuating the difference in size between the sexes.

Undoubtedly we come from a polygynous or promiscuous stock and our bodies still carry the tell-tale evidence. Yet we can develop an intense bond of attachment, usually to somebody of the opposite sex, so that at any one moment most men are monogamously bonded to a single woman, and vice versa. We can and do behave as a monogamous species for much of the time. Men are fertile from puberty to the grave, whereas in women fertility is restricted to the period between menarche and menopause, and this means that men have a much longer fertile life than women. Even in a monogamous society, some men are likely to produce more offspring by more partners during a lifetime than are most women: that is the essence of polygyny. Often the passion of sexual love weakens after several years and new relationships can become established. Perhaps serial monogamy is our subtle compromise between strict monogamy and polygyny.

Thus when Mrs Amos Pinchot awoke from her dream, she had genuinely transcribed something very profound about human experience: there is indeed some truth in the shorthand that men are polygamous and women are monogamous.

3 SEX AND GENDER

'Nuptiall *love* maketh Mankinde; Friendly *love* perfecteth it; but Wanton *love* Corrupteth, and Imbaseth it.'
Sir Fracis Bacon, *The Essyes or Counsels, Civill and Morall*, 1625

Peter Stirling is looking forward to his silver wedding anniversary. He is balding, has a salt-and-pepper beard and has had one heart attack. Mr Stirling had his first menstrual period at the age of 15 years and was delivered of a healthy baby girl at age 22.

Most people sometimes wonder what it would be like to be a member of the opposite sex for a while. Peter Stirling knows. He was born an apparently normal girl and christened 'Jean' in Sydney, Australia, in 1936. During her adolescent years at school the choir mistress asked Jean not to sing in the school choir because her voice was a little deep, and she was playing soccer with the boys when her first period began. Jean married Robert in 1957. The marriage broke up and Jean, feeling awkward and confused, sought medical help. She was referred to specialists in London. They found that her male sex hormone levels were abnormally high and rising with time so she had a hysterectomy, her breasts were removed and she became Peter. Thus Peter

Bride or groom? Jean Stirling married Robert at the age of 21 (*left*). They were divorced. Jean became Peter, and married Barbara at the age of 31 (*right*).

[Peter Stirling.]

Stirling lived the first part of his life as a normal fertile woman, but he has lived the second as a happily married man, with a little help from some additional male sex hormone injections.

Sex describes our anatomical and genetic make-up – our chromosomes, our gonads and our genitalia. Jean had female sex chromosomes and ovaries, but she also had tissue that made a great deal of testosterone. As the ovaries and testes have a common origin in the embryo, it is perhaps a wonder that such errors of gonadal development are not more common.

Gender is the sex we perceive ourselves to be and how we express our sexuality in our dress, our gait, and our very name. Gender is society's stereotype. Animals have sex, but they do not have a gender. In some cases a person may seek to change their gender without any abnormality of their hormones. The fact that we can choose to change our gender tells us much about the degree of social control we can exercise over our sexuality. In Jean's case, however, her hormones overrode everything else. Jean was brought up as a girl, and initially she was unambiguously a girl, but, as she developed, male sex hormones gradually changed her gender to that of a male. She left Australia as her mother's daughter and returned some years later as her son, Peter. He married Barbara, and it was as a proud father that Peter gave away her/his daughter to be married; he was genetically her mother, but socially now her father. Peter Stirling suffered a great deal during the transition when his hormonal sex and his assigned gender did not fit. He is a generous man, willing to share his story because he would not like others to suffer as he did.

In 1963 a little boy had a circumcision that went horribly wrong. On the advice of his doctors at Johns Hopkins Medical School, Baltimore, the damaged penis was removed, surgery was performed to fashion a vagina and female hormones were given. At the time the experts sincerely believed nurture would triumph over nature, and the parents were persuaded to bring the child up as a little girl called Joan. Even as a toddler, Joan felt different, ostentatiously playing with guns, standing up to urinate and tearing off frilly dresses. Joan was not told of her real history until she was aged 14. Then, 'for the first time everything made sense'. A second set of operations was conducted and now John is married and has three adopted children. In this case of medical folly, nature was much stronger than nurture.

Reinforcing gender

Cultural reinforcements of gender start in the cradle and end in the grave. We are assigned our gender at birth, as the obstetrician or midwife announces the appearance of our genitalia. In the modern world, the mother may be shown her fetus's scrotum on an ultrasound screen, or told the genetic sex after chromosomal analysis even earlier in pregnancy. Our gender is broadcast to the world as soon as our arrival is announced to relatives and neighbours. Most of us are given a sexually dimorphic name and often we are dressed in colour-coded clothing. Although this makes no direct difference to the babe in arms, the indirect effects are enormous, since gender radically alters the behaviour of everyone who comes into contact with the child, including the giving of presents; witness the hesitancy of the stranger approaching a baby whose sex they do not know, or worse still, the embarrassment of one who gets it wrong. Once we have been assigned a sex it is difficult to change it.

Hunter–gatherer and peasant societies often define sexual roles even more sharply than does modern society. Each sex is given its own well understood tasks, such as making pottery, killing game, weaving, preparing food, tending the animals or tilling the fields. While such sex roles may not be consistent across cultures, there are often strong taboos against mixing up or altering sexually defined tasks in a particular society. The word 'taboo' is Polynesian. In ancient Hawaii women were not allowed to eat with men and were forbidden to eat pork, coconuts or bananas. Those who broke a *kapu* (the Hawian variant of taboo) could be clubbed, strangled or buried alive. The *kapu* system ended in 1819 when King Liholiho, encouraged by some of his chiefs and his mother Keopuslani, ate with the women at a feast. Segregation of this type makes men and women more dependent on one another than in a sexually egalitarian society such as ours: it is more difficult for a wife to walk out on her husband if society has ensured she has no experience in earning a living.

'Genderlects'

We extend gender beyond the sexual, and conversation, gossip, oratory, gestures and the very way we frame our communications are all suffused with the colours of sex and gender. French, Russian and many other languages assign gender to everything. English does the same but more discreetly. 'Spinster', meaning unmarried woman, is clearly derived from the mediaeval division of labour, where unmarried girls did all the spinning of yarn. When it comes to stringing words together to convey ideas, the differences between the sexes are so great that misunderstandings are almost the norm. Just as there are geographical dialects, so in linguist Deborah Tannen's word there are 'genderlects'.

Tannen's book *You Just Don't Understand* analysed male and female conversation with great insight and became a best seller. It is unlikely a man

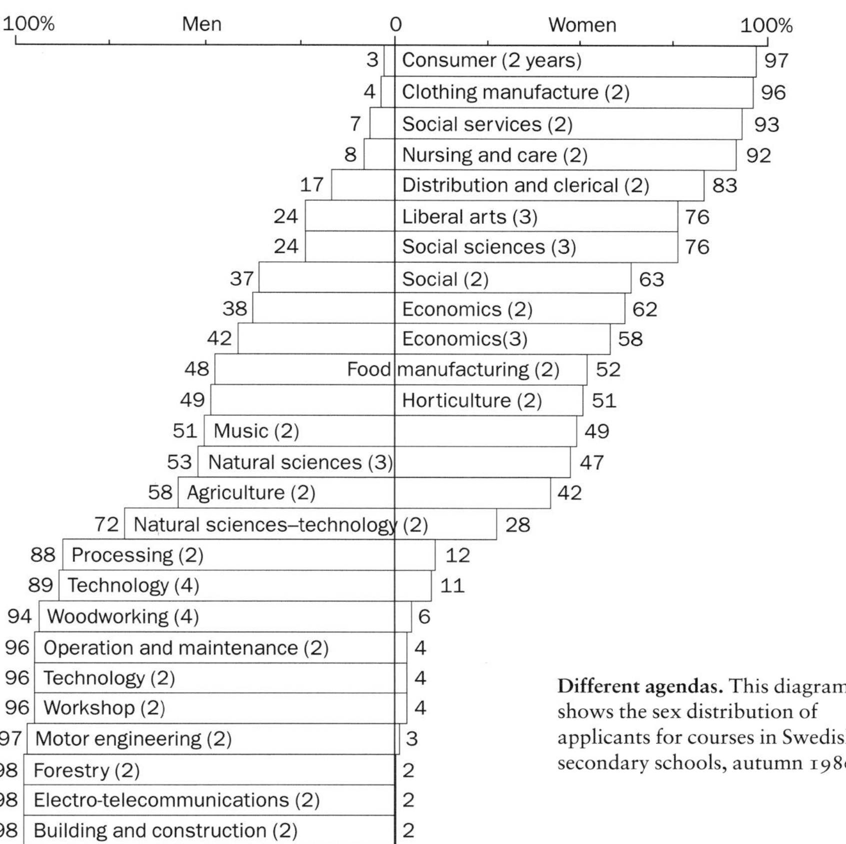

Different agendas. This diagram shows the sex distribution of applicants for courses in Swedish secondary schools, autumn 1980.

could ever have written a book half as good. Yet, nowhere does Tannen explore explanations for the differences between the way in which the two sexes use language, other than some oblique references to cultural influences in childhood. As male authors, we would have given a poor account of women's use of language, but we would have struggled to seek an explanation: the sexes do indeed think in different ways.

Tannen observed that women use language for rapport, understanding, and to reassure. Men, she showed, more often use language to report, to gain attention, to assert independence and to define their position in the social hierarchy. Men like to lecture and are talkative in public, women are expected to listen but are talkative in private. A man more often talks to transmit information and instruction, while women are better at using language to establish intimacy. A man may perceive that not to know something is humiliating, while for a woman it is a trivial shortcoming to be acknowledged honestly. In the particular area of sex, women are more likely than men to discuss emotional or sexual problems. Men are reluctant to share intimate details with one another, let alone discuss any aspect of sexual failure.

Going beyond Tannen, we suggest that genderlects reflect the different ways men and women have evolved. Men are competitive among themselves and especially eager to impress the opposite sex, and the more they inflate their place in the world, the more likely they may be to acquire mates. Women

Arnolfini Wedding Portrait, **Jan van Eyck, 1434.** One of the most famous marriage portraits in the history of art, as well as a major masterpiece of the period. The painting presents a young couple exchanging marriage vows in the privacy of the bridal chamber, not an uncommon practice at the time of the painting. They seem to be alone with the painter, as indicated by the Flemish phrase above the mirror, 'Jan van Eyke was here'. In other words, the painter was a witness to the wedding and this picture functions as a pictorial marriage certificate. The setting, however realistic it appears, also is replete with disguised symbolism of a very subtle type which conveys the sacremental nature of marriage. For example: the single candle in the chandelier burning in broad daylight stands for the all-seeing Christ – also note the scenes of passion in the frame of the mirror; the shoes that have been removed are an indication that they are standing on holy ground; even the dog is an emblem of marital faith, as are the furnishings throughout the room.
The natural world is made to contain the world of the spirits so that the two actually become one. Also, note that the bride is not pregnant, but wearing the very full dress typical of paintings of the period. The marriage was childless and ended in the husband going off with another woman.

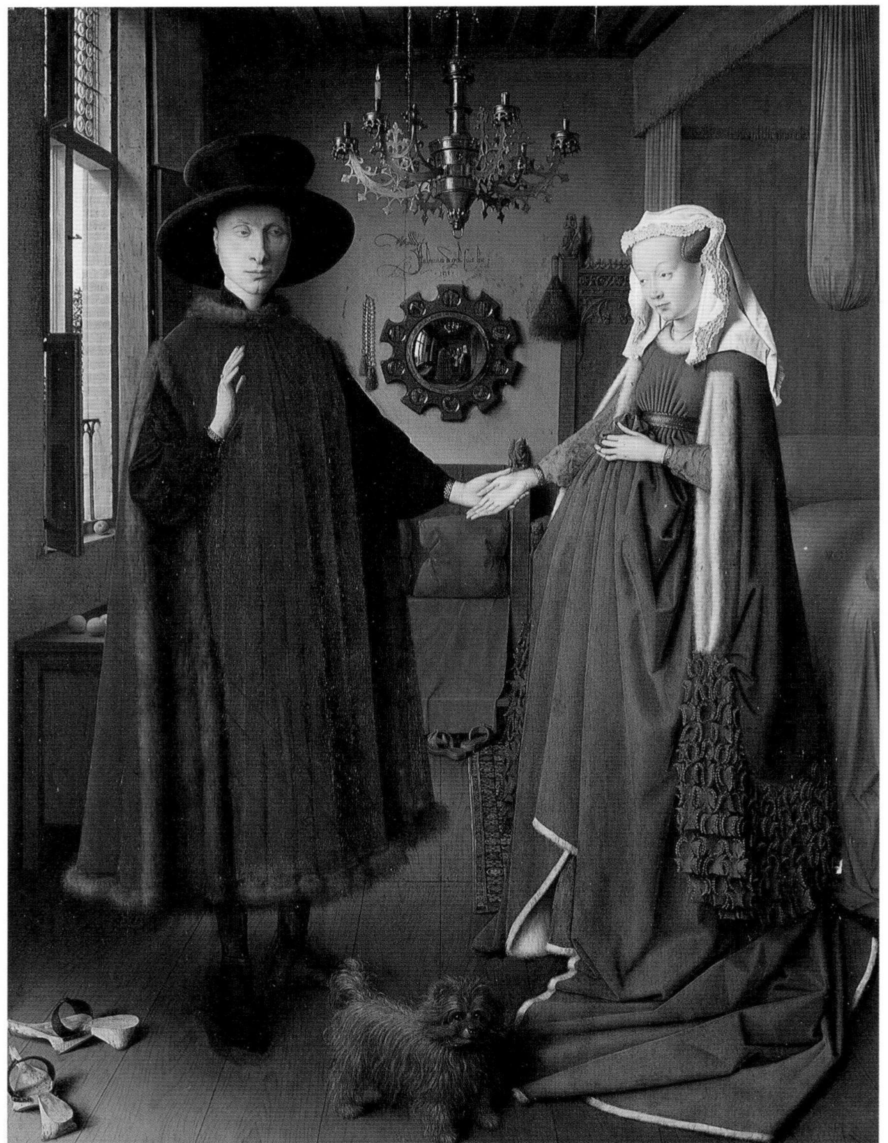

[The National Gallery, London.]

are more likely to be supportive, as helping one another is a reasonable strategy for the sex that must carry the burden of pregnancy and that is most directly involved in child rearing. Tannen suggested that conversation between men is asymmetrical and part of the contest of daily living, while women's is symmetrical and builds closeness: hence a man may interpret his wife's request to do something as an order, while she will have seen it as a perfectly reasonable suggestion. A woman will provide helpful feedback to a conversation that a man may misunderstand as unnecessary interruptions. Women in an effort to be cooperative will consult over a course of action and ask an outsider the way, while men will avoid consulting and consider asking for help to be demeaning. Of course, as with all the differences between the sexes, there are a thousand exceptions to this series of contrasts; yet there are also truths. How often will a man drive the extra mile rather than stop to ask the way? It is important to understand the different ways each sex uses language, since we can enrich our lives by learning the other sex's approach to communication.

The fashion of gender

Every morning, on waking, we set about making a carefully nuanced statement of our gender and reproductive potential. We get dressed. Clothes allow us to wear the antlers of a deer, the breast of a robin, the genital swelling of a baboon and the mane of a lion all in the same day. In societies with great differences in wealth, rich men may decorate themselves rather in the way male birds compete for mates, with colourful plumage. Such male decorations were seen in French aristocrats before the Revolution, in upper class Victorian England, as well as among the Aztec and Inca nobility. Today, men express their wealth by a well cut suit or handmade shoes. A uniform is a cliché – often a successful one – for authority. The remarkable global uniformity of the man's business suit is broken by subtle differences in cut, fit, cufflinks and tie, in attempts to signify wealth. A male who flaunts his success is likely to increase his allure to females. An expensive suit, and not just one, but many, set off by a chauffeur-driven Rolls Royce is designed to impress, at least initially. It may even mean taking risks, and it is not unusual for men to overreach themselves and to be declared bankrupt. A new generation of business consultants have emerged, mostly women, who advise public figures, especially politicians, about 'power dressing'. For men, ill-fitting suits, tight collars, double chins, obesity and club ties are out. Minute attention to detail – the pattern of shoes you wear, the size and colour of the handkerchief in your breast pocket – can all convey powerful images to a television audience of millions who are probably more impressed by what you look like than by what you say. After all, we are all in awe of peacocks, in spite of their monotonous, raucous, squawking calls.

But if these interpretations are correct then biology has also been the great leveller, as all this male strutting, preening and decoration is ultimately controlled by the opposite sex. Darwin wrote of the 'great eagerness' of males to compete for mates, and compared it with the relative caution of females. Women learn to gently accentuate whatever competitive advantage they have in the triggers and symbols of reproductive potential: a trim ankle, a coy cleavage, the flow of fabric over a rounded buttock, or a tangle of glistening hair. As a result of the high investment a woman makes in reproduction, and her lesser interest in being opportunistic, she must signal a continuous attraction – or availability for sex – but only according to strict conditions and rules. Female dress says: 'I'll show you this much but if you want the rest you must make a commitment.' It is a fine balance: a young woman may dress 'to turn a man's head', but for the man to stare too long would be rude. A world of nudists would be exceedingly dull, missing all the non-verbal messages we transmit so clearly in the way we dress.

The ratio between the sexes

Sex is unambiguous, unlike gender. We share our division into male or female with all other vertebrates and much of the rest of the natural world. Unless we are unlucky enough to suffer from some congenital abnormality of the reproductive tract, or an abnormal division of chromosomes, we know what sex we inherited.

As female mammals make a much greater investment in the next generation than males, it might seem a good idea biologically to flood the species with females and have relatively few males who would still compete with one another to inseminate females whose offspring would in turn produce mostly females. Yet, in almost all mammals, the sex ratio at birth is close to 50:50. An analysis of forty-six million human births in western Europe showed that 51.43 per cent of the offspring were male and in another study of 1.6 million cattle, 52.57 per cent were male. However, among 317 000 sheep only 48.7 per cent were male. These tiny but consistent differences may merely reflect differences in the primary sex ratio at fertilization, or a subsequent change due to differential death of one sex over the other during embryonic development, but in general the 50:50 ratio persists.

The explanation for equal numbers of males and females, like so many other things, goes back to the competition between individuals that is the basis of Darwinian evolution. R. A. Fisher, the great British statistician and geneticist, first pointed out in 1930 that natural selection will always tend to produce a sex ratio that approximates to equality. If one sex is produced in excess, while there might be some short term advantage, in the long term there will always be an advantage for the next generation to produce the rarer sex and over time an almost perfect balance will be established.

The alternation of generations

Our sex is determined by our gametes. All eggs have one X chromosome, while half the sperm have one X and the other half one Y chromosome. A combination of X and X in the fertilized egg will give a female and X plus Y a male. As we shall see, the germ cells that will ultimately produce the single-celled gamete (an egg or sperm) are set aside very early in embryonic life. If we are born to a middle-aged mother, we may have lived almost as long as an unfertilized egg as we do in the form of a multicellular organism. In reality, each of us leads a double life. There is the romantic life we know, that of a thinking, moving, feeling individual, and there is that secret life lying dormant within us, the sexual life of our gametes – thoughtless, senseless sperm or eggs, waiting for a rare opportunity provided by their host to meet with a gamete of the opposite sex and produce a new individual, thereby handing down the thread of life from one generation to the next. One world is familiar to us, the other alien and mysterious. One is a brief spark of sentient life, the other tied to thousands of millions of years of slow continuous evolution. For the mature sperm, life is nasty, short and brutish. It lives only for a few days and it is a trillion to one chance that it will fertilize an egg. Few will even make it into a woman's vagina. The vast majority are destined to be washed out of the man's reproductive tract each time he urinates, to be flushed down the toilet, ending their days amongst the detritus of civilization in the sewers of some city, or spilled upon the ground, where they die like stranded tadpoles. A woman begins life with millions of eggs, each unique, but virtually all of them die inside her body and, of the tiny fraction that are released, most go unfertilized and are incinerated with menstrual pads. Our gametes are our birthright, but we are unaware of their presence and accord them scant respect.

This alternation of the generations between a mortal soma and immortal germ plasm has fascinated philosophers, theologians, poets and scientists for generations, and will continue to do so long into the future. For it deals with the very nature of life, and death, and the transmission of our DNA, from generation to generation. At one extreme, there are those who like to think that a chicken is merely an egg's way of making another egg. Or maybe, as Richard Dawkins would have it, the soma is merely the product of an ageless battle between selfish genes, striving for mastery and seeking propagation through succeeding generations. William Wordsworth wrote in *Ode on the Intimations of Immortality*,

> *Our birth is but a sleep and a forgetting;*
> *The Soul that rises with us, our life's Star,*
> *Hath had elsewhere its setting,*
> *And cometh from afar:*
> *Not in entire forgetfulness,*
> *And not in utter nakedness,*
> *But trailing clouds of glory do we come*

Our life on Earth has not been a series of discontinuous acts of creation, but is an unbroken thread tying us all to our ancestors and with the potential of linking us to innumerable future generations. We are indeed trailing clouds of glory – the glory of billions years of continuous evolution. We do not create life: we have only the privilege of passing it on.

A sexually reproducing organism passes on only half of its DNA to each sperm or egg, in preparation for the doubling-up that will occur later when the sperm and egg fuse at fertilization to create a new individual. This unusual form of cell division is called meiosis and it is limited to the germ cells. Our DNA is packaged into forty-six chromosomes and each cell in our body has twenty-three pairs of chromosomes, half derived from our father's sperm and half from our mother's egg. During the process of meiosis, when the number of chromosomes is halved, chromosomes making up each pair wrap around one another and exchange sections of DNA. It is the process of chromosomal exchange and gamete fusion that gives genetic variability between individuals. This may be why sexual reproduction, for all its complexity, has been so successful.

Animals that reproduce sexually, like ourselves, end up leading double lives, alternating between sex and soma. We also are infected by a little intracellular parasite-like organelle, called a mitochondrion (plural mitochondria), that multiplies asexually in the cell sap. It probably represents a bacterium that invaded one of the ancestral forms of life around 1.5 billion years ago. It has since become an essential part of the make-up of all cells throughout the body of all higher forms of life, where it regulates the energy metabolism of the cell in return for free board and lodging. But whether by design or accident, this 'parasite' has not learned the trick of sexual reproduction, and hence appears to have no DNA recombination mechanism. Its DNA is very different from that of the cell nucleus, being much simpler in structure, and containing a mere thirty-seven genes, compared with 100 000 or more genes coded by our chromosomes. Mitochondrial DNA appears to accumulate mutations over time at a rather constant rate, and hence can be used as a molecular 'clock' to determine the time-course of evolution in a particular species. The intriguing thing is that our mitochondrial DNA is inherited exclusively from our mother, and so it tells us something about Eve, our common maternal ancestor. Although the sperm is surrounded by a spiral of mitochondria that provide the energy for the beating of the tail, and although these male mitochondria enter the mammalian egg at fertilization, they do not survive in the cytoplasm of the egg, which is packed with its own mitochondria. There is evidence that the metabolic activity of the cell produces toxic waste products which in turn damage the mitochondrial DNA and, if this damage is severe, it may ultimately contribute to the death of the host. Evidence is also accumulating that mutations in the mitochondria may be the cause of some forms of Alzheimer's disease, of diabetes that occurs late in life, and of rare cases of blindness and of muscular wasting in young adults.

Comparisons of the DNA from different groups of people allow us to say something special about our evolutionary origins. In the spiral staircase of molecules making up mitochondrial DNA there are 16 569 steps. About every 2000 or 3000 years a mutation takes place in one step and by counting and comparing mutations we can trace our ancestry as a species. On the basis of this evidence, as a species we originated in Africa about 130 000 years ago; by 70 000 years we had spread to much of Asia, and then 60 000 years ago humans crossed the Torres Strait to Australia. About 12 000 to 15 000 years ago they crossed the Bering Strait into the Americas. Efforts have been made to compare the DNA sequences in mitochondrial DNA from Neanderthal skeletons and modern humans. It seems that there was no interbreeding between these two exceedingly similar species, even though they lived side by side for tens of thousands of years. Have we always been predisposed to divide those we see around us into in-groups and out-groups, as chimpanzees do and as we seem to do so often in wars and on other occasions? If so, perhaps we always saw Neanderthals with their different physiques as a hateful enemy (as they may well have also perceived *Homo sapiens* to be). Neanderthals had bigger brains than we do, but perhaps for some reason we won more of the battles. Did we exterminate our cousin species?

Sex invades the embryo

Nature's prescription for passing on our genes to the next generation is that we share the task in precise, mathematical equality with another human being: only two can tango reproductively. The two halves of the gynandromorphic Adam are restored. The sperm and the egg become one flesh when they form a single fertilized cell, or zygote, similar to but distinctly different from either of its parents and with an intimation of its own future sexuality conveyed by the single X or Y chromosome from the sperm that helped to form it. A critically important function for the sex chromosomes is to regulate the development of the gonad, turning it into a testis or an ovary. The gonad in its turn disseminates a sense of sexuality to the whole of the developing embryo. The males testis releases hormones into the circulation, suffusing all the organs and tissues, stamping them with the imprint of masculinity. In the absence of a testis, the embryo will develop as female, for femininity is the neutral state upon which masculinity is superimposed.

I am the love that dare not speak its name

Male homosexuality, as an exclusive lifestyle, appears to be limited to our species, and it has been found in all societies and at all times in history. Among those who are thought to have been gay are princes and paupers, artists and aggressors, soldiers and spies, and kind men and cruel.

Alexander the Great was devastated when his lover and general, Hephastion, died of a fever, and he designed a vast monument, to be built from stones taken from the walls of Babylon, in Hephastion's honour.

King Richard the Lionheart regarded it as a penance when ordered to sleep with his queen. Frederick the Great was an enlightened and successful, if joyless, monarch who as a young man was forced to witness, on the orders of his father, the beheading of his homosexual lover Hans von Katte.

Erasmus was the illegitimate child of a priest, the founder of modern Biblical criticism and a homosexual. Christopher Marlowe, who, had he not died in a tavern brawl, might have outshone Shakespeare, quipped 'all they that loved not tobacco and boys were fools'. At the age of 24, Leonardo da Vinci was imprisoned for having sex with a youth and when he died he left his papers to his closest male companion, Francesco Melzi. Michelangelo, tortured genius and rival of Leonardo, celebrated male beauty in his statues and in his poetry:

The love of which I speak aspires
on high;
Woman is too unlike and little
does it agree
With a wise and manly heart to
burn for her.
The one draws up to heaven, the
other down to earth,
The one inhibits the soul, the
other the senses.

The composer Tchaikovsky was totally immersed in his music, 'if it had not been for my music I should have become mad.' At age 32 he fell in love with 19 year old Vladimir Shilovsky and was inspired to compose *Swan Lake*. At age 36 he tried to cure his homosexuality by an impetuous and unwise marriage and then attempted suicide – pathetically, by trying to catch pneumonia by standing up to his neck in the frozen Neva. In America, Herman Melville wrote the macho parts of *Moby Dick* while in love with Nathaniel Hawthorne, who was already famous for his attack on sexual hypocrisy in *The Scarlet Letter*. Oscar Wilde, the perpetual adolescent, married and had children, but his most successful plays such as *The Importance of Being Earnest* were written during a phase of homosexual experiment and extravagance (earnest was used as a synonym for homosexual, just as gay is used today). 'Beautiful sins, like beautiful people, are the privilege of the rich. The only way to get rid of a temptation is to yield to it', he wrote. He received two years hard labour in Reading Gaol for sodomy, having invited prosecu-

When scarcely six weeks old, the tiny embryo, just over a centimetre in length and not yet recognizably human in appearance, suddenly becomes invaded by sex. Sex enters the body of the embryo as a group of very specialized cells, the primordial germ cells, that initially develop outside the embryo. The germ cells have to push and squeeze and shove their way into the embryo, eventually coming to rest in the region of the future gonad. They are the very soul of the embryo, its life's star, for eventually they will produce the gametes that, in turn, will give rise to the next generation: they are the hidden unicellular life in the multicellular host.

One of the most compelling pieces of evidence for hormonal control of gender comes from people who spontaneously change sex as a result of altered hormone secretion. We have already discussed Peter Stirling, who changed from a fertile female to a male, as a result of increasing male hormone secretion, but even more remarkable are people suffering from a single gene defect called '5α-reductase deficiency'. These individuals were initially

tion by bringing a libel case against his lover's father, the Marquis of Queensberry. It was his lover, 'Bosie', Lord Alfred Douglas, who penned the poem with the line 'I am the love that dare not speak its name'. Bosie's father, the Marquis, remembered today for his boxing rules, had accused Oscar Wilde of 'posing as a sodmite' (he couldn't even spell it correctly).

Somerset Maugham overcame a stammer by becoming a fluent writer; of his homosexuality he wrote, 'I tried to persuade myself that I was three-quarters normal and only a quarter queer, whereas really it was the other way round.' When E. M. Forster wrote *Passage to India* he already had in his drawer an explicitly homosexual novel, *Maurice*, which was published posthumously: 'I want to love a strong man of the lower classes and be loved by him, and even hurt by him.' One of Ivor Novello's most popular musicals, *Perchance to Dream*, was making a record run of 1000 performances while he was spending a month in Wormwood Scrubbs prison for an 'offence'.

Alan Turing, the brilliant mathematician, who broke the code used by the Nazis to transmit messages in World War II, may have contributed more than perhaps any other single person to the Allied victory. Unrecognized for his work, he was arrested as a homosexual in 1952, and 'treated' with oestrogen to stifle his urges. Two years later, after his 'treatment' caused obesity and breast development, he committed suicide. The spies who passed atomic secrets from Britain to Russia in the 1950s, Kim Philby and Sir Anthony Blunt, were also gay.

In Germany, Ernst Röhm joined the National Socialist Party even before Adolf Hitler. An organizer and propagandist, he put together the Nazi Storm Troops, the SS. When Hitler ordered his murder on the Night of the Long Knives, Röhm was in bed with one of his SS troops.

John Maynard Keynes revolutionized modern economic theory; he married when he was 42 but had more fun with the 'Cambridge Apostles', and his private diaries record his conquest of little boys and male street prostitutes. T. E. Lawrence, Lawrence of Arabia, once said of his leadership in the Near East Campaigns of World War I, 'I liked a particular Arab, and I thought the freedom for the race could be an acceptable present.'

AIDS has decimated much top talent in fashion, theatre and the arts, bringing attention to the homosexuality of its victims. Among these were: the actor Rock Hudson, who came out of the closet as he was dying; the attorney Roy Cohn, who worked with Senator McCarthy in his 1950s witch hunt against communists; pianist and entertainer Liberace; and acclaimed theatrical director and choreographer Michael Bennett. In their togetherness, many of these men learned to face death with grit and gallantry.

Herculine to Hercule

Herculine Barbin was born in La Rochelle, France, in 1838 and her personal diary reveals an amazing story. Seemingly a normal girl at birth, when she was still a child her father died and poverty forced her mother to send her to a Catholic orphanage at the age of 7; later she entered a convent. Deeply religious, Herculine became increasingly disturbed by the nature and strength of the emotional attachments she started to form with other girls in the convent.

At the age of 17, she was sent to a new convent to train as a teacher. To her shame, she began to grow a beard and a moustache. Coarse hairs also began to grow on her arms and legs, so she did not like to go swimming with the other girls out of embarrassment. Her menstrual periods never started, and her breasts failed to develop. When she was 19, Herculine was sent to teach in a girl's boarding school, and she almost immediately fell passionately in love with Sara, another teacher, who was only 18. Soon, she began to help Sara to dress and undress, and she would kiss her breasts, to their mutual embarrassment. Eventually, the two girls began to sleep together, and became lovers.

Herculine evidently had some degree of hypertrophy of the clitoris that made some form of sexual union possible. The two girls then had a terrible fright; Sara feared that she might be pregnant. They went through agonies of conscience as they wondered how they would cope with the situation. But all was well; Sara's periods resumed. But then another crisis arose. Herculine had been experiencing pains in her groin, which were becoming more frequent and more intense by the day. Fearing appendicitis, Sara insisted that they summon the doctor, something that Herculine dreaded, for fear of the consequences. But her pleadings were in vain; the doctor came, and as was the custom, began to examine her beneath a coverlet. Realizing that something physical was seriously amiss, he felt bound to inform the Mother Superior of the convent, who forbade the two girls to continue sleeping together; they chose to ignore the edict and resorted to subterfuge.

Tormented by self-doubt in the weeks that followed, Herculine eventually sought an audience with the bishop and confessed everything to him. He listened compassionately and immediately asked his personal physician to examine Herculine in the presence of her mother. Telling her that she had 'lost a daughter, but found a son', the doctor reported his findings to the bishop, who allowed Herculine to return to her school for a few days to collect her belongings and bid a last, loving farewell to the heartbroken Sara.

Herculine's name was then changed on the Civil Register to Hercule. But the local gossips were soon hard at work, and the good nuns in the convent were quite scandalized at the thought of their former intimacies with their pupil, now officially a man. Hercule was dispatched to Paris to work on the railroad, and left the convent, never to return.

At this point, the tone of the diary changes abruptly, it now becomes full of despair, remorse, shame, sorrow and self-pity. In the month of February 1868, the corpse of Hercule Abel Barbin, aged 30, was found in a room in Paris, alongside the diary documenting this tragic life. Hercule had committed suicide by carbon dioxide asphyxiation from a charcoal stove.

The published diary ends with the French doctor's autopsy report. Hercule was of male physique, having an imperforate penis 5 centimetres in length and an imperfectly formed scrotum containing a normal right testicle and an undescended left testicle. No spermatozoa were present in either of the testicles or their ducts. No uterus was present.

These findings are consistent with a diagnosis of 5α-reductase deficiency, a genetic condition in which males are unable to convert testosterone into the hormone dihydrotestosterone, which is responsible for masculinization of the external genitalia. Males suffering from this therefore look like girls at birth, but usually develop male behaviour at puberty. The condition was first recognized from a spate of cases in the Dominican Republic. The death of Hercule Barbin was due to a fatal conflict between nurture and nature.

identified in the Dominican Republic in the Caribbean, but we now know that this condition occurs sporadically, but fortunately rather rarely, all over the world.

Affected individuals are genetic males, with normal X and Y chromosomes, but they lack a vital enzyme which is responsible for converting the testosterone produced by their testicles into a more active form, called 5α-dihydrotestosterone, or DHT for short. Although testosterone itself is responsible for masculinizing the internal genitalia of the undifferentiated embryo to give it a male reproductive tract, the development of the penis and scrotum is dependent on the prior conversion of testosterone to DHT in these target tissues. If the enzyme responsible for that conversion is lacking, then the person will have female external genitalia, and hence will be christened and raised as a girl. But as puberty approaches, the increasing secretion of testosterone from the testes (which remain caught in the abdomen) appears to act on the brain, causing the individual to start behaving sexually as a male. In the Dominican Republic, where a number of families have this condition, it is now recognized and accepted by the community, and such affected young 'girls' can relatively easily change gender at puberty and become the 'boys' that they really were all along. They may even go on to get married, although unfortunately the fact that their testes have been retained in the abdomen all this time means that they are not capable of producing sperm.

Another interesting example of a single gene defect that can alter hormone action and hence change a person's gender is seen in the case of testicular feminization syndrome. Once again, affected individuals are genetic males, with an X and a Y chromosome, but one of the genes on the X chromosome is defective, and as a result neither testosterone nor DHT can bind to any of its target tissues. Thus the whole body is blind to the male sex hormones that the testes are producing. The external genitalia are therefore female and, as with the 5α-reductase deficiency, the affected individuals are christened and reared as girls. But they completely lack hair in the armpits or pubic region, which is normally developed in women in response to a little bit of male hormone secreted by their ovaries. Their testes remain in the abdomen, or may even be palpable in the groin, and since they do not have a uterus, they never menstruate. But one female attribute they do have are particularly well developed breasts, a response to the small amounts of oestrogen secreted by the testes. The reason that men do not normally develop breasts is that their testicular oestrogen is counterbalanced by the much larger amounts of testosterone they are producing, and this inhibits breast development. But since testicular feminization individuals cannot 'see' their testosterone, excellent breast development occurs. So attractive do these individuals become that they often end up winning beauty contests; some become glamorous airline stewardesses, and one even became a queen, until the king divorced her on the grounds of her infertility. But although they may be men at heart, chromosomally, gonadally and hormonally, all the evidence suggests that they can lead perfectly normal, happy, well adjusted lives as women.

So not only is our gender at the mercy of our hormones, it is ultimately governed by our genes. No doubt society reinforces gender stereotypes, but more and more evidence points to important and immutable differences that depend on hormones. For example, little girls with abnormally high levels of testosterone, given a choice of toys, will pick up the same fire engines and sports cars that little boys prefer. But this is not to dismiss nurture as a most powerful factor determining our sexuality: we must remember that many people who decide to undergo gender reassignment, and change from male to female or vice versa, have no known genetic or hormonal condition that could account for this compelling urge to change sex.

As the abnormality of 5α-reductase deficiency shows, maleness is something that is imposed on the neutral female state by the secretion of male sex hormones. Male sex hormones imprint male patterns of response on the brain during fetal life. The relevant behaviour may become evident only in childhood and can persist even if the hormone supply is cut off. Thus young boys show patterns of play very different from those of girls, often described as 'rough and tumble'. Female rhesus monkey fetuses that are experimentally exposed to male sex hormones show this type of behaviour as they grow up, even though the male sex hormone has long since vanished from their circulation. (As an adolescent girl Peter Stirling was playing football when she first menstruated.) As in other animals, there is now evidence that male sex hormone is present during a critical phase of prenatal human brain development and it is able to bring about permanent alterations in the wiring diagram, which in turn cause lasting changes in behaviour.

Societal sex preferences

Society may value one sex – usually but not always the male – more highly than the other. The value societies ascribe to a particular sex can change the biologically determined sex ratio through neglect and death, or deliberate killing. All other things being equal, little boys succumb to accidents and infection slightly more frequently than little girls, but if in any society this natural pattern is reversed and the death rate for girls is higher than that for boys, this is *prima facie* evidence of social pressures favouring male offspring.

Girls may simply be abandoned, or more indirectly they may be fed less and receive less medical care, putting up the infant death rate. More recently, new reproductive technologies have been developed that enable people to give birth to a preferred sex. There is concern in India at the moment that the high cost of marrying off a daughter, with her mandatory dowry, is resulting in antenatal sex diagnosis by ultrasound, for those who can afford it, to detect the presence or absence of a scrotum, with consequent selective abortion of female fetuses. Similarly in China, where sons have long been preferred, the one-child family policy puts additional pressure on the couple to dispose of an unwanted daughter by selective abortion or female infanticide. A recent Chinese census revealed that instead of the normal sex ratio at birth, 106 males per 100 females, it had suddenly jumped to 112 males per 100 females, suggesting that in any given year there are about half a million females 'missing'. Some of this may be due to selective abortion and female infanticide, but it also seems probable that, under the one-child rule, many female births just go unregistered.

Supposing in South Korea, which is notorious for its preference for sons, if the next generation really did have 10 or 20 per cent more boys than girls. Probably, just as biological evolution eventually settles for a 50:50 sex ratio, so would 'social evolution'. When the time comes for men chosen by sex selection to marry there would be a shortage of potential brides, so that in the succeeding generation it is likely that parents would rapidly come to value girls more highly and a self-adjustment would take place. Indeed, as men usually marry women younger than themselves and as fertility has fallen rapidly in many countries, there is already a 'shortage' of brides simply because fewer babies are born each year. As a consequence it seems women are becoming more valued.

In a number of human societies boys are also breastfed longer than their sisters, and amongst some Guatemalan Indians, mothers may even contrive to suckle a son after a younger sister has been weaned. The Cambridge scientist Tim Clutton-Brock has observed Scottish red deer on the Isle of Rhum, and he has also found that hinds (female red deer) will suckle their male calves more frequently and for longer than they will female calves. The underlying biological reason is perhaps the same for deer and for human beings: in the race to reproduce in the next generation, a male that is given the advantage of extra nutrition from its mother's milk may grow up to be stronger and more competitive and hence able to sire a larger number of offspring, thus replicating his mother's genes more effectively than a female would have done. In the case of deer, a successful stag may produce around thirty surviving offspring in his lifetime, whereas even the most successful hinds seldom produce more than nine.

A particularly vivid and interesting example of sex preferences comes from an unusual historical source: an extensive set of Portugese genealogical records of noble families born between 1380 and 1580. In this *Peditura Lusitana* the relative wealth of each family member can be identified by their titles from duke and baron to ecclesiastical or military positions. James L. Boone III of the University of New Mexico in Albuquerque has shown that human parents, like other mammals, will invest in whichever sex is most likely to produce the most descendants, thereby increasing their own reproductive fitness. As with stags and hinds, a man of high physical and social status has the potential to father and support more children than a woman. Therefore low status families sometimes favour daughters in the hope that they will marry up the social ladder, while higher status families favour sons who can use their wealth in the competition to beget more children. Amongst the Portuguese aristocracy, the eldest sons of the most wealthy and powerful were those most likely to marry and have the largest families. Their sisters were often put into nunneries and a remarkable 40 per cent of upper class families sequestered their daughters in this way, thereby avoiding subdivision of family wealth among many offspring.

In the lower status Portuguese families, the number of daughters becoming infertile nuns was half that in the more prosperous households, but sons then became something of a liability. Whereas the elder sons of upper class families stayed at home on the family estates, the later born sons of high ranking families, together with all the sons of lower ranking families, were both more likely to enter the military and more likely to die in warfare. Well over a quarter of lower class family men were killed in battle. Not only were these redundant sons more likely to be slaughtered, they were more likely to die in far flung Portugese possessions, such as India. Between 1380 and 1480 in mainland Portugal, the competition for resources became increasingly intense and the numbers of daughters being cloistred in nunneries and of sons dying in warfare increased further. Indeed, after adolescence, young men entered into what might be termed professional vagabondage and it was this group that provided the core of Christian knights for the *Reconquista* (the Christian expulsion of the Arabs from the Iberian Peninsula) as well as for the Crusades against the Ottoman Turks.

Eckart Voland of Göttingen University has studied church records of births, deaths and marriages from Ostfriesland, along the northern coastal region of Germany, as these records also show interesting sex differences in survival. The analysis of records from the eighteenth and nineteenth centuries turned up a couple of hundred cases where one spouse died, leaving a number of living children. In this monogamous, Christian, agricultural society, if a young wife lost her husband she almost invariably became very poor. Any sons that she had were unlikely to compete adequately with boys from richer families, but her daughters, like the daughters of low ranking hinds in Clutton-Brock's studies, always had some chance of marrying up the social ladder. An investment in daughters in this particular social situation had an adaptive biological significance and, as evolutionary biology would predict, the sons of widows were 36 per cent more likely to die in infancy and childhood than the daughters. When men lost their wives, however, their economic status did not change and they often had the opportunity to remarry; the sons of widowers were no more likely to die young than their daughters.

The investment a woman makes in her children may also be greater as her own reproductive value diminishes: in other words, a young woman, with many years of fertile life ahead of her, is likely to take more risks with her children than an older woman nearing the menopause, who may not have the opportunity to conceive again. To return to the monogamous agricultural society of eighteenth century Ostfriesland, a widow with children was considerably less likely to remarry than a widow without children: the children of widowed mothers were 25 per cent more likely to die if the mother was under the age of 25 than if she was in her late thirties, while the children of men who were widowed were no more likely to die whether their father was young or old. These statistics about the effect of sex and maternal age on child mortality, patiently gleaned from dusty church records, give verisimilitude to family nursery rhymes and fairy tales. In 'Hansel and Gretel', and in the early nineteenth century version of 'Snow White', it is the evil mother who denies her children food and is jealous of them. The wicked step-mother we all recognize in today's story of Snow White is an interesting late nineteenth century corruption of the story, no doubt to conceal the unpalatable truth that human parental behaviour, like that of other animals, can be driven by ruthless imperatives which we may not always wish to recognize but which are not too far below the surface.

Clearly the individual actors in these dramas extending over many generations and involving very different cultures were completely unconscious of the biological drives that appear to have influenced their behaviour. Certainly, it is likely that the widows of Ostfriesland wept like any other mothers over the deaths of their children. Nevertheless, there is something compelling about the fact that biologists can chart the same patterns of parental investment for the Portuguese nobility or the farmers of Ostfriesland as they can for herds of deer on the Isle of Rhum.

Nature and nurture

The extent to which nature (our hormones and our genes) or nurture (our cultural upbringing) controls our sexual behaviour is a fascinating conundrum. The sexes are anatomically different and a biologist, understanding the different roles male and female mammals play in reproduction, would also expect the two sexes to show different behavioural predispositions. A physiologist would look first at the sex hormones as possible mediators of anatomical and behavioural differences in both animals and humans. Social scientists often emphasize the similarities between the sexes, asserting that cultural influences determine almost all the differences relating to the behaviour and the perceptions of the genders. In fact, both nature and nurture are powerful influences.

As they evolved, men and women carried different reproductive burdens, and therefore they engage in different mating strategies, as well as having different average body sizes and secondary sexual characteristics. It is possible to demonstrate differences in the skill with which different tasks are performed by the two sexes, and it may be possible to trace these back to differences in the anatomy of the brain. When presented with photographs of actors portraying a variety of emotions, women outscore men in interpreting

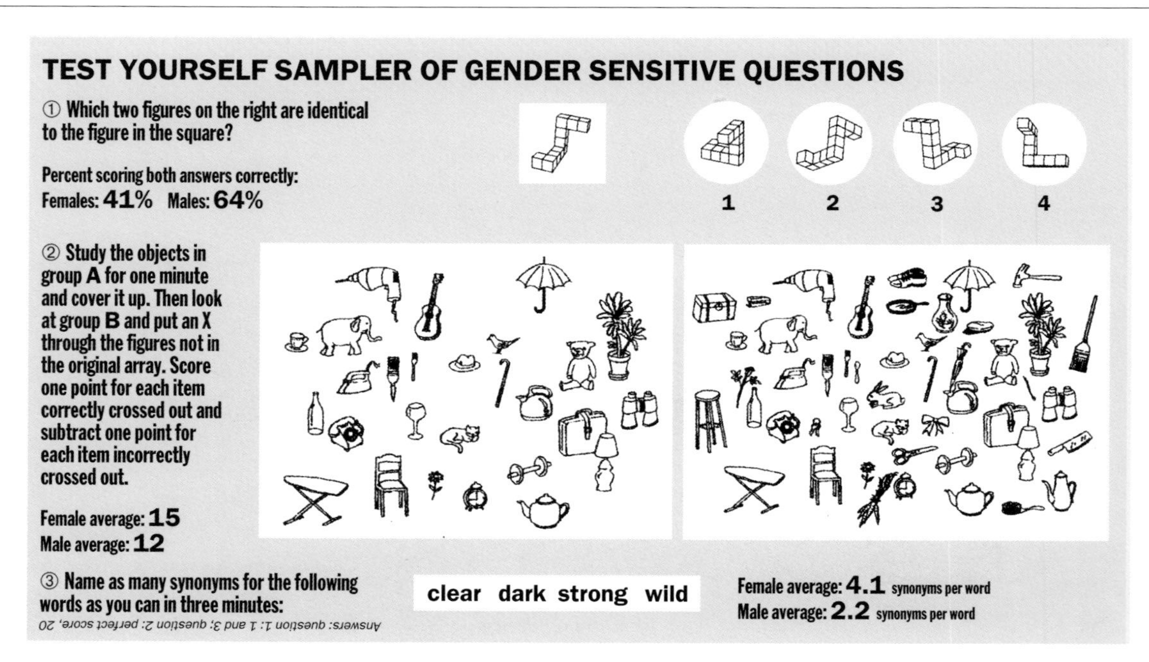

TEST YOURSELF SAMPLER OF GENDER SENSITIVE QUESTIONS
① Which two figures on the right are identical to the figure in the square?
Percent scoring both answers correctly:
Females: 41% Males: 64%
1
2
3
4
② Study the objects in group A for one minute and cover it up. Then look at group B and put an X through the figures not in the original array. Score one point for each item correctly crossed out and subtract one point for each item incorrectly crossed out.
Female average: 15
Male average: 12
③ Name as many synonyms for the following words as you can in three minutes:
clear dark strong wild
Female average: 4.1 synonyms per word
Male average: 2.2 synonyms per word
Answers: question 1: 1 and 3; question 2: perfect score, 20

[*Time* magazine, 20 January 1992.]

the picture. Women are considerably better than men at remembering physical relations, for example the location of objects on a desk top, but less adept at rotating imaginary three-dimensional objects in their brain. A well known curiosity of the human brain is that language is localized mainly in the left hemisphere (which controls the right side of the body) and spatial abilities in the right hemisphere. It seems that the sex which places the greatest emphasis on language or spatial ability is also the one that is most vulnerable if the brain is damaged: a stroke affecting the left hemisphere in men took away the ability to speak in only 3 per cent of subjects, whereas in 13 per cent of women similar damage was associated with loss of speech. Neurologist Christine de Lacoste studied the brains of men and women recovered at post-mortem and found that parts of the bundle of neurones tying together the two sides of the brain (the corpus callosum) were larger in women than in men.

A number of studies have been designed to test male and female differences in spatial and language abilities. Tests of spatial ability require a volunteer to duplicate a pattern with coloured shapes, read a map or solve a maze. Such tests have many limitations but, overall, relatively little difference in ability is found before puberty, while from about age 11 onwards boys begin to perform in spatial tests slightly better than girls. Conversely language skills

Playing footy footy. Human feet show a marked sexual dimorphism in size. This is an advertisement for a well-known brand of condoms.

[Advertisement for 'Mates' condoms.]

seem more highly developed in women. Women also perform certain linguistic and other tasks differently at various stages in the menstrual cycle. The tests are subtle and at first sight comic: women at the time of ovulation can say tongue twisters about 10 per cent better than at other times in the menstrual cycle, whereas their spatial ability tends to be reduced at this time. Boys are four times as likely to stammer as girls and boys outnumber girls 3:1 in remedial reading classes in American schools.

The longest official road race in the world is from Pietermaritzburg to Durban in South Africa, a hilly 56 miles (90 kilometres) – or more than twice as long as the Olympic marathon. In 1993, the first international competitors entered the race. The fastest male runner completed the distance in 5 hours 39 minutes and 41 seconds. The first woman to cross the line did so in 6 hours 55 minutes and 7 seconds. And, as if to emphasize the difference between the sexes, 277 other men finished the race before the first woman did. Men outperform women in all tests of physical strength such as running, jumping and swimming, and in the Olympic games women do not enter some events, such as wrestling, boxing or weight lifting. There are, however, Iron Man (or Iron Woman) triathlon competitions, where a woman's greater stamina may eventually give her the edge for swimming, running and cycling incredible distances – not in five or six hours as in the Pietermaritzburg race, but actually over twenty-four hours. Testosterone is the hormone driving male libido, aggression and competition. The reason why we do not allow any athletes of either sex to take anabolic steroids, which are merely synthetic derivatives of testosterone, is that it would give them an unfair muscular and behavioural advantage. In addition, when a sportsman uses illegal injections of testosterone he may not only be using the hormone to build up his muscle mass, which is one of its actions, but to change his temperament and give him that aggressive urge to win. But since there are considerable differences in normal testosterone levels between men and women, should they be handicapped accordingly? Or should athletes resort to behavioural practices such as sexual stimulation to boost their endogenous male hormone production?

In most polygynous species such as deer or lions, males range more widely than females during the breeding season. The greater the territory they cover, the more likely they are to meet possible mates. Chimpanzee males range around the periphery of their communal territory, which they defend, while the females tend to cover a more limited range nearer the centre. For females, the availability of food for them and their offspring is the limiting resource with respect to reproduction, so they have evolved to maximize their ability to find what they need in as small an area as possible. For males, the limiting resource is access to females, so they have evolved to establish as large a territory as possible. Greater spatial skills, therefore, would be an advantage to the male. Barry Hewlett of Oregon State College followed the wanderings of Aka pygmies in Central Africa and found that men, on average, strayed 38 miles (61 kilometres) from their base camp while women only averaged 25.5 miles (41 kilometres). Similar studies of Mexican immigrants in Texas, Kenyan tribes, African-American school children in the USA, children in Puerto Rico and the Kalahari San Bushmen all showed that boys ranged further than girls and this tendency became apparent as the boys approached puberty. The fact that measured differences in performance and behaviour accelerate at puberty, when the sex hormones begin to be secreted in greater amounts, is strong evidence for genuine biological differences in behaviour.

One behavioural difference between males and females that we can measure in both men and monkeys is the risk of dying from accidents. Young male macaque monkeys in the wild, and little boys in modern society, have more accidents than their sisters. Monkeys and apes do indeed fall out of trees and injure themselves. In a study of young chimpanzees, males had three or four times as many accidents climbing trees as did females – and all falls of more than 11 yards (10 metres) were by males. In a study of subadult macaque monkeys, six times as many males as females died. In Australia between three and four times as many boys and young men (aged 15 to 24) die from accidents as females of the same age. In Japan twice as many teenage males die in road accidents as girls. The fact that adolescent males take more risks and suffer more accidents among human and non-human primates is strong testimony that there is a biologically based sexual difference in behaviour, even though it may be exaggerated or diminished according to the cultural overlay. Even under the age of 1 year little boys manage to poison themselves more commonly than little girls. Mothers will often attest to the fact that little boys crawl off and open cupboards and find their ways into dangerous places more often than little girls do. The consistency of findings across different cultures, along with the fact that there are biologically plausible explanations why males should wander further than females, strengthen the arguments in favour of sex-linked behavioural differences.

Such observations, however, are often countered by suggestions that most cultures encourage little boys to be more exploratory than little girls, and therefore opportunity and training may be the cause of differences in spatial or language abilities between the sexes. Could the differences in mortality be culturally imposed because mothers tolerate their sons running farther afield than their daughters? How then do we sort out the effects of culture and biology? To some extent we do not need to. Most functions of the human brain have an anatomical aspect, derived from the blueprints encoded in our genes, and a learnt component determined by the world in which we grow up. For example, if the eyes of a kitten are covered up for a critical stage in its development it will behave as if it is blind, even though the anatomy of its eye and brain appears to be perfect – it has not learnt how to use these structures at the critical stage. It is misleading to insist that only genetic or cultural factors are at work. It is silly, for example, to suggest that the only reason more boys attend remedial reading classes is because gender-biased teachers pay less attention to girls who are poor readers. That is something that may also occur – and it should be remedied because many schools may indeed undervalue the teaching of girls – but it is unlikely to be the cause of a three-fold difference. Similarly, it is highly likely that the more exploratory behaviour of young boys reinforces their spatial ability, while girls spending more time at home with their mothers may reinforce their language skills.

Differences do not mean inequality. It is also essential to emphasize that while genuine differences may appear in statistical comparisons of a large number of individuals, any one woman or man may perform much better than the average for the opposite sex, or indeed than their own sex. Difference between the sexes add to the richness of life and do not imply that one is inferior to the other. Women and men are different: one is not better than the other. Biologically women are the limiting factor in reproduction, but historically they have often been undervalued. All studies show that male and female skills are likely to overlap to a great extent. Some of the leaders among scientists working on sex differences in brain anatomy have been women. Even measurable anatomical differences in neuroanatomy, however, have aroused opposition from gender flat-Earthists, who reject the idea of sex differences in the brain for ideological reasons. 'How dare you work in this area when the politics are such?', one man in the scientific audience accused Christine de Lacoste when she reported her studies on the corpus callosum. The sexes are different and it does not advance the cause of equal opportunity and equal recognition to overlook the fact that there are certain things which, on average, each sex does somewhat better than the other.

Evidence from the kibbutzim

The Israeli kibbutzim are close-knit farming communities based on collective ownership of land, community governance, communal eating and recreation areas, and nurseries and day-care facilities for all children of the kibbutz from an early age. Part of the creed of the kibbutz movement was to eliminate as many gender and social differences as possible. Boys and girls have the same toys and are dressed similarly when young. Adult men and women have equal opportunities, pay, and access to the political structure. Originally part of the Jewish settlement of Palestine, kibbutzim have survived over eighty years as one of the most radical experiments in communal living ever attempted. Early in this century they practically obliterated the family to the extent that marriage itself became rare. The kibbutz experiment permits a more convincing analysis of biological and cultural influences on gender perceptions than almost any other in society. Is the newborn infant the *tabula rasa* suggested by the philosopher John Locke – a neutral, blank sheet on which society imprints culturally determined stereotypes – or are there biological differences in how the sexes organize, communicate and behave as well as anatomical and physiological differences?

Sociologists Lionel Tiger and Joseph Shepher looked at over 34 000 case histories and a great deal of administrative data from the kibbutzim. When they were first launched, all kibbutzim placed infants in dormitories away from their mothers within a few weeks of birth. Over four generations of kibbutz life the family has re-established itself, although emphasis remains on social and sexual equality. Today, although children tend to spend more time with their parents, they continue to be educated communally. When girls from the kibbutz join the Israeli army they find themselves in one of the few armed forces where women carry rifles and train with live ammunition. Nevertheless, Tiger and Shepher found that generation by generation sex stereotyping **increased**. Before World War 1 women helped to build roads and men did the washing up; today, sex roles are more marked in the kibbutzim than in the rest of Israeli society. The feminist complaint that a patriarchal society teaches the next generation to be sexist is reversed in the kibbutz, where a society that tried to do without sex roles rapidly reinvented them. Of course male and female behaviours overlap. Yet in the kibbutzim, where infants begin life in an identical environment and where children grow to maturity in a society sincerely and demonstrably committed to sexual equality, more boys enter engineering and more girls enter social work.

In a kibbutz community goals continue to take precedence over private needs and in one population of over 100 000 only one case of embezzlement was reported. Yet men spend more time in the assemblies and are six times more active in the government of the kibbutz than women. Men may well have conspired to prevent the advancement of women in many other societies, but, in the kibbutz, women have proved reluctant to accept political leadership. It was the women, however, who initiated the re-establishment of the family: again and again they voted – often in opposition to the men – to take their children out of the dormitory system and bring them up at home.

As sex roles became more distinct over the years, the birth rate also rose, even though the women had easy access to contraception and abortion. Sexual expectations changed from austerity and modesty to romance and comfort. The cultural fundamentalist could argue that the most radical attempt to remove sex stereotypes in the education of children failed because it was not radical enough; a sociobiologist would argue that with the passage of time parents and children reverted to their natural predispositions.

The homosexual conundrum

Many mammals, especially when young, engage in homosexual play: bull calves, puppies and monkeys will mount each other regardless of their sex. Bonobo chimpanzees, as we have seen, engage in a great deal of deliberate, same-sex activity, but bonobos also remain enthusiastically heterosexual. We are the only species where a small proportion of individuals are exclusively and consistently oriented towards their own sex. Biologically this is a profound puzzle. Evolution, as has been said so many times, is driven by the successful transmission of an individual's genes to the next generation: homosexual behaviour is the antithesis of reproductive success. Is it an altered

Buggery

By the late nineteenth century, the kingdom of Buganda, on the western shore of Lake Victoria, was a centralized, hierarchical state ruled by a king, or *kabaka*. Like the Egyptian pharaohs, the ancient Babylonian kings, or the Incas, the *kabaka*'s word was law. In 1884, the 18 year old Mwanga was elected *kabaka*. He ruled a court of thousands consisting of bureaucrats, wives, concubines, warriors, slaves and about 500 young pages. The pages were the sons of aristocrats, who made up the *kabaka*'s bodyguard. It was traditional for the *kabaka* to have anal intercourse with the pages, and Mwanga seems to have preferred this partnership to his wives or concubines.

Both Protestant and Catholic missionaries were entering for the first time what is now called Uganda. Mwanga became interested in the new religion and began to receive instruction prior to baptism. When he was told that the Bible condemned buggery – and he checked the teaching with especial care – he was outraged and turned his back on such a crazy and unrealistic religion. Some of the pages, however, did convert to Christianity and began to refuse to satisfy the king's sexual demands. In January 1885, Mwanga had three pages who had converted to Protestantism decapitated for refusing anal intercourse. One year later, 31 boys aged 13 to 18 and mainly Catholics were burnt alive. The boys could have saved their lives at any time by accepting anal intercourse. The fathers of the boys consented to the executions, promising the king they would replace them with more obedient pages.

In 1964, twenty-two of the Catholic pages were canonized as saints.

physiology, like the inability of some men to manufacture sperm? Is it a social condition facilitated by cultural change which takes away the desire to reproduce? Or is it a subtle type of altruism, like the infertile worker bee who through her efforts enhances the reproductive capacity of others? There is no consensus about the answer, although the presence of homosexual behaviour across cultures and throughout history underscores the reality of the question.

Failure to reproduce is death to the line, and if homosexual behaviour were encoded in our genes then it is a trait that would have become extinct long ago. Individuals with a homosexual orientation must be continually recruited by some process from parents with a normal heterosexual orientation. Despite extensive studies no consistent differences in sex hormone levels have been found between homosexuals and heterosexuals. The pituitary gland of gay men seems to respond to injections of oestrogen in a way that is half way between that of heterosexual men and women, but whether this is a cause of their lifestyle or a consequence remains unknown. In recent years publications by gay scientists have argued that microscopic differences in the brains of gay men suggest that there are underlying genetic or hormonal explanations for homosexuality and there is even some evidence for a 'gay gene' on the X chromosome. Some people think that the community at large would find homosexuality more understandable, and hence more acceptable, if it was the inevitable biological consequence of some congenitally acquired condition. However, the neurological differences that are claimed for brains of gay men are even less than those observed between the brains of men and women. Both the science and the statistics have been attacked. Even if the microscopic differences in brain structure are accepted, and that is still debatable, it is possible that any such changes are a consequence rather than a cause of the homosexual behaviour.

In the early nineties, the USA and Britain carried out the largest randomized studies of sexual behaviour undertaken to date. The British questionnaire assumed, as did Alfred Kinsey in the USA in his famous 1948 study, that human sexual behaviour is a continuum, with some people preferring to have sex exclusively with those of the opposite sex, and others preferring exclusively those of the same sex, and all gradations in between. The British study showed that 93 per cent of men and 95 per cent of women were attracted exclusively to people of the opposite sex. At the other extreme, only 0.5 per cent of men and 0.3 per cent of women were attracted exclusively to people of the same sex, a much lower proportion than was found by Kinsey, but confirming more recent data from elsewhere. In the US study by researchers from the University of Chicago, 7.1 per cent of men said they had had sex with someone of their own sex since puberty and 2.7 per cent had done so in the past year. Only 1.2 per cent of women said they had had sex with another woman in the past year. While men in Britain are most likely to have their first homosexual experience during adolescence, for women it could occur at any age after puberty. The survey confirmed that there is no such thing as a 'typical' homosexual profile, and that, for many people, homosexual experience is transitory, and unlikely to lead to a permanent behaviour pattern.

Homosexuality occurs in a great many very different cultures and the response of heterosexual onlookers to homosexuality has varied from applause to lethal condemnation. The ancient Greeks expected a man to engage in homosexual behaviour, but to limit his attention to young men 'without beards'. Unlike the modern world, homosexuality in the classical world occurred against a background of strict sex roles. Although men alone could rule a city or build a temple they could also be bewildered and afraid of women. The mythical Medea was half demon, half woman, who cooked people in cauldrons and knew things that men would never know, while the fictitious Antigone was possessed of a terrifying purity. Among tribes in Papua New Guinea and in the Siwan in North Africa, anal intercourse among young men is almost universal, although all seem to marry subsequently. The Lango in East Africa not only permit homosexuals to dress as women and become the wives of other males, but they even goes so far as to simulate menstruation. In Oman there is a third gender: the zaniths are biologically men but work as domestic servants, wear distinctive clothes and are basically homosexual prostitutes. In contrast, some Bedouin tribes in the Near East still make buggery a capital offence.

Some of the world's most famous soldiers may very likely have been gay or bisexual, including Alexander the Great, Richard the Lionheart and Lawrence of Arabia. It has been suggested that, in the former USSR, 'sexual relations of a man with another man' were punished by discharge from the service and up to five years' imprisonment. It has been said also that in the USA, between the end of World War II and the mid 1990s, the Department of Defense discharged 80 000 to 100 000 members of the armed forces for gay or lesbian activities. Vice-squad detectives looked for soldiers in gay bars, and women were threatened with loss of custody of their children unless they identified lesbian colleagues. Under President Clinton a 'Don't ask' policy was initiated. By contrast, in Japan, France and South Africa, homosexuality, of itself, is not a reason for discharge from the armed forces.

India is probably the only country in the world that has created a special social category, the *hidjra*, for individuals who may be homosexuals, or intersexes, or transvestites, or even some male castrates or eunuchs. The *hidjra* make their living by travelling through the countryside in small groups, offering entertainment at birthdays, weddings and funerals for a small fee – and subsequently having sex with the guests. With the advent of the acquired immune deficiency syndrome (AIDS), this now poses a major health hazard. Sadly, the *hidjra* are the lowest of the low in society, below the Untouchables; hence they are denied any information about the risks they run, and do not protect themselves from infection with sexually transmitted diseases in general, or the human immunodeficiency virus (HIV) in particular.

Some *hidjra* castrate themselves, or are castrated by their peers. If they receive insufficient gifts for a performance, their ultimate sanction is to sweep up their skirts exposing their mutilated genitalia. The ranks of *hidjra* are constantly replenished because of the custom that any child born with abnormal-looking genitalia will be given to the *hidjra*, who will rear it as one of their own. Each year, the *hidjra* from all over India meet for an annual festival, attended by thousands, when they regard themselves as Brides of Rama for the night. What an opportunity such a gathering could provide for education to help these poor people climb out of the pit of despair that has become their lot in India's caste-ridden society!

No need to compromise

In a way, recent human evolution is characterized by a set of sexual responses and emotions which are increasingly similar for both sexes. Female orgasms have been observed in bonobo chimpanzees, but, as far as is known, orgasm is a rare accompaniment of female sexual drive in other mammalian species. Human sexual behaviour is also unlike behaviour in other animals in that we find so many areas of our body and our partner's body (the breasts, the buttocks, the thighs, the hair on the head) to be erotically stimulating. Is it possible that the strength and symmetry of the human sexual drive in the two sexes and the ability to turn so many parts of the body into erogenous zones also predisposes our species to homosexual love-making? Men are more easily aroused by visual stimuli, seek more sexual partners and more frequent orgasmic physical relationships than do women. Women look for long term, emotionally supportive relationships, characterized by faithful companionship. Same-sex relationships between men are often passionate but relatively brief, and even when two men are emotionally bonded together for long intervals they often accept each other's tendency to seek short term erotic release with other men, driven by physical attraction. In the era before AIDS, some homosexual men in San Francisco had more sexual partners in one night at a bathhouse than many heterosexual men have female partners in a lifetime. One gay man reported physical encounters with forty-eight different men in one evening. Gay male sex can be brief, all fantasy and no conversation, focusing on youth and perceived beauty rather than on social status. Lesbian lifestyles are fundamentally different. Gay women more often put loving relationships ahead of physical experiences, and when two women live together their partnership is more likely to be sexually faithful and last much longer than when two men live together. For lesbians, the warm bonds of human companionship become increasingly important with the passage of time, while the physical aspects of sex may become correspondingly less important and less frequent.

Homosexuality expresses the reproductive agenda of each sex in the absence of the compromises that are necessary for heterosexual partnerships. When two men or two women have a sexual relationship, they seem to act out their own unmodified reproductive agendas with particular clarity; perhaps that is why some heterosexuals feel so threatened by homosexual behaviour. The huge differences in lifestyles between gay men and gay women underscore the biological nature of sexual drives. If adult behaviour were merely a result of the fact that parents emphasize the 'sugar and spice' in girls and the 'slugs and snails' in boys, according to the old rhyme, then this degree of variation would be unlikely. It seems clear that male and female homosexual couples act in different ways for innate biological reasons; homosexuals merely do what biology programmes any man or woman to do in the absence of the need to modify their behaviour to the agenda of the opposite sex.

The flowering of the soma

For multicellular sexual creatures, such as ourselves, whether we die of old age, or prematurely of AIDS, or as the result of an accident or cancer, the thread of life passes unbroken from generation to generation. From a biological perspective, we must ask whether our brain reached its present state of development merely to promote the survival and transmission of a unique pattern of DNA to the next generation? Is the soma, or body, little more than a vehicle for handing on our genes? Are the love and passion of the sexes and the rich and complex patina of our gender no more than a half ruthless, half ridiculous mechanism to carry our genetic material on its endless, slowly altering journey? We are aware that sexual drives may sometimes overwhelm our intellect, perhaps for example exposing us to a sexually transmitted disease or an unwanted pregnancy. But from an evolutionary perspective, we have been constructed by our genes to give our eggs or sperm the best possible chance of surviving to the next generation, and it is in no way surprising that

The heinous sin of self-pollution

Onania, or the Heinous Sin of Self-Pollution and All its Frightful Consequences in Both Sexes was published in 1700, and was one of a flood of books on masturbation phobias. This anxiety-making literature reached its apogee in a work by the Reverend John Todd (1800–73), a Congregational minister from Massachusetts who, in 1835, published a book entitled *The Student's Manual*. Todd recommended reading, exercise and cold showers to avoid the vicious act of Onan, but he faced a conundrum: how to write about masturbation without putting the very idea he was trying to avoid into innocent growing minds. He solved it by writing the key passage in the book in Latin! Translated, it reads:

> *No light, except that of the ultimate God, can uncover the practice of pouring out by hand, in spite of its frequency and constancy. No light can reveal as many modern adolescents as one can imagine, debasing themselves day by day in that way, and doing so over many years… Those people taught by the light of nature have reproved the crime with many words. 'Hand – stay your lasciviousness! Do you think this nothing? It is a viscious act, believe me! An enormity, how great can scarcely be conceived by a soul; restrain your unfortunate hand. More than perpetrating an enormity of young boys, it SINS!'*

According to Todd, masturbation caused a debilitated memory, a weak mind, and ruined a soul. It was something God punished with death. Todd was obsessive and eccentric (he had a mania for collecting guns which he named like pets), but his *Student's Manual* went through twenty-four editions and sold 100 000 copies in Europe.

Masturbation has a rich and varied cultural history. The ancient Egyptians celebrated it as the way in which the Sun God, Re, created the first couple, Shu and Tefnut, whereas Judaic writers regarded it as a crime warranting the death penalty. Saint Thomas Aquinas condemned masturbation as a 'sin against Nature,' and hence worse than adultery or rape. Nineteenth century nutritionists devised diets aimed at combating masturbation. Sylvester Graham advocated a high fibre diet to quell this 'unspeakable vice', and 'Graham Crackers' remain popular in the USA to this day. John Harvey Kellogg perfected the Granola cereal for the same purpose, founding the Kellogg empire whose headquarters are still in Battle Creek, Michigan, where he was superintendent of the local sanitarium. Writing about 'cures' for masturbation in *The Home Book of Modern Medicine: A Family Guide to Health and Disease* (1896), Kellogg suggested,

> *A remedy which is almost always successful in small boys is circumcision, especially when there is any degree of phimosis. The operation should be performed by the surgeon without anaesthetic, as the brief pain attending the operation will have a salutary effect upon the mind, especially if it be connected with the idea of punishment as it may well be in some cases.*

Philip Roth made literary history by making masturbation the theme of his novel *Portnoy's Complaint* in 1969,

> *Then came adolescence – half my waking life spent locked behind the bathroom door, firing my wad down the toilet bowl, or into the soiled clothes in the laundry hamper, or splat, up against the medicine-chest mirror, before which I stood in my dropped drawers so I could see how it looked coming out.*

Kinsey estimated that at least 92 per cent of all US males and 58 per cent of all females had masturbated to orgasm at some time in their lives, and in Britain mutual masturbation is the commonest form of sexual activity after heterosexual vaginal intercourse. Self-masturbation has been described as having sex with the person you know best and love most of all.

our brain and its view of the world are so dependent on the sex hormones our gonads pour out.

However, knowledge is freedom. The more we understand about the machinery of our bodies and the greater the insight we have into our evolution, the less likely we are to be slaves of our reproduction. We can devise ways to separate sex from pregnancy. Perhaps we can understand marriage better. When a man and a woman fall in love they would do well to remember how much they will never understand the world the one they love inhabits. We can describe the differences between men and women, but can we really feel them? Peter Stirling prefers not to talk of his early life as a female, including the birth of his daughter or when he had his first period, although the memories are vivid enough. He says, 'There were two people in one body and Jean had to leave so Peter could emerge.'

The alternation of the generations gives a rhythm to life: 4 generations to a century, barely 80 generations since the birth of Christ; 200 000 since we shared a common ancestor with chimpanzees. Life is an unending game of cards: shuffle and deal, shuffle and deal, always hoping for a better hand in the next generation, although the pack of cards remains virtually unchanged. Double and halve, double and halve: haploid gametes to diploid individuals, then back to haploid gametes once more. In the space of fifty days, a man produces as many sperm as there are currently people in the world: each one is genetically distinct from all its fellows, and potentially another human being.

In the last analysis, life at many levels of complexity is a struggle for existence. There are selfish genes, fighting for expression; there are selfish male mitochondria, endangering the egg cell that they enter; and there are selfish individuals, trying to ensure that their gametes are passed on to succeeding generations by sexual reproduction. Although the flowering of the soma may represent the triumph of evolution, it is destined to wither and die. It is only the cells that produce the gametes, the germ cells, which have the secret of immortality. But even if the ultimate aim of the gene is simply self-perpetuation, it is surely the flowering of the soma that gives the gene its chance for self-expression. As human beings, we add the unique richness of gender to the sexual distinctness of the sperm and egg. It is much more fun being a person than a gamete.

4 LOVE AND MARRIAGE

'When two people are under the influence of the most violent, most insane, most delusive, and most transient of passions, they are required to swear that they will remain in that excited, abnormal, and exhausting condition continuously until death do them part.' George Bernard Shaw, *Getting Married*, 1911

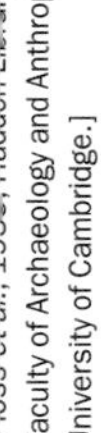

A mediaeval marriage. A woodcut of 1483 showing the marriage bed, where the ceremony took place.

Quickly cam Raymound,
in the bedde him laide
By fair melusine, the suete
doucet made.
Forsoth A Bisshop which
that tyme there was
Signed and blissid the
bedded holyly.

Marriage is found in all human societies. It is the civilized and social definition of mating. A male chimpanzee may take a fancy to a female and spend time grooming her and then try to sneak away from the rest of the troop with her when she ovulates, but a close sexual relationship that separates a pair of adults from the rest of the troop and which lasts for years – and often a lifetime – is not found among chimpanzees or other apes.

In the West we marry for love. The bridal gown, gold ring and the honeymoon are imbued with romance. Yet the 'white wedding' is largely an invention of this century and the combination of love and marriage is by no means universal. Among the Manus people, who inhabit the lagoons of the Admiralty Islands north of Papua New Guinea, marriage for the girl is shame, pain, loneliness, a shaven head and little more than socially sanctioned rape. Yet, however different the experience, a marriage ceremony is recognizable in virtually all cultures and it links the interests of different families and clans. One of the many curious things about human mating is that we often leave the choice of sexual partner to others, so that parents, relatives, astrologers – or in these days even computers – can arrange marriages. In all other species each individual animal makes its own mating choice.

The key to understanding human marriage is not that it permits sex but that it limits it: marriage does not offer the bride and groom sexual access to one another – they could have taken that anyway – but it defines and separates their sexual partnership from all the other sexually active adults in their community. Human marriage makes sense only if a couple is part of a larger group: it is about the relatives and in-laws as much as it is about the bride and groom. Marriage gives social definition to private sexual acts and generates a structure for bringing up children. The apocryphal shipwrecked couple alone on a desert island would have sex, but marriage would serve no useful function.

As we have seen, when it comes to reproductive strategies men and women behave almost as though they belonged to two separate species: the erotically driven male forever reviewing the reproductive potential of women

'The Wedding Dance', after Pieter Breughel the Elder, 1566

[Germanisches Nationalmuseum, Nürnberg.]

and the more cautious female attempting to judge the wealth and status of men. Marriage is a compromise the partners must make in order to invest in the extraordinarily demanding task of bringing up children, yet the sexual bond that unites them will be frequent episodes of usually infertile sex. Marriage is the badge of a polygamous animal struggling to be monogamous.

Marriage is a cultural manifestation of an amazingly bold step in reproductive behaviour, rich in opportunities but replete with problems. Most, although perhaps not quite all human societies, recognize that sexual relations between a man and a woman, at least for an interval of time, may be characterized by extraordinary passion and desire for sexual exclusivity, even in a polygynous society. Epidemiological studies show that married men aged 35 to 44 years and married women aged 29 to 34 have half the death rate of unmarried individuals of the same age. Unmarried women aged 29 to 34 are three times as likely to attempt suicide as married women of the same age. Marriage is eternally popular, and by age 27 three-quarters of all women in the USA have married and by age 29 three-quarters of all men. Eventually 93 per cent of Western adults marry. Yet one-third of all American marriages end in divorce, and when marriage goes wrong it commonly causes more pain

Here comes the bride

Our innate biological drives are nearer the surface in the case of marriage than in many other family activities. As among chimpanzees, so in nearly all human cultures, the bride leaves the 'troop' of her birth to join that of her husband. In ancient Rome, and for the first thousand years of Christianity, marriage was a private contract, sometimes literally conducted in the bedroom, in which the head of one extended family 'gave' the bride (and a dowry) to another. Later a priest might bless the bed, but the marriage agreement remained a family affair and easily broken. Even in the tenth and eleventh centuries the Church was slow to condemn bigamy but concentrated on avoiding marriages between genetically related individuals – another biologically driven aspect of marriage. At one time even a seventh degree of consanguinity came to be labelled as incestuous. By the thirteenth century marriage had been elevated to a sacrament, like baptism, and the Church was less intent on banning relations between remote relatives and more interested in the *stabilitas* – the indissolubility – of marriage. The ceremony moved from the privacy of the home to the public arena, outside the church door. The priest replaced the father in uniting the bride and groom. But not until the seventeenth century did the wedding begin to take place inside the church in France and England. By this time the European colonists in North America were already established and the older tradition of marrying in the home lives on in America to this day.

than any other error in human relationships. Nevertheless, following divorce many individuals remarry. Biology can provide many useful insights into this event, which captivates us so much but fails in its potential so often. At the same time, the variety of marriage structures and the range of cultural expectations associated with marriage underscores how much of human behaviour is determined by our upbringing.

The evolution of love

The basic unit in mammalian society is the mother and her offspring. The bond between the two, which commences with physical attachment at the nipple, may last from a few days to a lifetime. Evolution is about getting the most out of your environment and out of your competitors, including parents, kin and non-kin of your own species. Pregnancy, lactation and the care and feeding of the young are physically demanding efforts, and at first sight it might seem that having a hungry adult male about the place can only make life more complicated. After all, the female's most immediate competitor in the struggle for existence is often a member of the opposite sex of her own species who almost invariably eats exactly the same food that she is seeking for herself and her offspring.

Males can provide protection from predators, or help to give one social group the edge over rivals of the same species. Within groups of social primates, subtle relationships sometimes arise between the two sexes. Adult male and female baboons often establish 'friendships' prior to sexual relations. A new male trying to join an established troop will scrutinize all the adult members carefully and then select a female not obviously under the control of a resident male, establish eye contact with her and befriend her prior to any sexual contact. Chimpanzees go one step further. The males band together and hunt and kill other primates or forest mammals. The victims are torn to pieces and eaten raw and such episodes also generate a great deal of excitement among the females. Meat is shared between individuals and ovulating females are more successful than non ovulating females in begging for meat. In the words of Donald Symons from the University of California at Santa Barbara, 'female sexual overtures may have been motivated more often by pragmatism about protein than by sexual emotion'.

When our Australopithecine ancestors moved from the forest to the open savanna of Africa about five million years ago, they changed from knuckle-walking, quadrupedal apes into upright creatures: bipedalism made it easier both to find and to carry food. A female's reproductive success would be determined by her skill at feeding herself, and females may have used sticks to dig up plant roots and containers to carry food and water before, to borrow a biblical phase, men turned their plough shares into swords. *Australopithecus* males, like chimpanzees and unlike human beings, had large canine teeth. They were physically more dimorphic than we are, the males being perhaps 35 per cent larger than the females. Some of this dimorphism may have been lost as we began to use tools and weapons to express aggression. The fossil teeth of both sexes atest to a varied diet of plants, fruits, grubs and animal meat – a lifestyle that encouraged good topographic memory and an ability to communicate. Was it on the African savanna also that we evolved the fatty deposits on the thighs, buttocks and breasts so characteristic of the sexually mature woman? Fatty stores would indicate reproductive potential in an animal exploiting an environment sometimes subject to drought. But fat all over the body would be a disadvantage, especially in a hot climate, so perhaps women were selected because they had fat in localized areas and, as the manufacturers of T-shirts appreciate, one of the best places to advertise a message is on the human chest.

Fossils belonging to the genus *Homo* have been traced back 2.4 million years in Kenya. About 1.6 million years ago *Homo erectus* appeared, named for his upright stance. Again skeletons are clearly dimorphic, suggesting a division of labour perhaps associated with sexual bonding between individuals. *Homo erectus* used tools, and we can infer that they engaged in cooperative and foraging parties, perhaps returning to a home base at night.

The concept of paternity

It's a wise man that knows his own father, or so the saying goes. But unlike the males of other large primates, men show a willingness not only to defend children but to help to nourish and nurture those born to a woman with whom they have had intercourse. Do we have to understand the relationship between intercourse and pregnancy to do this? Probably not. In some preliterate societies sexual intercourse was not necessarily associated with conception: imagine intercourse commencing as a girl entered puberty, but the first ovulation not beginning for another year or so. How would you ever know which act of intercourse resulted in conception? It is said that Australian Aborigines did not associate intercourse with pregnancy until they domesticated the dingo. Since dingo bitches came into obvious oestrus, the only time when they would permit the male to copulate, and gave birth sixty-four days later, these dogs possibly taught the Aborigines the facts of life.

It is only when you know these facts that the male can begin to get concerned about paternity. A wise English Law Lord once said, 'Maternity is a matter of fact; paternity one of mere inference.' With the advent of genetic markers, and now DNA fingerprinting, it becomes possible to establish paternity with almost complete certainty, and there have been a number of surprises. One study in Romford, England, after World War II, accidentally revealed that at least 25 per cent of children born were not sired by their legal fathers. Human beings are not alone in their infidelities, and DNA fingerprinting in birds is showing that even the seemingly most monogamous species, which we romantically imagine pair for life, obviously have a number of fertile encounters outside the pair bond. The cuckoo is not alone in cuckolding her partner.

Although there is only one hominid species alive today – ourselves – in the past there were sometimes several alive at the same time. Neanderthals, as we noted earlier, lived side by side with *Homo sapiens* for tens of thousands of years.

Skeletal evidence of sexual dimorphism, along with indirect evidence from archaeological excavation, may be the nearest we will ever get to 'fossilized behaviour'. Speculations are rarely, if ever, open to validation. What we can be certain about is that love, based on sex, brings human parents together and helps to sustain them during the often tiring process of child rearing. It is the key factor separating the human family from that of the apes. Did evolution conceal ovulation and make our hominid ancestors willing to have non-productive sex in response to a social system where males controlled and distributed females? Was it a response by females to the threat of new males killing existing offspring? As hunting became an increasingly important male activity, did the loss of external signs of ovulation make our female ancestors better at begging for meat throughout the menstrual cycle?

[Finnish National Gallery.]

The Bride's Song, **Gunnar Berndtson, 1881.** In this Finnish painting the bride is singing a farewell to family and home. The wedding feast has been cleared away and the celebratory wine remains; an admiring husband sits on her right and the father who 'gave her away' on the left.

Or was it a growing awareness of paternity, or a little bit of everything, that led to the evolution of human marriage? Or did evolution encourage females to exchange sexual favours for the care and protection of one mate and the benefits that follow from each sex exploiting special food sources? Whether any of these, or some as yet unthought of explanation is true, we may never know for certain, but thinking through possible scenarios can help to sharpen insights into our own behaviour.

A variety of marriages

We can grow as children, mature as adolescents or have fulfilling lives as adults only by being part of a family, albeit in modern industrialized nations often a single-parent family. Outside some sort of family, we are more likely to become vagrants, bag people, hermits, down-and-outs or just 'bums'. When an animal is taken out of its own social structure, individuals fail to thrive and often reproduction becomes impossible. We need only look at monkeys in zoos or in isolated laboratory cages, listless, reluctant to breed and often incapable of rearing their young.

A blot on one's escutcheon?

In mediaeval times, when most people were illiterate, a family's coat of arms was a unique heritage. The bar running from bottom left to top right across the sixteenth century coat of arms of the Viscount de L'Isle, denotes his illegitimate birth. However, it was not always a symbol of shame. To this day the wealthy often by-pass social restraints on monogamy by keeping mistresses and supporting their illegitimate children, in the same way that a man keeps a harem in a polygamous society. English kings since 1066 have totted up about 100 royal bastards. Usually a bastard had no chance of inheriting the throne (although William the Conqueror, also known as William the Bastard, was an exception). As a result, a bastard might receive more love and trust from the king than would a legitimate child, who was always the centre of political intrigue.

[The College of Arms, London.]

The kaleidoscopic range of human marriage patterns is remarkable. In contemporary Sweden, for example, 40 to 50 per cent of all births are outside marriage, and it might seem as if marriages were disappearing. Yet most Swedish children are born into stable partnerships, with many of the social characteristics of marriage, even if they lack a civil or religious ceremony. In many non-Western cultures, marriage is not only about children, but also about the acquisition of land or the union of different families. In some hunter–gatherer societies, young people choose their partners on the basis of romantic attachment, but in many settled agricultural communities, marriages are arranged by parents, or the older men in the group, and the bride joins the extended family of the groom, living in daily contact with her in-laws.

The modern ideal of marriage, based on the two people falling in love before the event, is a relatively recent social invention, but it is a popular and infectious one, spreading rapidly in the modern world. Arranged marriages persisted in Britain until relatively recently. The marriage of social equals was common and, for example, in seventeenth century England, one-third of clergymen's children married other clergy. In Elizabethan times, through the Puritan Commonwealth and into the eighteenth century, family structure was of the extended type. Dowries were given and parents chose the bride, sometimes with the help of marriage brokers. Even in the early nineteenth century the perceptions of marriage differed from those of today. Society gave men a great deal of power over women, and women were seen as either Madonnas or whores.

A mid-Victorian woman wrote to her daughter, 'After your wedding, my dear, unpleasant things are bound to happen, but take no notice. I never did.' At the other extreme women were so sexual they had to be watched closely to avoid sliding into nymphomania and hysteria.

We will never know when the two sexes began sleeping in the same nest: it is something adult chimpanzees or gorillas never do. Sometime in the nineteenth century it became almost universal for the married couples to sleep in the same bed. When Mme Pariset wrote her popular *Manual for the Mistress of the House* in 1821 she recommended separate bedrooms for the French bourgeoisie; in 1913 the book was still in print, but this recommendation had been deleted. Honeymoons first became fashionable among the European upper classes in the 1830s. A Frenchman wrote, 'The English have an excellent custom, which is to spend this month of happiness in the remote countryside'. By the second half of the century the rich were travelling to Italy. As intimacy between marriage partners increased, so men became more involved in the nurturing of their children.

[The Bodleian Library, Oxford; MS. Arch. Seldon. A.1, fols.60r, 61r.]

An Aztec wedding. The Aztec Empire evolved in total isolation from the rest of the world outside South America prior to its overthrow by the Spaniards in 1521. But, in this illustration from the Codex Mendoza, the institution of marriage is instantly recognizable. The garments of the bridal couple have been tied together to represent marital union; the same symbol is used by Hindus and Zoroastrians in India. Other aspects of Aztec social structure and religion are incredibly foreign, and there was, for example, a well-defined merchant class that despised wealth, used no money and gained social status by giving away the goods they traded. But the Aztecs used a marriage match-maker (seen at the bottom of the picture carrying the bride on her back) in exactly the same way as did the mediaeval Jews. The four persons around the bridal couple – two of each sex – were witnesses, also a virtually universal feature of marriage in Asia, Africa and Europe. When it came to the institution of slavery, Aztecs once again lived in what seems to be an upside-down world, where slaves were not treated with undue cruelty and where free men occasionally made a voluntary choice to take up slavery as a profession. Yet traders, in an ostentatious show of wealth, occasionally sacrificed slaves and ate their flesh. In an extraordinary piece of parallel evolution, Aztecs took as much interest in an astrologer's interpretation of the bridal partner's horoscopes as any contemporary Buddhist in Sri Lanka. We can immediately recognize the normal feasting and drinking associated with marriage (see food in the centre of the picture), although no society other than the Aztec threatened the death penalty for anyone getting drunk under the age of 60, while those over that age were positively encouraged to consume alcohol.

Anthropologists have documented great variation in human marriage patterns. The Australian Tiwi Aborigines on Melville Island, north of Darwin, live in clans and count their inheritance through the female line. Women are assigned a marriage partner even before they are born, indeed before they are conceived. At the time of the girl's puberty ritual, her father selects a man and gives him a ceremonial spear, as a sign that any girls his daughter may be delivered of later will eventually become wives of that man. But first the girl herself must marry and she will marry the man who was selected at the time of her mother's puberty ceremony. The man who was given the spear becomes what we would call the mother's son-in-law. When the daughter reaches puberty and then conceives, her girls will grow up to be his wives. In what to us seems an odd system, the man contracts to supply his mother-in-law with food, clothing, money and tobacco, even though she is about to marry someone else, namely an older man who has been waiting for her since before she was conceived.

A Tiwi man will receive the wife he has been married to since before her conception when she is about 10 years old, by which time he is likely to be at least 30. Life for the prepubertal girl continues much as before, except that she now owes allegiance to her husband and any wives he may already have, rather than to her parents. As puberty approaches, the husband begins the sexual education of his child bride, starting with a digital deflowering. Intercourse takes place later, although it may still be before puberty is completed. Indeed, the Tiwis believe that puberty is not a spontaneous process, but that the development of breasts and menstruation are consequences of the husband's sexual advances. In the words of one Tiwi wife, her husband 'took me as a daughter ... he grew me up ... and made me a woman.' When a man dies, his wives pass to his brother, thus most men have a succession of brides and most women a succession of husbands. Extramarital affairs are relatively common, as young women are attracted to partners of their own age and most eligible young men are either unmarried or have wives who are toddlers or still at their mother's breast. If the young people go into the bush for an illicit tryst, the boy is said to step carefully in his girl's footprints to obliterate her tracks so the husband will not suspect the union.

Some human marriage patterns may be advantageous in a biological sense but others, provided they are not frankly contrary to survival of the species, may survive as quirks of cultural tradition. It is said that the Manus mentioned above have no word for love. They sing no romantic songs and expect no tenderness in courtship; it is taboo for a girl to mention the name of her betrothed, and after marriage she is forbidden to look her father-in-law in the face, even though they may live in the same house for years. The Manus are indulgent parents and childhood is a carefree experience until a girl is betrothed, usually before puberty. Mothers do not teach their daughters about sex, except with an aura of pain and disgust. Marriage is an exchange between families in a people who are inveterate traders, and even the bride's costume is little more than a walking bank, hung with seashells and dog's teeth that make up the local currency. The wedding begins with an assault on the bride by her in-laws who tear her costume apart looking for hidden wealth and grumbling aloud 'she hasn't brought enough'. The husband will have intercourse without foreplay or affection. If life becomes too intolerable, wives will turn to their brothers for help and to pressurize their husbands to be more reasonable.

An emphasis and investment in siblings with whom you share 25 per cent of your genes is a reproductive strategy that is a viable alternative to a commitment to a wife whose child will carry 50 per cent of your genes. The Manus way of marriage with virtual hostility between the husband and wife, but continued trust and dependence between brothers and sister makes sense as a biological strategy. Among the Marri Baluch of Pakistan, many of a woman's lovers will also be her close kin, and any offspring are

Egyptian marriage

On the day of my wedding I was ready in the usual way. My face and body were cleaned and depilated, and henna was applied on my hands. In our village we like to sign the marriage contract and consummate the marriage on the same day in order to ensure there will not be a change of heart on the part of the groom or his family... That same night we went through the customary show of blood which proves to the groom, and to all, the bride is a virgin. The midwife, my mother and married female relatives were in the room with me for the defloration. Two lengths of clean white gauze shawls that are normally used as turbans were made ready for the ceremony. The groom wrapped one around his finger and entered me until he drew blood. When he was satisfied of my virginity the midwife said to him, 'Congratulations. Now go sit at the other end of the room while I do what remains to be done.' She then inserted her finger into me several times, taking blood and spotting with it the two white shawls until they were adequately decorated. She hiked them on sticks, and they were carried out of the house for all to see, then taken as a procession to the groom's house. This is called the ritual of exhibition.

After the ceremony the groom lay with me, but it took seven or eight days for me to get used to him. He was patient, but he wanted what he wanted... I sat in pans of water after sexual intercourse to relieve the pain, but by and by, after a time, I became hardened to the process and felt nothing.

Om Naemma describing her marriage in Egypt at age 15: Nayra Atiya, *Khul-Khaal: Five Egyptian Women tell their Stories*, 1982

[Popperfoto.]

The Taj Mahal. The Taj Mahal is an astounding monument to sexual love, wet-nursing and the risks of childbirth. Mumtaz Mahal was a consort of Emperor Shah Jahan. She was not his first wife, but she was his unquestionable favourite. As Mogul emperor he had a seraglio filled with young dancing girls and experienced concubines, but he always went back to sloe-eyed Mumtaz. She bore her first child when she was 16 and it, like those that followed, must have been put to a wet-nurse because Mumtaz had one child nearly every year until she died having her fourteenth child on 28 June 1631. She probably had a post-partum haemorrhage, a common event in women who have given birth many times, because history records that there was time to summon Shah Jahan and she died in his arms. The emperor was grief stricken and abstained from fine clothes and food for two years. Mumtaz's mausoleum was built explicitly as a place of pilgrimage in the midst of large formal gardens beside the River Yamuna because in Islam a woman who dies in child birth becomes a *shaheed*, or martyr. It took 20 000 men twenty years to carve the white marble with its inlaid precious stones. Today the population of India increases by 20 000 people a day and the country has enough spare labour to build a new Taj every twenty-four hours.

always identified with the woman's husband. Tiwi adults also remain close to their blood relations throughout adult life. As among the Manus, emotional relationships in the Tiwi are often closer with kin than with the marriage partner. The same was true of marriage in preindustrial England. One seventeenth century writer, William Stout, said of a marriage in 1699, that the couple 'lived very disagreeably but they had many children.' An extended family works well in a society where law and order is uncertain and loyalty to one's clan important. Prior to the sixteenth century in England, 92 per cent of homicides were directed outside the family and, as present-day writer Lawrence Stone has quipped, 'The family that slayed together stayed together.' The nuclear family, where young men and women choose their own marriage partner, is a product of a society where law and order are enforced by civil authorities, where literacy is expected of women as well as men and where couples live apart from their parents in individual economic units. Since the seventeenth and eighteenth centuries, the percentage of homicides in Britain involving marriage partners or blood relations has risen.

Polyandry, where one female has several males mating with her, appears to be an adaptation to particularly serious shortages of resources, or to some other environmental challenge. The nests of the American jacana bird are often attacked by predators and the hen mates with several males, probably so that if a clutch of eggs is lost it can be replaced easily. Human societies have to respond to scarce resources in harsh mountain terrains. In the Swiss Alps the tradition of primogeniture operated, where the eldest son inherited the farm and his brothers were forced to migrate to the valleys. In parts of Nepal and Tibet, fraternal polyandry, where several brothers share one wife is still practised. The men provide the labour to cultivate a limited and stony environment, the farm is transmitted *en bloc* to the next generation, and the number of women who reproduce is limited, thus controlling population size. The surplus women leave the high valleys to seek mates and some, in times past, were literally sold to wealthy city merchants. Careful enumeration of children and grandchildren shows that polyandrous marriages in Tibet reproduced more successfully than monogamous or polygynous ones.

Males controlling females

Marriage patterns change with the increasing complexity of society. In hunter–gatherers, such as the San Bushmen, young people make a relatively free choice about their sexual partner, marriages break up and new partnerships arise fairly easily. In a subsistence agricultural community, where women often do the planting with a hoe, as in much of Africa, there is often

[Germanisches Nationalmuseum, Nürnberg.]

A chastity belt. It is thought that chastity belts first came into use in the time of the Crusades, but they were still being used in the present century. They were not always made of iron; the Pennsylvanian Dutch settlers had their wives wear 'day belts', which were heavy leather girdles, studded with rivets and padlocked. In December 1933 the League of Awakened Magyars put forward a National Programme that all Hungarian girls of 12 and upwards who were unmarried should wear girdles of chastity, the keys being kept by their fathers.

In Indonesia today, chastity belts have become a popular sale item in the Chinese community, fearful of further ethnic riots.

also some degree of individual choice and both men and women may have numerous sexual partners. Prostitution is unregulated and there are no pimps. In agricultural societies, where land is inherited by sons and men both own the land and labour behind ploughs pulled by farm animals, then a harsher control of women commonly arises, the dual standards of sexual behaviour are exaggerated, divorce (at least for women) may be difficult, and women unlucky enough to be prostitutes are controlled by pimps or corralled into brothels. Such societies put great emphasis on female virginity, marriage at an early age and parental choice of marriage partners, and in nearly all cases girls live close to the groom's family after marriage. The tendency to treat women as chattels arose once men owned land or cattle.

In the majority of societies nubile young women usually leave home and move into their husband's family group. The traditional Christian marriage service asks 'Who gives the bride away?', but not 'Who gives the groom away?'. In the contemporary West, nearly all wives wear a wedding ring, but only some husbands.

Chimpanzees, as we have seen, live in troops of related males and at puberty females usually leave their natal troop and migrate to another, whereas the males remain in the troop of their birth. Men, like chimpanzees, also form coalitions and work together on tasks with a common goal, such as hunting. Most businesses are of the type *Smith & Sons*, and although *Smith & Daughters* is possible it is less common. Many of the politicians and

Match-making

Even among the wealthy and educated in India, the family still chooses most marriage partners, and advertisements appear in daily newspapers promoting the physical attractiveness of potential brides and the educational achievements and earning potential of the men.

Human mating is more of a market than we sometimes wish to acknowledge. Newspaper advertisements are also used in the West by those looking for romance, in everything from free magazines on airlines to widely read weekly pulp magazines in supermarkets. Perhaps the next true revolution in marriage will be more and more computer match-making. In America, it is already possible to make your own videotape as a way of introducing yourself, and some television cable stations already carry advertisements. But present systems lose track of the happy couple after they first meet – what would happen if they could be programmed to follow-up the outcome of the marriage? Would electronic machines be able to seek out and match those characteristics most likely to lead to a happy marriage – or would the battle between the sexes continue to outwit such an electronic defence system?

leaders in Britain went to a relatively small number of famous schools and universities, which socially (although not genetically) is pretty close to being brought up in the same family. The children of King Fahd, king of Saudi Arabia since 1982, include the Ambassador to the USA, Chief of the Air Force and Deputy Chief of Foreign Intelligence, while the king's six surviving brothers have been Minister of Defence, Prime Minister, Minister of the Interior and a couple of provincial governors.

Who marries whom?

The reproductive agendas of men and women are particularly transparent when it comes to choosing our marriage partners. Men look for 'good looks' or 'physical attractiveness', that are really measures of age and health – smooth skin, lustrous hair, sprightly gait, flashing teeth. The emphasis men put on the bust and hips in their perception of a woman's figure are clearly biological criteria: the Western focus on a 'tiny waist' could be a clue derived from the male's need to prove paternity, namely that the woman is not pregnant. Women look for ambition, industriousness, and financial prospects. Over the years, several sociologists have asked US college students to describe their ideal partner. They have found consistent differences in male and female ideals in different localities and across several generations. In one study, female 'attractiveness' proved to be more correlated with the husband's

Royal nuptials

A mystic thread of unspun cotton is wound around the bed seventy-seven times, and the ends held in the hands of the priests, who, bowing over the sacred symbols invoke blessings on the bridal pair. The nearest relatives of the bride are admitted... these salute the bed, sprinke it with consecrated waters, festoon the crimson curtains with flower garlands, and prepare the silken sheets, the pillows and the cushions; which done, they lead in the bride, who has not presided at these entertainments, but waited with her ladies in a separate apartment.

Thus Anna Leonowens described the wedding of the king of Siam to one wife when she tutored the royal children in 1860s.

occupational status than with the woman's intelligence quotient, or social class. Richard Udry, from the University of North Carolina, devised a way in which male college students could score the attractiveness of the women in their class: when he followed up the women many years later he found that a one point difference on the quantitative scale used by the researchers in college was associated later in life with an increase of US$3000 in average income of their husbands.

Of course, social class, wealth, race, IQ, religion and even political persuasion, remain important components in the selection of marriage partners. In a study of marital preferences based on 10047 people in thirty-seven developed and developing countries, David Bass of the University of Michigan found women more 'choosy', looking at a broader range of social, economic and personality factors than men, whereas men sought youth and physical attractiveness.

In Sri Lanka the traditional matchmaker, or *magul kapuwas*, is being replaced by the anonymous efficiency of a newspaper advertisement. When 2000 of these advertisements were analysed, 80 per cent of the advertisements about brides were placed by the girl's parents, but only one-third of the advertisements about a groom were placed by the man himself or his friends. Many overseas families advertise back home for brides, showing the human tendency to marry into one's own group, while at the same time avoiding very close relatives. Among those marrying locally, most mentioned their caste, again emphasizing the tendency of mating within the same group. Older individuals who advertised for mates almost invariably emphasized that they looked younger than their years: one man of 53 said he looked the reverse of his age. The youth and beauty of the brides, euphemisms for reproductive potential, were nearly always emphasized: 'fair', 'attractive', 'beautiful' were common adjectives. Only 17 per cent of men claimed to be 'handsome', but most gave an impression of wealth and power, such as professional qualifications and four out of ten advertisements for brides specified that they wanted a professional man. To meet the male need to prove paternity, the newspaper codes for virginity were 'pure', 'unblemished', 'unstained character', and 'convent educated'. Three or four divorced women made out their marriages were 'unconsummated'. Most of those men who specifically said they would consider marrying divorcees were careful to mention she should have 'no encumbrances'.

The polygamous primate's commitment to sexual dimorphism can be seen inside and outside marriage. In the Sri Lankan advertisements, short men went to considerable lengths to warn prospective brides about a perceived defect they would not be able to conceal, while still trying to camouflage the fact: they revealed their height, but in inches – 62 inches (or 158 centimetres) looks better than 5 foot 2 inches (or 1.58 metres). Shortness in a man is, indeed, generally a disadvantage. All US presidents save two have been of above average height (Lincoln was 6 ft 4 inches (190 centimetres)), and with one exception the taller candidate for president has always won. Conversely, tall women are at a disadvantage and some doctors will try to curtail excessive height by giving oestrogens from about age 12. When oestrogen is secreted from a girl's ovaries after puberty it naturally stops the growth of long bones and artificial sex hormones (such as the contraceptive pill) do the same thing.

***Judah and Tamar*, Émile Vernet, 1840.** The patriarch Judah had several sons. Judah's firstborn 'was wicked in the sight of the Lord; and the Lord slew him. And Judah said to unto Onan, "Go in unto thy brother's wife, and marry her, and raise up seed to thy brother."' But whenever Onan slept with his brother's widow 'he spilled [his seed] on the ground' and the Lord 'slew him also'. The rest of the story in Genesis 38 is less well known but makes a television soap opera look tame. Judah became alarmed that his youngest son, Selah, might also be cut down by God and ordered his eldest daughter-in-law Tamar to 'remain a widow'. But she, still childless, disguised herself as a prostitute and, covering her face with a veil, tricked Judah, her father-in-law, into having sex. Vernet's painting shows Judah and Tamar discussing the price. 'What wilt thou give me that thou mayest come in unto me?' she asks. 'I will send thee a kid from the flock.' Tamar demands more than a promise and bargains Judah's ring, bracelets and staff before agreeing to sex. Three months later the servants tell Judah, 'Thy daughter-in-law hath played the harlot.' He shouts, 'Bring her forth, and let her be burnt,' but Tamar produces his ring, bracelets and staff. Judah changes his tune and Tamar's pregnancy ends in the delivery of twins.

Theologians are divided on whether Onan's sin was practising coitus interruptus or disobeying his father, yet the whole of the Christian condemnation of contraception is based on this single story. The implicit approval of the old man using a prostitute and the threat of burning his daughter-in-law to death for being one is hardly an uplifting beginning for something as important as the Papal encyclical *Humanae Vitae* (see p. 297ff.).

[National Gallery of Art, Washington / Bridgeman Art Library.]

***Lot and His Daughters*, Albrecht Dürer, *ca.* 1505.** Dürer's neat little picture portrays the story of Sodom and Gomorrah with an appropriate lack of seriousness. Lot's wife is a smoke-blackened pillar of salt in the middle distance, while Lot himself is plodding stoically forward followed by two deceptively demure daughters, carrying the household belongings. Mushroom clouds of fire and brimstone rise over the walled and towered cities of Sodom and Gomorrah.

Sodom's sins are described by Ezekiel (16:49–50): 'Behold, this was the iniquity of thy sister Sodom, pride, fulness of bread, and abundance of idleness was in her and in her daughters ... And they were haughty, and committed abomination before me.' In the Genesis account of the myth, homosexuality is more explicit, and when the citizens of Sodom surround Lot's house they say, 'Where are the men which came in to thee this night?' (Genesis 19:5). But the real insight into the sexual attitudes of a patriarchal society was when Lot tried to placate his neighbours by offering them his daughters, whom he clearly regarded as property, not as loved ones. 'Behold now, I have two daughters which have not known man; let me, I pray you, bring them out unto you...'

Later, Lot's daughters got their father drunk and committed incest with him, which is why in Dürer's painting he is carrying the wine bottle and they the money box.

Incest

While we tend to marry into our own group, we avoid marrying those who are closest to us. If close relatives reproduce then some of the many deleterious recessive genes we all carry may express themselves; in one series of 161 incestuous human matings, 71 abnormalities and malformations were recognized, compared with five in a control group of 95 children born to parents who were not genetically related. Most mammals leave the parental nest and are dispersed before they are mature sexually, so that closely related individuals are unlikely to meet and mate. But among the apes and human beings the strong family ties that persist throughout life have made it essential to evolve behavioural mechanisms to reduce incest. We appear to share with other apes a built-in mechanism, based on the recognition of family members, to discourage mating between parents and children and between siblings. Jane Goodall says she has never seen an adult male chimpanzee mate with his mother. Kelly Stewart has observed gorilla troops in Rwanda and noted how they become artificially separated from other troops when the tropical forest is cut down to make fields for human agriculture. If a maturing female remains trapped in the troop of her birth, instead of leaving to join another troop as is natural, then father–daughter matings become inevitable. Among such matings the first baby is born later than average. Are there more spontaneous abortions in these incestuous matings or, like Lot's daughters, are incestuous matings a tactic of last resort?

As noted in Chapter 3, in Israeli kibbutzim children of different parents are brought up in close association with one another, just as if they belonged to the same household. In a study of 2769 marriages of couples who had grown up in the kibbutz system, Joseph Shepher found not a single case of marriage from within the same peer group. In some areas of Taiwan it used to be the custom for parents to arrange marriages very early in life, and actually to give their daughters to be brought up in the household of the prospective groom very soon after birth. As the infant bride and groom were brought up together they came to recognize each other not as potential man and wife, but as brother and sister. Studies show that, when such couples eventually married, on average they were 30 per cent less fertile than partners who met later in life (probably the result of behavioural rather than physical factors), they divorced three times as often, and there was an increased risk of adultery. As in the kibbutz, these effects occurred only when the children lived together before age 4 or younger. Apes and people seem reluctant to mate with those with whom they grow up.

A similar in-built mechanism may also prevent father–daughter and mother–son incest. Sexual abuse much more commonly involves a step-parent

– usually the father – than a natural parent. Interestingly, when it does involve a biological parent, then it is sometimes a man from a religious group who believes in a strict division of labour in marriage, and who never changed his daughter's nappies or gave her a bath, and who has therefore avoided the close physical contact that is probably the basis of the protection against incest.

History contains some notable cases of incest. No doubt Pope Alexander VI, who fathered a child by his natural daughter and announced the fact in a Papal Bull, had had his daughter wet-nursed, probably outside the Vatican, and had little or no contact with her as a baby. The Egyptian pharaohs sometimes married their sisters, but they had probably also led separate lives in the royal household, with little except ceremonial contact. Dynastic incest led to some odd relationships: in Eygpt the eighteenth dynasty Queen Hatshepsut was aunt, step-mother and mother-in-law to Pharaoh Thutmose III, all at the same time.

Divorce

The intensity of sexual desire dims with familiarity, and changes its character with the passage of time. Love may last a lifetime, or succumb to the proverbial 'seven year itch'. With relative affluence and lack of social opprobrium, divorce is becoming increasingly common in Western countries. It is also relatively frequent in countries with a different cultural tradition, such as Bangladesh and Egypt. Statistics from the contemporary USA show that, when couples separate, those without children have been together for an average of just under five years, and those with children about seven. Sexual love, it seems, binds for long enough to meet the woman's need for

Proof of impotence

Indissoluble monogamy became the ecclesiastical goal of mediaeval Europe and the only grounds for divorce were impotence, or evidence that the marriage was invalid in the first place – something King Henry VIII contrived to show with Queen Catherine of Aragon.

Proof of impotence was tested in an earthy, direct way. In the case of a man called John, involved in a divorce case in York in 1433, a woman, other than his wife, 'exposed her naked breasts, and with her hands warmed at the said fire, she held and rubbed the penis and testicles of the said John, and stirred him up as far as she could to show his virility [but] the whole time aforesaid, the said penis was scarcely three inches long, remaining without an increase or decrease.'

Fornication

First offence – fine, prison and pillory.

Second offence – heavier fine, longer prison sentence, pillory with head shaved.

Third offence – fine, prison and pillory as set out above together with ducking in the foulest pool of water in the town or parish, and banishment.

The Privy Council, Edinburgh, 1564

In the Nor' Loch (drained to build the railway) in Edinburgh, Scotland there was a hole for ducking fornicators prior to imprisonment.

monogamous support during the difficult days of pregnancy, the strain of breastfeeding and the early years of intensive parental care. Then infidelities sometimes begin, and partnerships break up.

Over the past century Western countries have slowly moved away from Christian teaching on the indissolubility of marriage. The ban was never total and divorce was permitted if the marriage was unconsummated, or if a Christian was deserted by a non-Christian spouse (the so-called Pauline Privilege after 1 Corinthians 7:15). Henry VIII's need to untie the marital knot led to the English Reformation. He had his marriage to Catherine of Aragon annulled on the grounds that she had been his dead brother's bride, and that to Anne of Cleves on the novel grounds that he found her so ugly it made him impotent and unable to consummate the marriage.

Prior to the Industrial Revolution, couples often delayed marriage until their mid or late twenties and many marriages were cut short by the death of one partner: marriage today can last three times as long as those two centuries ago. This, together with a weakening of the religious ideal of an indissoluble marriage, has led to a redefinition of marriage in the Western world. Divorce is almost as common as marriage is popular. The number of divorces in the USA has risen from 400000 in 1960 to 1.2 million a year in the 1990s, and 8 per cent of American adults now have three or more marriages. At one level, society's refusal to countenance divorce upheld the woman's biological agenda to the extent that it was supposed to compel the man to care for his children, but the costs could be unacceptably high. Until the eighteenth century, for example, the courts could order reluctant wives to return to their husband's beds. The wives of adulterous or physically abusive husbands often could do little more than pray. The mediaeval world did indeed have a saint to whom unhappy wives could pray: Santa Wilgefortis was the daughter of a king of Portugal who was betrothed against her will to the king of Sicily. She prayed to become unattractive and by divine intervention grew a moustache. When the Sicilian king then refused his bride, her father had her crucified. In England Santa Wilgefortis was known as Saint Uncumber, and in France as Sainte Livrade.

The English Protestant parliament, in the seventeenth century, introduced the option of civil marriage and the possibility of divorce. The poet John Milton in his *Doctrine and Discipline of Divorce* (1643) argued that divorce should be possible on grounds of incompatibility. He considered adultery 'a transient injury ... soon repented, soon amended'. In 1792 the Revolutionary French Assembly did add incompatibility to adultery as grounds for divorce, yet until the 1900s divorce was difficult to obtain and unusual in any European country. English aristocrats might take their problems all the way to the High Court of parliament. For the poor, a marital relationship might be ended by the simple practice of the husband taking his wife to the marketplace with a halter around her neck and then selling her like a cow. In the nineteenth century there were 268 accounts in English newspapers of such sales – some, it seems, involved the transfer of an adulterous wife to her lover, the price being perceived as compensation for the aggrieved man. Today, divorce is permitted in every Western society, except Ireland and Malta.

The compromise of marriage works best where tolerance and understanding are either socially expected, as among the Tiwi, or are reinforced by some degree of compatibility brought about by an appropriate choice of marriage partners. Whether marriages break up in hot passion, or fall apart like an old rag, each partner usually has a litany of things 'they never liked about the other'. The habits that irritate most are often as much general attributes of the opposite sex as manifestations of the individual partner: 'You never understood me', 'I want my space', 'I sacrificed myself to bring up the children', 'I gave you a good home; what more do you want?'. When divorce reaches the courts the man's first question is usually, 'What will it cost me?', while the woman asks, 'What is going to happen to the children?'.

The same reasons for divorce are found in both sexes, but a shadow of each sex's biologically differing investment in reproduction still shows through. Men are more sexually restless and a survey of American divorce found that 23 per cent of men but only 4 per cent of women felt something was amiss by the end of the first year of marriage. Couples who get married under the age of 20 are twice as likely to divorce in the next five years as those who marry later. In court, women of all ages frequently complain of marital infidelity, whereas men more frequently petition on grounds of unreasonable behaviour. Given greater wealth and social mobility, many human societies have drifted towards serial monogamy. The rich or famous set the trend: Chairman Mao was divorced three times and President Reagan twice. Women who come to great public wealth and visibility, such as actresses Elizabeth Taylor and Joan Collins, also often have serial marriages. While divorce has become more common in the West, the frequency of remarriage has also increased: divorce is seen as a failure of the specific marriage and not of the general idea. Those who stay together do so for positive reasons.

Divorce can lead to a great deal of long-term unhappiness. If we think about it, in most marriages (once the honeymoon is over) each partner could write the script for their own divorce, were it not for the tolerant and mature companionship that husband and wife develop. But marriage as an institution also has a great ability to fight back. Whatever way we look at it, marriage,

Marriage

Then Almitra spoke again and said, And
what of Marriage, master?
And he answered saying:
You were born together, and together
you shall be for evermore.
You shall be together when the white
wings of death scatter your days.
Aye, you shall be together even in the
silent memory of God.
But let there be spaces in your
togetherness.
And let the winds of the heavens dance
between you.
Love one another, but make not a bond of
love:
Let it rather be a moving sea between the
shores of your souls.
Fill each other's cup but drink not from
one cup.
Give one another of your bread but eat not
from the same loaf.
Sing and dance together and be joyous,
but let each one of you be alone,
Even as the strings of a lute are alone
though they quiver with the same
music.
Give your hearts, but not into each other's
keeping.
For only the hand of Life can contain your
hearts.
And stand together yet not too near
together:
For the pillars of the temple stand apart,
And the oak tree and the cypress grow not
in each other's shadow.

Kahlil Gibran, *The Prophet*, 1926

based on love, is a cultural ideal of increasing power in the global village to which so many of us now belong. The happy marriage between equal partners is more and more the standard for all cultures and religions. Monogamous marriage is a persuasive idea that reaches from the kings of Nepal and Thailand (who now have only one wife, in contrast to their recent ancestors who had many wives and concubines) to the teenager daughter of a landless labourer who has just migrated to a shack in a *favella* in São Paulo, Brazil, or a *bustee* in Calcutta, India.

Some remarriages work well for the children from a previous partnership, while others are disastrous. Step-children are usually better off financially than children living with a single parent, but in the United Kingdom boys with a step-father are twice as likely to be brought before a juvenile court as those living with their natural father. Girls with a step-mother are four times as likely to get into similar trouble. Children with step-mothers, however, attend school far more assiduously than those with their natural parents and the aspirations – and possibly the realism – of the remarried family is as high or higher than a first marriage. Serial monogamy can be a learning process and there is evidence of greater sexual fidelity between partners of the second marriage than the first, although the cynic might say it is just because they are a bit older.

Intimate strangers

Sex inside marriage is the glue that unites two very different species. There will always be tension between the sexes, stemming from the different investments each makes in reproduction. In some situations that tension is transformed into a loving partnership, whereas in others it ends in fear, inequality, bitterness and even brutality. Women are more consistent in their friendships, but also more bitter if a relationship is broken after years of trust. Yet it is the very compromise that is built into marriage that provides much of the richness of adult life. It was heterosexual cooperation, propelled by evolution's need to secure access to adequate food without overmuch competition from males, that set us on the long road to civilization.

The union of two such different animals is a wonderful thing. Though marriage arrangements and expectations differ widely around the world, practically all human societies recognize the emotional attachment that sexual fulfillment promotes. Unlike male chimpanzees, men have a sense of paternity and invest in their children, although the amount of time and energy they spend varies greatly between cultures and families. As we have seen earlier, the bond between parents depends upon concealed ovulation in women combined with receptivity to sexual intercourse throughout the menstrual cycle, privacy of intercourse and covering up the genitals. It is these behavioural characteristics that form the basis of our family life, adult sexual love, and the love and care of children by their parents. The woman promises to limit her sexual favours to one man, while he commits to care for the children he sires. This relationship is built around frequent, private sex, most of which occurs when the woman is not ovulating and unable to get pregnant. The human use of infertile sex is unique. Among bonobos, same-sex relationships bond females in long-term partnerships, but heterosexual intercourse, while common and apparently often pleasurable, does not bond males and females in stable relationships. Among Japanese macaque monkeys, which breed seasonally, sex helps to define the social structure, but their society does not fall apart during the four to nine months of the year when no matings occur.

Although evolution has manipulated human sexuality to make it the foundation of family life, it has left the details of domestic living up to cultural modification: many different cultural interpretations of marriage are possible, but none is perfect, since male and female reproductive agendas are in intrinsic conflict. Yet the fact that sexual behaviour can be shaped by culture in so many different ways tends to make us anxious about behaving correctly. Religion often attempts to provide the missing assurance. Christianity, for example, in the Middle Ages slowly turned marriage from a secular event, celebrated outside the steps of the church, into an explicitly religious ceremony, literally and spiritually housed inside the church. In the present century, it has been partly turned back into a civil event, in the British registry office or, in the USA, commonly in the home.

Our contemporary world gives us a confusing array of choices. What is a good age to marry? Should we live together before marriage? Should the wife follow her vocation and postpone childbearing, or have her children early and then start her career? Should a couple with marital problems stick it out or try to make a new start? Jobs in the workplace are increasingly similar for men and women, but women continue to carry the burden of labour in the home. In the USA alone, thirty-three million women are cast in this dual role: half of all the women with children under 1 year old, and three-quarters of those with children under 6, work outside the home. Men come home to relax; women to care for their children, attempting to combine a career and the 'mummy touch'.

One thing we can do for ourselves and others is to strive to see problems in a long term perspective: we tend to see our reproductive lives as a series of snapshots – of pregnancy, of birth – when we need to see it portrayed cinematically. The continuous progression of adult sexuality makes sense only when all the component parts are put together. We can seldom think ahead and anticipate the full extent to which one single event may change the whole course of our lives. Some couples desperately want a baby, but they remain quite unrealistic about how it will change their lifestyles as they embark on the long years of care and expense associated with having children. Moralists get hopelessly lost when they ask the meaning of a single act of intercourse, instead of analysing the significance of many such acts throughout life that bond the couple together.

The bond of love transcends the other differences produced by evolution, permitting a man and a woman to gain most from their environment and from each other, and to share in the long, slow process of bringing up their children. Sex is evolution's imperative, driving us to perpetuate our species: love trades on *Homo sapiens*' recognition and respect for individuality. As a species, we commonly put our greatest investment of time and thought into family relationships. Sexual love is evolution's most intriguing and preposterous creation, and marriage one of culture's most universal and popular inventions. Selfish genes have culminated in a primate that often feels impelled to put his or her sexual partner's interests first. Love can couple two people together so we come to believe the statistically improbable suggestion that 'we were made for each other'. Love and marriage are a curiously wonderful mixture of Nature and nurture binding together a pair of intimate strangers.

5 SEX AND PREGNANCY

'and then I asked him with my eyes to ask again yes and then he asked would I yes ... and first I put my arms around him yes and drew him down to me so he could feel my breasts all perfume yes and his heart going like mad and yes I said yes I will Yes'. James Joyce, *Ulysses*, 1922

When we make love we are in naked communion with the first ancestral *Homo sapiens*. If we could be transported back 100 000 years we would lack our ancestors' skills to find food or build appropriate shelter, just as our progenitors from the last ice age would find themselves equally bewildered and helpless in a world of concrete and computers. But we would certainly know how to have sexual intercourse across the centuries, and might well fall in love.

Sexual intercourse can be the most intimate sharing two people have with one another, or it can be the most brutal collision between the two sexes – a man raping a woman. The vivid awareness of sexual union signals a momentous but momentary step in the transmission of life: the orgasm men seek so avidly does no more than carry already formed gametes from a duct in the male into the vagina. The female orgasm, although equally satisfying, is in no way essential to conception. Biologically, intercourse is the one moment in our lives when we, the adult organism, make a choice essential to the survival and further evolution of the genes we carry. All the other necessary steps in reproduction take place at the cellular level, silent, unseen and totally beyond our control. They are as unconscious as the first evolution of self-replicating molecules and cells on the Earth billions of years ago.

The molecular processes that rearrange our genes and the microscopic machinery that isolates the chromosomes in the cells and sorts one member from each pair to form the sperm and egg belong to an unimaginably tiny world. Suppose we take an apple and enlarge it until it is as big as the Earth. On that new scale, one atom would now be a large as one apple! When our DNA is duplicated, every atom in the DNA molecule must be copied correctly. In a man the key steps that pack the chromosomes tightly into the head of a wriggling sperm begin more than three months before ejaculation. In the woman the division of the chromosomes to make the egg occurred while she was still in her mother's womb, up to fifty years before the egg was shed. In the first half of each sexual cycle an egg is readied for release in a liquid-filled chamber, or follicle, that also secretes the hormone oestrogen into the

'The Imperfect Enjoyment'

Naked she lay; claspt in my longing arms,
I fill'd with love, and she all over charms,
Both equally inspir'd with eager fire,
Melting through kindess, flaming in desire;
With arms, legs, lips close clinging to embrace,
She clips me to her breast, and sucks me to her face.
The nimble tongue (love's lesser lightning) play'd
Within my mouth, and to my thoughts convey'd
Swift orders that I should prepare to throw
The all-dissolving thunderbolt below.
My flutt'ring soul, sprung with pointed kiss,
Hangs hov'ring o'er her balmy limbs of bliss.
But whilst her busy hand wou'd guide that part
Which shou'd convey my soul up to her heart,
In liquid raptures I dissolve all o'er,
Melt into sperm, and spend at every pore.
A touch from any part of her had done't:
Her hand, her foot, her very look's a —.
Smiling, she chides in a kind murm'ring noise,
And sighs to feel the too too hasty joys,
When, with a thousand kisses wand'ring o'er
My panting breast, and 'Is there then no more?'
She cries: 'All this to love and rapture's due,
Must we not pay a debt to pleasure too?'
But I, the most forlorn, lost man alive,
To show my wisht obedience vainly strive:
I sigh alas! And kiss, but cannot drive.
Eager desires confound my first intent,
Succeeding shame does more success prevent,
And rage, at last, confirms me impotent.

John Wilmot, Earl of Rochester, *ca.* 1675

woman's blood stream. After the release of the egg, the follicle turns into a solid mass of cells, the corpus luteum, that secrets the hormone progesterone.

The sexual bond

The passion of sex is focused on the exit from a unicellular phase of life, and heralds the onset of a new diploid existence, when each cell in the new body will contain a paired complement of chromosomes donated by each parent. At another level, sexual intercourse must define the different sexual agendas of men and women. Ideally, regular intercourse should express the love of the two partners as they care for the offspring to which intercourse occasionally gives rise. For some, it is filled with the joys of anticipated parenthood, but for hundreds of millions of couples around the world, sex is darkened by the fear of unwanted pregnancy. For the man, an erection lasts a few minutes and ejaculation a few seconds, while for the woman pregnancy persists for nine months and breastfeeding and child care can go on for many years.

It is common in evolution for the same organ to perform more than one purpose: feathers insulate a bird's body and help it to fly; our larynx helps to direct our food and drink down our gullet and away from our windpipe, and also permits us to speak or sing. In primates, the same act of sexual intercourse serves the totally different purposes of reproduction and social bonding. Among bonobos, sexual intercourse can reduce aggression at a crowded fig tree; among human beings, sexual intercourse not only gives rise to pregnancy but it also underpins the affection that ties the man and the woman as they bring up the next generation. In identifying with and caring for their own children, men are moving away from their polygamous ancestry where paternity was an unknown concept.

The mechanisms of sex

Virtually all men, and more than 98 per cent of women, experience sexual arousal sometime during their lives. The basis for sexual desire appears to be hard-wired into the nervous system, but also open to great modification by the environment. Male chimpanzees go from penile penetration to ejaculation in only 90 seconds, but seven out of ten American adults questioned about the duration of sex say they spend between 15 minutes and 1 hour making love. The machinery of orgasm, at least in the male, existed long before we developed insight into the emotional context of sexual relationships. Male infants often have erections in response to non-sexual stimuli and it is not unusual for a mother to discover a hard phallus while bathing her baby son. Some boys learn to masturbate before reaching puberty and since they are not yet producing any semen they experience a 'dry orgasm'.

On average, women have a less intense physical sex drive than men, and are usually aroused more slowly. From an evolutionary perspective they need to be more cautious, and avoiding the 'quick-fix' male orgasm may be to their

Viagra, a hard luck story

Some years ago the Pfizer pharmaceutical company began investigation a compound called sildenafil citrate that improved the blood flow to tissues. It was thought that this ability to improve blood flow might help to treat heart diseases, where lack of adequate supply causes the pain of angina, but it was soon noticed that it had a particular effect on the genitalia. Viagra was born. It does not initiate sexual desires, but it facilitates penile erection in men, and may also cause clitoral engorgement and improve sexual responsiveness in women. In the USA, between March 1998, when Viagra was first approved for use, and May in the same year, 1.7 million prescriptions were given. Sixteen men died, although it is too early to say whether this was random chance or evidence of serious risk. What is certain is that Viagra is being smuggled (a US $ 10 tablet sells for US $ 40 in Bangkok and over US $ 100 in Dublin), it is being imitated and it has aroused intense interest. Italians are selling Viagra pizza, and Mexicans say Viagra is short for *vieja agradecida* (= grateful wife). General Abacha, the Nigerian dictator, is said to have died *in flagrante delicto* whilst under the influence of Viagra.

In the USA, many medical insurance schemes do not cover the cost of oral contraceptive pills for clients, but the companies are being lobbied in favour of paying for Viagra. As in other mammals, so in *Homo sapiens*, it seems that the drive for sex may be stronger than the drive to think through the consequences.

Samson and Delilah, **Peter Paul Rubens,** ***ca.*** **1609.** Samson is physically and emotionally in the post-orgasmic phase of exhaustion, and Delilah, with flushed cheeks and half-closed eyes, also looks ravished. She rests a tender hand on his shoulder whilst a male servant carefully cuts off locks of Samson's hair to weaken him for the Philistines, who are waiting in the doorway to capture him (Judges 16:8). Although Rubens undoubtedly painted a picture of Samson and Delilah, art critics have suggested that the original was lost and this is a copy.

[The National Gallery, London.]

may i feel said he

may i feel said he
(i'll squeal said she
just once said he)
it's fun said she

(may i touch said he
how much said she
a lot said he)
why not said she

(let's go said he
not too far said she
what's too far said he
where you are said she)

may i stay said he
(which way said she
like this said he
if you kiss said she

may i move said he
is it love said she)
if you're willing said he
(but you're killing said she

but it's life said he
but your wife said she
now said he)
ow said she

(tiptop said he
don't stop said she
oh no said he)
go slow said she

(cccome? said he
ummm said she)
you're divine! said he
(you are Mine said she)

e.e.cummings, *Complete Poems 1904 – 1962*

advantage. A 1992 survey of US sexual behaviour showed that women think about sex less than men do. Only four out of ten US women claim they usually have an orgasm when they make love, and fewer than one in three women says she always has an orgasm. One-fifth say they have trouble lubricating, and over 30 per cent say they have lost interest in sex. Donald Symons captured the asymmetry in human sexual relations with the aphorism, 'When marriages are founded on love, women give sex for love and men give love for sex.' In all animals the clitoris is the female analogue of the penis and has the same rich nervous innervation and erectile tissue, although it is not clear whether any species other than humans, chimpanzees and some monkeys actually have orgasms. The human clitoris is sited more fully outside the entrance to the vagina than that of the chimpanzee, making it difficult for the penis to stimulate the clitoris during penile intercourse. This apparently annoying oddity may be an evolutionary adaptation to the fact that the human baby has a much larger head than a chimpanzee, and childbirth would damage so vascular an organ as the clitoris if it had not migrated out of harm's way during recent evolution. At the same time, the female orgasm is manifestly an important part of the sex bond, and women, unlike men, have an ability to have repeated orgasms within a short time.

Data on the frequency of human intercourse rely mainly on self-reporting but whatever way we count it, married couples have intercourse far more often than is needed to procreate – several thousand times in a lifetime to produce very few offspring. In Northern Ireland, H. G. Tittmar devised an objective way to gather anonymous data on the private act of sexual intercourse. He used the municipal sewerage system as his social test-tube, maintaining a daily log of the number of condoms passing through the Belfast drains. He found the highest number on Sundays and Mondays and the lowest on Wednesdays and it seems likely the articles being analysed took about twenty-four hours to complete their journey. Over the year the highest number of condoms was recovered in April, oddly appearing to confirm Alfred, Lord Tennyson's more poetic sentiment 'In the spring a young man's fancy lightly turns to thoughts of love'.

Intercourse is a simple, physical, sweaty episode and something we have in common with all mammals. Sexual love is complex, all embracing, uplifting, elusive but real, and it is a uniquely human characteristic. Human sexual love is highly selective – usually limited to one person at a time. It involves an intense desire for prolonged, close proximity with a person who is the object of affection. We are 'broken hearted' ever to be parted and 'can't wait' to be together again. We talk of 'falling in love', emphasizing the instinctive nature of the process. Passion leads to intimacy and commitment, which vary in their orchestration as the music of love proceeds. Although the desire for a child may be strong, the internal drives which control our behaviour focus largely on a desire for sexual intimacy. Sex itself is driven primarily by the desire for personal physical satisfaction, but it can also lead to what may be the strongest form of altruism we show to another adult who is not genetically related to us. Over the years, passion may subside, but still retain a latent potential for eruptive resurgence. In extreme circumstances, love can be so strong that it can endure for long intervals without genital consummation. Certainly, a stolen kiss or the touch of a hand may be remembered longer and as more significant than some episodes of naked intercourse.

Fantasies and fetishes

Beginning in early adolescence, we think more and more about sex when we are awake and we may dream about it while we slumber. Most men have penile erections two or three times a night while asleep, accompanied by dreaming (not always about sex) and rapid eye movements. Although less frequent than in men, female erotic dreams may lead to muscular spasms of orgasm that waken the dreamer. Nearly all men and most women learn to masturbate, although societies differ in how they view this practice. Young male langur monkeys have been observed to masturbate in the wild, and to eat their own ejaculate. In captivity, male chimpanzees masturbate often, but gorillas never do, even though they are deprived of other sexual outlets.

We can never know whether other apes engage in sexual fantasies while having intercourse, but humans commonly enter a secret world of fantasy when making love. They may recall a real sexual event, sometimes far removed from the immediate situation, or string together a fantasy that has never been and never will be put into practice. Some people screen a whole range of potential partners and choose a location for their fantasy with all the care of a Hollywood producer. Our sexual fantasies, like so much else, may be a window into some of our deep-seated biological drives. Symons has shown that male fantasies often revolve around visual images of the female body, and frequently involve more than one woman. Female fantasies often put more focus on the character of the fantasy partner and the emotional setting of the intercourse. E. Barbara Hariton and J. L. Singer, of Long Island Jewish Hospital, sampled the coital fantasies of women in a New York suburb, including parent teacher association members and regular church-goers. Half or more of them fantasized about imaginary lovers or some form of forbidden sex. A few envisaged being a whore. Fantasies about forced sex were frequent.

Fantasies, instead of being a prelude to sex, can also become a fetish, where an object or part of the body becomes a substitute for sex. At one time or another, human beings have managed to make practically anything from animals to chain saws into erotic objects. The great philosopher René Descartes is said to have been sexually aroused by women who squinted. A case has been reported where a man reached orgasm by following women whose shoes creaked.

Human beings, with their remarkable interest in sex, are unique in the variety of other species with whom copulation occurs. Alfred Kinsey reported that as many as 17 per cent of boys raised on farms had had at least one sexual encounter with an animal. Bestiality has been condemned by the Churches and, for example, in 1750 one Jacques Ferron was hanged for having intercourse with a female donkey; several people, including the local abbot, testified to the honour of the donkey, who was assumed to have been raped and was acquitted of any part in the crime. In 1991, an Englishman, Alan Cooper, was brought to court accused of an 'act of lewd, obscene and disgusting nature and outraging public decency by behaving in an indecent manner with a dolphin' in the sea off the British coast. Unlike Ferron's donkey, the dolphin, called Freddie, appears to have been a consenting adult and a defence witness described Freddie as 'extending the finger of friendship' for masturbating by Mr Cooper. As we have seen, dolphins are highly sexual animals and do indeed use their penises to explore the environment, sometimes springing them out like a jack-knife. Mr Cooper was acquitted.

Norms and rules

We are interested in how our peers behave and we often crave rules and norms to help to define how we 'ought' to behave. Yet, it is more difficult to quantify human sexual behaviour than it is to collect anecdotal stories of extreme or unusual behaviours. In the 1990s large surveys of sexual behaviour involving many careful samples of many thousands of adults have come from Britain, France and the USA. They were put together in the face of controversy. The British government under Margaret Thatcher withdrew financial support for the British survey, and the US government never even considered supporting work of this type. The costs had to be picked up by philanthropic foundations. Not surprisingly, in all surveys, vaginal intercourse was the most common form of sexual activity. Eighty-two per cent of men and 75 per cent of women reported masturbating. Seventy per cent of men and women had some form of oral sex, male oral contact with the woman's genitals (cunnilingus) being slightly more common than female oral contact with the penis (fellatio). In the USA in 1992, a research team from the University of Chicago questioned a sample of 3500 adults over the age of 18 on their sexual behaviour. Americans appeared to be more open than the British in reporting masturbation (one in four men and one in fourteen women reporting doing it once a week) but half said they felt guilty. Heterosexual anal intercourse, in which the man's penis is inserted into the woman's rectum, is low on the list of heterosexual preferences; it was reported by only 14 per cent of British men or women, and only one in twenty heterosexual US men found anal intercourse 'very appealing', and only 1 in 100 women reported that they enjoyed receiving anal sex.

Most sexually active gay men give or receive anal sex, while a small number engage in more unusual, but well documented, practices such as 'fisting' and 'felching'. Fisting involves inserting the clenched hand into the anus. Perforation of the rectum can occur. Felching is the practice of inserting a live animal into the anus. Gay males in America have put gerbils in a plastic bag and then, using the cardboard tube from inside a roll of toilet paper, have had the animal inserted into the rectum. In short, there is almost no end to the strange and unusual, comic and curious, trivial or cruel, silly, bestial, dangerous, stupid, harmless or imaginative things people will do to act out their sexual fantasies, make money, amuse those they love, or exploit those over whom they exercise power.

In the Chicago study conducted in 1992, 21 per cent of men and 3 per cent of women said they had had twenty-one or more partners since age 18. College graduates were slightly more conservative than the population at large. Twenty per cent of men and 30 percent of women reported having had only one partner since age 18. In Britain today, 30 per cent of men but only 10 per cent of women in their 30s report having had more than ten sexual partners. This imbalance is because a small number of women (often, but not always, prostitutes) have a large number of partners but may not be adequately captured in surveys.

Interpretations

As we have noted, there are good biological reasons why humans studiously try to avoid having intercourse within sight or sound of other people. But the privacy of human sex also condemns each new generation to be perplexed and insecure. Prior to the circulation of sex hormones at puberty, love and intercourse are incomprehensible. The mystery is also part of the fascination: we are curious about such a compelling experience, yet we desperately want to conform to the norms and rules expected of us. Consequently, intercourse can be a lonely experience and cause anxiety as well as pleasure. While sex is a source of jokes and swear words, normal intercourse is seldom a topic of frank and open discussion. This thing that may be so often on our minds is traditionally *verboten* on our lips. Inadequate communication between the two partners is one of the commonest causes of stress in marriage: how difficult it can be to ask your spouse about a sexual practice you think may cause embarrassment.

From an evolutionary perspective it is easy to see how sexual activity in humans serves the dual purpose of procreation and parental bonding, but many ancient cultures came up with conflicting interpretations of the meaning of sex. In ancient Egyptian mythology, masturbation was celebrated as the way the Sun God, Re, created the first couple Shu and Tefnet. By contrast, Saint Thomas Aquinas condemned masturbation as a 'sin against nature' and as worse than adultery or rape. In 1986, the United States Supreme Court interpreted a broadly worded law against sodomy to include fellatio. Yet the Bible literally sings the praises of fellatio. The 3000 year old Song of Solomon is thought to be a compilation of sexual songs to be sung at weddings. It begins, 'Kiss me again and again for your love is sweeter than wine', while later the woman's voice speaks of going down to a man's 'garden of nuts' (Song of Solomon 6:11). Ancient Hebrew beliefs held a mystical, almost holy view of the sexual climax, teaching that intercourse should take place only at night, and when the moon shone through the window a bed sheet was to be hung up. If the moon was likely to move across the bed while the couple made love, the position of the bed was to be changed. These instructions stemmed from the sacredness of the act and the belief that the eyes were a window into the soul. As scripture forbids anyone to look into the face of God, so the couple was forbidden a light to look into one another's eyes at the moment of orgasm in case they caught a glimpse of the divine. At the other extreme, the Christian Saint Clement of Alexandria taught that the moment of ejaculation represented such uncontrolled passion in the very presence of transmitting original sin that the soul actually fled from the body during orgasm.

Miracles and mistakes

Our multicellular life begins not as a person but as a cell: the fertilized egg is individually different from all other cells that have existed before or will come afterwards. The human egg is only one-tenth of a millimetre (0.004 inches) across, barely visible to the naked eye, and the sperm is 100 times smaller than that; yet the sperm and egg hold all the information required to coordinate the development of myriad cells that will become the assortment of organs composing the mature body. The processes that occur during pregnancy are awesome both in their complexity and lifelong consequences. They are also processes where natural mistakes are almost as common as the miracle of normal development.

Over the ages, the misinterpretation of some aspects of pregnancy – like the misinterpretation of intercourse – has caused a great deal of misery. Reproduction, because of its discontinuous nature, complexity and wide variation between species, has been difficult to study. The light of science has only slowly illuminated the fog of superstition. Most preindustrial societies regarded congenital defects either as a punishment from God, or a consequence of breaking some taboo. In the sixth century, Saint Gregory of Tours described how the mother of a blind and crippled child confessed in tears that she had conceived it on Sunday. 'Let it suffice,' Gregory told his flock, 'that you indulge your lusts on other days and leave this day unsullied to the Glory of God, else the children born to you will be crippled, or epileptic or leprous.' The irrational guilt of a woman burdened with an abnormal child, that the bishop so cruelly exploited, can be all too real even today and it is something sympathetic friends and loved ones of those unlucky enough to carry a congenitally abnormal child should understand.

We no longer believe, as did our mediaeval ancestors, that a woman has

A large family

When Samuel Pepys, the diarist, visited Holland in 1660, he made a pilgrimage to Lansdune near the Hague. In a church he saw the memorial to 365 children said to have been born to the Countess Margaret, daughter of the Earl of Holland on Good Friday, 1278. 'We saw the hill where they said the house stood ... Wherein the children were born. The basins wherein the male and female children were baptized stand over a large tablet that hangs upon the wall, with the whole story in Dutch and Latin.'

Clearly the Countess had had a hydatidiform mole and the priest, unaware of this condition, took each grape-like vesicle, diligently examined it, adjudicated whether it was male or female and then, with somewhat less imagination, baptized 182 vesicles baby Elizabeth, 182 baby John and left one unbaptized hermaphrodite condemned to spend Eternity in Limbo.

Hydatidiform moles are well described by Aristotle. Today, we know that they contain only the DNA of the father's sperm, with none contributed by the mother who produces the egg. Hydatidiform moles are usually genetically male, and the vesicles are merely swollen pieces of placental membrane without any sign of an embryo. Although the product of sexual intercourse, moles have no legal or moral status, other than to remind us that we should be careful not to assume that fertilization of an egg by a spermatozoon necessarily results in an embryo.

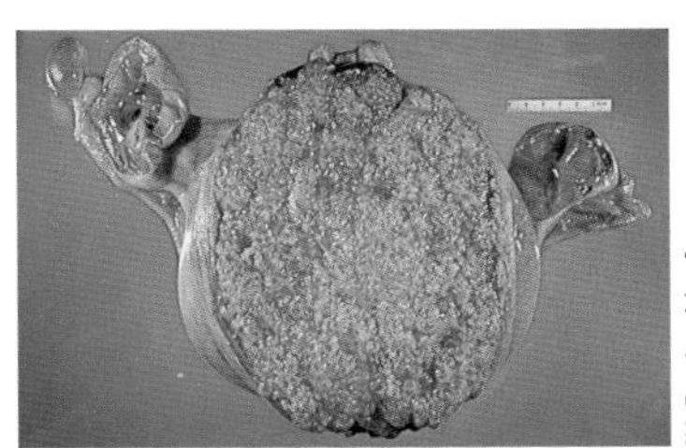
[K. Benirschke.]

Hydatidiform mole, occupying the whole of the cavity of the human uterus. The scale is in centimetres.

a child with a hare-lip because she saw a hare crossing a field during pregnancy. At the same time, another ancient belief, that whatever enters a woman's body during pregnancy affects the fetus, has been partially substantiated by modern research. Excess alcohol consumption by the pregnant mother can produce fetal damage, and the example of thalidomide, a drug used to prevent morning sickness which caused fetal limb malformations, underscores the need for great care and study before pregnant women are given any drugs. Smoking has been shown to have particularly deleterious effects on placental development and in the USA approximately 2000 newborn babies per year die as a result of damage to the placenta associated with maternal smoking. In 1991, a US woman was brought to court charged with providing addictive drugs to another individual when she used 'crack' cocaine during pregnancy and injured her child.

Today, much is understood about abnormalities of development and more and more insight is being gained into Nature's all important quality control mechanisms. Quality is achieved partly by a massive overproduction, followed by selective elimination of errors. The human female fetus has six

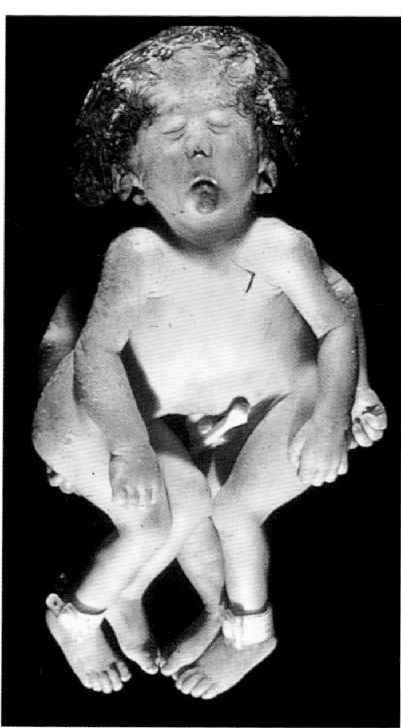

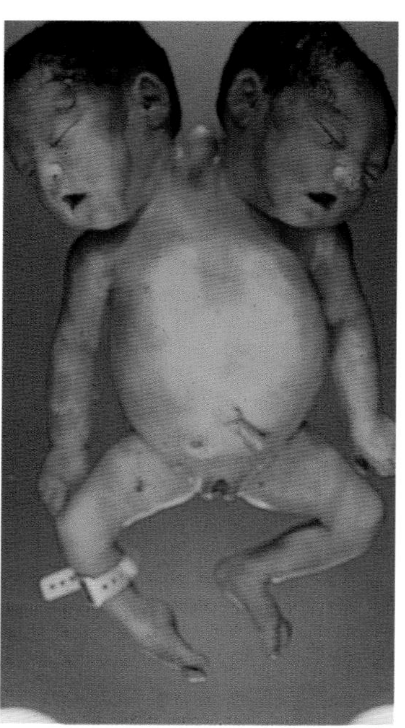

[K. Benirschke.]

How many souls? Intuitively, most people think that the human fetus on the left is one individual with four legs, whereas the one on the right is two individuals with only one pair of legs. Are we merely counting heads? Genetically, both developmental accidents have occurred to a single fertilized egg.

million eggs in her ovaries, but by birth a newborn girl has only two million and by puberty she is down to a few hundred thousand of which only a few hundred will ever be shed and only a handful can ever become fertilized. A man produces about 100 million new sperm each day – over 1000 per heart beat, or over a trillion in a lifetime – and each is genetically unique. The egg has a greater chance of being fertilized, but even so the overwhelming majority perish before ovulation, or are flushed out of the uterus at menstruation.

The female reproductive tract is more of an obstacle course than a sperm-friendly passage from the vagina to the fallopian tube where the egg is fertilized: the ejaculate is deposited in the neck of the womb and the cervix itself is filled with thick, sticky mucus which is hostile to sperm for much of the menstrual cycle, and even at the time of ovulation slows their progress. As a high proportion of sperm in the ejaculate of a healthy young man appears abnormal when looked at under the microscope, the female reproductive tract may represent a selective filter ensuring that only healthy sperm reach the vicinity of the egg. However, it is sobering to realize that we still have no

It's all in a word

Our attitudes are often determined by the words we use. By the same token, our attitudes to the early stages of human development are strongly influenced by the nouns we use. *Webster's Dictionary* defines a human embryo as 'the developing human individual from the implantation to the eighth week after conception,' whereas the *Complete Oxford Dictionary* defines it as 'the fetus *in utero* before the fourth month of pregnancy'. To the person in the street, a human embryo is something with arms and legs and sensations and movement, recognizably a little person – a newborn baby seen through the wrong end of a telescope. One can imagine the concern, therefore, when scientists announce their intention to perform experiments on early human embryos.

But what often interests the scientists is not the embryo itself but the fertilized egg before an embryo has begun to appear. Unfortunately there is no generally acceptable way to describe this stage of development, other than with scientific jargon such as zygote or blastocyst. Perhaps we should call it a 'pre-embryo'? After all, until the primitive streak first makes its appearance at about fourteen days after fertilization, we do not know whether there is even going to be an embryo; the fertilized egg may merely degenerate into an amorphous mass of placental tissue or it may die because it has one chromosome too few or one too many.

In Aristotlean times the early embryo was thought to have only a vegetative soul. Performing experiments on pre-embryos is a far cry from cutting up wriggling little human beings, and in Britain the Warnock Committee (1985) recommended that experiments on human embryos should be approved in principle, but only up until the fourteenth day after fertilization. Perhaps if we said that experimentation was allowable only on pre-embryos, never on embryos, it might allay public misgivings. But that would require rewriting our dictionaries.

The one word we have for abortion is even more limiting. Women all over the world distinguish between 'My period is late', 'I may be pregnant', and 'I am expecting a baby'. However, with our unimaginative vocabulary we are forced to use 'abortion' for everything from the possible action of an intrauterine contraceptive device a few days after fertilization to the delivery of a potential viable baby at twenty-seven weeks of pregnancy.

idea what a 'normal' sperm looks like. The so-called abnormalities that we see under the microscope are mostly in the shape of the sperm head or in its motility. This tells us nothing about its DNA blueprint. Although we know that the occasional very large sperm is diploid, carrying a double set of chromosomes, and hence incapable of producing normal fertilization, most of the rest may be genetically normal.

The human embryo is immensely complex and abnormalities are indeed common. Even today, however, our knowledge of the very early human embryo is based on a few tens of cases. In the 1940s John Rock and Arthur Hertig in Boston, Massachusetts, explored human wombs removed after hysterectomy (for good medical reasons) at various times after presumed fertilization. In over 100 cases, they found just over thirty embryos in the early stages of development. Microscopic examination suggested that one in ten would have failed to survive the first 100 hours of development, and four out of ten appeared unable to attach to the uterus and six out of ten were lost by twelve days after fertilization. Even amongst pregnancies that survive long enough for a woman to miss her period and recognize she is pregnant, approximately one in five embryos will abort spontaneously. A great many, possibly a majority, of these spontaneous abortions involve defective embryos, often with chromosomal abnormalities. Spontaneous abortion, therefore, is a natural, necessary process without which all these pregnancies would turn into nightmares with a likelihood of perhaps a third or more of all babies being not merely abnormal but grossly deformed.

The afterbirth

A woman's ability to retain a fertilized egg and nurture the early stages of development within her own body is shared with a curious zoo of other viviparous animals (those who bear their young alive). It includes some species of cockroaches, fleas, some sharks, certain snakes and all mammals, save two Australian egg-laying mammals, the spiny anteater and duck-billed platypus. Eggs that are laid outside the body have evolved to store a lot of yolk to nourish the developing embryo. The eggs of viviparous animals contain only a fraction of the nourishment found in a hen's egg or even a frog's egg, but they have a similar set of enveloping membranes that surround and protect the embryo. They first evolved about 200 million years ago as vertebrates moved out of the water and onto dry land. All of us spent our early life in an inner watery space capsule, the amnion, which in evolutionary terms represents a fragment of the aquatic environment in which our ancestors first developed. It is the same placental membrane that obstetricians refer to as the amnion

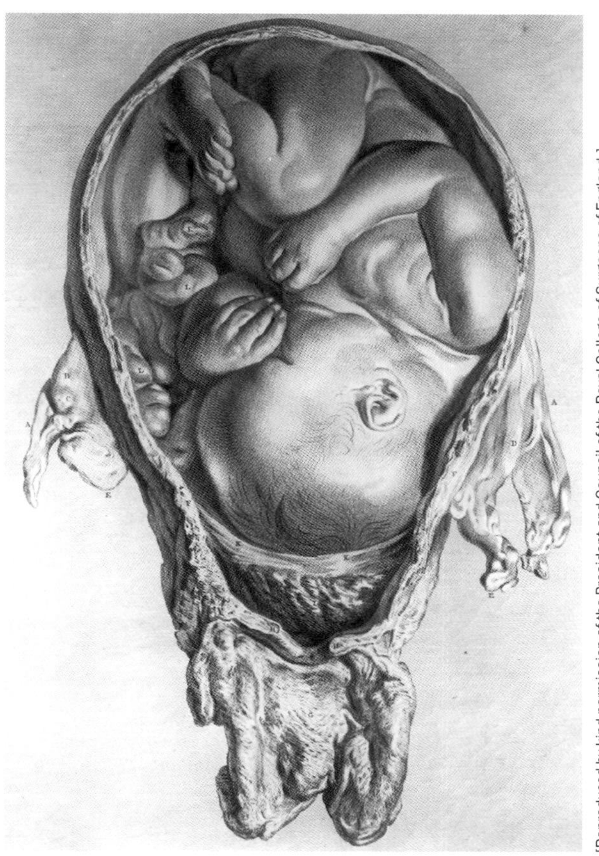

The fetus in the womb. In 1774 William Hunter, the Scottish obstetrician, published his illustrated *Atlas of the Gravid Uterus*. This illustration is of 'a woman who died of a flooding [haemorrhage] in the ninth month of pregnancy'. Part of the placenta can be seen just below the child's head and it is abnormally situated over the cervix (referred to as placenta praevia). No doubt it was from this point that the lethal bleeding occurred.

and they talk about the amniotic 'waters' breaking during labour. From an evolutionary viewpoint these are exceedingly 'ancient waters'. In reptiles and birds, these membranes permit the embryo to breathe through the porous eggshell and to store waste products prior to hatching, while in viviparous animals they provide the interface with the uterine tissues that allows food and oxygen to pass from the mother to the growing embryo and removes waste products and carbon dioxide for excretion by the mother.

The fertilized egg can grow outside the uterus just as well as it does inside the uterus. In rare cases a fertilized human egg enters the abdomen and attaches to some organ such as the liver or gut. Occasionally such an ectopic pregnancy may develop a working placenta, permitting the embryo to continue development, but usually the tissue to which the egg attaches, such

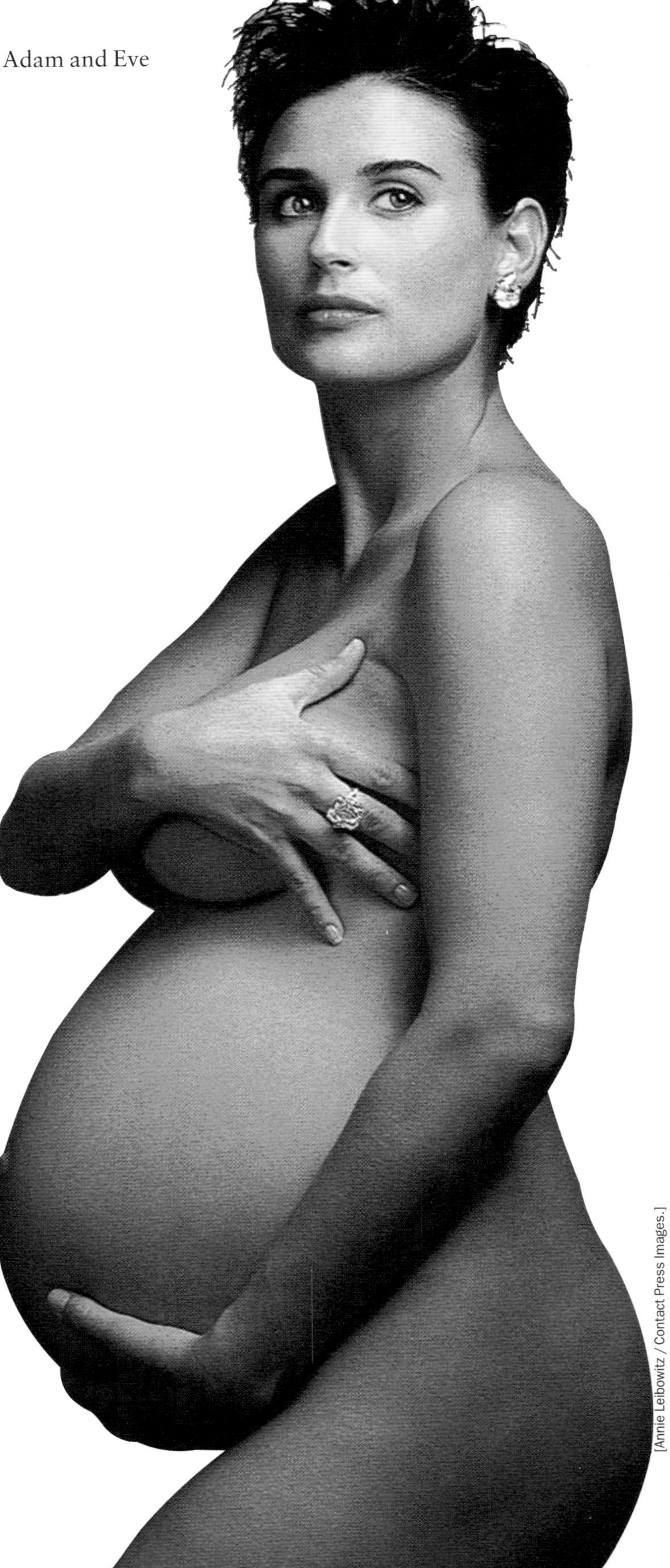

Demi Moore pregnant (*opposite*). Why does a picture of a naked pregnant woman cause such controversy? When film star Demi Moore had this photograph on the front cover of *Vanity Fair* magazine in 1991, it generated a heated debate on both sides of the Atlantic.

as the fallopian tube, ruptures, bringing about death of the embryo as well as threatening the life of the mother. Nevertheless, there are a small number of individuals alive in the world today who never entered their mother's womb, but developed in her abdominal cavity, and were delivered surgically in the later months of pregnancy (see p. 159). The commonest site for an ectopic pregnancy is in the fallopian tube, where internal bleeding can threaten the woman's life. Even the most conservative religions justify surgery to terminate ectopic pregnancies, yet biologically such operations are abortions, since they destroy a potential human life. We have to recognize that in human reproduction there are few absolutes and we are all forced to be pragmatists. It would be manifestly absurd to abandon to virtually certain death thousands of women with ectopic tubal pregnancies because the odd one might occasionally develop into a normal child, and everyone recognizes this. Whatever our philosophy, or basic religious belief, in the case of ectopic pregnancy we all give the life of the mother priority over that of the embryo: those who confront one another in Right-to-life and Pro-Choice politics are separated not by moral absolutes, but by probabilities.

Variations on a theme

The size and number of our offspring and the duration of pregnancy have been tailored by evolution to maximize reproductive performance. The long-nosed bandicoot (an Australian marsupial) delivers several immature babies after a mere twelve days of pregnancy, while the elephant carries a single fetus for twenty-two months. The honey possum (another Australian marsupial) gives birth to an infant weighing 5 milligrams, little bigger than a full stop, while a fin whale delivers a baby weighing 200 million times as much. Human beings produce a baby about one-thousandth of the weight of a newborn whale, but they take almost as long to do it. All these mammals use the same basic reproductive mechanisms (the sex hormones are of identical chemical structure, the uterus, ovaries and testes develop in the same basic ways, and the afterbirth of each has the same anatomical elements); yet their diversity illustrates the range of strategies evolution has created to solve the basic problem of delivering the next generation into the world alive and wriggling.

Once the onset of labour has been triggered by the fetus, a maternal hormone called prostaglandin plays a role in delivery. This chemical was first thought to be made by the male prostate gland, but it is now known to be produced in the uterus at the time of menstruation, spontaneous abortion and delivery. That it might play a role in female physiology was first suggested by Sultan Karim, who, while working in Uganda, was intrigued to hear women say they sometimes drank their husbands' semen to induce labour. Prostaglandins may also trigger maternal behavioural responses.

The human placenta manufactures high levels of a hormone that maintains the production of progesterone by the ovary and so prevents the next menstruation from occurring. It is this rapid build-up of placental hormone production in the first weeks after fertilization that is the tell-tale clue used in pregnancy testing kits. Changes in circulating hormones also give rise to the nausea and sickness that are relatively common in early pregnancy. The growing uterus may press on the bladder, leading to a frequent desire to urinate. The pregnant woman may also be aware of changes in the breasts including increased blood flow, enlargement, and darkening of the nipples and surrounding areola.

Decisions

When pregnancy goes wrong, and it does quite frequently, then it can present parents and health professionals with harrowing decisions. Our burgeoning technology is solving old problems and creating new ones. More and more congenital abnormalities are being diagnosed before birth, and may result in an abortion being proposed. Since the placenta and embryo come from the same egg and have identical chromosomes, conditions such as Down's syndrome can be detected by taking cells from the embryonic membranes with a long needle passed through the woman's abdomen and then growing them in tissue culture for chromosomal studies. The level of a particular protein called alpha-fetoprotein is raised in the mother's blood when the fetus has an abnormality of the nervous system, such as spina bifida. Ultrasound examination can reveal serious deformities, such as enlarged fetal kidneys, early in pregnancy. The risks of congenital abnormality rise with maternal age, and in Britain it is recommended that all pregnant women over age 35 be tested for fetal abnormality.

Nowhere are the consequences of abnormality sadder than in the case of the nervous system. About three weeks after fertilization the cells that will form the embryo are arranged in sandwich-like layers. A trough appears in the outer layer that soon forms a closed tube which will become the brain and spinal cord. The formation of this neural tube can go wrong in several ways and defects occur in about 1 in 200 births in Britain, and about 1 in 1000 in the USA. It may fail to fuse properly, leaving nervous tissue exposed to the outside world, as in spina bifida. If the defect is not closed surgically, infection may enter the nervous system causing the infant's death. If the defect is mild then surgery may leave a scar but no loss of function, but in other cases there may be permanent paralysis of the legs and an inability to control the bladder or rectum. If the forward end of the neural tube fails to develop properly an anencephalic baby is born – a baby literally without a brain. Anencephalic newborns usually die rapidly and there is no way, and never will be, of replacing the missing brain tissue. It has been shown recently that many neural tube defects are the result of lack of sufficient folic acid in the diet. Such abnormalities can be largely prevented, but the woman must begin to take the folic acid supplements before she conceives.

Errors in the development of the nervous system demonstrate the full range of physical and ethical issues presented by congenital abnormalities. The anencephalic newborn has a face but no top to the head and it invariably dies quickly. Some people reason that an infant without a brain cannot qualify as 'a person' and no-one has seriously suggested that anencephalics should be resuscitated. But their other organs are usually perfectly normal and can be a source of organ transplants. Is this a reasonable thing to do? What rights do the parents have? To some extent, it is the continuity of biological problems which bewilders us. It explains, for example, the apparent paradox that a mother might reasonably decide to have an induced abortion if she knew her baby had spina bifida in the fourth month of pregnancy, but use surgical repair and invest a lifetime of love if a child is born with the same defect after nine months of pregnancy. Where absolutes are lacking, the law finds it difficult to balance society's interest in protecting the helpless fetus against the parents' autonomy and decision-making. Perhaps the best that can be done is to create a framework within which those closest to such agonizing issues can make sincere decisions using the best scientific information available. Many people in industrialized nations are worried about abortion as a general possibility, but they are sympathetic when presented with an individual hard case. For example, in 1987, by a 2:1 majority in a secret ballot, the people of Ireland amended their constitution so as to protect the life of the 'unborn child'; yet when a 14 year old girl became pregnant as a result of rape in 1992, the polls showed a 2:1 majority in favour of permitting the young woman to travel to London for an abortion. It is not unreasonable to be ambivalent about something as complex and emotional as abortion.

When did I begin?

One of the reasons sincere people differ over abortion is because they have different images of embryonic development. Those who believe a pregnancy should never be terminated typically perceive the early embryo as having all the features of a newborn child, but seen as if through the wrong end of a

Birth. The Arrival and Trials of the Soul, ca. 1160–80. For thousands of years the action of the soul in embryological development was compared to that of rennet on milk, doubtless derived from a passage in the Book of Job (10:10): 'Hast thou not poured me out as milk, and curdled me like cheese?' This concept was passed on by later Jewish thinkers into Christian thought and so into the vision of Saint Hildegard of Bingen (1098–1180), who saw the soul, containing all the elements of wisdom, being passed into the infant's body whilst it was still within its mother's womb. The Wisdom of God is represented as a square object with its angles set to four quarters of the Earth, this being the symbol of stability. From it a long tube-like process descends into the fetus, which 'illumines the whole body', and becomes the soul. The ten attendants are apparently carrying cheeses, and in the top left the Evil One interferes with one of them and is a corrupting force throughout the rest of adult life (*panels on right*).

Fertilization

2 weeks

6 weeks

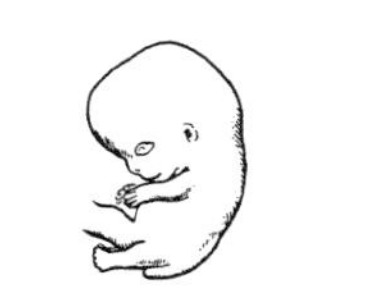

9 weeks

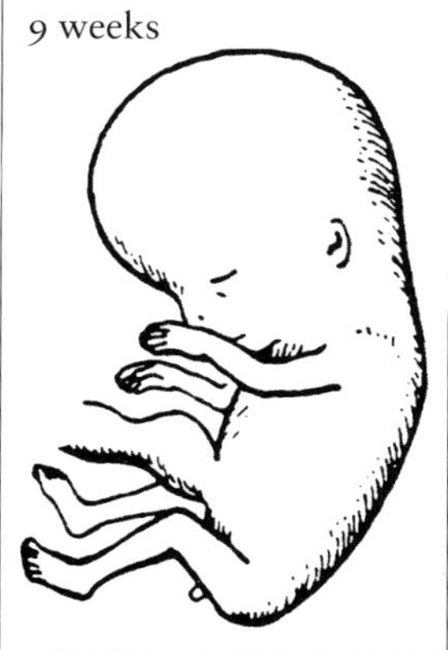

The human conceptus, life size. A newly fertilized egg is too small to be seen by the naked eye (*top*). When the mother's first menstrual period is missed, the embryo is 2 weeks old and about 1 mm in length. By six weeks, it is 1.5 cm long and by nine weeks 4.5 cm.

telescope. This is misleading. During pregnancy the embryo grows in both size and complexity. The question of whether the embryo is preformed at the time of conception and merely grows in size, or whether it becomes more complex with the passage of time is an ancient one. 'The problem before us', wrote Aristotle, 'is not out of what, but by what, are [embryos] formed? Either something external fashions them, or else something present in the semen or something that possesses the Soul.' Aristotle's idea of the soul is not too far removed from the modern embryologist's use of the term inducer, or the biochemist's enzyme. Anyone who opens a series of chicken eggs at regular intervals after laying, which is exactly what Aristotle appears to have done, can readily see with the naked eye that all embryos begin as simple structures which become increasingly more complex with the passage of time. Very early in development, each of the cells that make up the embryo are capable of giving rise to a full range of both placental and body tissues. As every cell in the body carries the same coded information in its DNA, so every cell, even in the adult, has all the information needed to make a whole new person. Embryological development is associated with the shutting down of information no longer needed on the voyage of development.

Non-identical human twins are formed when two eggs are released and fertilized at the same time. They are no different from other siblings of the same mother and there are even cases of women whose non-identical twins had different fathers. The tendency to have non-identical twins is inherited and is common, for example, in West Africa, but relatively rare in East Asia. Identical twins are totally different and are the product of one fertilized egg. One egg can split into two very soon after fertilization, giving rise to identical twins with separate placentas: they are true clones. Over 60 per cent of identical twins, however, appear to be formed much later, two to three weeks after fertilization, when two primitive streaks develop in the same embryo, attached to a shared placenta. If by some mischance the two streaks run together, then conjoined or Siamese twins are formed. It is even possible to get identical triplets, quadruplets or even quintuplets from a single fertilized egg. The Dionne quins, discussed later, are a case in point.

Thirty days into development the embryo is about 0.3 inches (8 millimetres) long and the different organs are beginning to function, albeit in simple ways. The heart begins as a simple tube which starts to contract and continues to function and pump blood even as it increases in complexity, eventually forming a four-chambered heart. In the second half of pregnancy, the kidneys of the fetus secrete a dilute urine which is passed into the amniotic fluid separating the fetus from the extra-embryonic membranes. The fetus 'drinks' this fluid, which is also formed by the developing lungs.

[J. W. McArthur © 1938 the American Genetic Association.]

The Dionne quintuplets at 3 years of age. Born in Canada in 1934, the Dionne quintuplets, unlike the seven babies born to Bobbi and Kenny McCaughey in the USA in 1997, were conceived naturally and all derived from a single fertilized egg, having a single shared placenta, and identical fingerprints. They are therefore an example of natural cloning.

By twelve weeks, the basic architecture of the embryo is complete and so we now call it a fetus. Some of the most complicated aspects of development are over, even before the woman begins to let out her waistband. The last two-thirds of pregnancy are taken up mainly with growth of the organs that have been established early on, with one exception – the brain. The brain takes longest to reach its full size and complexity and new brain cells are formed at the staggering rate of 250000 for every minute of pregnancy. Unlike a computer, the brain cells begin to function as development is proceeding. There is no sudden 'switching on' of the nervous system, and the unbroken, continuous processes of embryonic and fetal growth pose difficult problems for moralists, lawyers and for any woman carrying an abnormal fetus or an unwanted pregnancy: when does life begin?

Father Norman Ford of the Catholic Theological College, Melbourne, Australia, has pointed out that the Christian concept of a unique human soul is difficult to apply to human development prior to the formation of the primitive steak, when identical twins can still occur. Can one soul be shared between two twins? Theologians have always taught that the soul is indivisible. In the laboratory, reproductive scientists have fused the cells from two or more early embryos and produced a chimaera, which has at least four

A

SHORT, but concise account of ELISABETH and MARY CHULKHURST, who were born joined together by the Hips and Shoulders, in the Year of our Lord 1100, at BIDDENDEN, in the COUNTY of KENT;

COMMONLY CALLED THE

Biddenden Maids.

THE Reader will obſerve by the above Plate of them, that they lived together in the above ſtate, Thirty-four Years; at the expiration of which Time, one of them was taken Ill, and in a ſhort time died; the ſurviving one was adviſed to be ſeparated from the body of her deceaſed Siſter, by diſſection, but ſhe abſolutely refuſed the ſeparation, by ſaying theſe words, as we came together, we will alſo go together, and in the ſpace of about ſix hours after her Siſter's deceaſe, She was taken Ill, and died alſo.

BY their WILL, they bequeathed to the *Churchwardens* of the Pariſh of BIDDENDEN, and their ſucceſſors *Churchwardens* for ever, certain pieces or parcels of Land in the Pariſh of *Biddenden* containing twenty Acres, more or leſs, which now lets at £.31 10*s*. *per Annum*. There are uſually made in commemoration of theſe wonderful phænomena's of nature, about 1000 Rolls with their impreſſion printed on them, and given away to all Strangers, on *Eaſter Sunday*, after Divine Service in the Afternoon; alſo about 300 Quartern Loaves, and Cheeſe in proportion, to all the poor Inhabitants of the ſaid Pariſh.

BIDDENDEN: PRINTED AND SOLD BY R. WESTON.—1806. [PRICE TWO PENCE.]

The first Siamese twins? Poster advertising the Biddenden Maids, born in AD 1100. They were derived from a single fertilized egg, and hence were clones.

different parents. There is genetic evidence that such chimaeras may also occur by accident on rare occasions in human development: could two souls commingle?

It is difficult to imagine an 'incomplete person', yet nature forces us to think in this direction. The problem is that biological development is a gradual process, but social and legal forces demand absolute distinctions. The same problems arise in the less contentious areas of biological maturation during life after birth. Intellectual and emotional development in young people, like embryonic development in the womb, is a continuous process, yet society has to choose a specific date when someone becomes legally competent. It would be stupid, for example, to legislate so that 6 year olds could vote in an election. Equally, it would be absurd to forbid the franchise until someone is 60. Yet nations at different times, and for valid reasons, have chosen 18, 21 and 30 as the age when someone can vote: it is easy to exclude the extremes but in the end the exact time selected as a cut-off date is an arbitrary choice. Similarly, during development before birth it is also easy to exclude extremes. Few people consider an intrauterine contraceptive, which can occasionally destroy the fertilized egg, as inducing an abortion. Conversely, no sensible person wishes to call the destruction of an abnormal fetus in the fifth month of pregnancy a contraceptive procedure. The difficulty is that there is no Rubicon between fertilization and birth, before which we can say the embryo is as trivial as a nail paring and after which it must enjoy the full ethical and legal status of a child. We cannot escape making pragmatic, and to some extent arbitrary decisions, but we can still make those decisions based on prudent interpretations of the biological facts.

Manipulating human reproduction

Over the last century, a great deal of insight has been obtained into the development of other animals, and in the last two decades human reproduction has been manipulated in a number of new ways. Eggs and sperm are relatively easy to sustain in an appropriate liquid medium kept at body temperature, and artificial insemination using fresh or stored sperm is a common veterinary practice. *In vitro* fertilization (IVF) and embryo transfer have been common procedures used for many years. The first embryo transfer was performed in the rabbit by Walter Heape in Cambridge, England, as long ago as 1890. By the 1980s, 100 000 calves a year were being delivered following embryo transfer.

On giving birth to one's self

It is now theoretically possible for a woman to give birth to herself. All the technology is now in place and the process would be something like this: following fertilization of an egg *in vitro*, the zygote is allowed to cleave to the two-cell stage. Then, like the primal Adam, the two halves are separated from one another to create identical twin embryos. One of the blastomeres is then deep frozen in liquid nitrogen, whilst the other half is transferred to the uterus of the egg donor, where it develops into a baby. If it is female, then as an adult the woman could give birth to herself following transfer of the deep-frozen embryo to her uterus. In other words, it would be possible to produce identical twins by splitting the egg, and then separating the twins in time by the chill of the deep freeze. As the first-born twin aged in the natural environment, she could be reborn, hopefully avoiding all the pitfalls and mistakes she had experienced. What lessons one might be able to teach one's self!

Of course, the other way of giving birth to one's self is by cloning from the nucleus of a cell in the body of an adult. This is discussed in more detail on p. 282.

It took unusual persistence, however, to make IVF and embryo transfer work in human beings. Robert Edwards, who like Heape worked in Cambridge, and an obstetrician, Patrick Steptoe, from Oldham, England, began trying to achieve human IVF and reimplantation of the embryo in the late 1960s, but did not have a successful outcome until the birth of Louise Brown on 25 July 1978 – a perfectly normal child except that she was conceived by Mr and Mrs Brown outside their bodies, in order to by-pass Mrs Brown's blocked fallopian tubes. For IVF to be carried out, a long needle guided by ultrasound is used to puncture the ovarian follicles just before the egg would normally be released. Sperm are added to the eggs in a special dish outside the body and when the egg, or eggs, have been fertilized they are injected into the uterus. The surgery and biochemical tests to predict follicular ripening are expensive, and the whole thing is a bit of a palaver, but is well worth it for loving parents who can afford it and who would otherwise have been childless; about 40 000 IVF babies had been born by the late 1990s. On average, it costs approximately US $5000 for every menstrual cycle during which an infertile woman is treated by IVF, and there is only a 10 to 20 per cent chance of success during each cycle. It is worth emphasizing that the most common use of IVF is to by-pass blockages of the fallopian tubes. Much tubal blockage is the result of infection, commonly due to a mild sexually transmitted disease such as chlamydia, which may even have gone unnoticed earlier in the woman's life. A wiser use of condoms in non-monogamous partnerships would save a great deal of suffering and expense later.

When a couple's own egg and sperm are used the child born by IVF is as surely and naturally theirs as if it had been conceived in the normal way. More challenging situations arise when we start switching eggs and sperm between natural and surrogate parents. An egg taken from one woman's ovary and fertilized can be implanted into another woman's uterus. Such a procedure may be done for financial return, or for reasons of altruism. American surrogate mothers usually earn from US$5000 to US$10 000. Should a rich woman, for reasons of convenience, be permitted to pay a poor woman to carry her child for financial reward – a womb to rent? An example of altruistic surrogate parenthood is that of a 42 year old woman from Minnesota. IVF was used so that she could be delivered of her own grandchild. Her original daughter was born with functioning ovaries but no uterus. Her daughter's husband's sperm was used to fertilize four of her daughter's eggs removed by operation and implanted into the woman's uterus. She delivered non-identical twins, who were in a very real sense her own grandchildren. Another variant is when a woman has an inherited disease and takes an egg from another woman to be fertilized by her husband's sperm and implanted into her own uterus; this is adoption into the womb instead of the home. We are familiar with adoption, but IVF is relatively new and therefore more frightening. Pregnancy lasts only for nine months and as far as we know one womb is very much like another, while adoption lasts a lifetime and the love and care available in different families varies enormously. Perhaps we should be as concerned about the statutory regulation of day-care centres as about surrogate mothers. Finally, the technology of IVF also makes it possible, using hormones, to prepare the uterus of a women well past the menopause to receive and carry to term an IVF embryo conceived by using an egg donated from a younger woman. One of the oldest women to have an IVF baby of this type is Arceli Keh, who was 63 when her baby was born. Pregnancy at this age carries considerable physical dangers for the woman and some problems for the growing child, who, when she needs her mother most, will find she has an old and possibly rather frail parent.

In the 1970s, Ralph Brinster of the University of Philadelphia took malignant cells from an experimentally produced tumour in a mouse and injected them into a mouse blastocyst in the first week following fertilization. The cancer cells lost whatever properties first made them malignant and reverted to normal tissue in the maturing embryo, which survived to adulthood and was fertile. If, as was sometimes the case, the malignant cells ended up as sperm or eggs, then it was true to say that the next generation had a cancer as its grandparent.

To keep these remarkable discoveries and possibilities in perspective, we also need to remind ourselves of the many things modern biology cannot do. A fertilized egg can be cultured outside the body for only four or five days, and there is no way that current technologies could be used to let it develop into an embryo or fetus outside the body, since for the foreseeable future it will be impossible to replace the complex workings of the living placenta. In biological terms, the high technology of an IVF clinic achieves little more than mating frogs do in a muddy pond every spring. However, we can culture cells from the early human embryo, so-called embryonic stem cells, and these may one day enable us to culture differentiated cells for transplantation.

Pregnant males?

As we have seen, the fertilized egg occasionally implants outside the womb, and in exceedingly rare cases such ectopic pregnancies may survive the full nine months. In the 1960s, the late David Kirby of Oxford University began transplanting fertilized mouse eggs not only into the wrong site, such as the kidney or the brain, but also into the wrong sex: they developed particularly rapidly when placed in the testis. Ectopic pregnancies usually end in serious haemorrhage because the growing placenta damages whatever organ it invades. In theory, however, a fertilized egg placed in an ectopic site in the male could last the whole of pregnancy and produce a viable offspring, just as it sometimes does in a woman. Already some gay men have asked scientists to explore the possibility of doing what has been done in mice – creating a pregnant male by implanting a fertilized egg in the abdomen. There is no reason why in the end a man should not deliver a child by abdominal operation nine months after his sperm might have been used to fertilize a donor egg, but hundreds or even thousands of men would have to risk their lives before one pregnancy, by some lucky chance, survived. What might be physiologically possible would be biological and social nonsense.

Unequal investments

For the foreseeable future, child bearing will remain an exclusively female occupation, and the huge difference in investment in time and energy the two sexes put into reproduction (we will see in Chapter 6 that lactation requires an even bigger investment than pregnancy) will continue to shape the behaviour of each sex. In evolution, the critical issue is the transmission of the genes to the next generation. Put bluntly, from a biological perspective, if the opportunity arises and he is not stricken by conscience or hobbled by convention, it is always in the male's interest to spend a few hundred million sperm in the hope of propagating his genes, putting sex first and leaving love

Cuckold

To be called cuckold is perhaps one of the most derogatory taunts that can be directed against a man; to rear a cuckoo in your nest, thinking it is genetically one of your own, wasting all your resources propagating the genes of a rival male, ignorant of the infidelity of your Mona Lisa of a wife – shame upon you! Hence the extraordinary lengths men have taken, and continue to take, to ensure their paternity.

A man's best guarantee of paternity is female virginity at marriage. In societies where wealth is inherited by male line of descent it therefore became particularly important to ensure paternity. Jack Caldwell, an Australian demographer, has pointed out that in communities that do not inherit land, because soil fertility is so low that it is almost worthless, there is no concern about paternity. Thus, throughout sub-Saharan Africa, with its poor clay soils, puberty in both sexes is celebrated as the time of acquisition of potential fertility, but sexual relationships are relatively unrestrained, and the concept of no sex before marriage was unknown prior to the coming of Christianity. But when humans walked out of Africa, and encountered the rich fertile soils of the great river valleys – the Nile, the Tigris and the Euphrates, the Indus and the Ganges, the Rhine and the Rhône – they cherished the land and wished to pass it on to their extended families. All the great religions have insisted on female virginity at marriage, so that the man can be sure that it is only his own children that inherit his estates.

to sort itself out later. The predispositions that affect our sexual and other behaviours are not always conscious and the same innate drive may well manifest itself in different ways in different settings. We are interested in exploring the evolutionary origins and development of human sexuality for the very reason that we may want to try to modify some of the behaviours.

To the effort of pregnancy and the investment of breastfeeding common to all mammals has been added the extra burden of bringing into the world a helpless child with a brain that is only one-quarter grown. As our brains evolved to their present size over the last few million years, so the time taken to fully programme them rose from a few years, as in most other primates, to almost two decades. Human parenting is something to exhaust even the strongest woman and it is a reasonable speculation that the development of an increasingly helpless infant has resulted in some key changes in mating behaviour. One strategy that men can follow in this situation, which will help to maximize the chances that their genes will survive to the next generation, is to invest directly in the protection, feeding and nurturing of their children. Yet it is intrinsically difficult to evolve behavioural strategies that link the different investments that male and female mammals make in reproduction. The passion of sex can indeed weld together the strong but differing behavioural agendas of men and women; however, sex can also end up blowing relationships apart with explosive violence. Later chapters explore both sides of this paradox.

6 BIRTH AND BREASTFEEDING

'Nature has so wisely ordered things that did women suckle their children, they would preserve their own health, and there would be such an interval between the birth of each child, that we should seldom see a houseful of babies.' Mary Wollstonecraft, *Vindication of the Rights of Woman*, 1792

Birth is hard work for large mammals with big babies. For the offspring its birth day is usually the most dangerous of its whole life. For the mother it can be painful, life threatening, and can cause serious injuries. We have no comfortable verb to describe human birth. The words we use for our livestock such as foaling, farrowing, whelping, calving, kidding and lambing strike a tender note, but for human beings the verbs labour or delivery convey threatening overtones. Delivery in apes and women is strikingly similar. Chimpanzees and gorillas deliver in the sitting position. The baby has a smaller head than the newborn human and labour lasts only about two hours, but even so it appears to be painful and it is associated with some of the same dangers as human delivery, such as breech birth or haemorrhage.

Birth signifies the entrance of a new actor into the world, whose life may be determined in large measure by the circumstances of that entry. Birth has a profound effect on the social and personal situation of the parents and the other children in the family. The birth of the first child transforms the parents; they achieve a new social status, with new expectations, rights and responsibilities. It marks their sexual and social maturity and the visible consummation of a marriage. The birth of a son – especially the first born – is regarded as particularly important in some societies. In the West, as noted, expectations of marriage are changing rapidly, but in many parts of the world a birth outside marriage may at best be a source of problems and at worst a cause for exile and death. Births to the unmarried are often more physically dangerous for the mother and child than to the married. The stigma of illegitimacy may cling to a child for the rest of his or her life. Illegitimacy is an expression of a man's alternative reproductive strategy – the 'sneaky rutter' of red deer society that lies hidden in the hearts of all men. Societies may recognize that a child born into an unstable sexual partnership will cost them more than one born into a stable partnership, but they typically punish the woman and the child rather than the man when the birth occurs outside wedlock. In many societies a failure to conceive, 'the barren wife', may be the subject of pity, or even condemnation. In biological terms sterility of either one of the couple condemns them to genetic oblivion. In the words of Ecclesiasticus (44:9), 'For some there be which have no memorial, ... who are become as though they had never been.'

Successful birth is the dawning of new hope. In evolutionary terms, it is the first presentation of a genetically unique individual to a potentially hostile environment. The human baby is more dependent on its mother than the offspring of most other species, and it will prosper most if it has the love and care of two parents for two decades or more. From the point of view of our selfish genes, parenting is the most difficult thing we do, and in evolutionary terms it is the only thing we do.

Mary Toft's rabbits

Mary Toft was the rather simple-minded wife of a poor journeyman clothier, Joshua Toft, living in Godalming, Surrey, England. The couple had been married for about six years and had had three healthy children when, quite suddenly, in the first week of November 1726 Mary Toft gave birth to a rabbit! This all seemed to relate back to the fact that on 23 April, when she thought she was five weeks pregnant, she had been surprised by a rabbit jumping out at her when she was weeding in the fields. Thereafter, she began to dream about rabbits, and for the next three months she developed a craving to eat rabbit, only the family was too poor to afford such a luxury.

Mary Toft went on to give birth to several more rabbits in the days that followed, and Mr John Howard, a highly reputable and experienced man-midwife from neighbouring Guildford, was called in to witness these strange goings-on. He attended a number of deliveries, describing how one rabbit 'had leaped in her belly for the space of eighteen hours before it had died, and the moment it was taken away another was perceived to struggle for birth.'

News of these events soon reached the ears of King George I and Queen Caroline, who were most intrigued. They sent for W. St André, Surgeon and Anatomist to the Court, to investigate the matter. He arrived just in time for the delivery of the fifteenth member of the litter, which appeared to be about four months old and devoid of any skin. St André demonstrated his forensic skills by seeing whether the lungs floated in water: they did, proving that the animal had breathed. St André was convinced that he was witnessing a most amazing natural – or rather unnatural – phenomenon. The king, however, was less gullible, and sought a second opinion from London's most distinguished man-midwife, Sir Richard Manningham, FRS, who arrived on the scene on 28 November. When Mr Howard proudly produced what he said was part of the placenta from Mary Toft's vagina, Sir Richard dismissed it as merely a piece of pig's bladder. St André disagreed, and so it was decided to bring Mary Toft to London for further investigation. When she once again began to have labour pains, Sir Richard was indeed able to palpate a swelling in her lower abdomen. And then the story broke. One of the servants volunteered that Mary had secretly persuaded him to obtain a rabbit for her, ostensibly to eat. Sir Richard summoned Mary before him:

> *I urged her very much to confess the Truth; and told her I believed her to be an impostor, and that she was differently formed from other Women, having some peculiar way of conveying pieces of rabbets into her Uterus and of imposing upon the World, and therefore, I was resolved to try a very painful experiment on her.*

The threat worked, and Mary confessed. She had had a miscarriage and while the cervix was still dilated, one of her female accomplices had placed in her uterus the claws and body of a cat and the head of a rabbit, which had caused her great pain. Thereafter, she had had a succession of rabbets placed in her vagina. 'so many pieces of Rabbet as would make up the number of Rabbits which a Doe Rabbet normally kindles at one time', in the belief that the resultant fame would ensure her a good living for the rest of her days.

Mary Toft was briefly imprisoned for her fraud, and died in 1763.

H. Graham, *Eternal Eve*, 1950

Labour

The fossil record shows that our brains have enlarged rapidly during the last few million years of evolution, from about 30.5 cubic inches (500 cubic centimetres) of brain tissue in Australopithicine fossils, such as 'Lucy', to 92 cubic inches (1500 cubic centimetres) today. Most mammals are born with brain development almost complete, but the fully developed human brain is so large that it would exceed the anatomical limits of the birth canal. The solution evolution has given us is to leave 74 per cent of brain growth and development to take place after delivery. Relative to the other apes, we produce a premature baby that is uniquely dependent on maternal care, and needs breastfeeding to supply the vital extra nutrition for the final explosive growth of the brain.

It is quite common for children to believe that the baby is delivered through the navel, and certainly an inventive Creator could have made some improvements on the current system. Some marsupials develop the birth canal only shortly before delivery, and there is nothing special about the physiology of the muscles or the lining of the reproductive tract that would prevent such a straightforward solution to the anatomical problems of human parturition. As it is, we enter the world squeezed uncomfortably between the rectum and the bladder, and jammed between the unyielding walls of the bony pelvis. The problems that we have with delivery began when our earliest aquatic ancestors took a particular fork in the evolutionary road about 350 million years ago. At that time, evolution hijacked a couple of tubes that collected the urine from the kidneys and used them to carry the eggs and sperm to the watery world outside. The Blind Watchmaker of evolution could not foresee that inextricably mixing the excretory and reproductive organs would lead to serious dangers for big-brained, viviparous land animals hundreds of millions of years later, or that those same animals might come to associate sex with dirtiness and perceive birth as the ultimate form of excretion.

When some fish began to struggle onto land and became the first four-legged creatures, the bones that supported the hind fins developed into a sturdy ring, the pelvis. This presented no problem when only urine, sperm and tiny eggs had to find their exit this way, but during recent human evolution a serious conflict of interests has arisen in the design of the pelvis: if the bony ring is too large, then the individual will tend to waddle like a duck and walking is hampered, but if it is too small then birth becomes impossible. Caught between an evolutionary rock and a physiological hard place, women came to face more danger and difficulty in delivery than any other mammal.

Midwifery

A baby is born only once, but a woman can have many pregnancies, dangerous deliveries and unsafe abortions. In contemporary sub-Saharan Africa, a woman has a one in twenty-one lifetime risk of dying from pregnancy, childbirth or abortion, while for a Western woman it is 1 chance in 9850. While the history of midwifery is not without its mistakes, and insensitive things still happen, there is no doubt that scientifically based obstetrics is one of the triumphs of modern living. Several species of big-brained, social mammals take an intense interest in birth. Female elephants, chimpanzees, whales and dolphins all gather around their sisters during delivery. 'Midwife' dolphins help to nuzzle the newborn to the surface for its first breath. Juvenile langur monkeys fight to be near a parturient mother and to handle the newborn within minutes of birth. The human midwife is ubiquitous in human societies. Phaenarete, the mother of the philosopher Socrates, was a midwife. Even in the 1980s, a traditional midwife named Etta Nicols was still delivering women in the mountains of Tennessee – for less than the cost of a laboratory pregnancy test in a US city hospital.

The modern triumph of birth. In some Western countries, caesarean deliveries are becoming increasingly common. Perhaps the profit motive of private obstetrics needs to be viewed with some suspicion?

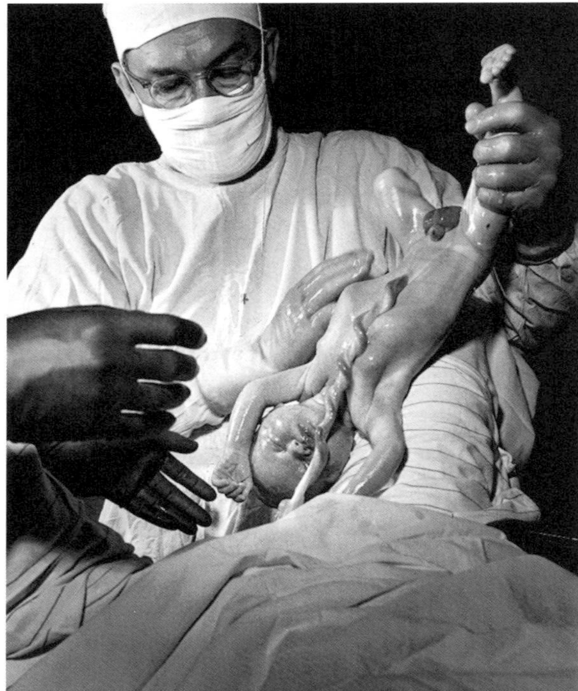

[Wayne Millar / Magnum Photos Ltd.]

Childbirth has always been both magical and threatening. Many cultures consider it polluting. In the Indian subcontinent traditional midwives have a low status because they are 'contaminated' by the blood and amniotic fluid at delivery. In some preliterate societies, the mother retires to a specially built hut to deliver her baby. In precommunist China, men were never permitted to enter the delivery room, which was usually also the same room where women were sequestered during their menstrual periods. After childbirth Chinese women had to avoid raw and cold foods and they were forbidden visitors. Even today, 90 per cent of obstetricians in China are women. Until the early seventeenth century in England, 'Churching' was an obligatory part of a woman's re-emergence into the world after childbirth, because until that ceremony she was considered unclean. The woman, accompanied by her midwife, entered the church veiled, a symbol of the perceived need to isolate the parturient woman from the rest of society. In the interval before 'Churching' took place, it was believed that the fairies might steal the new baby, or if an unbaptized baby died it was thought it would go to hell. Therefore babies were often baptized quickly after birth and commonly the

The martyr

The midwife alone had the management of the lying in: she took charge of the household, prepared food and massaged the patient's belly. If the birth was delayed, the woman was given a draught made from cuiapatli [Montana tomentosa], *which, taken as an infusion, causes strong contractions: if this did not answer, then they turned to the last resort, a drink made of water in which a piece of the tail of a* tlaquatzen, *or opossum, had been mixed. This brew was thought to bring about an immediate and even violent delivery.*

If baths, massages and medicines had no effect, the midwife shut herself into a room with the patient. She invoked the goddesses, particularly Ciuacoatl *and* Quilazti. *If she saw that the child was dead within its mother, she took a flint knife and cut the fetus to pieces. It was clearly understood that a woman who died in childbirth was upon the same footing as a warrior who died in battle or as a sacrifice…*

It was said that the woman [dead in childbirth] *did not go to the underworld but into the palace of the sun, and that the sun took her with him because of her courage… The women who are killed in war or who die at the first lying-in, are called* mocivaquetzque *(valiant women), and they are numbered among those who die in battle. They will go to the sun, and they live in the western part of the heavens; and that is why the old people called the Occident* ciuatlampa *(the women's side).*

Fr. Bernadino de Sahagun, *Florentine Codex: General History of the Things of New Spain*, tr. A. O. Anderson & C. E. Ribble, 1961 mother was not allowed to attend if she had not been 'Churched'. The Catholic Church taught that the corpses of women who died in childbirth could not be brought into church because the baby in the womb was unbaptized. Of course, the dead baby could be removed with a knife and buried in unconsecrated ground while its soul went into limbo, and the dead mother alone was interred in the churchyard. Such parcels of unconsecrated ground can still be identified in Ireland.

Superstitions about pregnancy and childbirth have been chains controlling women. For example, in several parts of Africa today, a prolonged labour is regarded as a punishment for sexual infidelity, and women may delay going to hospital when obstetric complications occur because to admit to a prolonged labour would suggest to her family and neighbours that she had been unfaithful to her husband. In mediaeval Europe, ignorance and religious superstition, combined with the harsh realities of life, made the suffering of women unusually terrible. A tragic clash occurred between the female peasant healer and men of the Church. 'No one does more harm to the Catholic

Taboos on intercourse during lactation

In many traditional human societies, there are taboos on intercourse for a varying period of time following birth. Even in our own Christian culture, the service for the Churching of Women in the prayer book is probably a reflection of this practice. In Islam, there is a forty day post-partum taboo. By making comparisons between different communities, anthropologists have sought to uncover the reasons underlying the taboo. Was it a primitive attempt at family planning? Was it found only in polygamous societies, where the man could go and live with another wife during the period covered by the taboo?

The longest taboos, of one to two years' duration, are found most frequently in Africa and Indonesia and are associated with polygamy, so the man could turn to another wife. Shorter intervals, of six months or less, are commoner in North and South American tribes, in some of the Pacific Islands, in Eastern Europe and Asia, and in the Mediterranean Basin. In Africa, the reason most commonly given by traditional societies for the existence of the taboo is that it is in the interest of the child, since the postponement of another pregnancy preserves lactation. A number of societies believe semen can be transferred to the milk, 'poisoning' the baby, but in Rwanda tradition has it that since semen and milk are white and similar, intercourse is encouraged during lactation in the belief that it enhances milk production.

It is interesting that traditional hunter–gatherer societies like the San from the Kalahari Desert had no such taboo, and yet they achieved four-year birth intervals through the contraceptive effect of frequent (four times an hour) breastfeeds. Perhaps these taboos developed in an attempt to counter the rise in fertility associated with agriculture and horticulture, which provided early weaning foods and hence eroded the natural contraceptive effect of breastfeeding.

Western civilizations, with their disapproval of polygamy, and the promotion of bottle-feeding or early weaning, have unconsciously been responsible for stimulating fertility in parts of the developing world.

Recent studies of the sexual feelings and behaviour of breastfeeding mothers in Western society have shown that over 50 per cent may experience some loss of sexual interest during lactation, compared to women who bottle-feed their babies. Does the lactating breast become too sensitive to be manhandled or does the inhibition of ovarian activity result in a vagina that is too dry? It is interesting that the mean time elapsed before the resumption of sexual intercourse by breastfeeding mothers was found to be just over six weeks, so the forty day taboo stated in the Koran had it just about right.

Church than midwives', wrote the Chief Inquisitors Kremer and Springer in their guide for bringing women to the stake, threateningly called the *Hammer of the Witches* (*Malleus Maleficarum*). 'All witchcraft comes from carnal lust', they maintained, 'which in women is insatiable.' Illiterate women, under torture, confessed to a bizarre range of improbable sexual activities, and were burnt alive in their thousands. In 1522 Dr Wertt of Hamburg was burnt at the stake for a more unusual reason – he had attended a birth disguised as a woman. Today, the situation is commonly reversed, and in the West the majority of obstetricians are male.

Men killing women

Sadly, the advent of the male midwife, like the advent of the missionary, did not always improve the lot of the average person he was dedicated to help. In the eighteenth century, as more and more women were delivered of babies in large city hospitals, there were increasingly common outbreaks of 'puerperal

Virgin birth

In 1984, in Bulawayo, Zimbabwe, knives were drawn when two men fought over a 15 year old girl in a bar. The teenager had been born without a vagina, but with a normal uterus and ovaries. She satisfied her boyfriends by performing oral intercourse, and she had just fellated one lover when a second man came upon the couple and the fight broke out.

During the fracas, the 15 year old was stabbed. She was taken to a hospital and recovered rapidly after repair of the stab wound which had penetrated the stomach. Two hundred and seventy-eight days later she came back to the hospital with episodes of severe abdominal pain – to everyone's astonishment she was in labour and a healthy boy was delivered by caesarean section.

It is known that, in animals, fertilization can be achieved by injecting sperm into the abdominal cavity, where they will swim the wrong way down the fallopian tubes to fertilize the egg. The stabbing must have released sperm from the girl's stomach immediately after she had swallowed the man's ejaculate, but before the stomach's acid could kill them. Equally remarkable, it may have been her first ovulation, as after the child was born she had to have a hysterectomy, because the menstrual blood had no route of escape and the surgeons were unable to create a satisfactory artificial vagina.

The father accepted the child, and some cattle were exchanged in the tribal tradition as bride price. Dr Douwe Verkuyl who did the surgery ended his scientific description of the case with the comment, 'The fact that the son resembled the father excludes an even more miraculous conception.'

pestilence', or fever, following childbirth. At delivery it is easy for infections, such as the *Streptococcus* bacterium, to enter the large areas of raw tissue left in the uterus and local wounds in the birth canal. In the crowded, unhygienic conditions of the first lying-in hospitals, if one woman carried a fatal bacterium then it spread rapidly to others. The great American physician Oliver Wendell Holmes observed, 'puerperal fever is so far contagious as to be frequently carried from patient to patient by physicians and nurses', but his peers were bitterly reluctant to accept the idea that the doctors themselves could be the carriers of disease and death.

In the Paris Maternité between 1860 and 1864, 9886 women gave birth and 1226 died. In the Vienna lying-in hospital, 7 to 30 per cent of all women who entered the hospital to give birth died of puerperal fever. A Hungarian, Ignaz Phillip Semmelweis, working at that hospital, observed that three times as many women died in the wards attended by the medical students as in those looked after by the pupil midwives. He began telling his students to scrub their hands in a solution of chloride of lime before they examined any patient: the death rate plummeted from 1 in 6 women dying from puerperal fever to 1 in 100. But statistics, even today, are not always successful at driving out superstitions and it was Semmelweis, not puerperal pestilence, who was forced out of Vienna. He returned to his native Budapest, where he again convincingly demonstrated the virtues of simple hygiene, only to be rebuffed a second time. He had fits of depression and, poignantly, died from a cut in the postmortem room that gave him the same streptococcal infection that caused the puerperal fever he had spent his life trying to prevent.

'In sorrow shalt thou bring forth children'

Science and conservatism clashed almost as cruelly over the relief of labour pains. God had told Eve in the Garden of Eden, 'I will greatly multiply thy sorrow and thy conception; in sorrow thou shalt bring forth children'. (Genesis 3:16). Ether had been discovered in the thirteenth century and its anaesthetic effects were noted in the sixteenth century. Nitrous oxide, or laughing gas, was used as early as 1722 by Joseph Priestley to put people to sleep. But when Walter Channing in Boston, USA, began to use ether to relieve the pains of childbirth in the middle of the nineteenth century, he was strongly resisted. 'The very suffering which a woman undergoes in labour is one of the strongest elements in the love she bears her offspring', claimed one of his critics. Dr Meigs of Philadelphia described pain in childbirth as 'a desirable, salutary, and conservative manifestation of the life force.' In Edinburgh, Sir James Young Simpson (a pioneer in the use of chloroform for pain relief in

Fistulae

During prolonged labour, the baby's head may crush the mother's tissues creating a fistula, or hole, connecting the rectum or the bladder with the vagina. The fistula never heals spontaneously, but continues to drain urine or faeces into the vagina. The woman's clothes are continually soaked in excreta, so she is offensive to herself and to others and may be thrown out of her family and the community, like a leper. Investigation of the mummy of Princess Henhenitt from ancient Egypt shows she suffered from this calamitous condition. In parts of Africa the traditional birth attendant may actually produce a fistula in attempts to relieve a full bladder during labour, and in the Sudan, fistulae are more common in women who have undergone ritual female circumcision.

Before anaesthetics were developed the surgical treatment of fistulae was as dreadful as the disease, and the first successes were obtained by a brutally obsessive doctor, the nineteenth century American surgeon J. Marion Simms. He made his mark in the competitive surgical world by operating on women's reproductive organs, and he once confessed, 'If there was anything I hated, it was investigating the organs of the female pelvis.' In the 1840s he began collecting slaves afflicted with fistulae from his native Alabama, keeping his 'guinea pigs' for several years in a 'little building in his yard.' Sustained by a sense of 'Divine Mission' he made innumerable attempts to repair the fistulae, operating on one poor slave called Anarcha thirty times before succeeding. One of his other specialties was what he chose to call 'vaginismus' or spasm of the vagina, and he arranged to have one patient anaesthetized two or three times a week so her husband could have intercourse with her. He quipped about her 'ethereal copulation' when she became pregnant.

Fistulae still occur in many developing countries and, although effective surgical treatment is now possible, there are still too few surgeons in the right place to meet the need. The tragedy afflicting such women resulted in the opening of the world's first fistula hospital in Addis Ababa, Ethiopia, by the late Dr Reginald Hamlyn and his wife, from Adelaide, Australia. They recounted how one of their patients, a young Tanzanian girl who had become a social outcast, had walked all the way to Addis Ababa, wandering from village to village with a piece of paper that just said 'Hamlyn, Addis'. Another of their patients, Nametee, was not accepted by her husband, even after the fistula was repaired. Instead of going home Nametee stayed on, doing odd jobs at the hospital, then she began passing instruments in the operating room. Today, she is a competent surgeon repairing fistulae in other women and performing operations that would defeat many Western surgeons.

childbirth) countered his religious critics by pointing out that God had caused 'a deep sleep to fall upon Adam' (Genesis 2:21) when he removed his rib to make Eve. The great debate about relieving pain in childbirth only ended in 1857 when John Snow gave chloroform to Queen Victoria as she gave birth to Prince Leopold.

Ancient and modern practices

From the viewpoint of the woman's welfare, and sometimes even technically, modern obstetricians may still have some things to learn from traditional midwives. Many traditional midwives deliver a baby with the woman in the sitting or kneeling position, supported by one or more other women, or the husband, or leaning against a wall or a post, or even hanging on to a rope suspended from a beam in the roof – the *habil* or rope midwife of the Sudan. Studies show that women who are free to walk about during labour deliver

***L'Adoration des Bergers*, Robert Campin, *ca.*1440.** This painting tells us something about childbirth, and much about Christian teaching on sex and sin in mediaeval Europe. The Virgin Mary, who has just given birth to Jesus, is in a kneeling position, common at the time for birthing. Her serene freedom from the pains of childbirth is because, in the words of one theologian, 'she alone conceived without pleasure'. The aged, bearded Joseph further emphasizes Mary's virginity. The right hand of Salome, the midwife, has become paralysed, because she was said to have doubted Mary's virginity and attempted to examine her after delivery.

[Musée des Beaux-Arts, Dijon.]

their babies slightly quicker and need less pain-relieving drugs. As the modern midwife or obstetrician (male or female) has moved centre stage, so the labouring woman has been in danger of becoming a depersonalized, anatomical obstacle course.

Apes will drag the placenta around on the end of the umbilical cord and may eventually bite it or eat it. Human beings seem to be so strongly impelled to sever the umbilical cord that 'cutting the cord' has become an everyday metaphor. Yet it is neither necessary nor always a good idea. As the cord cools, the blood vessels inside it constrict automatically and no harm will follow if the placenta is left attached to the baby for ten or fifteen minutes. If the cord is cut too soon there can be spontaneous bleeding. Perhaps the greatest risk of cutting the cord in traditional societies is that of infection. In Bihar, India, it is common to cut the cord with the same blunt instrument that is used for digging up the vegetables from the ground, and tetanus takes the lives of up to one in ten infants. It was probably a similar practice that almost wiped out the population of the island of St Kilda off the west coast of

A gorilla gives birth

Labour started at 12:55 h when the pregnant female gave several sharp grunts. They sounded very long and strained. She moved to the birth site 11 minutes before parturition and gave continual loud grunt-screams for 5 min. At 13.24 h she sat up and broke branches around her, making a rough nest. She grunted briefly, put her hand down to her perineum, and then lifted both hands to her mouth. They were covered with blood, and the infant's head was just visible in her lap. After delivery she licked the blood from her hands and sucked it from the long fur of her arms for 3 min. Then she grunted softly, reached down to her perineum and pulled up the placenta, which she began to eat immediately, consuming the entire mass in 4 min. It was only then, after she had eaten the placenta and 7 min after parturition, that she lifted the infant to her arms and held it to her chest. She also groomed the newborn twice and licked it four times.

The neonate first cried 24 min after birth. The sound was a squeak-whine and later it occasionally graded into a squeal. The next morning, the infant had dry fluffy fur and was being nursed. The mother seemed tired. Although she kept up with the other gorillas, she ate very little, sitting frequently and making a rough nest whenever she did. It was as if she wanted a cushion to sit on.

During her labour certain other animals were clearly interested in her or excited by her behaviour. She was followed to the birth site by two adult females and several immatures of both sexes, including her son. In the 4 min before parturition, however, all the gorillas left except a female infant and her mother, who remained behind for 30 min, peering at her and her newborn, but making no attempt to touch the infant.

The birth seemed to alter the course of group travel for that day and they stopped feeding and drifted back to the mother and her newborn. As members of the group arrived they showed an interest in the mother by standing or sitting within five metres and looking at her intently. The immatures, but not the adults, showed great interest in the birth nest, touching the bloody leaves and then sniffing and licking her fingers, or picking up leaves and licking them.

Kelly Stewart, 7 October, 1982, Rwanda, Africa

Scotland in the nineteenth century. Even without bleeding or infection, if the cord is cut too soon the baby is deprived of that extra supply of blood that remains trapped in the placenta until the uterus contracts and squeezes down on it like a sponge.

In north-east Brazil, the traditional birth attendant lets the baby suckle even before cutting the umbilical cord. The stimulation of the nipple sends messages, via the nerves, to the mother's brain, which in turn releases a hormone causing the uterus to contract, expelling the afterbirth and controlling blood loss. If the placenta is expelled from the uterus, but then remains in the vagina, the woman is encouraged to blow across the top of an empty cola bottle, so as to make a musical tone, when the raised pressure in the chest and abdomen will help her to expel the afterbirth from the vagina. Exactly the same technique is used in KwaZulu, Natal, in the Republic of South Africa. Delivery of the placenta is a comparatively gentle process under such circumstances. In Bangladesh, the same goal is achieved in a less tender way, and the parturient woman may snatch a braid of her own long hair and swallow it until she is sick; women call it 'vomiting out the placenta'. In Bali, Indonesia,

Eating the placenta

A custom that is catching on with some exponents of natural childbirth is placentophagy – eating the placenta. Anecdotal evidence suggests that this can be a natural cure for postnatal depression. Wendy Jackson, who runs antenatal classes, ate her placenta after her third and fourth children were born. The effects, she says, were astonishing:

> *I suffered from terrible postnatal depression after the birth of my first two children, who are now 16 and 12 years old. I felt tearful, overwhelmingly tired and unhappy. I was plagued with the thought that life would never be the same again. I felt terribly, terribly inadequate.* [These feelings lasted between the second month after birth and the seventh.]
>
> *When I became pregnant with my third child I made a few enquiries to see whether there was any natural remedy available. I knew that Culpeper, the chain of herbalist shops, offered a freeze-dry placenta service – they don't any longer – so women could sprinkle a bit of their dried, powdered placenta on their food. I had heard of the beneficial effects of eating the placenta, for restoring the hormone balance after the birth. After all, other mammals did it, so why shouldn't I?*
>
> *I had my third child, now six, at home. After the birth, the midwife cut off a few very small pieces of the placenta and placed them in my mouth. It was like no other taste. If I had to describe it I would say it was like a rich mushroom and wine paté, very creamy and luxurious and not a bit like liver. Then my father, who has a very strong stomach, cut up some more and I ate it with cucumber on rye bread.*
>
> *I continued eating it for every meal for about three or four days. I had it fried with bacon and salad. I loved it. I used to wake up at night craving it. When I had finished it, I really missed the first meal I had without it, but after that I didn't mind. I felt extremely healthy and fit and the dreaded depression never arrived.*

The Independent on Sunday, 3 April 1994

Wendy Jackson did the same with her fourth baby, now 3 years old; once again she did not experience postnatal depression.

where rather unusually the traditional birth attendant is a man, the woman's nipples may be stimulated digitally to produce the same effect.

Other mammals, including the leaf-eating gorillas, consume the placenta, giving the mother an added source of nourishment and perhaps also concealing the birth from predators that might otherwise be attracted by the smell of blood. Eating the placenta is the only time in its life that a herbivore like a cow or sheep ever eats meat, and it may also play a role in the 'bonding' process that unites mother and infant. In sheep it has been shown that the passage of the lamb through the birth canal sends nerve impulses to the brain which cause an instantaneous change in the mother's behaviour, so that she develops an absolute craving for the taste of amniotic fluid. This causes her to lick the newborn lamb, thereby stimulating it into activity and encouraging it to find the teat and begin to suckle. Since the placenta is soaked in amniotic fluid, the mother licks that as well and consumes it. One or two American counter-cultures have taken to cooking the afterbirth and eating it, but no society does this regularly, suggesting that our loss of the instinctive desire to eat the placenta is another of the steps in evolution which separates us from chimpanzees and other primates.

Many societies ritualize the disposal of the placenta. The Ostik peoples from the Russian Urals shrewdly referred to the placenta as 'the nourishing mother of the child' and dressed it in a special shirt, treating it like a close relative. A palm tree is planted over the burial site of the placenta by the Buganda of Uganda, as well as in far away Indonesia. Hanging the afterbirth of a foal in a tree was a way to bring luck in Yorkshire, England. In times past, the Japanese buried a boy's placenta with a writing brush and a girl's with a needle and thread, in the hope of producing industrious children. A folk tradition in the Czech Republic maintained that infertile women should eat a placenta, while in Hungary the ashes of a burnt placenta were a supposed contraceptive. Even the modern word has not abandoned its belief in placental magic, and creams made from the afterbirth are on sale in many European countries in the belief that they are good for the complexion.

Mammalian reproductive strategies

When a bird or reptile hatches, typically it finds its own food or is brought food by its parents. A few birds, such as pigeons and penguins, secrete a sort of milk-like fluid from the crop, but it is among mammals that the ability to lactate gives a whole new flexibility to reproducing. The mother can turn whatever she eats into a food specially tailored to her offspring's needs. Marine mammals, for example, which give birth at sea or on an exposed

[unicef.]

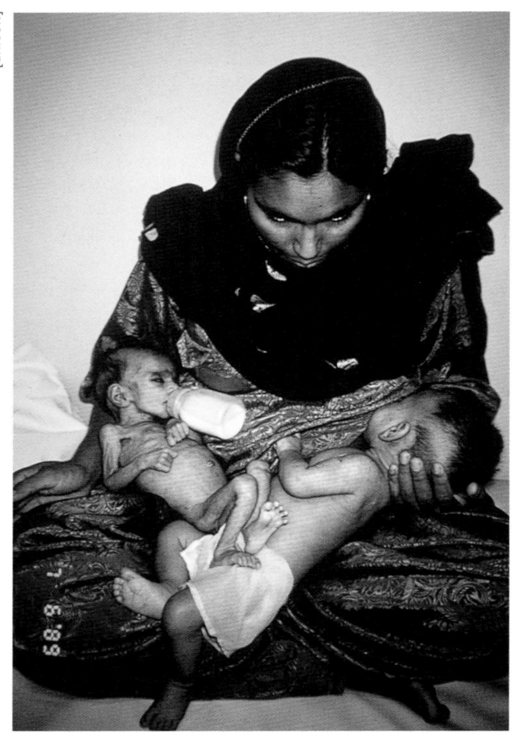

A fatal controlled experiment. This Pakistani mother gave birth to twins, a boy and a girl. Knowing that breast was best, she breastfed her precious infant son, who thrived. In the mistaken belief that she would not have enough milk to breastfeed two babies, she bottle-fed her daughter with infant formula, with tragic consequences. The little girl died the day after this photograph was taken.

coast, produce precociously developed young. Harbour seals shed their puppy coat and even their milk teeth before birth, only to swallow them so that they are born constipated with toothy, hairy faeces. By contrast, the polar bear, which delivers its baby in a cave dug in the snow, has a helpless cub weighing just a few ounces. The human baby is at neither of these extremes but it is much closer to the polar bear than the guinea pig in its immaturity and complete dependence on the continuous attention of the mother.

The milk composition of any particular species is tailor-made to the needs of its infant, so to feed the babies of one species with the milk of another is likely to be fraught with problems. Romulus and Remus may have survived on wolf's milk, but their infant digestive tracts would have had problems coping with its high fat and low sugar content. Cow's milk is for cows, and human breast milk is the best milk for human babies. The exquisite adjustment of the quality of milk to meet the baby's changing needs may be one explanation of recent studies suggesting breastfed babies have a higher IQ than bottle-fed infants. In a study by the Dunn Nutrition Unit of Cambridge University it was found that 8 year olds who had been premature babies had

Witch's milk

The hormones produced by the placenta during pregnancy prime the breasts for subsequent lactation; the onset of milk secretion is triggered by the sudden withdrawal of these hormones at birth. But since these hormones also circulate in the blood of the fetus, where they reach far higher concentrations than in the mother, it should perhaps come as no surprise that the breasts of some newborn baby boys and girls may become quite swollen and engorged with a secretion that is not unlike the first milk or colostrum produced by the mother. However, this transitory breast development soon subsides of its own accord, and there are no adverse consequences.

In ancient times, this precocious lactation became a focal point for many a myth and superstition. During the Middle Ages, there was a widespread belief in, and fear of, witchcraft throughout Europe. Any unpopular woman in the community, particularly if she was elderly and inclined to be a bit eccentric in her ways, was likely to be accused of being a witch. King James I of England even wrote a book entitled *Daemonologie* in which he set down the diagnostic criteria of a witch. High on the list were 'Witch's Marks' – warts or other excrescences that might represent a teat with which she could suckle her impish offspring or 'familiars'. If any such telltale signs were seen on the body of a woman suspected of witchcraft, she would often be put to torture; after the inevitable confession had been obtained, she would be hanged on a gibbet or burnt at the stake. It is estimated that as many as 30 000 women were put to death for witchcraft in England alone.

In addition to suckling their familiars themselves, it was thought that witches also made use of newborn babies for this purpose. Their imps, often in the guise of some animal such as a toad or frog, would come to the sleeping babe during the night to obtain the 'Witch's Milk', 'Lait de Sorcière', or 'Hexenmilch' from its swollen breasts. In the early days of American colonization, a terrifying episode of witch-hunting took place at Salem in New England. Cotton Mather recounts how in 1693 'Amongst the Ghastly Instances of Success that these Bloody Witches have had, we have even seen some of their own Children so dedicated unto the Devil, that in their Infancy it is found that the pups have suckled them, and rendered them venomous to a Progeny.'

Such was the fear surrounding Witch's Milk, and its attraction for these children of the Devil, that throughout Europe midwives and grandmothers assiduously expressed any secretion from the newborn baby's breasts. In Westphalia, it was common practice to make a puppet or caricature in the likeness of the child out of rags and straw, and to place it in the baby's cradle as a decoy, to divert the imp's attention. Perhaps today's dolls have a somewhat sinister ancestry.

an 8 point IQ advantage if they had been fed breast milk rather than infant formula made from cow's milk. Studying IQ is difficult even when social factors are taken into account, nevertheless there may be a simple explanation for this. As noted earlier, the human brain is unusual in that so much of its growth has to be completed after birth, so not only has breast milk evolved to contain all the fats and fatty acids required to build the brain, but the composition of the milk alters with time so as to fit the exact needs of the baby's growth. Human milk is relatively dilute compared with many other mammals; it is low in protein but high in carbohydrates, particularly lactose. The cow's brain, in contrast to the human's, has almost completed grown at birth, so cow's milk has a different composition, and contains ten times as much protein, two-thirds as much lactose and four times as much minerals as human milk. Cow's milk formulas modify these proportions, but never really come near mimicking human milk.

The milk of human kindness

Milk is the one bodily fluid that is symbolic of all that is clean, fresh, wholesome, pure and good. The image of a goddess nursing her offspring appears in ancient Ur, in pre-Columbian Mexico and in Hindu mythology. The Roman goddess Juno nursed the infant Hercules, and one night sprayed her milk across the heavens, creating the Milky Way. Mediaeval churches were filled with paintings and sculptures of Maria Lactans – the Blessed Virgin Mary nursing the infant Jesus at her breast. With the commercialization of religious relics for sale to pilgrim tourists in the Middle Ages, phials of Mary's milk soon began appearing in shrines all over Christendom: Walsingham, Chartres, Genoa, Rome, Venice, Avignon, Padua, Aix-en-Provence, Toulon, Paris and Naples all claimed to have samples of the Virgin's milk. In

Virgin and Child before a Firescreen, **Robert Campin**, *ca.* 1430. At the beginning of the fifteenth century it was common to represent Mary in the act of breastfeeding the infant Jesus; it underscored woman's humility in accepting the full human condition. Mary's milk was attributed with miraculous powers of healing, drawing Calvin's sarcastic reproof 'There is no town so small, nor convent ... so mean that it does not display some of the Virgin's milk ... There is so much that if the holy Virgin had been a cow, or a wet nurse all her life she would have been hard put to it to yield such a great quantity.'

[The National Gallery, London.]

Bethlehem there is a grotto on the site where a few drops of Mary's milk were said to have been spilt on the ground.

It is no accident that we now use the word 'nursing' in a much wider context to describe the whole profession devoted to the care of others. A mother nursing her baby is the ultimate expression of love, tenderness and caring. 'Mum–mum' words are rather like the suckling noises babies make and they are among the first words uttered by babies in any language, and mama, mammae (the mammary glands), mummy, mammal all have the same linguistic root. We are mammals because we suckle our young with milk, but our language continues to make a link our culture has often broken. Breastfeeding is the one part of our reproductive lives that has been most altered by 'civilized living'. Societies that we in the West call 'primitive' often do a far better job than we do of breastfeeding their babies.

It seems likely that human breastfeeding involves both innate and learnt processes. If a 5 year old boy and girl were shipwrecked alone on a desert island then, as they grew older, no doubt hormone-driven desires and experimentation would lead them to have intercourse, and the woman would certainly push in the second stage of her labour. But, lacking the advice and shared experience of older women, she might not breastfeed her infant very well. To some extent breastfeeding is a learnt process. A striking feature of the female breast is that the small, knob-like nipple is surrounded by a large circular area of thin pigmented skin known as the areola, making the nipple look rather like the bull's eye in the centre of an archery target. Designers of artificial teats for babies' feeding bottles and of babies' 'dummies', or 'pacifiers', have usually copied the shape of the nipple but ignored the areola. Little do they realize that, during breastfeeding, when the baby's mouth is wide open and its head tilted slightly back, the nipple lies deep in the mouth against the soft palate, well behind the gums, and the protractile areola is also drawn into the mouth, almost disappearing from sight and becoming an extension of the nipple. This is very different from the sucking activity of a bottle-fed infant with a relatively rigid milk-filled rubber teat clamped between its gums from whose orifice (often enlarged by impatient parents with the aid of a hot needle) milk pours out at a prodigious rate. No wonder babies become confused if they are made to change from bottle to breast.

The human breast is designed for frequent feeding and, unlike the cow's udder, lacks a reservoir to store the formed milk. Milk production is a simple process: the more frequently the breast is emptied the more milk is secreted. Unfortunately, the breast is not always emptied because the mother has pain, or is simply harassed by too many things going on in her life. Sore and

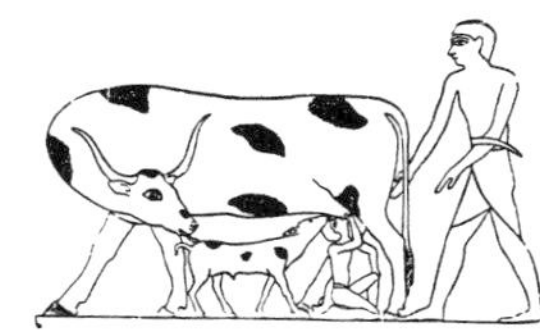
[Ploss et al., 1935.]

Cow's milk. It was not long after the domestication of the horse, cow, sheep, goat, donkey and camel that their milks started to be used for feeding human infants. An early Egyptian hieroglyph shows how the cow was allowed to suckle her calf, thereby producing the let-down reflex which enabled a child to suck the milk from one of her other teats. Interestingly, this drawing also displays how the calf raises its tail and may defaecate whilst suckling (the gastro-colic reflex), and the cow sniffs its anus, and should the calf start to scour, the cow will lick up its faeces. This in turn triggers the release of antibodies into the cow's milk, which will neutralize the organisms in the calf's intestine that were the cause of its diarrhoea – the so-called entero-mammary circulation.

cracked nipples are one of the commonest reasons for abandoning breastfeeding. When the baby is correctly positioned, contact with the nipple is limited to the soft tissue at the back of the tongue and the soft palate. If this is done correctly, many cases of sore nipples can be avoided. When this does not happen the breast becomes distended and further milk production is inhibited. Sadly, many a woman has given up breastfeeding because she believed she was 'making too little milk', when in reality she had too much.

Milk is much more than a food finely adjusted to the needs of the offspring. It is a living secretion, rich in antibodies that protect against disease. For example, the mother stores up an immunological 'memory' of all the disease-producing organisms she has met during her life, a memory that is retained in special lymph nodes lying in the wall of her small intestine. When she is lactating, cells from these lymph nodes are shed into the circulating blood, and come to rest in the breast, where they are transformed into antibody-producing cells that secrete an enormous amount of an antibody called immunoglobulin A into the breast milk. Scarcely any of this is absorbed, but it remains within the infant's gut, where it stops any disease-producing organism attaching to the gut wall and setting up an infection that could result in diarrhoea, the major cause of death in human infants. The mother is constantly sampling the environment through the food she eats and, if she swallows one of these harmful organisms to which she has already become sensitized, she will immediately start secreting large amounts of the right antibody into her breast milk to protect her baby from the infection. These natural defences against infant infection are so strong that, even in the cleanest Western home, bottle-fed babies are at a substantially higher risk of acquiring gastrointestinal and respiratory infections than are breastfed babies. Milk formula simply cannot give the baby the unique immunological protection afforded by its mother's milk. In 1772, Hugh Smith in *Letters to Married Women on Nursing and the Management of Children*, astutely observed:

> *The thrush and watery gripes are, in the author's opinion, artificial diseases, and both of them occasioned by improper food, such as all kinds of pap* [baby food].

The 'artificial diseases' are tragically common in the contemporary developing world, where poverty drives women to make up formula with bacterially contaminated water in bottles that have not been properly sterilized. One enlightened country, Papua New Guinea, has had the foresight to make all feeding bottles and teats available only on medical prescription, in an attempt

[Mary Evans Picture Library.]

The Remmingtons of Yorkshire, *ca.* **1647.** In the East Riding of the county of Yorkshire, England, in the seventeenth century, Sir Thomas Remmington and his wife produced fifteen surviving children, five still-births, and one fetal death, as indicated by the skull in the bottom left corner of this engraving. Such high fertility would only have been possible if they had employed wet-nurses to rear their children.

to curb the abuses that have earned powdered milk the name 'baby killer' in the developing world. It has been shown by Peter Howie in Aberdeen that, even if the baby receives breast milk only for the first three months, it is still at a reduced risk of diarrhoea throughout the whole of the first year of life.

The human baby can prosper solely on its mother's milk until six months after birth and, even in the tropics, does not need any supplementary liquids, let alone solids. Unfortunately, even among those women who do breastfeed, sales pressure for commercial weaning foods often leads to mixed feeding at an unnaturally early stage. The newborn's intestinal tract is particularly permeable during the early months of life, and breast milk contains a growth-promoting substance that assists in the maturation of the infant's gut lining. If the mother starts to give baby foods other than breast milk too early, the foreign protein in the food is able to enter the baby's circulation and sensitize its developing immune system, and the baby will be more susceptible to allergies later in life. Recent research suggests that the antibodies the baby may form against this foreign cow's milk may accidentally damage the developing pancreas, giving rise to insulin-dependent diabetes – a high price for a child to pay for the rest of its life for the questionable convenience of the bottle over the breast. Babies that have been given supplementary feeds in the first few months of life are much more prone to a potentially fatal gut infection known as necrotizing enterocolitis and are more likely to succumb to SIDS (Sudden Infant Death Syndrome).

Nature's contraceptive

Breastfeeding is a two-way process: the mother gives food and protection to the infant and the process of suckling acts as a contraceptive for the mother. Hunter–gatherer societies, such as the San Bushmen of the Kalahari Desert, or the nomadic slash-and-burn agriculturists of the Highlands of New Guinea, carry their babies with them wherever they go and put the child to the breast several times an hour. They sleep with the baby beside them at night, when it can feed at will. They often continue breastfeeding until the third year of life. Chimpanzees, gorillas and orangutans also breastfeed several times an hour and lactate for three to four years. In human beings and apes alike, long

Lactating fathers

John Hunter, the British eighteenth century anatomist, recorded a fascinating case of one Anthony Lozana, of Pamplieya in the diocese of Burges in Portugal, who was married to Maria Parejo. She bore him twins, a boy and a girl. Hunter recounted how

> *to soothe the cries of the male child, the father used to apply his left nipple to the infant's mouth, who sucked and drew milk from it in such quantity as to be nursed by it in perfect good health. He treated all his other children, eight in number and all alive, in the same way, always dividing with his wife the business of nursing the children and taking care of their domestic concerns. But, what is very remarkable, is that ever since, he has had a constant flow of milk from the left nipple, whereas, in women, it always ceases soon after they give up nursing.*
>
> *The man has been subjected to various trials, and examined very accurately by Messers Castallar and Caballero, physicians and surgeons to the army. His genitals were particularly inspected, but there was not the least appearance of his being an hermaphrodite or of any difference from other men ... The father himself remarks that his nipples were more turgid, and that the flow of milk was more copious, of a whiter colour and thinner, when he suckled his first child than at the time of his examination, ... and that he had not the least appetite for venery for several months after. On the 4th of March, 1786, in the city of Cumana, before the commandant of the town, Colonel Lascanotegui and the Leut-General Bailets, and several others, Mr. Lozana filled a spoon with the milk of the left breast, which was of a yellowish colour; and he drew a small quantity from the right nipple.*

J. Hunter, *Essays and Observatons on Natural History, Anatomy, Physiology, Psychology and Geology*, 1861

It is interesting that Lozana's wife produced eight single offspring and one pair of twins in the space of less than fourteen years. Presumably her husband's activities as a wet-nurse had enhanced her fertility without diminishing his.

intervals of lactation evolved to nourish the child and to space births about four years apart.

Throughout the ancient Egyptian, Babylonian, Hebraic, Graeco-Roman, Byzantine and Arabian eras, babies were breastfed from birth and supplements were not introduced into their diet until after the eruption of the milk teeth (baby teeth) at around six to eight months of age, presumably as Nature would have intended. Aristotle stated in *Generation of Animals* that, 'while women are suckling children, menstruation does not occur according to nature, nor do they conceive; if they do conceive, the milk dries up'. He imagined that milk and menstrual fluid were similar secretions, and if one was being produced it must be at the expense of the other. Leonardo da Vinci perpetuated this myth in his famous drawing of human intercourse, which depicts a hypothetical duct connecting the womb to the nipple, since he thought milk was actually made from menstrual blood (see p. 14).

The process by which the baby suppresses fertility in its mother is now

Kwashiorkor. The evil eye of the child in the womb upon the child already born. This Zambian mother's older child, in the arms of a relative, died from kwashiorkor soon after this photograph was taken. Note the pot belly, swollen legs, depigmented skin around the mouth, and bleached hair, all signs of gross protein and energy deficiency. His mother had become pregnant with twins whilst still breastfeeding him, and this would have dried up her milk supply, thus depriving him of his main source of nourishment.

[D. Morley.]

well understood. When the baby suckles on the nipple, nervous impulses pass from the breast to the brain, to inhibit the release from the pituitary gland of the hormones responsible for ovulation. Breastfeeding is Nature's contraceptive, and in parts of Africa and Asia, the natural suppression of fertility during lactation has been calculated to prevent far more births than the use of modern methods of contraception.

Statistics on infant and maternal mortality show that when the natural four-year birth interval is reduced, then the risks to both the mother and her child rise. The effect is small but measurable in developed countries. In developing countries, infants born less than two years apart have approximately double the risk of death in the first year of life compared with those born after a longer birth interval. The risk of death for the mother also rises significantly with short birth intervals. A new birth too soon also hazards the health of the older sibling. In West Africa, the word 'kwashiorkor' means 'the evil eye of the child in the womb upon the child already born'. The children have

Smothering

Our primate cousins, the great apes, always sleep with their babies in their nest at night. Similarly in human hunter–gatherer societies and many other traditional cultures it is the custom for the mother to sleep with the baby beside her at night, lying on the ground. If it wakes, the mother can easily get it to sleep again by putting it to the breast. As the baby gets older, it may learn to suck from the breast without even waking its mother. All the evidence suggests that these night-time feeds are extremely important for maintaining the contraceptive effect of breastfeeding. Once night feeds are abandoned, so that the mother may go for six or more hours without putting the baby to the breast, ovulation is likely to return.

One of the main reasons Western women give for not wishing to share their bed with their baby is fear that they may smother it. This appears to be a hang-over from fear of 'overlaying' which was widespread in the Middle Ages. It was said that careless parents could accidentally kill their children by lying on them in bed; worse still, that parents who wished to dispose of an unwanted child could most easily do so by smothering it with pillows. Perhaps this fear of smothering was occasioned by what we now called the Sudden Infant Death Syndrome – the unexplained and tragic death of a sleeping child in the first few months of life with no apparent cause. It appears to be commoner in bottle-fed than in breastfed babies, which has led some authorities to suspect that a milk allergy may be involved.

Whether a healthy baby could be smothered to death by the bedclothes when sleeping besides its mother seems highly unlikely. In the 1940s an intrepid American paediatrician, Paul Wooley, from Portland, Oregon, showed that it was virtually impossible to reduce the oxygen or increase the carbon dioxide inspired by a baby by covering it with ordinary bedding – it was necessary to add a rubber sheet, tightly tucked in around the edges, to produce any undesirable effect. Wooley was even unable to produce anoxia by placing mattresses or pillows over the nose of sleeping babies, noting that 'here again we were unsuccessful since the smallest was capable of rolling to obtain an airway'.

In addition to fear of smothering, other modern deterrents to sleeping with the baby in bed with you are fear that the baby will fall out of bed – something that did not exist when we slept on the ground – and objections by the husband, who may resent the disturbance to his sleep, or feel embarrassed by the presence of a baby when making love to his wife.

characteristic pot bellies (a result of gross enlargement of the liver produced by the malnutrition), the hair of the scalp is scanty, straight, and depigmented, giving it a bleached appearance often with a reddish tinge. There is swelling, or oedema, of the legs, but the rest of the body is extremely emaciated. Around the world, adequate birth spacing, of the type that was once achieved with natural patterns of breastfeeding, could prevent perhaps a million infant deaths a year.

If a woman is breastfeeding her child without adding any additional liquids or solids, and if menstruation has not returned, then she has only a 2 per cent chance of conceiving in the first six months after delivery. Such a failure rate compares well with other methods of contraception, yet everyone seems to know someone who became pregnant while breastfeeding, and some Western women – and physicians – even deny that breastfeeding has any contraceptive action at all. The limitation of breastfeeding as a contraceptive is that it is difficult to predict when ovulation will return, so in order to

***Visit to the Child at Nurse*, George Morland, *ca.* 1788.** The elegant mother and her two older children make one of their rare visits to the wet-nurse, who is breastfeeding her infant, and also has an older child in her care. The infant clings to the wet-nurse, no longer recognizing its natural mother.

[Fitzwilliam Museum, Cambridge.]

[Samuel H. Kress Collection / National Gallery of Art, Washington.]

***Diane de Poitiers*, François Clouet *ca.* 1571.** Diane de Poitiers was the favourite mistress of King Henry II of France. A peasant wet-nurse suckles her infant while Diane herself sits in her bath, her non-lactating breasts clearly visible to the King.

guarantee adequate spacing of pregnancies, even a woman who is amenorrhoeic and breastfeeds on demand should start using a modern method of contraception by about six months after the birth of her child.

Wet-nursing

The pharaohs gave their babies to others to wet-nurse, and the natural child of a royal wet-nurse was forever allowed to call herself 'milk sister' to the infant king with whom she had shared the breast. Some societies even went so far as to consider as incestuous sexual intercourse between biologically different children that had suckled at the same breast. According to tradition, both Moses and Mohammed owed their lives to wet-nurses after they were rescued from the bullrushes. At the opposite extreme, Plato advocated that children should be wet-nursed and 'every precaution [taken] that no mother know her own child.'

Until the eighteenth century, it was common for the European aristocracy to pay village women to act as wet-nurses for their children. Not only were their wives relieved of the inconvenience of frequent breastfeeding, which they hoped would also preserve the beauty of their breasts, but this also greatly increased their fertility. As soon as the baby was removed from the breast, ovulation returned. Having a large family made it possible to increase your power and influence by suitably arranged marriages for your children. It was not uncommon for an aristocratic woman to have twenty children, and there is at least one recorded case of a family of thirty. Conversely, the wet-nurses might feed one infant after another and go for literally decades without becoming pregnant. The choice for many wives in the Western world during their fecund years, before contraceptives were easily available, was to have a infant in the womb if you were wealthy, or one at the breast if you were poor.

It would be difficult to imagine any régime more likely to disrupt the family bonds than wet-nursing. The mother was subjected to the stress of separation from her infant within a few days of birth, and was never exposed to the bonding associated with suckling. In preindustrial Europe, city women often sent their children considerable distances into the country to be wet-nursed, so they would scarcely have an opportunity to see their baby again until it was returned two or three years later. When the child was returned to its biological mother, it was subject to a triple emotional trauma: separation from the wet-nurse whom it would regard as its natural mother; its initial resentment on being returned to its real mother who was virtually a complete stranger; and the mother's own difficulty in accepting the unwilling child back into her family, having had one or two more children since its birth. It may be no accident that the age of wet-nursing among European aristocrats was also a time when the world's first great explorers set off on voyages of discovery to the remotest corners of the Earth, leaving behind their wives and children for years on end, seemingly with never a backward glance.

Dry-nursing

In 1748, William Cadogan, the doctor in charge of London's Foundling Hospital, published a highly influential *Essay upon Nursing and the Management of Children from their Birth to Three Years of Age*, in which he advocated scheduled feeds and the abandonment of all night-time feeds:

> *Four times in four and twenty-hours will be often enough to give suck.*

Little did Cadogan realize this was a perfect recipe for eroding the contraceptive effect of breastfeeding. Other social developments reinforced these changes: husbands and wives began to sleep in the same bed, raised off the floor, and so the baby was banished, first to an adjacent cradle and later to a separate nursery, thus making night-time breastfeeds most inconvenient. At about the same time, a technology developed to supplement breastmilk with pap, made from animal milk, cereal flour, sugar and spice, or with panada made from broth, breadcrumbs and flavouring. By the sixteenth century in

Europe, the average age of weaning had fallen to just over a year, and by the eighteenth century it had declined to eight months. By the seventeenth and eighteenth centuries the majority of medical writers recommended the introduction of weaning foods at two to four months – a tradition which has persisted to this day.

In 1688, an experiment in human reproduction was first performed which was more profound in its biological implications than some aspects of *in vitro* fertilization or surrogate pregnancy in the twentieth century, and certainly more challenging in its ethical implications. King James II decided that his infant son should be 'dry-nursed', because several of his previous children had died at the hands of wet-nurses. The child was fed with pap from a spoon from the day of birth onwards. The experiment was nearly a disaster, and by the age of seven weeks the child was so close to death that he had to be returned to a wet-nurse, but others began to follow the king's example and dry-nursing became quite common in preindustrial Europe. It was also adopted as the commonest method of infant feeding in many of the Foundling Hospitals for orphaned or abandoned children established in eighteenth century European cities. The death rate was appalling: in the Dublin Foundling Hospital 10 227 babies died between 1775 and 1796, a mortality rate of 99.6 per cent.

The decline in breastfeeding resulted in great increases in fertility, although these were initially counterbalanced by corresponding increases in infant mortality. Then, as medical care and hygiene in the home improved, more and more children survived. In a traditional, preliterate society a woman often had no more than four or five live-born children in a lifetime, all adequately spaced by breastfeeding. Wherever family size is very large, as in Victorian times, or in contemporary Angola (where the average woman has over seven children), we can be certain breastfeeding practices have changed so as to undermine the natural contraceptive effect of lactation. Queen Victoria herself was an example of what happens when a woman neither breastfeeds nor uses contraceptives. Records show that she first conceived on her honeymoon, and then became pregnant again within six weeks of the birth of her firstborn, since she had put the baby to a wet-nurse the day it was born. She produced nine children in twenty-one years. Victoria wrote to her uncle, King Leopold, 'You cannot really wish me to be the "Mamma d'une nombreuse famille" ... men never think, at least seldom think, what a hard task it is for us women to go through this *very often* ... '.

La Charité Romaine, **Nicholas Regnier,** *ca.* 1620 – 60. The famous Dr John Caius, the leading medical man of his day and founder of the Cambridge college of that name, was suckled on his deathbed in 1573 by wet-nurses.

The quintessential bond

Are breasts symbols of sex or motherhood? Attitudes towards breasts and breastfeeding have changed over time, and they have often been arbitrary and ill informed. As sex objects, breasts have come to symbolize the male's short term interest in sex, while breast feeding is a measure of a woman's long term investment. Society's changing attitudes to breastfeeding have made a deep impact on us all. For some Christians, breastfeeding was regarded as an act of humiliation, a reminder of the Fall from Grace. From the fifteenth century onwards a growing sense of shame at the beauty of the naked female body made it indecorous to show the Virgin with bare breasts. One of the few survivors of earlier attitudes is in the name of the popular German white wine, Liebfraumilch, literally the milk of the blessed Virgin Mary.

Our vocabulary often mirrors our attitudes: we use the words tits, boobs, mammaries, knockers, melons, which, although belittling, are not demeaning like our slang for the genitalia, but we never call the breast an udder, even in jest. Yet we are probably the only species in which the breasts have an erotic significance. We are the only species in which the breasts develop at the beginning of puberty, long before the first menstrual period or ovulation. Enlargement of the nipple and the adjacent areola is the first sign of impending puberty in a young girl. Once a young girl's breasts start to enlarge she becomes self-conscious and men take notice. Among our cousins the chimpanzees the breasts do not develop until during the first pregnancy. Perhaps early breast development is a trade-off for the suppression of ovulation: if a female is to be continuously attractive to the male, instead of periodically so, perhaps she needs some erotic adornment, at least to announce sexual availability after puberty. In all cultures, the young female breast appears to have an erotic significance.

Some modern women seek to augment or reduce breast size to bring it into conformity with perceived norms. There is as yet no unambiguous scientific evidence that silicone breast implants, unless they actually burst, cause long term illness (even though American juries have been of the opinion they do and huge legal settlements have been made). Nevertheless, breast implants are a branch of surgery where exploitation and unsatisfactory practices sometimes occur. Some of the operations that are performed may damage the milk ducts and interfere with subsequent breastfeeding. Even after death silicone implants are inappropriate since they leave a gooey mess in the crematorium, when all that was natural has been turned to ashes. In 1992 the USA placed a moratorium on the use of silicone breast implants, as a result of uncertainty about their long term adverse effects.

At the other end of the spectrum, some women have argued that the encouragement of breastfeeding is yet another example of a male-dominated society's none-too-subtle attempts to subjugate women because of their biology. Such women therefore welcome the alternative of being able to feed their babies, or get their male partners to do so, with artificial milk formula delivered from a bottle. Others, rightly incensed by society's failure to recognize that men and women are indeed different, feel cheated when no provisions are made for paid or even unpaid maternity leave as a woman's statutory right following childbirth, and when there are no facilities available in the workplace that will enable a mother to fulfil her biological role by breastfeeding her baby whenever it is so desired. The tender human breast has been just that; the supreme symbol of femininity in art and literature around the world, the infant's pillow, the quintessential bond that links one generation to the next, the bosom of the family.

Today's challenges

The USA in particular needs to re-examine its priorities relating to pregnancy, childbirth and infant care. US Federal Regulations demand that hospital staff strive to keep every newborn baby 'alive' with tubes and surgical procedures,

There are no absolutes

On 5 March 1984 a little boy was delivered in l'Hôpital de Gisenyi in Cameroon, West Africa. His mother was 25 years old and had been divorced by her husband five years previously because she was infertile. She did, however, eventually get pregnant and came into hospital with an unusually swollen abdomen and constipation. The baby's heart could be heard but the cervix did not show the normal signs of pregnancy. The surgeon, Dr Bugingo, performed a caesarean operation and found a perfectly normal baby, weighing 1.5 lbs (3.4 kilograms), that had been dead just a few hours. The baby and the placenta were entirely outside the uterus and enclosed in a cyst attached to the ovary.

The mother had almost certainly had a sexually transmitted disease earlier in life (most likely caught from her husband), which had damaged the fallopian tubes but not enough to make her entirely infertile. There are a tiny number of children alive today who have developed normally, although never having been in their mother's womb.

In the West, such an extrauterine pregnancy would have been diagnosed in the first two or three months of pregnancy and removed to pre-empt the likelihood of lethal internal haemorrhage. The hospital had no X-ray or ultrasound and a caesarean operation was performed only when the heart sounds stopped. Every surgeon, whatever their religious beliefs, and with the blessing of all theologians and moralists, including the Pope, would abort the fetus when it is diagnosed as developing in an extrauterine position. There are no absolutes in reproductive biology, and ultimately neither can there be any moral absolutes in the area of abortion.

regardless of their subsequent quality of life, or their parents' feelings, yet tens of millions of women in the USA do not have affordable access to antenatal care, which can do a great deal at very low cost to prevent death and morbidity in newborn babies. Similarly, while the average European woman in a steady job can expect several months' paid maternity leave, many US women have no right to maternity leave, even when it is unpaid. Finally, child care facilities in the USA are often too expensive for many people who need them.

But whatever our problems in the West, they are dwarfed by those of the developing world. Globally, one woman a minute dies from a complication of pregnancy and childbirth. About one-third of these deaths result from unsafe abortion. Ninety-nine per cent of these deaths occur in the developing world. This toll of maternal deaths is equivalent to a jumbo jet of women crashing every four hours and killing all aboard. Even if, for just one day, four or five jumbo jets were to crash in remote places that most of us never visit, the news would surely make the local papers and the television news. But because women suffer and die one at a time, first in this village and then in that slum, we take no notice and we are not stirred to action. The situation is getting worse and as a result of rapid population growth in the next decade, more women are likely to die from complications due to pregnancy, abortion and delivery than in any period of human history. Infant deaths are falling more rapidly than maternal deaths, but remain tragically high. Eight million babies a year – almost 1000 per hour – die before their first birthday, and in parts of West Africa one in five babies dies in the first year of life.

7 GROWING UP

'Children begin by loving parents; after a time they judge them; rarely, if ever, do they forgive them.'
Oscar Wilde, *A Woman of No Importance*, 1893

Wittingly and unwittingly, the Western world is changing how we bring up children in a number of profoundly important ways. We are altering the timetable of natural development, separating mothers and children in unnatural ways and depriving some children, perhaps particularly in the USA, of the opportunity to grow up into adults who can function fully in modern society.

The age of maturity

Johann Sebastian Bach was born in 1685 and lived in Leipzig from 1723 until his death in 1750. Among his responsibilities was training choirboys for three churches. Bach wrote a list of when the boys changed from singing treble to alto – it averaged around 17 years. Today in the famous boy's choir at King's College Chapel, Cambridge, England, the voices of the singers usually break at around 13, and in some individual cases considerably earlier than this.

The age at which a boy's voice breaks is one of the many changes associated with puberty and, with good reason, we call the prominent male larynx the 'Adam's apple'. Of course, the key event at puberty is the onset of potential fertility. It would be unacceptable to ask young boys to masturbate in order to detect when the testicles first manufacture sperm, but if urine samples are collected and centrifuged to collect the sediment, it is possible to recover sperm if present. Workers in Scotland and Israel have found sperm in the urine of boys aged 11 to 12, sometimes even before the first pubic hairs appeared. In 1997 in Britain, a boy of 12 years fathered a child. In women, the onset of the first menstruation is easier to track and there are records from Scandinavia which show that the average age of first menstruation has fallen from about 17 1/2 years in 1850 to between 12 and 13 today. Throughout the Western world, there has been a marked and well documented fall in the age of sexual maturity over the last few centuries, and over much of this century the age of first menstruation fell by as much as six months in a decade.

Today, legislators in the developed world commonly define the age for voting and legal autonomy as 18. It is also the age when the nation can call on young men to die for their country in war. Earlier in this century maturity was deemed to occur at age 21, an age derived from mediaeval times, as it was only around this time that a young knight was big enough and strong enough to wear a full suit of armour on horseback. Throughout this century, each new generation of teenagers in Europe and North America has been on average a little bit taller and a little bit heavier than its parents at a comparable age. Exactly the same changes are occurring in countries such as Japan, where body size is increasing and the age of fertility is falling even more rapidly than the comparable changes occurred in the West.

In the forest-clothed mountains that make up the backbone of the great island of Papua New Guinea, there are tribes who were entirely cut off from contact with the external world until the 1950s. They hunt forest game, keep pigs and farm vegetables. One of these tribes, the Gainj, has been studied in meticulous detail by James Wood of Pennsylvania State University and Kenneth Campbell of Boston University. They found that the average Gainj woman did not have her first period until somewhere between 18 and 20 years of age. They also discovered that the later a woman began to menstruate the more infertile cycles she was likely to have before conceiving her first baby. Among the Gainj, and other groups with late puberty, children eat less, weigh less, and are shorter than most children in the modern world.

[L. A. Malcolm.]

Coming of age in Papua New Guinea. Children from the Bundi tribe in Highland Papua New Guinea. The youngest girl standing on the left is 2 years old, and the others are arranged at two-year intervals. The first signs of breast bud development occur at age 14; this is more pronounced by age 16 and, by age 18, the ovaries would be producing sufficient oestrogen not only to complete the development of the connective tissue of the breast but also to stimulate the uterus into its first menstrual bleed, referred to as menarche. By the age of 20, height growth is complete, and the young woman will have started to ovulate.

In the Western world, everybody would move three places to the left, thanks to improved health and nutrition in infancy and childhood.

But it was in such a world that we evolved, and it is as if our genetic make-up is put together to give young women a time when they can learn their own emotions and the subtleties of heterosexual interactions before becoming parents. Thus, in a traditional society with a subsistence economy, young women, who have never seen a modern contraceptive, are having their first baby at about the same time that Western women graduate from college.

A unique investment

Despite the tendency to become sexually mature at a more juvenile age, human beings still take longer than any other animal to make the transition from dependence to independence – from being a cared-for child to being a caring parent. Even the largest whales mature sexually more rapidly than we do. The female stoat, or ermine, actually matures before it is weaned, and is impregnated by a male who enters the burrow and also mates with the newborn's mother. The rhesus monkey is physically mature and learns all that it needs to know about how to reproduce by about 3 years of age. In chimpanzees, growth accelerates in both sexes at age 9 or 10, and females begin to bear young at 11 or 12. Interestingly, animals kept in zoos, like many contemporary human beings, eat more and exercise less than in the wild, and therefore tend to become sexually mature earlier than those living in the wild.

Nature can construct all the wondrous anatomical complexity of the human heart or nervous system in a mere 280 days of pregnancy, but it takes 7000 days or more of parental investment, individual experiment, growth and maturation to raise a dependent infant into a self-sufficient adult. The uniquely long interval between birth and sexual and emotional maturity is one of the few characteristics that clearly distinguishes us from our great ape cousins. We have a shorter lifespan than some tortoises, but we take longer to grow up than any other animal. Why?

If, as we believe, evolution judges us by the ability of our genes to survive into the next generation, then a prolonged childhood and slow adolescence is a daring and costly investment for any animal to make. The long, slow process of human infancy and childhood exposes us to death before we have the chance to reproduce and hence to genetic oblivion. Equally important, the parent's ability to rear additional offspring is severely limited by the children they already have.

Before puberty, we learn to manipulate things. The babe in arms becomes a crawling infant and then a toddler on two legs. Verbal and linguistic skills develop rapidly. The infant learns to make a variety of sounds, turns them into words, makes words into sentences and in a few years is using

[Harlow Primate Laboratory, University of Wisconsin.]

Harlow's monkeys. An isolated baby rhesus monkey in researcher Harry Harlow's laboratory clings to its terry cloth 'mother' while drinking from a bottle attached to its wire 'mother'. Yet 'social pathology' is reversible and when these same monkeys were released into the wild their behaviour reverted to normal. 'The real questions for historians of science,' Allison Jolly observed in *Primate Behaviour*, 'are why we had to look at monkeys to find all this out? Why were we ever surprised at the results? And once the first dozen rhesus monkeys had been reared in isolation and the first surprise was over, did the later results justify the misery knowingly inflicted?'

sentences to express abstract thoughts. The growing child discovers how to select safe food and how to avoid dangerous situations, and by the age of 7 or 8 we are usually eager and adept at exploring our environment. Mediaeval theologians defined the 'age of discretion', when children could distinguish good from evil and therefore could take their first communion, as 9 to 14 years. In 1910, Pope Pius I pushed the age down to 7 years. The second decade of life seems to be devoted to learning to manipulate our fellow human beings, in everything from sex to corporate takeovers and politics, while we continue to develop physical control of the world around us.

Hugs and cuddles

Growing up normally begins in the same way for all mammals – with a warm, close, totally dependent relationship between the mother and her offspring. Physical contact between mother and child is especially important among the monkeys and apes. Cuddling and hugging are profoundly significant for human beings.

In a notorious series of experiments on primate behaviour carried out by Harry Harlow at the University of Wisconsin in the 1950s and 60s, rhesus monkey babies were separated from their mothers at birth and allowed to choose between a pair of inanimate 'pseudo-mothers'. One pseudo-mother was a bare wire dummy, but with a built-in feeding-bottle. Next to it was another dummy, lacking the bottle, but this time covered with soft terry cloth. Harlow found that deprived babies clung to the softer dummies, even though they lacked an artificial breast, reaching across to drink from the bare wire surrogates. Like mentally retarded humans, the motherless infants sat forlornly rocking back and forth in their isolation, occasionally biting their own hands and feet. Harlow's experiments were repeated many times and bizarre refinements added, such as designing pseudo-mothers that actually extruded spikes when the pathetic infants clung to them. When these isolated infants grew up, deprived of any peer group contacts, they had no idea how to mate. If the abnormally reared females were strapped to a 'rape rack' and put with normal males they conceived, but they then proved incapable of feeding or handling their children, treating their newborn babies like intruders. However, in subsequent pregnancies they slowly learned to do better.

Fortunately these deeply disturbing and seemingly cruel experiments had a happy ending: on Harlow's retirement, a young colleague, Dr Suomi, inherited the socially deprived animals and released them into the Wisconsin countryside, while continuing to provide food and shelter. Amazingly, their reproductive behaviour returned to normal. This should give new hope to

Wolf children

In the autumn of 1920, in a village in Orissa, inland from Calcutta, there were reports of ghosts running about the forest. The Rev. Singh, an Anglican missionary, intent on putting this superstition to rest, accompanied a posse of men into the forest. The 'ghosts' were two children living in a wolf's lair. When the lair was dug open, two wolf cubs and two little girls were uncovered, all in one terrified embrace. The mother wolf defended her lair with great ferocity. The children had matted hair, ran on all fours, bared their teeth, growled, and bit their captors. They had to be transported in a bamboo cage and would drink only milk. One appeared to be about 3 years old and the other 5 or 6, and the Singhs called them Kamala and Amala.

The Rev. and Mrs Singh ran an orphanage and they made a humane attempt to care for the children. The children preferred to live in the dark, and they were most active at night. They refused to stand up, or run on two legs. They ate raw meat, chewing it away from the bone like a dog, and growling if approached. To the Singhs' distress the two children ate any carrion they could find, and topped off many meals with a hearty dose of stones and dirt. They showed no emotions and made no effort to communicate. They ran from other children and attacked anyone who tried to wash or dress them; 'They wanted to be all by themselves and shunned human society altogether', said Rev. Singh.

[Maclean, 1977.]

Less than a year after they were found, the younger child Amala died of a gastro-intestinal infection. Kamala showed no emotion but clung to the corpse and remained immobile and morose for weeks after Amala's death. Slowly Kamala began to take an interest in other children. She accepted food from Mrs Singh's hands. Rather like a circus animal she was trained to stand upright with rewards of raw meat held above her head, but she always walked poorly. After three years she began to spend more time with other children, showed signs of understanding her name and began calling out 'Ma' to Mrs Singh. She eventually developed a vocabulary of a few dozen poorly pronounced words, although she would spend long intervals chanting softly to herself. She died at the end of 1929, when she would have been perhaps 14 years old.

There are over forty stories of wolves adopting children, from Romulus and Remus onwards, but none as well authenticated. The story of the Orissa children leaked into the Indian and British Press. In 1977 Charles Maclean gathered together all the written material he could, including the Rev. Singh's detailed diary, and he interviewed eye-witnesses. The results were published as *The Wolf Children*. Wolves quite often killed babies in Orissa and sometimes desperate women abandoned their children in the forest. How and why one wolf adopted two children is a mystery. Were they collected at different times? But the message is that the growing human brain is programmed to receive a complex pattern of inputs early in life, and once certain windows of opportunity are closed they can never be re-opened.

zoo-keepers, as failure to care for newborn young is a common occurrence among captive animals, and maybe it also provides us with hope for the future of socially deprived children.

In modern hospitals a great deal of high technology is used to keep premature babies alive. Very little research has been done on the effect the bright lights and almost cage-like apparatus found in modern intensive care nurseries may have on the development of the baby. In the USA, suicide among teenagers has quadrupled in the last twenty-five years and adverse experiences at the time of birth, such as a premature delivery or respiratory distress, are more common in those who subsequently take their own lives. Mothers isolated from their premature babies by the plexiglass of an incubator may also face difficulties relating to their child when he or she leaves the hospital. Although the vast majority of premature infants survive to lead normal lives and to be loved by their parents, we should never overlook the biological oneness of mother and baby, as well as the exciting human potential – unique among primates – for intense inputs from the father.

Adoption

Monkey mothers have been observed to share infants, rescue each other's children from danger, and band together to fight infanticidal males. But among monkeys, custodial mothers are also observed to treat their non-biological children more harshly, particular if they have several children of their own. When a juvenile monkey in the wild loses its mother it cries, stops

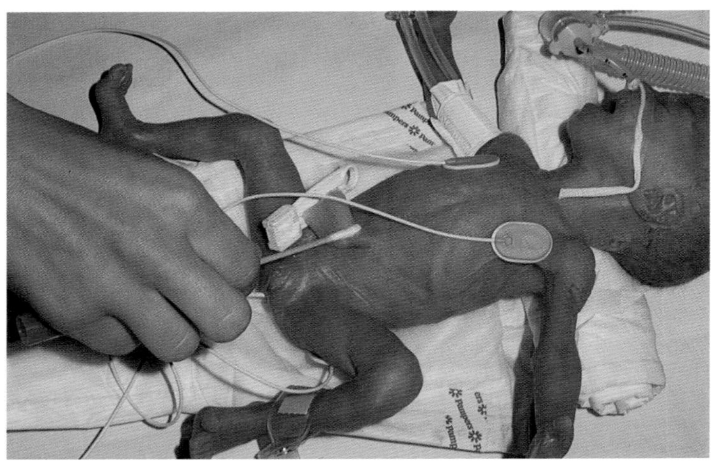

[C. Morley.]

Touch and go. Neonatal intensive care units now work wonders to save the lives of premature babies, even those weighing less than 18 oz (500 grams). But only time will tell whether they will suffer any handicaps in later life. Evidence is accumulating which suggests that birth weight may be positively related to life expectancy, those born small being more likely to die at an earlier age from cardiovascular disease.

playing and searches for her. The youngster may become depressed to the point of death, or may try to attach itself to another mother, a grandmother, a sibling, a young female or even to a playmate. A chimpanzee over the age of 3 may survive if adopted in this way, but commonly it 'regresses' to more infantile behaviour for a while and may always remain less adept at learned skills, including the ability to be a good mother. In one study of Japanese macaques in the wild, nearly all the infant mortality in the troop was concentrated in the newborns of females who had lost their own mothers during childhood.

Human beings, with our great plasticity of behaviour yet lacking the instinctive bonding at birth of some species, have a remarkable ability to adopt and share children. Informal adoption, particularly among relatives, is common in many societies. Our industrialized society has gone a step further, passing children from woman to woman in crêches and in day-care centres for children. Child care has become a necessity for many working mothers. Modern society invariably pays university professors more than kindergarten teachers, but from what we have discovered about human development we may need to rethink how we train and what we pay those who care for the young. At a minimum, a child care system with stable staff is surely preferable to one where a toddler meets a new surrogate mother each week.

Parent–child conflict

Evolution operates at the individual level. In the 1970s, Robert Trivers of the University of California at Santa Cruz developed a biological explanation of parent–child conflict. Evolution, he suggested, will select those parents who invest equally in all their offspring and so ensure their survival into the next generation, but it will also select those offspring that secure the greatest parental support for as long as possible and who defend themselves best against sibling competition. Thus, Trivers postulated, evolution has programmed conflict into our very genes; the same individual when a child and when a parent will adopt opposing biological strategies to maximize survival. Deep down, biologically, every child wants to be an only child, or at least a favourite child, while parents seek to share their love and resources equally among all their children. Without doubt children can be very demanding of their parents, and sibling rivalry is often desperately real. Plainly, it is in the parents' interest to give the utmost help to their offspring when they are most helpless and vulnerable, and parental care invariably wanes with the passage of time. Sooner or later it will be in a mother's biological interest to wean her child, so that she can begin ovulating again and have

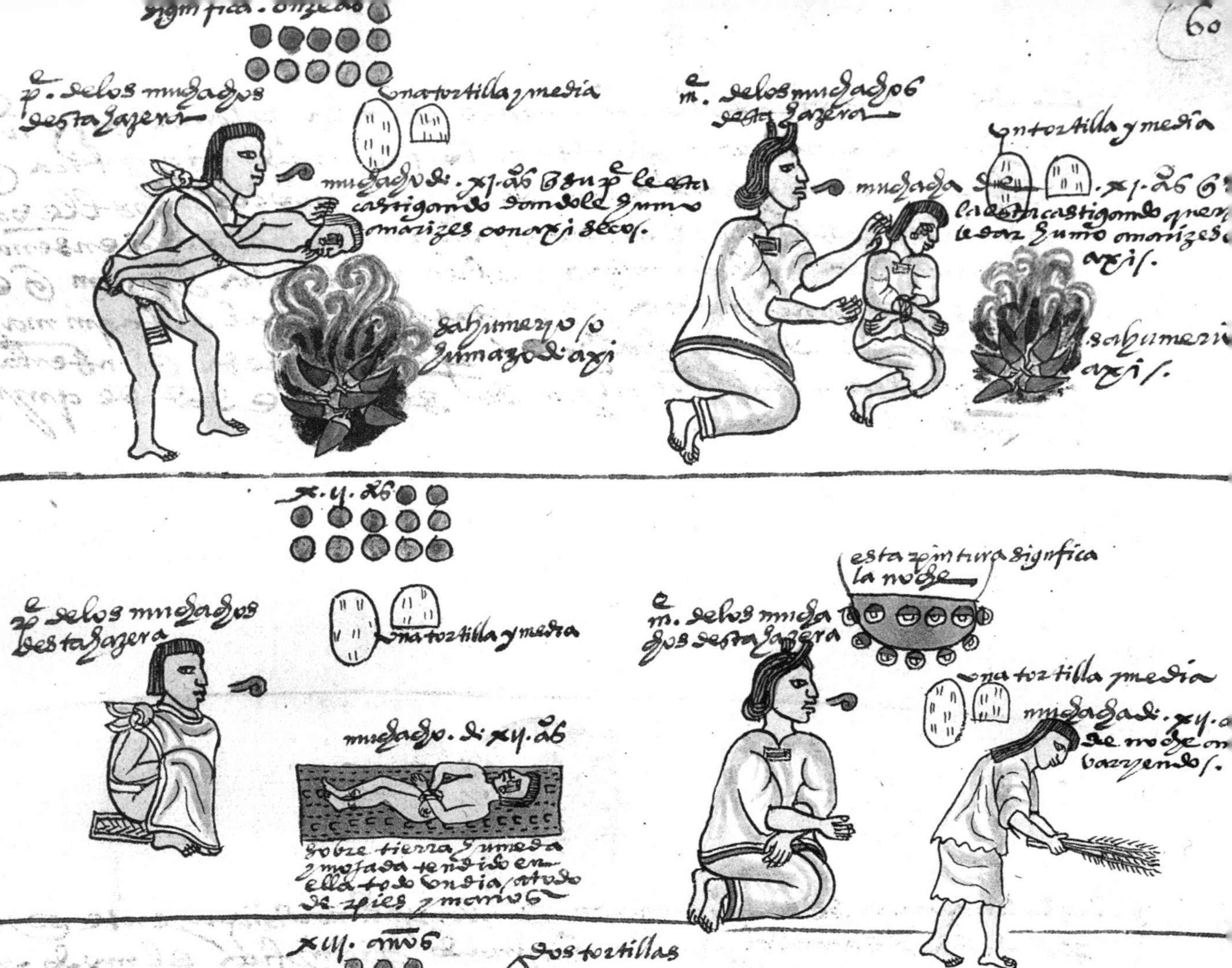

Discipline in childhood. The war-like, human sacrificing Aztecs brought up their children with harsh discipline. For openers, (*top left*) a father holds a naughty son over a fire, while his wife (*top right*) merely threatens a daughter with the same fate. For more severe punishment a boy is tied up and left in the damp cold all day (*bottom left*). Sometimes thorns were thrust under the skin of recalcitrant children. A daughter is woken at night (*bottom right*) and made to repeat her household chores such as sweeping.

another chance of passing on her genes to the next generation. But it is always in the offspring's interest to postpone weaning for as long as possible: mother's milk is a cheap, easy and nutritious way of feeding yourself, far preferable to going out and searching for a few scraps to eat. When the mother reproduces again, the child will suffer additionally from a rival who will compete with the elder sibling for attention and resources. Among mammals, weaning appears to be more and more traumatic with the rising intelligence of the species.

As a woman grows older, her prospects of having additional children decline, so biology would predict that a 40 year old mother, or an ageing chimpanzee, would be willing to invest much more in her latest and possibly last child, than a 20 year old, where it may be a reproductive advantage to cut back on her investment in the current child in order to free herself for the next pregnancy. Jane Goodall describes how chimpanzee Flint, the child of an ageing Flo, refused to be weaned at the normal age of 3. When Flo eventually had her last child, Flint continued his infantile behaviour, perhaps contributing to his younger sister's death only three months after her birth. He was still sharing his mother's nest at 8 1/2 years when she died. Although other chimps at that age would be able to survive on their own, when Flo died Flint went into a deep depression and himself died six days later. Flint and the spoilt child of an indulgent older human mother are immediately recognizable stereotypes. Of course, such evolutionary influences are largely subconscious and not every parent or child will follow its biological script.

The miracle of speech

The acquisition of language is something children do outstandingly well, and we need to remind ourselves how extraordinary it is that any young child can learn any language, from Afghan to Zulu, apparently effortlessly and nearly always flawlessly. By contrast, most adults must struggle to learn a new language and rarely speak it without an accent. Our brains seem to be 'hard-wired' to learn a language very early in life. The brain has evolved to hear and to imitate sounds with an especial facility: think of the amazing ability we have to recognize the voice of a friend on the telephone within a few syllables of opening a conversation. The developing fetus lives in a pool of liquid which is an excellent sound conductor and no doubt hears its mother talking, laughing, and perhaps crying. The response of a newborn baby to stimuli can be measured by recording the pressure with which it sucks on an artificial teat, and studies show that an infant responds more vigorously to hearing – literally – its mother's tongue, compared with a language it has not come across before. Long before we learn to talk, we learn to distinguish the melody and individual sounds, or phonemes, of our own language. Clumps of neurones begin to respond to each individual phoneme. If, as in English, it is important to distinguish sounds such as ra and la, then the neurones responding to these sounds seem to be far apart. But if, as in Japanese, these sounds are not distinguished from one another, then the responding neurones may be close together.

Parents in all cultures make cooing noises to a baby's face, which reflects an adult predisposition to accelerate learning in the baby. This singsong speech or 'parentese' exaggerates vowel sounds and helps the baby to learn the fine distinctions between the sounds making up any language, while disregarding any auditory information that is not absolutely necessary. The more the parents talk to a child, the more rapidly the child learns new words. By age 2, normal infants know perhaps 20 words, but by 3 as many as 1000. In the case of the English language, by the sixth year the vocabulary explodes to between 10 000 and 20 000 words, and by age 18 to around 60 000. A child learns a new word about every ninety minutes that it is awake. But learning requires human contact and emotional content, and an infant lying alone in front of a television dismisses the babble on the tube as just some sort of background noise. Television has been described as chewing-gum for the brain.

Distinguishing sounds is only the first step on a long and remarkable road. What do the sounds mean? Again, the child's brain seem to be hard-wired both to categorize objects, and to associate particular sounds with each class of object they see. The brain assumes a sound refers to a class of objects, and not that each ball, for example, has its own name. It also assumes that the name is constant and that something called a ball on Wednesday will still be called a ball on Saturday. It is known that some key functions of both spoken and sign language are analysed in the brain's temporal cortex in an area called the planum temporale, and this part of the brain is larger on the left than on the right. Interestingly, Patrick Gannon of Mount Sinai School of Medicine, New York, has shown that chimpanzees also have a similar asymmetry of the brain in this area.

Despite a seemingly endless variety of languages, children learn to modify and string words together, according to sets of rules that cross language frontiers. Therefore, certain aspects of grammar also appear to be built into the brain. Between 3 and 3 1/2 years, children begin to use tenses correctly, then to distinguish between the singular and plural, and they come to understand that the position a word has in a sentence determines its meaning: do you do something to somebody else, or do they do something to you? Similar rules appear in all languages, even in sign languages used by the deaf and in 'pidgin' languages that develop to ensure at least minimal communication between different language groups. Very occasionally a child is born with a specific neurological defect called Specific Language Impairment, where it lacks the circuitry for creating a grammar.

Poetry is part music and part language and a stroke may take away a person's power to speak, but leave them an ability to recite nursery rhymes. Poetry and music processing areas, unlike those for language, are nearly always localized on the right side of the brain. But while women, on average, have more facility with language, there are more male composers than female. Is this because women are kept out of music classes, or is there perhaps a biological reason? Geoffrey Miller, an evolutionary psychologist at University College London speculates that composing music allows a man to show off and impress potential mates. Male rock stars seem to demonstrate the point by always having access to young women. The age when male rock and jazz composers are most likely to write a hit record coincides almost exactly with

Children

As a woman who held a babe against her bosom said, Speak to us of Children.
And he said:
Your children are not your children.
They are the sons and daughters of Life's longing for itself.
They come through you but not from you,
And though they are with you yet they belong not to you.

You may give them your love but not your thoughts,
For they have their own thoughts.
You may house their bodies but not their souls,
For their souls dwell in the house of tomorrow, which you cannot visit, not even in your dreams.
You may strive to be like them, but seek not to make them like you.
For life goes not backward nor tarries with yesterday.
You are bows from which your children as living arrows are sent forth.
The Archer sees the mark upon the path of the infinite, and He bends you with His might that His arrows may go swift and far.
Let your bending in the Archer's hand be for gladness;
For even as He loves the arrow that flies, so He loves also the bow that is stable.

Kahlil Gibran, *The Prophet*, 1926

the age when men are most likely to be convicted of murder. It is not to be suggested that rock stars murder – in fact the very opposite. As noted in Chapter 2, when a man kills another man it is often an expression of sexual competition between men. Therefore, it could make sense that statistics concerning men who are at the bottom of the social pile, and are driven to murder, and men who are highly successful at musical composition should match so closely.

Puberty

Puberty in both sexes involves a cascade of hormonal, bodily and behavioural changes that takes several years to complete. It is associated with physical growth and change and with the explosive appearance of new emotions that create tensions between the child and its parents. Puberty is a breaking-away, a severance of the parental bonds in preparation for leading an independent reproductive existence. Castrate a male red deer at birth and it will never leave its mother's side for the rest of its adult life, whereas normally the young stag leaves his mother at puberty to seek his sexual fortunes over the hill.

The clock that controls the timing of sexual maturity is located in the brain, and the cells that will ultimately trigger the release of sex hormones from the ovaries or the testes are well developed at birth. Indeed, the testes are particularly active in fetal and early neonatal life, laying down the anatomy of

[The Lewis Carroll Picture Book / Mary Evans Picture Library.]

Alice in Wonderland. Nearly the whole Western world read *Alice in Wonderland* when it was published in 1865, but the photographs the Rev. C. L. Dodgson (Lewis Carroll) took of little girls were by no means intended for publication. While there is no evidence that the shy bachelor clergyman and Oxford university lecturer sexually assaulted any of the prepubertal girls he befriended, there is a great deal of fetishism in this carefully posed picture of Alice Liddell (the girl for whom he wrote *Alice*) as the 'young beggar'. Indeed, Mrs Liddell objected and Dodgson explicitly asked other mothers, 'Are [your daughters] kissable? I hope you won't be shocked at this question, but nearly all my girl friends are on these terms with me.' Dodgson's latent paedophilia waned as the girls passed through puberty, 'About nine out of ten of my child-friendships,' he wrote, 'get shipwrecked at the critical point where the stream and the river meet'.

the male reproductive tract and the brain, and then become quiescent in childhood. Puberty is not the first sexual awakening for the male, but a reawakening at the end of a long period of sexual dormancy and suppression. In both sexes these momentous transformations begin during the silent watches of the night, when the brain first begins the slow tapping out of the hormonal messages that stimulate the pituitary gland and hence the testes and ovaries. Eventually the messages get more urgent and the hormonal clock ticks throughout twenty-four hours, the body responding maximally to the brain's bidding. If, for some unusual reason, the restraint on the brain hormones controlling the ovaries or testes is lifted during childhood, then precocious puberty occurs. In the 1970s, a Peruvian girl just under 6 years of age gave birth to a living child. The brain hormone controlling puberty has been synthesized artificially, so it is now possible to use it to treat cases of delayed puberty.

The first sign of impending puberty in girls is enlargement of the nipple and surrounding areola and growth of the breast tissue due to increasing oestrogen secretion from the ovaries. Growth accelerates, the hips broaden and more contoured body fat is laid down. Menarche in girls, the time of the first menstrual period, is merely an outward and visible sign of an inward and invisible change that has been going on in her body for several years. The ovaries also make small amounts of testosterone which is responsible for the development of hair in the armpits and in the pubic region. Testosterone also drives the girl's emerging interest in sex. The timid girl becomes the subtle woman, rounded, romantic before conception, tough in childbirth, sensitive and sensible, resolute in motherhood. Boys begin their growth spurt later than girls but eventually grow taller and more muscular. The testes and penis enlarge and hair appears in the armpits, on the face and in the pubic region, turning Shakespeare's 'whining schoolboy with his satchel and shining morning face' into 'the lover, sighing like a furnace' in *As You Like It*.

Puberty is the time when each of us is driven out of the Eden of childhood by our emerging sexual awareness. Strong new loyalties are formed and it may be more important to conform to the world of your peers than to that of your parents. Every parental rule is systematically tested to the limit and key adult behaviours, especially sex, begin to be conducted in secret away from the parents, although sometimes discussed at length with peers. Styles of music and dress become symbols of a tangible break with the older generation. Each generation seems to have a particular attachment to the music we heard during adolescence, thus today's parents might listen to beach music while their teenagers enjoy rock. All who have ridden out the turbulent excitements and torments of adolescence have vivid memories of that time of life.

It can be hard trying to live by an adult and a childhood rule book simultaneously. A teenaged girl or boy, physically larger and stronger than mother or father, may suddenly act in a trying, moody, apparently childish way, while the same person at another time may respond to a challenging situation with more sagacity than their elders. Roller coaster emotions, driven by a hormonal upheaval in a free-wheeling inner world of rich imagination, in the twinkling of eye may pass from know-it-all confidence to frightened vulnerability, or from soaring elation to deep depression. Such mood swings and their frequent unmanageability may end in tragedy. In the USA today, murder is the commonest cause of death among inner city 15 to 19 year old males, and suicide the second. A study by the US Centers for Disease Control in Atlanta, Georgia, in 1990 found that each year a quarter of adolescents thought about suicide, 1 in 50 attempted it and 1 in 10000 died. Suicide, which is practically unknown before puberty, becomes more common in adolescence, although important sex differences exist: self-inflicted death is three or four times more common in boys than in girls; girls are more prone to attempt suicide but survive ('pseudocide') while boys are more likely to succeed.

Dieting and dancing

The best understood factor influencing the age of puberty is body weight. Children are rather like little atomic bombs – when they reach a certain critical body weight they explode sexually. There is an obvious evolutionary importance in ensuring that a young woman is capable of withstanding the strains of pregnancy and lactation and that a young man is capable of competing with other males for sexual access to females; hence evolution has seen to it that there is a close relationship between physical maturity and sexual maturity. Rose Frisch of Harvard University observed that when a growing girl weighs about 106 lbs (48 kilograms) she begins to menstruate. A portion of this body weight must be laid down as fat, which is an excellent way of storing calories against possible food shortages. About 35 lbs (16 kilograms) of body fat, or 150 000 kilocalories (627 000 kilojoules) of reserves, seems necessary to trigger menstruation. Weight and exercise, however, are not the only factors determining the age of puberty but they are the most important. Blind girls tend to menstruate later than sighted ones. Purely social factors also interact with the age of puberty in an interesting biological way. If a girl loses her mother through death (or her father through divorce) shortly before puberty and is suddenly forced into a parental role bringing up her own younger brothers and sisters, then her own puberty may be delayed. It may be to the advantage of her selfish genes to instil a behaviour that delays fertility a little in the interests of the survival of her siblings, with whom she shares 50 per cent of her genes.

If a woman who has begun to menstruate loses body weight through illness, starvation, or of her own volition then she will cease to menstruate. The dictates of fashion are often exaggerated in the young, and in recent decades enthusiasm for slimness has sometimes turned into virtual emaciation. A survey in Australia found that 85 per cent of 14 year old girls consider themselves overweight, and for 1 in 100 adolescents in the Western world, fighting flab and dieting away cellulite turns into anorexia nervosa. The singer Karen Carpenter died from this sad affliction in 1983, aged 32. Anorexia nervosa is twenty times as common in girls as in boys and usually begins at age 16 or 17. Anorexic girls are often of above-average intelligence, compliant and loving in nature, and they may disguise the early stages of their self-imposed starvation as a health or food fad. They enjoy food, but feel guilty eating: sometimes they will eat in company, or binge in private, only to vomit the food when alone – bulimia. Sometimes bulimics vomit twenty times a day. All the while, an anorexic's self-perceived body image is often that of a normal or even an overweight person. Jane Fonda and the late Diana Princess of Wales were each bulimic for many years.

***Le Foyer de la danse à l'Opéra de la rue le Peletier*, Edgar Degas, 1872.** The performance of Degas' short, well-rounded ballerinas would be considered timid by today's standards. Ballet changed irrevocably when the Sergei Diaghilev's Russian Ballet toured western Europe and America in 1909. They demonstrated spectacular *entrechats* and *grand jetés* as a group of strong young men threw a troop of relatively small young girls about the stage. Western girls were beginning to grow taller and heavier and the only way western ballet companies could compete was by selecting fragile, slight, ballerinas.

Ballerinas express an art form which developed in the eighteenth and nineteenth centuries before young women were as tall or heavy as they are today. Some contemporary ballets companies require young women to sign a contract agreeing to stay below a specific body weight. Modern, professional ballet virtually demands that a girl attempts the painful process of turning back the hands on the clock of puberty. It is well nigh impossible to become a professional female ballet dancer unless a girl begins serious training several years before puberty. A mother's desire to see her child as the Sugar Plum Fairy combines with the girl's idealism and naïveté to fuel a ten hour working day and a weekend of non-stop coffee and cigarettes. Like her hunter–gatherer ancestors of tens of thousands of years ago, the contemporary ballerina eats a subsistence diet while exercising a great deal and, as a result, most have highly irregular periods and ovulation commonly occurs much later than in other young women.

Sex and intellect

On average, boys are more noisy, more rumbustuous and more likely to get into trouble than girls. But in the USA a 1997 poll showed that 61 per cent of parents believe the differences in behaviour between boys and girls are the result of the way they are raised. Evolutionary biology suggests that both innate biological predispositions and environmental factors underlie behavioural differences between boys and girls.

'no egg for you girls'

Kulsum was serving eggs to her small son Shoukat. Standing by her side were her two young daughters, crying. Kulsum shouted at them not to bother her while she was preparing their brother for school.

Five-year old Seema protested: 'You give him egg every day, but never to us.'

A sharp slap landed on Seema's right cheek; 'How many times do I have to tell you that there are no eggs for you girls? Don't ask again.'

The mother's explanation for her apparent favouritism was the conventional one. 'Believe me', she said, 'they are all my children and I love each one of them dearly. But I have no means of buying eggs for all of them. The son has to be fed properly so that he grows up strong enough to bear the family responsibilities.'

Tahmina Ahmad, Bangladesh, *The Indonesian Times*, May 1989

Ngweko, or fondling

The word ngweko *(fondling) is used in its real Gikuyu* [or Kikuyu] *sense and not as the loose term* ngweko ya gecomba, *employed by missionaries and detribalised Gikuyu, which means full sexual intercourse.*

In a dance a getharia *can be recognised, for he dances with several girls around him, but in order that he will not have a monopoly, a kind of Gikuyu 'Paul Jones' dance,* gothombacana, *is repeated very often so as to allow the less attractive men an opportunity of dancing with nice girls. Girls visit their boy-friends frequently, especially during the dancing season. The boys also visit the girls in their homes and take them to dances and escort them home afterwards.*

Ngweko, *or fondling, is looked upon as a sacred act and one which must be done in a systematic, well-organised manner ... After partners have been arranged, one of the boys gets up, saying:* 'Ndathie kwenogora' *(I am going to stretch myself). His girl partner follows him to the bed. The boy removes his clothing. The girl removes her upper garment,* nguo ya ngoro, *and retains her skirt,* mothuru, *and her soft leather apron,* mwngo, *which she pulls between her legs and tucks in together with her leather skirt,* mother. *In this position the lovers lie together facing each other, with their legs interwoven to prevent any movement of their hips. They then begin to fondle each other, rubbing their breasts together, while at the same time they engage in love-making conversation until they gradually fall asleep. Sometimes the partners experience sexual relief but this is not an essential feature of the* ngweko.

Many Gikuyu have been punished and regarded as 'sinners' by missionaries simply for having been found sleeping in the same room with a girl, for in their eyes such an act is sinful.

The Gikuyu who have not been brought up under the missionaries' influence find it difficult to understand this sort of European puritanism, for a Gikuyu man has been taught from childhood to develop the technique of self-control in the matter of sex. While the missionaries' idea is that, since a white man would not be able to restrain himself under these circumstances, so the African would not be able to, and must be forbidden to sleep with a woman-friend in the Gikuyu fashion.

Jomo Kenyatta, *Facing Mount Kenya*, 1979

Modern living has created a maturity gap. Teenagers, their bodies stimulated prematurely by sex hormones, find themselves in a society that adds its own external ambivalence to their internal tensions. American society dresses 13 year old girls as mini-adults, expects young people to 'date', allows them the freedom and adult symbolism of a driving licence when only 16, yet still expects intercourse not to occur, or – worse still – when it does take place, pretends it never happened. The denial of sex among those with whom we grow up is all too easy. Teenagers cannot believe their parents still make love. They know the facts of life, but surely mum and dad did it only once for each of their children: they can't still be doing it! Parents often find it just as difficult to accept that their children are sexually active. In one US study conducted in 1990, eight out of ten women over age 40 admitted that they had had sex before marriage, but two-thirds of the mothers hoped that their own daughters would be virgins when they were married. Were they denying their previous experience, or did they think they had made a mistake earlier in life? In public, some Churches may still adhere to sexual chastity before marriage, yet only 3 per cent of Americans and fewer than 1 per cent of Britons delay the first intercourse until their marriage night.

If we reproduce prematurely, then we do it badly: Western society is burdened with a fearful load of adolescent misery – unintended pregnancies, inadequate parenting, abortion, drug abuse, accidents, suicides and sexually transmitted diseases and most recently of all the lethal threat of AIDS. Teenage marriages are twice as likely to end in divorce as marriages contracted by partners over the age of 20. One in five American girls has had intercourse by age 15 or younger and in Britain 19 per cent of girls have sexual intercourse before they are 16 (the legal age of consent). In Baltimore, Maryland,

50 per cent of African-American males are sexually active before age 13. One factor leading to the earlier sexual debut of many African-American adolescents may also be biological. By age 10 in the USA 1 per cent of white girls but 25 per cent of African-American girls have breast and pubic hair development. The difference cannot be explained by differences in weight, socioeconomic status or even the age of first menstruation, and therefore may be genetic. But, as with nearly all human behaviour, social and biological factors still interact in complex ways. African-American teenagers are also more likely to come from single parent families, and to live in poorer conditions with fewer chances of acquiring an interesting and rewarding job.

Urbanization makes the expression of teenage sexuality much easier. In a small village community, characteristic of most of Western history or much of today's developing world, everyone knows everyone else; everyone is interested in everybody else's business – especially their sexual business. In such a community, teenagers are in a minority. Embedded in the claustrophobic familiarity of the extended family there is little privacy. If you sneak away with someone of the opposite sex, the chances are that somebody will notice and before you know it you will be behind bars of gossip. Authoritarian expectations to behave oneself are unlikely to restrain the human libido as

Guarding his progeny

Every day for six months, anthropologist Mark Flinn from the University of Missouri, walked along the same 3 mile (5 kilometre) route in a village in Trinidad. He knew everyone individually and every time he passed someone in the street, in the garden or in their home he noted what they were doing. Flinn entered 33 000 observations into the computer. He found that fathers spent very little time with their daughters in infancy, but suddenly, as they approached and went through puberty, fathers and daughters were very much more likely to be found together. Men who had fertile young daughters were also much more likely to be found quarrelling and arguing with either their daughters, or their daughters' boyfriends, than were men without teenage daughters. About half the young girls in the village had been abandoned by their fathers and lived in one parent families. Mark Flinn found that he met these fatherless girls further from their homes and in unchaperoned situations more frequently than those with a resident father.

Why should fathers guard their daughters but not their sons? The more a boy sows his wild oats the more likely he is to pass on his father's genes. But a female, with her high investment in reproduction, will benefit from a more stable relationship with a richer man. The evidence from Trinidad was that girls with resident fathers who were likely to 'guard them' as teenagers, made more stable relationships and were five times as likely to mate with richer men with a great deal of land than girls who lacked resident fathers. The men with greater wealth, for their part, preferred the more chaste women because they would not have to spend their wealth on caring for other men's children. They would also have a high confidence of paternity of any children born to them, who would subsequently inherit their wealth.

effectively as the chastity belt of gossip. Today's anonymous urban world is as socially different as it is physically distinct from yesterday's village. In today's inner city, large numbers of individuals of the same age or lifestyle congregate together, yet around the next corner, no one knows you. A Papua New Guinea Highlander, a youth of Shakespeare's time, a Newcastle coal miner's son in 1950, or an Idaho farmer's daughter in 1960 – like other young primates – all grew up with a well defined pattern of social and family expectations. Late twentieth century society has bulldozed many of these different lifestyles into one open, fast-paced, individualistic society. In a traditional society, children may have known their parents have sex, from sleeping in the same room, but they were not exposed to images of young people getting into bed together or media discussions of the sexual proclivities of national leaders. Sex loses its mystery.

Self-reporting of sexual activity always contains uncertainties, but it seems that the age of initiating sexual intercourse has fallen considerably in Europe and North America over the past quarter of a century. Older males often coerce young females into having sex both among such primates as orangutans and in our own society. A recent nationwide survey of sexual behaviour in Britain has shown that 75 per cent of women reported having

The *ghotul*

The *ghotul* is a building that is the centre of village life for the Muria, a tribal people in southern India. It is a single, large, bare room that is the repository for the village orchestra. It is where village disputes are settled, government bureaucrats are entertained and feasts celebrated. Dancing and feasting by members of the *ghotul* are an essential part of any wedding. The *ghotul* is also the dormitory where twenty to thirty young people of both sexes are expected to sleep after puberty and before marriage. At first glance, it might seem that a society which requires unmarried teenagers to set up house together would dissolve into orgiastic hedonism.

In reality, *ghotul* life is hedged around with a variety of interesting restraints. Boys can enter or leave the *ghotul* at will, and they become full members only when they bring a sleeping mat woven by their mothers. The boys establish the *ghotul* government, and levy mild punishments, such as collecting firewood, for breaking any rules. Girls can also decide when to enter the *ghotul*, but once they do so they must continue to sleep there (except when they are menstruating) until they marry. They are not allowed to mix with boys from a *ghotul* in another village. When a girl joins the *ghotul* she must indicate with whom she intends to sleep. This can be embarrassing and humiliating: embarrassing because a girl must identify the boy in public, and humiliating because the boy may feign lack of interest. 'I will not sleep with her', said Karu when Maina shyly selected him. He was fined by his peers for refusing her.

When a partnership, or *jor* (Hindi word for 'pair'), is established, the girl must share the mat of the boy she chooses. When two young people sleep together, antagonism is as common as romance. When affection does develop, it must not be displayed in front of others. Girls may massage boys while they sit round the fire at night, but never their own *jor*. If the boy fails to come to the *ghotul* on any night, the girl may sleep with another boy. She can also publicly announce she wants to end a *jor*, at which point she must find another boy.

their first intercourse with a partner older than themselves, and 51 per cent of these partners were already sexually experienced. In one US study, it was noted that teenage girls usually went around with boys an average of three years older than themselves. None of the girls reported that they had been raped, but most said that there were occasions when they had been 'forced to have sex'. The informants did not consider it rape if they knew the man, and if he had invested dollars in giving them a good time. In addition to the earlier appearance of sexual drives, contemporary adolescents have greater wealth and mobility than their parents, calling their car a 'sin bin'. Between the two World Wars the opportunities for premarital sex were more limited; perhaps a week's summer holiday in Blackpool for the British, or a day trip to Coney Island for New Yorkers. It was more difficult to have sex when your parents were at home and your younger brother was doing a jigsaw in your shared bedroom. Furthermore, the penalties for a premarital pregnancy were much greater. When she was 96 years old, Gina Baker told author Steve Humphries what it was like to be an unmarried English mother in 1919.

> *When I had to tell my family they were furious. Especially my mother. She shouted at me to pack my bags and take my troubles elsewhere. Eventually I made my way to the Church Army and they sent me to a home in Brighton. Every day there we were marched through the streets, for everybody to gaze at us, and know we were single women expecting babies.*

In some Muslim countries sexual intercourse also often begins in the early teens, but here it is only after early marriage, and loss of virginity before the wedding may be still punished by death – a close male relative may kill the wayward girl. The father of one young woman in Upper Egypt, whose husband doubted her virginity on her wedding night, locked her in a small room and dropped scorpions through the window until she died.

It is hardly surprising that one out of ten US teenagers becomes pregnant every year, and half those pregnancies end in induced abortion. More than a million births annually, or about one in five of all deliveries in the USA, are to single women. Unmarried women receive less antenatal care, are more likely to abuse drugs or alcohol and have more low birth weight babies.

Female infanticide

Most mammals abandon or kill abnormal offspring, and there has probably never been a time in the journey from apes to humankind when we have not, under certain circumstances, killed or let die our infants. Most traditional societies also realize that congenitally abnormal children are destined to die, and simply abandon them or kill them at birth. A surprising number of societies, however, have also been prepared to kill healthy children. The contrast between the love parents and onlookers normally shower on a new baby and the brutality of infanticide is harsh and dramatic. Yet even societies that make murder a capital offence are usually more lenient to the mother who kills her newborn.

Infanticide is practised in many hunter–gatherer societies, from Inuits to the San of the Kalahari Desert. Women know they are unable to sustain a second pregnancy until the youngest child is about 4 years old. In such an environment a child is so dependent on its mother's ability to carry it and to suckle it that if she were to have too many children too close together she would end up raising fewer to maturity. In San society, women were traditionally delivered of their babies under a tree outside the village and the newborn was not considered a true person until it was brought back into the community. Therefore, infanticide was not equated with murder: when it came to a choice between hazarding the life of an existing toddler or killing a baby after nine months of pregnancy, the mother protected the greater investment.

Abandoning a baby at birth may increase the survival of older children, or a mother's chance of successfully reproducing later in her life. The Ayoreo Indians, who live along the border of Bolivia and Paraguay, vividly illustrate

The singer

By today's standards, Baldassare Ferri would have been classed as a megastar. When he sang in Florence, admiring fans met him a long way outside the city and escorted him along a flower-strewn path. He was employed by kings, and so great was his fame that warring armies stopped fighting to listen. Ferri was tall, with spindly legs, flat feet, a vast barrel of a chest and no beard. His voice ranged over four octaves, from A to high C. He had no testicles.

For over 300 years, during the growth and maturation of European opera, little boys were deliberately castrated before puberty to provide singers with the power of an adult voice and the range of a choir boy. Castrati were said to be able to hold a note for a minute and, before the age of the microphone, to fill an opera house with a supernatural quality of voice, depersonalized, and 'like a nightingale'. 'Viva il coltello' (long live the knife), the audience would cry.

Scarlatti and Handel wrote for castrati but as the supply dwindled, women were written into dual male/female roles such as Despina in Mozart's *Cosi Fan Tutte*.

From around 1500, European barber surgeons created castrati as singers. Poverty drove parents to offer their children for mutilation in the hope that, like a modern rock star, they might hit the jackpot. One technique was to give a 5 year old boy a hot bath to relax the scrotum, and then to press on the jugular vein until he passed out before snipping off the testes. The Catholic Church forbade castration, but when the deed was done they were happy to employ castrati to sing in the Sistine Chapel. The last castrato to sing in the Vatican made a record of the Ave Maria in 1902, which still exists.

the drive to optimize reproduction over a fertile lifetime. Until the 1950s, the Ayoreo were forest migrants who gathered food and practised a primitive agriculture. In the 1980s, Paul Bugos and Lorraine McCarthy of Northwestern University interviewed a number of older Ayoreo women. They found 54 cases of infanticide out of 141 births. They found the infanticide rate was highest (over 50 per cent of all births) among teenage mothers. Bugos and McCarthy commented, 'Even when trained as anthropologists, it is difficult to believe that someone one knows as a charming friend, devoted wife and doting mother, can do something that one's own culture deems repugnant.' Unlike many preliterate tribal peoples, the Ayoreo marriages were based on love. Women initiated romantic relationships and, like contemporary Western teenagers, tended to have a number of affairs before settling down with an individual man. But the tribe also had a taboo against sexual relationships during pregnancy or lactation which would last for up to three or four years. If a woman was involved in an unsatisfactory relationship and yet had a child and breastfed it, then, in view of the taboo against sex during pregnancy and lactation, she would not have been able to establish a new, stable relationship for several years. It was therefore in her long term interest to trade the life of her newborn infant to give herself a chance for a successful marriage. However, for the older woman, with less reproductive life ahead, the sacrifice of a child made less and less reproductive sense, and Burgos and McCarthy found the infanticide rate amongst Ayoreo fell with increasing maternal age. The age distribution of Western women accused of infanticide is very similar to that of the Ayoreo Indians, and is highest among teenage mothers who have the most to lose by being 'tied down by a baby' but who also have the greatest likelihood of conceiving again in the many years of fertile life still ahead of them. In Wilson and Daly's Canadian data referred to earlier, the chance of a natural parent killing a baby or a toddler was five to ten times higher than the risk of killing a child later in life. Fewer than one parent in one million killed their own child immediately before or during their child's puberty. In contrast, someone *in loco parentis* was ten to twenty times as likely to murder a child as the genetic parent. Parents may joke about wanting to kill obstreporous teenagers but they almost never carry it out; however the murder rate of teenagers by unrelated adults rises in the younger teens when adolescents are indeed most annoying.

Battered children

Sadly, for every child that is killed, a great many are ill treated. Again, our biology shows through and for every preschool child with two natural parents that is abused, forty are battered by step-parents. Occasionally, women will join in battering their own children, presumably, from an evolutionary point of view and like an Ayoreo woman killing a child, judging the long term security provided by a new mate to be worth the short term sacrifice of a young baby. The pain and horror of child battering and murder highlights the value of evolutionary insights: it is not our purpose to excuse murdering parents, but to protect children. Just as medical scientists strive to understand high blood pressure in order to cure hypertension, so we can use the insights from the behaviour of other animals to help to civilize ourselves. Social workers have often found it difficult to screen out those at risk of damaging their children. Sometimes they have arbitrarily sequestered children from loving parents, while at the same time returning children to abusive parents only to see the young ones killed or seriously injured. Biology would say that if a woman with young children marries or begins to live with a new man, and if there is evidence of physical injury to the children, then social workers and neighbours should be alert to the possibility they are dealing with battering by one or both parents.

In the developing world, poverty and lack of access to contraceptive choices and safe abortion is creating armies of abandoned and battered children. There are more children living in the streets of Latin America than there are people in Venezuela. Most people call them *pivetê* or urchins. The story of the children is often the same. They begin by spending more and more time on the streets, perhaps earning pennies shining shoes or selling newspapers. There is a row at home and a beating, and the child decides it is better to sleep rough. Most of the murders of street children are by death squads hired by hotels or shop keepers to rid an area of petty criminals. The corpses are often mutilated and sometimes dropped back at the slum the child came from as a warning to others. More street children are murdered in Rio each year – about 500 – than the total number of children living on the streets a couple of generations ago.

Investing in the future

Biologically, bringing up our children is not only the most important thing we do, but in a strictly evolutionary sense it is the only thing we do. Much of the waking activity of a child can be described as play but the aphorism, 'animals do not play because they are young, they are young because they must play' has a good deal of truth in it. Learning new motor skills and coordination is a repetitive, integrated and seemingly happy activity. Our near miraculous ability to manipulate our environment to our advantage –

resulting in an overabundance of food, extreme mobility, and the opportunity to work and create unprecedented wealth – has not been as good for children as it has been for adults. The Aka, who have few maternal resources, invest time in their children: an Aka woman says the best husband is one who is a good father. The more wealthy we are the less time we tend to spend with our children. Today's urban living and the nuclear family deny children the continuous attention they would receive in a preliterate tribe. Geographical mobility removes grandparents and uncles and aunts to distant places. Divorces fragment families further. Altogether there are 9.5 million households with children in the USA where the father is not present, either because of divorce or birth out of wedlock: 60 per cent of these mothers are due support from the child's father, but only 30 per cent receive the full sum awarded and 14 per cent receive nothing.

History, economics, the pressures of urban living, and prejudice have combined to break the links between parents and children and selectively disadvantage poor ethnic minorities. In the USA over 50 per cent of African-American women and 38 per cent of Hispanic women giving birth are unmarried. There is a stronger relationship between juvenile crime and not having a father at home than there is with adverse economic circumstances. There are more young African-American men (25 per cent of those aged 20 to 29) in prison or on parole than are in college: a generation of husbands, brothers and sons is being lost. The one thing we can be certain of is that many of the next generation will also grow up seriously disadvantaged.

Practically no modern parents give their children the continuous, undivided attention a chimpanzee mother gives her offspring for the first few years of life. We no longer carry our children as much as our ancestors did, and mothers rarely share their beds with infants and toddlers. Instead of being watched over by kith and kin, today's child is shuttled from home to day-care, to kindergarten or, when it is older, comes home from school to watch the television, while mother and father are still out earning. We should, indeed, use more of our wealth to improve life for our children.

In a world of equals, many men could do much more for their children, but there is no escaping the fact that nothing can substitute for the time mothers and their children spend together, particularly in early life. Women deserve equality in the workplace, but children deserve to grow up in a caring society that makes it easier for women to be at home for the brief but critical years when preschool children, through play, cuddles, adventure and attention are perfecting their unique primate skills. As family size gradually falls in many parts of the world, women concentrate childbearing increasingly into two or three years of adult life. Women live longer than men but in some countries are encouraged to retire earlier. A concerned and rational society could develop mechanisms where women took time off work to be with infants and toddlers without losing seniority in their jobs.

As children grow older they need more time with their peers. Through specialized teachers and facilities, the modern world can impart skills of which our ancestors never dreamed. Education outside the family is a good example of a function that is biologically 'unnatural', but which, nevertheless, is one of the foundations of modern living. Where many nations fall down is in their reluctance to pay for the quality of education that the next generation needs and deserves. Paradoxically, it is another Darwinian trait that has been partly responsible for these sad and destructive trends. We may be a social animal, but we are still more concerned about our kith and kin than the children of others, which is surely the reason why we are reluctant to pay the taxes needed to alleviate poverty and poor housing, or provide adequate child care and good education for others. Yet in modern society, with ever-increasing specialization in its industry and services and ever more complex interlinkages at home and around the world, we are more and more dependent on the successful parenting of all children, not just our blood relatives.

8 THE CIVILIZATION OF SEX

'Some races increase and others are reduced, and in a short while the generations of living creatures are changed and like runners relay the torch of life.' Titus Lucretius, *De Rerum Natura* [On the Nature of Things], 1st century BC

At one level, the complexities of the modern world seem so far removed from the hunter–gatherer world in which *Homo sapiens* evolved that it is easy to dismiss the insights of evolutionary biology as largely irrelevant to life today. Yet at another level, the more insight we gain into our own evolution – and it is sex that has been the powerhouse of that evolution – the better we can understand our history, and the more realistically we are able to confront some of today's major problems. As emphasized previously, more than nine-tenths of the life of *Homo sapiens* on this planet has been spent in small hunter–gatherer communities. The development of settled agriculture just over 10000 years ago and the frenzied changes we have made in the past 200 years of human history have taken place so rapidly that they have had no time to have an impact on our genetic propensities for language, solving problems, making war or making love. In Chapters 9 to 12 we will look at these issues in relation to domestic violence, the dual standard of sexual morality that remains so pervasive around the world, the catastrophic spread of AIDS, and the explosion of the world's population. Here we want to explore how evolution has given us the building blocks of civilized living.

The origin of language

Speech is the most remarkable achievement of our species. For language to evolve we needed to develop a versatile voice box and a big brain. As we saw earlier, we seem to be 'hard-wired' to learn a language from infancy. But it takes many neurones to code and manipulate so much information, and a big brain is an expensive organ to evolve. At birth the baby's brain uses fully 60 per cent of the energy the mother makes available in the milk and even as adults, although our brains make up only one-fiftieth of the body weight, they consume one-fifth of the energy we use. In order to use our mouth and nasal passages to form sounds like an organ pipe, our larynx is higher up the neck than in apes. (The design of the larynx can be inferred from a tiny part of our skeleton called the hyoid bone, and evidence from Neanderthal fossils suggests that they also could talk to one another.) But the change in the voice box to produce speech is an evolutionary step that comes at a certain cost. Placing the larynx so high places us at risk of choking. Nearly every one of us has experienced the fear of choking at least once in our life, and old people sometimes die from pneumonia brought on as a result of food falling down the trachea and causing an obstruction of part of the lungs. When and why did this costly ability to speak evolve?

The answer lies in our pattern of reproduction. Like chimpanzees, we make relationships, have sex, become pregnant and bring up children inside a social group. As a general rule, for any animal a large social group has a number of advantages. In a community, defence against predators is easy: there are more pairs of eyes to watch for danger, and more teeth and claws to deter attack. But the larger the group the harder it is to find sufficient food. While a large group may offer advantages, it also forces competition with other members of the same species. Group size, like many other aspects of evolution, is the outcome of a subtle balance between opposing pressures.

One of the apparently odd things monkeys and apes do is to spend an inordinate amount of time grooming one another. Primates literally scratch one another's back for up to 20 per cent of their waking hours. This is more time than it takes to pick the nits out of a friend's fur, and ethologists have long recognized that grooming is also an essential social adhesive holding the group together. But grooming is not random. An adult male chimpanzee who spends a great deal of time grooming a particular female is more likely to mate with her than with a less familiar partner. A little vervet monkey that grooms a friend is likely to side with that individual if a fight develops in the troop. Grooming can be used as an act of reconciliation. Frans de Waal has pointed out that, after a bared-tooth screaming match, chimpanzees often turn, almost immediately, to grooming one another with great intensity. Finally, as we will see later, grooming seems to have evolved to help deter the freeloaders.

As human beings, we are unusually large animals and we live in unusually large and complex social groups. As early hominid groups expanded, so they began to outgrow the capacity of grooming to help to preserve the social order. If you tried to groom relatives and friends, and to reconcile antagonists in a very large group, then you would be scratching someone's back all day and all night. The Blind Watchmaker of random mutation had to come up with a alternative. Robin Dunbar of the University of Liverpool suggests that language fits the bill. You can groom only one person at a time, but you can talk to several. You must sit or lie down to groom, but you can walk about and do other tasks while talking. Meals are sometimes an occasion when conversation is most interesting. In Spanish, their word for 'gossip' translates as 'inconsequential talk', and in reality gossip seems to be a primary use of speech. Human conversations are rarely about relativity, or even about the stock exchange, but they involve gossip about other people, their foibles, their liaisons, their deceptions and how they relate to one another and to us. Speech, however trivial, dissipates loneliness, even if you are not part of the conversation, and it also reminds us of the pain of isolation.

If, as Dunbar suggests, language is the social glue replacing grooming, then we must also recognize that it has some limitations. Think how a conversation with eight people at a meal usually breaks into two talkative groups.

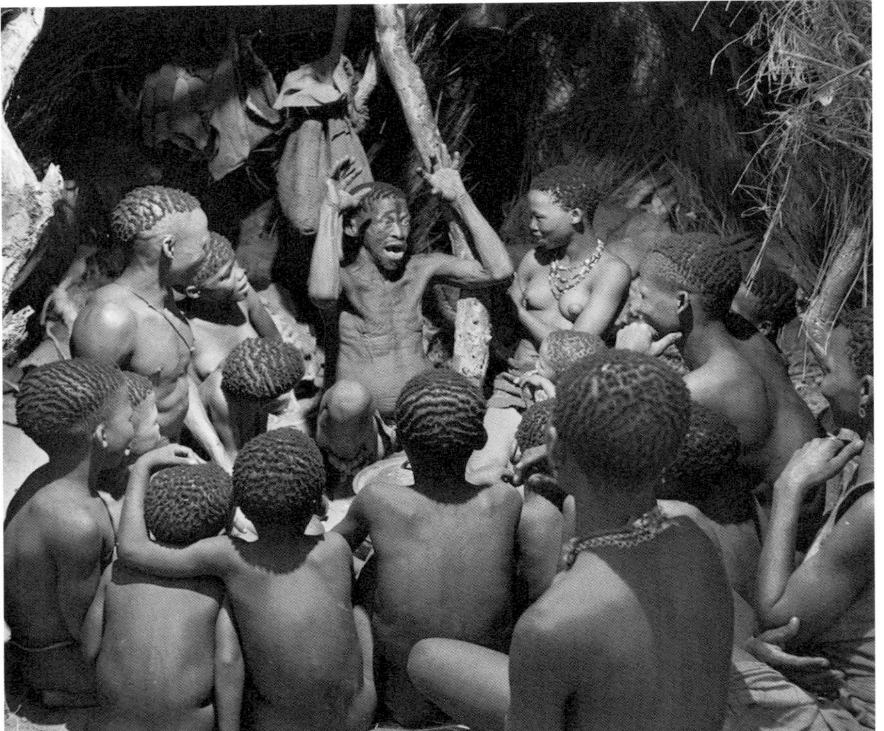

Grooming with words. A Bechuanan storyteller holds the group spellbound.

[M. R. Farbman / Katz Pictures Limited.]

The power of the spoken word. 'In human beings, exogenetic heredity – the transfer of information through non-genetic channels – has become more important for our biological success than anything programmed in DNA.'

Sir Peter Medawar,
In *Technology and the Frontiers of Knowledge*, 1975

It is language and learning that have enabled us to transmit knowledge from generation to generation independently of DNA.

If language is to be used to bind more than three or four people together then it needs to be combined with singing and dancing. Conversely, when two people want to be very close - whether a mother cuddling her child, or lovers caressing one another – then they revert to the more basic primate behaviour of touching one another. Like many ideas related to the evolution of human behaviour, Dunbar's speculation is impossible to prove, and alternative scenarios could be suggested. The important thing is that evolutionary theory can suggest plausible explanations for the origin of language: it is neither perpetually mysterious, nor an arbitrary creation, but in one way or another language increases our ability to survive and pass on our genes.

[A. Eisenstadt / Katz Pictures Limited.]

To some extent, the development of a child's mind as it struggles to understand the world, may recapitulate our own evolution as a species. In the first couple of years, an infant slowly works out that things fall to the ground, that sticks bend, and that cups spill over. It learns to distinguish between animate and inanimate objects, as do other mammals. It may pretend a doll is alive – but then most adults hold a doll the right way up, as if a little bit of our mind suspects that it may be alive. A child under 3 years sees the world at one level, as most animals do: you cry and someone picks you up. Older children, and some primates and whales and dolphins, think at a second level and work out the fact that other individuals are thinking creatures that can be manipulated. Children between the ages of 3 and 4 discover that other children and other adults want things and that they can be jealous. This is the age at which children learn to tell lies.

It is much more difficult to work out the rules governing the social world than those ruling the physical world. Most animals never get that far, but chimpanzees do. They deceive and manipulate one another and, whatever the intellectual capacity of our common ancestor compared with the chimpanzees, it must have travelled some way along the road of understanding the intentions of others. This noisy, social animal, had already accumulated a remarkably powerful combination of attributes: a vocal capacity to communicate simple information, a brain capable of working out what rivals and friends might be thinking, and the beginnings of a language structure.

The evolution of language probably reinforced other patterns of change. An external language to share with others can also be used as a silent, internal language, which we use to talk to ourselves to work out options, and to think through other people's patterns of behaviour. Indeed, it is difficult to comprehend how other big-brained animals analyse the world around them without using some sort of internal language. Does each chimpanzee or sperm whale develop a unique individual set of symbols inside its brain? Did the need for an internal, analytical language help to drive the remarkably rapid evolution of external speech?

Group size

Among primates (and also dolphins) which live in social groups, individuals recognize one another through their different appearance and variety of calls. Most primate societies are built around some sort of hierarchy, and it is very much in each individual's interest to track what his or her friends, relations and rivals are up to. It is a skill learnt in childhood and maintained throughout life. Moreover, we need to know not only how others relate to us, but how other individuals relate to one another. It follows that if the group becomes twice as large, then there are many more possible social relationships in the group and an individual needs much more brain power to compute what is going on.

Dunbar, whose speculations on language we have just met, also pointed out that there is a close correlation between the size of the social group in which primates live and the size of their brains – or more specifically, the area of the neocortex, the highly folded outer layer of brain only a fraction of an inch deep but packed with neurones. By working backwards and measuring the size of the human neocortex and comparing it with that of our primate cousins, Dunbar suggested that the average size of the human group in which we evolved was about 150 individuals. A clan of this size would have consisted of twenty to thirty families, many of them blood relations. It is a number that makes a good deal of intuitive sense.

It is part of the wonderful flexibility of the human animal that we make social groups of about the same size today, but not necessarily involving our close kin. One hundred and fifty is about the number of relatives and friends to whom a social person might send Christmas cards. It is the number of people who come to a wedding or a funeral. It is the size when a social unit, such as a church congregation or an Internet user group, tends to split into two. It is the size at which a business or professional group ceases to be run on handshakes and has to impose bureaucratic procedures, including forms, evaluations, and the rubber stamps of authority. One hundred and fifty is the number of friends and acquaintances we gossip about. It is the number of soap opera stars, television announcers and other media personalities we might be able to name. From the Roman army to a Battle of Britain fighter squadron, the upper limit of a close-knit fighting unit was about 150 people.

A plausible reconstruction of some aspects of the daily life of those small groups of about 150 human beings living a hundred thousand years ago can be attempted. Undoubtedly, individuals spent endless hours in each other's company. Everybody knew everybody else's business. We can be certain there was endless gossip. Occasionally, several small groups of hunter–gatherers would meet in larger gatherings. New sexual partnerships would have been established at this time, particularly as women reached sexual maturity and began to leave their birth-group to join men from other clans. Many small groups may have been strongly xenophobic: the tendency to form 'in-groups' and 'out-groups' is clear in chimpanzees and all too visible in human affairs. Raids on rival groups and small scale killings would be common. One hundred and fifty was probably the size of group in which children were socialized, learnt to speak and developed life's goals. Infants were never alone for more than a few moments at a time. Children grew up with relatively few friends of their own age group, but with a great deal of interaction with other children of different ages and with adults. In such a social world there was no room for any division of labour, and nothing to suggest change would ever be possible.

Suppose some time machine could transport us back in time to join a palaeolithic clan of *Homo sapiens* 20 000 years ago, and by some magic we could both speak their language and carry with us our individual knowledge of today's world. We might describe a steel knife to our new Ice Age friends, but we would be unable to find the iron ore, and unlikely to be able to make a fire hot enough to smelt it. There would be little or no useful knowledge a single person dropped into their world could give them. The cereals and fruits we enjoy in today's world would be represented by wizened, bitter, wild ancestors. We would be unable to use whatever tiny fragment of contemporary knowledge we had brought with us. Yet, if we were patient and worked hard, we might learn from our Old Stone Age ancestors how to knap a flint knife to scrape meat from a bone or clean animal skin. We might draw a picture of our world, but they would have to show us how to prepare the paints.

For civilization to take off, we had to begin to live in larger groups and to develop some division of labour. Even then change was imperceptibly slow. We all depend on others to teach us skills, and none of us has even a tiny fraction of the knowledge needed to make modern society function. Society functions because there is a critical mass of people to permit the division of labour, and that is one of our most precious social inventions.

Deadly skirmishes

Chimpanzees and human beings have one dramatic behaviour in common: members of one social group, or troop, will seek out and kill members of a neighbouring troop. It is a behaviour that separates us from all other mammalian species. Perhaps it is not an accident that we use the same word, 'troop', for human soldiers and to describe a group of chimpanzees. Like the use of tools, warfare among chimpanzees was first observed by Jane Goodall and her colleagues in Gombe National Park, Tanzania.

Many species of mammal will fight to defend or to extend a territory on which their survival depends. Among animals that live in herds or in social groups, individuals will sometimes fight among themselves. Male

The people who forgot how to light a fire

About 12 000 years ago the sea level rose and separated the island of Tasmania from the mainland of southern Australia. It is thought that Tasmania could support about 5000 hunter–gatherers. When the Europeans first reached Tasmania in the early nineteenth century, they found a group of Aborigines who were unable to make a fire, and who had no boomerangs, or fine stone tools like the people on the mainland. Their 'boats', made of bundles of reeds, became waterlogged and sank in a few hours, and they were astonished at the idea that anyone might catch and eat fish. The Tasmanians had brains as big as ours, and they could interbreed with us, yet, literally, they did not know how to rub two sticks together to make a fire.

Archaeological excavation shows that 7000 years ago these same people used a range of well-made tools, ate fish in abundance and probably knew how to start a fire. What happened? Not only are small groups of people unlikely to come up with new inventions, they can lose skills that we take for granted. A small population would fluctuate, due to the harsh climate or unusually vicious cycles of fighting. At some moment in the past few hundred generations, those who knew how to make a boomerang or start a fire simply died before they could pass on the skill.

Each clan kept a fire burning, but if it went out they had to eat uncooked meat and suffer the cold until they could replenish the flame. No individual reinvented fire, but the convention existed that every human group must share its fire with any group that needed it, even if they were bitter enemies who might have tried to kill one another the previous day.

The clash between the Tasmanians, who had the simplest material cultures known, and the Europeans, who had the most cruel, was particularly horrible. The English began bringing convicts to Tasmania in 1802 and some prisoners were still serving life sentences until the 1880s. Some brutalized convicts escaped, and shot or raped the natives. Free men, such as sealers, were no better, and one Tasmanian woman who tried to run away from her white captors had her ears cut off and was made to eat them. The Europeans thought 'there was no more harm in shooting a native, than in shooting a dog', and proclaimed 'it was preposterous to suppose they had souls.' Soldiers and constables shot whole tribes. A £5 bounty was paid for a dead adult, and £2 for a child.

In 1830, when the number of Aborigines had been reduced from 5000 to 2000, the lieutenant-governor, Sir George Arthur, decided to drive the natives across the island in front of a line of 2200 men, with 1000 guns and 30 000 rounds of ammunition. For seven weeks the English line marched across the country with the intention of corralling the natives on a tiny part of the island. The huge effort failed and only two men and a small boy were captured. The rest slipped through the lines, or died. In 1835, an Anglican missionary, George Augustus Robinson, who learnt some of the native languages, persuaded the last 150 Tasmanians to move to a small offshore island. In 1843, fifty-four were still alive, and in 1855 three men, two boys and eleven women survived.

One woman, named Trucannini, whose husband-to-be had had his hands cut off by two convicts, was raped and given gonorrhoea; she lived until 1876. Like many hunter–gatherers she was small in stature, being only 4 foot 3 inches (130 centimetres) tall.

chimpanzees compete for sex and status in their own group, and they very occasionally kill another member of the troop. Warfare, however, is very different from murder. In a war, individuals are killed simply because they belong to an alien group. Chimpanzee social structure, as has been emphasized previously, is built around a group of related males, who defend a territory they recognize as their own. The unique and bloody common characteristic of the chimpanzee *Pan troglodytes* and *Homo sapiens* is a propensity for a close knit group of mature males to drop what they are doing, venture stealthily and deliberately into the territory of a neighbouring group, seek out one or more individuals they can outnumber, and then beat the living daylights out of them. This behaviour has not been found in any other animal, and it has all the attributes of a war.

Sometimes, the warring chimpanzees attack individuals they have never met. Sometimes, a sort of 'civil war' develops, when a large troop (where each individual is well known to every other) splits, and then hostility arises as the two groups become fully separated. Under these circumstances, animals with a memory of one another may end up killing each other. As Richard Wrangham writes about warfare among two troops of Gombe chimpanzees who parted company a few years earlier,

> *It was hard for the researchers to reconcile these [raids] with the opposite but equally accurate observations of adult males sharing friendship and generosity and fun. We found ourselves surprised, fascinated, and angry as the number of cases mounted. How could they kill their former friends like that?*

War-like raids evolved in chimpanzees and humans because we have certain capacities and because, ultimately, such behaviour is to the advantage of the individual. A chimpanzee troop must control an area of forest large enough to feed the males, the mature females who usually migrate to join the troop, and their offspring. If chimpanzees destroy a neighbouring troop, then they can increase their access to resources by moving into the area of forest that the defeated group once held. Ultimately, more offspring can survive and more of the male genes will be passed to the next generation. It should not be assumed that chimpanzees – or human beings – sit and work through the consequences of their actions, or understand that such warfare is to their biological advantage. Nevertheless, from an evolutionary perspective it is a strategy that makes perfect sense. Maybe warfare has evolved only in species that recognize cooperation and develop simple communications. Attackers must know one another, act as a team and outnumber their enemy.

Chimpanzee warfare is brief, but if repeated often it can alter the balance of power in a forest environment. The first Gombe raid leading to the death of an adult male was observed in January 1974. It was another seven weeks before a second attack left an adult male mortally wounded. A year later there was a third killing. By 1977, one adolescent and six adult males had been killed in this sort of warfare. Some of the females of the defeated troop were also attacked, and at least one killed. Eventually, one troop was annihilated and one was victorious. The conquering troop expanded its territory and to some extent increased the potential of its children to survive. In the Gombe case, intermittent fighting went on for four years, and the payoff – if any – in improved reproductive performance may not have manifested itself for a good many more years. Human wars also often go on for long periods and the pay-off is not always immediately apparent.

The predisposition for warfare seems to comprise many of the same essentials in both human beings and chimpanzees. As human social groups have grown in numbers, however, so wars have also grown bigger and technology has become more lethal. It is moderately difficult for a group of chimpanzees to kill another individual with their teeth, bare hands and bare feet. The skirmishes observed by primatologists usually end in the injury of those attacked and, if death does occur, it tends to take place some days later, as a result of infected wounds, loss of blood and internal injuries. Chimpanzees will wave branches to frighten enemies and occasionally throw missiles at one another, but only human beings have come up with easy ways of killing their enemies immediately and in large numbers. Spears, pikes,

Jungle warfare

It began as a border patrol. At one point they [the Kasekela troop of chimpanzees in Gombe National Park] *sat still on a ridge, staring down into Kahama Valley for more than three quarters of an hour, until they spotted Goliath* [an old member of the Kahama troop], *apparently hiding only twenty-five meters away. The raiders rushed madly down the slope to their target. While Goliath screamed and the patrol hooted and displayed, he was held and beaten and kicked and lifted and dropped and bitten and jumped on. At first he tried to protect his head, but soon he gave up and lay stretched out and still. His aggressors showed their excitement in a continuous barrage of hooting and drumming and charging and branch waving and screaming. They kept up the attack for eighteen minutes, then turned for home, still energized, running and screaming and banging on tree-root buttresses. Bleeding freely from his head, gashed on his back, Goliath tried to sit up but fell back shivering. He was never seen again.*

R. Wrangham and D. Peterson, *Demonic Males: Apes and the Origins of Human Violence*, 1996 daggers and swords make killing easier, and bows, muskets, cannons, bombs and missiles make killing at a distance virtually certain.

Preliterate societies vary in their warrior traditions as a result of ecology and cultural traditions. The American Indians were hunter–gatherers and, like many similar groups around the world and throughout history, they fought their neighbours. The Mojave Indians of Southern California formed war parties of ten to fifty men, led by *kwanamis* or 'braves'. Each brave went to war carrying a bow and a club, and was naked except for a loincloth and sandals. Their arrows could kill at 10 yards and injure at 55 (about 10 and 50 metres, respectively). Scouts would reconnoitre enemy country, and the warriors would advance secretly, in order to surprise their enemy. Battles might last from a couple of hours to two days, and braves competed for the honour of killing the first enemy man. Scalps were carried home, after which the men sang and the women danced, mimicking the actions of warriors. It is difficult to estimate the population of Californian Indians before they were exposed to European diseases, but it probably did not exceed 250 000 and the Mojave may have numbered 5000. A raiding party might lose seven or eight warriors, and if fifteen out of fifty died it was indeed a disaster. Relative to the size of the population these were high losses.

The Yanomamo live in the forests that straddle the borders of Venezuela and northern Brazil, and the have been intensively studied by the anthropologist Napoleon Chagnon. The Yanomamo grow fruits and vegetables and hunt in the forests, and they live in villages of 100 to 300 inhabitants. They describe themselves as *waiteri*, or 'fierce people', and there is almost continuous hostility between villages. Fights are commonly said to break out over women. Fighting is usually over in a day, and always on a small scale. Some disputes are settled by ritual chest-slapping contests, or by teams of men who try to break one another's heads open with long poles. On other occasions, a party of ten to twenty men will leave the security of their own village, tramp through the forest and surprise their enemy. They may be so far from home that they need to camp at night and then attack at dawn. If they can find a man out alone, they will shoot him with poisoned arrows, and leave. If they are outnumbered they will fire arrows into the village, and disappear into the forest. If they capture a woman, the raiding party will rape her and take her back to their village, where the men who stayed at home also rape her, before she is given to one man as his wife. Of course, attacks of this type inevitably lead to retaliations. One way the Yanomamo take revenge on an enemy is to invite the whole of the other clan to a feast, and then kill the men and capture the women.

Language and warfare may interact in an interesting way. In preliterate societies, languages change and split into new dialects rapidly. There are 6000 to 7000 recognizable languages in the world, and half are in the island of Papua New Guinea. The hunter–gatherer Indians who lived in California before the Europeans came spoke 250 dialects, many of them unintelligible to one another. Like a banner carried into battle, speech identifies a group. One role of a dialect may have been to solidify a fighting group and identify aliens. Sinn Fein, the political wing of the IRA, use a knowledge of the Irish language, Gaelic, to pass information that guards and those outside the group will not understand, to build solidarity, and to exclude spies. If you cannot answer questions in Gaelic you are not one of us. IRA men in prison spend time learning Irish from a Dublin television channel called Teilifís na Gaeilge. In 1937 many thousands of Haitian sugar cane workers were massacred in the Dominican Republic. As the killings took place the Haitians were asked to say the Spanish word for parsley (*perejil*) and those whose pronunciation faltered were slaughtered.

Total war

In this book, we have used the word predisposition to describe behaviours that evolution has selected over the eons. Exactly how a mutation in our DNA is translated into a behaviour is not well understood. It is self-evident that neither people nor chimpanzees are mechanistic automatons, controlled purely by their genes. But it is equally obvious that there are some common threads in human behaviour, and in the case of warfare these threads are fairly near the surface, and very largely male. Many men get an almost visceral pleasure out of collecting and handling weapons. Numbers of young boys greatly exceed those of young girls in playing the more violent games in amusement arcades. Warships, warplanes and other weapons are regarded as female, unpredictable but seductive. In World War I, guns were given female names, such as Big Bertha and, in World War II, bombers were given names such as Tokyo Rose, Memphis Belle and Enola Gay and decorated with lurid pin-ups, but it was men who did the flying and the killing.

In addition to the two basic principles of surprise and outnumbering your foe, revenge is certainly a powerful element in many human wars, and it could be also in fighting between chimpanzees. Tit-for-tat killings remain a characteristic of modern warfare. Early in World War I, the Kaiser ordered the zeppelins to restrict their bombs to military targets. But the bombs were difficult to aim and inevitably civilians were killed. Reprisal raids were made by British aeroplanes against Germany. Retaliation led to retaliation; 'An eye for an eye and a tooth for a tooth is the only way we can treat the enemy', wrote the Cologne newspaper *Kolnische Zeitung*. World War II also opened with a commitment to limit bombing to military targets. Prior to this war, President Franklin D. Roosevelt called for no 'bombardment from the air of civilian populations'. Early in the war itself, the British Royal Air Force (RAF) lost twelve out of twenty-two bombers in one raid against German battleships, but even so the pilots were ordered to avoid dropping bombs on ships moored by a dock, in case they killed civilians. In the Battle of Britain in 1940, Hitler forbade the Luftwaffe to bomb London, and when the first bombs were dropped on civilian populations by mistake, the pilots were reprimanded. The British, however, had no way of knowing this and Winston Churchill ordered the bombing of Berlin. In three years the world went from a few accidental civilian deaths to the carpet bombing of cities in which 60 000 British and 300 000 Germans died. Yet the men who did the killing showed the greatest courage and, themselves, suffered appalling casualties. Over 47 000 RAF aircrew died over Germany. Only a quarter of the young men who flew in the American Eighth Air Force survived their twenty-five missions. In a strange way, a mixture of loyalty to fellow crew members and technological wizardry sometimes attenuated the actual desire to kill. 'I enjoyed map-reading', said one RAF crew member, 'and bomb-aiming was always an interesting challenge, though often I felt sorry for what happened below.'

The fire bombing and atomic attacks on Japan killed even more people than died in Europe. Fear, revenge, and the application of science and engineering drove a modern Armageddon. A Gallup poll conducted five days after the first atomic bomb fell on Hiroshima found that 85 per cent of Americans supported the attack. Five days after the Hiroshima bomb, and before the surrender of Japan, Dr Michihiko Hachiya was tending those whose skin had been burnt off and eyes liquefied by the flash, and those whose bones had been broken by the blast. A rumour began to spread among the injured that the Japanese had developed a similar weapon, but they had judged it too horrible to use until the Allies had dropped their weapon. Then, the rumour went, suicide pilots had flown across the Pacific in secret six-engined bombers and obliterated San Francisco, San Diego and Los Angeles with atomic weapons.

> *The whole atmosphere of the [hospital] ward changed, and for the first time since Hiroshima was bombed, everyone became cheerful and bright. Those who had been hurt most were the happiest. Jokes were made, and some began singing the victory song. Prayers were said for the soldiers. Everyone was now convinced the tide of war had turned.*

Chimpanzee males establish close alliances and may seek to revenge the loss of a friend. Both chimpanzee and human wars are primarily an activity of mature males at the fittest time of their life. Chimpanzee war parties commonly involve genetically related individuals who recognize each other because they have grown up together. Human troops are rarely genetically related, but basic training for the armed forces is explicitly designed as an intensely emotional experience to weld men into a single unit, each loyal to the others. Whatever the recruiting posters may say, men do not fight for 'King and Country', but they fight for their friends, as do chimpanzees.

The small groups of American Indians who fought for a few hours have been replaced by millions of men fighting for years at a time. But the basic fighting unit has changed much less: ten or twenty men in a platoon in a trench, five to ten men as the crew of a heavy bomber in World War II, or in the turret of battleship, and perhaps fifty to work a submarine. A psychiatrist writing about US bomber crews in World War II concluded:

> *So close are the men to each other, so bound together by a common purpose and common fate, that one individual's combat career cannot come to a different conclusion from that of his comrades without pain. This leads to innumerable situations where a man must choose between a hero's death, without in the least desiring to be a hero, or life in the future with a bad conscience and constant feeling of depression and guilt. If he chooses the first course of action, he may receive a posthumous decoration and a place of honor in that section of paradise reserved for airmen, but the act will have been due to the impossibility of leaving his friends or letting them down.*

An RAF bomber pilot wrote,

> *We were three to a crew, twelve crews to a squadron, and our lives depended upon one another. We reached out to one another for strength and support: when one was low, we tried to boost him up. I remember seeing many of them vomiting before getting into the aircraft – a sure sign of physical and mental exhaustion.*

If chimpanzees could read, they would probably identify with such statements: they can, for example, be literally sick with fear, vomiting up food when afraid.

Throughout history, leaders have exploited the human predisposition to

'Futbol' in Papua New Guinea

These football 'games' were not mere sport but a substitute for feuding, hina, *the forceful retaliation for injuries that disrupted the relationships of friendly tribes. Feuds were instigated by acts of adultery, by the theft of pigs, or by homicide, and unlike warfare,* rova, *the interminable hostility associated with enemy groups, the fighting ended when the injured party had redressed the wrong. Under the government-imposed peace feuding was proscribed, but groups that had been injured frequently issued a challenge to 'futbol', meeting their opponents in a contest that adhered to the traditional rules of redress... The game invariably degenerated into something closer to a hand-to-hand combat than organized competition, yet eventually the ideal was upheld. The contest ended when the elders of both groups, watching its progress from the sidelines, decided that the scores were even, and, honour satisfied, the challengers left the field.*

K. E. Read, *The High Valley*, 1966

fall into 'in-groups' and 'out-groups', and to engage in warfare. The patriot inflates the loyalties of the 'in-group'. Joseph Holper, a student at the University of Northern Illinois, compared the words and phrases used by US statesman Alexander Hamilton and James Madison in their private papers and when writing in *The Federalist*. *The Federalist Papers* were published in 1787 and 1788 to secure support for ratification of the US Constitution. Approval seemed particularly unlikely in New York State and it was the publication of *The Federalist Papers*, more than any other event, which changed public opinion. Holper found these two politicians were ten times as likely to use 'father', 'brother', 'mother' and other kinship terms in *The Federalist*, than when writing about private or business matters. Abraham Lincoln's Gettysburg address begins 'Four score and seven year ago our *fathers* brought forth on this continent a new nation (our italics).' Hitler used the term fatherland to great rhetorical effect.

Female chimpanzees may sometimes go along with a raiding party. Women have played a vital role in many wars, but primarily as supporters, not in the firing lines. Among the Mojave, women sometimes accompanied the men, although they did not take any direct part in the fray. Rosie the Riveter was both a symbol and a reality in the Allied war effort in World War II. Women were mobilized more slowly in Germany, where Hitler emphasized Kinder, Kirche, and Kuche (children, church and kitchen). At the height of the aerial bombardment of Germany, one wartime Nazi newspaper found time for invective against women who wore trousers on air raid duty. Recent US efforts to integrate women with men into front line units has resulted in a series of debacles and charges of sexual harassment, threats of life imprisonment for drill sergeants and resignations by senior officers.

The twentieth century has seen tens of millions of people die in two world wars and hundreds of other conflicts. In the World War II, out of sixteen million US men in uniform, 300 000 were killed in combat – a death rate of 2 per cent for fighting men, or of fewer than 1 per cent of all adult men in the country. Germany saw a third of her armed forces killed. Russia suffered most of all in what is still called the Great Patriotic War, and saw half its armed forces killed; perhaps 10 per cent of the total population of the nation died in that war. But even these horrific rates are lower than the 30 per cent death rate from fighting estimated among adult male chimpanzees in Tanzania and among Yanomamo men in Venezuela.

Cultural development

Over nearly four billion years the transmission of genetic information led to the evolution of our bodies and our big brains. Most of our cultural endowment has accumulated in a few thousand years, and much of it in the lifetime of people now living. More than half the scientists that have ever lived are alive today.

Today, our technical achievements are so staggering that they appear to overwhelm everything else and it seems preposterous, even perverted, to suggest that the brain that first circumnavigated the globe, understood chemical reactions, or wrote musical symphonies, evolved in the first place for the purpose of competing sexually. Yet, when we look back over history and prehistory it is humbling to recall with what painful slowness we have acquired our present supremacy. It took tens, or even hundreds, of thousands of years for one type of flint tool to replace another, while today we can create a computer industry with the capacity to double the power and halve the price of its product every three to five years. Technologies as stupendously expensive and original as that used to make the first atomic bomb in the 1940s have become something any oil-rich dictator might buy in a decade, if he chose to organize a group of technocrats to work together.

The history of technology is not that of an analytical animal perfecting one technology after another with objective logic. It is the record of a sexy ape using his or her big brain, evolved for sexual competition, in an unfamiliar field. After innumerable false starts, and a great deal of pain, technology and science have triumphed. There is not a shred of evidence that we are any more intelligent than our ancestors, or that we have evolved to act in any different ways: we are the same animal, but our technology has changed. Why? It has been a growth in human numbers, and the opportunity for a division of labour that has made this revolution possible. Small numbers of people, living in very small bands, did not come up with many inventions. When they did invent something better, the idea spread relatively quickly. For example, when the Magdalenian hunter–gatherers who lived in southern Europe 15 000 years ago perfected a fully barbed harpoon, it was soon adopted across the culture.

Given a critical mass of people, a division of labour and the transmission of experience first through language and later through writing, human ingenuity feeds on itself in an accelerating spiral of technical achievements. As we have emphasized many times in this book, society today has much to learn from preliterate cultures. In their human relationships such societies are no less rich than our own, and they may well do some things more effectively or more harmoniously than we do. Nevertheless, as a result of the great power of a well developed technology, less sophisticated technologies are easily overwhelmed – along with the culture in which such technologies were embedded. There seem to be no exceptions. It is, for example, easy to romanticize about the Inuit hunting bowhead whales in the Arctic wastes, but once a preliterate society has rifles, outboard motor boats, powdered milk and penicillin, then the culture that once held it together begins to dissolve, and it can survive only as a virtual image. It is unlikely that any significant preliterate culture has not been in contact with the modern world. The records of anthropologists, and especially the insights of anthropologists with an evolutionary perspective, will be analysed and reanalysed by future generations, but as cultures disappear little new knowledge will be added to anthropology.

The acceleration of technical innovation so characteristic of our world is a recent and remarkable thing. If we repeat the thought experiment of a machine that carries us back in time, together with the knowledge we have of today's world, and if we go back fifty years instead of 50 000 years, then the results would be profoundly different. While a Nobel Prize winner might be helpless in an Ice Age world, many a schoolchild with a basic knowledge of the structure of DNA could win a Nobel prize if transported back a few decades.

The technology boomerang

The boomerang is an example of one of the most sophisticated technologies discovered by prehistoric people. Most boomerangs are really aerodynamic throwing sticks and they are known from many parts of the world, but one group of Australian aborigines developed a curved throwing stick with asymmetrical surfaces that returns to the thrower. It was this invention that has become the metaphor for a technology that returns to hurt the person who devised it. In the past century the explosion of human numbers, our boomerang technology, and an extraordinary growth in economic affairs has begun to change the face of the planet. Long before the scientific or industrial revolution, however, human beings began changing their environment in a way no other animal had ever done. Even hunter–gatherers, living in small groups, were able to spread across the world. Small, nomadic bands, for example, reached Australia about 60 000 years ago. They found a parkland browsed by a hippopotamus-sized marsupial called *Diprotodon*, giant kangaroos, wombats and turtles, as well as a variety of flightless birds. Large mammals and flightless birds that have never met human hunters tend to be docile and easy to approach.

In Australia the extermination of the diprotodons changed the landscape, because these great herbivores played an essential role in fertilizing the ground and spreading seeds. When Captain James Cook voyaged to Australia in 1770 he wrote of 'This continent of smoke', because the aborigines spent so much time burning the undergrowth. (They also used fire as a weapon to flush out enemies and cover their retreat.) The extermination of whole groups of herbivorous mammals, the consequent loss of some plants, and the use of fire altered the environment so much that the climate changed: the parkland the first Aborigines found was largely replaced by near desert.

The story is the same everywhere. Paul Martin of the University of Arizona has suggested that when the first hunters entered the Western hemisphere they could have spread from Canada to the Gulf of Mexico in as little as 350 years, and to the tip of South America in 1000 years. The maximum population of people in North America, as the first immigrants hunted the easy-to-kill game, may have been about 600 000. More recently civilizations such as the Minoans, Hittites, Israelites, Phoenicians, Greeks and Romans changed the shores of the Mediterranean. They cut lumber for cooking, to build ships, to slake lime and to smelt metallic ores, for houses, scaffolding and for roofs for stone buildings. Over the centuries they changed wooded slopes with monkey-filled trees into sun-scorched, bare hillsides, grazed by goats. Over the centuries we have appropriated more and more of the plant and plankton food once used by other animals. We need to remind ourselves that where we now see people there once would have been mammalian herbivores and predators, birds, fish and marine animals. In the past there was a profusion and variety to life that is difficult to imagine and that we can never recapture.

A good deal of nonsense has been written about preliterate societies, such as American Indians, living in some sort of spiritual harmony with the land. In reality, the human animal has always exploited and destroyed its environment. Often the destructive phase runs its course in a few centuries. What we see today is an enforced harmony because any other balance of technologies has in the past – or may in the future – prove unsustainable.

The beginning of settled societies

Some hunter–gatherers began to hunt and follow herds of animals. By selection of wolf cubs for their loyalty, the dog became the first animal to be bred for domestication. The Laps of the European tundra still partially follow this way of life. They live among, and migrate with, the wild reindeer that provide their meat, milk, and clothes. They even castrate some male reindeer and use them as draught animals. About 11 000 years ago, a few hunter–gatherer communities began a fully settled way of life. They were able to harvest and store crops, domesticate animals, build permanent villages, and grow in numbers. Small villages developed in the Fertile Crescent stretching from the Tigris and Euphrates valleys in modern Iraq to the shores of the Mediterranean, and on into central Turkey. The people who lived in this area were lucky to find several varieties of grass with big rich seeds, and several species of wild animals (sheep, goats, pigs, cows) that could be corralled, fed, eaten and even harnessed to ploughs and vehicles. By about 8000 years ago barley, wheat and some pulses were being sown and harvested. The most productive of the self-pollinating plants such as wheat or peas were selected by farmers for increased yields. Even today the world feeds itself on about a dozen primary food crops. Early human settlements also occurred along the Indus, Yangtze and Yellow Rivers, and the Nile valley. Settled living also began in Central America and Peru in pre-Columbian times.

Hunter–gatherers also settled in other parts of the world many thousands of years ago, but as physiologist Jared Diamond of the University of California at Los Angeles has pointed out, they found less fortunate combinations of wild plants and animals. In Papua New Guinea they began to cultivate taro but it only has 1 per cent protein compared with 10 per cent or more for some grains exploited in the Middle East's Fertile Crescent, and Papua New Guinea had no wild animals of the size and pattern of behaviour that made them suitable for domestication. It was not lack of inventiveness but lack of opportunity that held back agriculture for so long and which limited its beginnings to so few places.

Domestication of the dog aided the hunter (*opposite*) Bechuanan hunters and dc bring a Kalahari gemsbok to bay.

Where settled agriculture and the growth of villages and small towns

> **Greetings in Papua New Guinea**
>
> *Their customary greeting, a standing embrace in which both men and women fondled each other's genitals, was an unfailing source of sniggering amusement to Europeans; but even in the villages, among people who saw one another every day, hands were continually reaching out to caress a thigh, arms to encircle a waist, and open, searching mouths hung over a child's lips, nuzzled a baby's penis, or closed with a smack on rounded buttocks.*
>
> K. E. Read, *The High Valley*, 1966

did occur, it created totally new opportunities for specialized crafts to develop. Population became more dense, although not always as well nourished as in nomadic hunter–gatherer societies. Hierarchies arose, chiefs gained power until they claimed to be the sons of god. Civilization took off, but at a cost. Settled agriculture led to land ownership and new technologies, such as the plough, that benefited from the greater brawn of the male. The 'immediate return' society of the hunter–gatherer was replaced by one in which wealth could be accumulated and even passed to the next generation. Rich and poor emerged. Societies developed fault lines according to lines of wealth, and now the rich élite could recruit other members of the same group to support the appropriation of resources by the privileged few. Although most of human history has been lived out in a materially egalitarian hunter–gatherer society, once technologies arise that permit wealth to be garnered and to be distributed to kin, then economically stratified societies invariably appear and develop their own internal stability.

New pressures were put on sexual relationships and, as we will see in Chapter 9, men commonly exercise more power over women in an agricultural society than among hunter–gatherer groups. As described in Chapter 10, the domestication of animals introduced new and lethal infections, and large populations enabled diseases to become endemic. Early agriculture in some of the irrigated parts of ancient Iraq collapsed due to over exploitation of the land. Today much land of the Middle East is degraded. Palestine, which the Israelites of the Old Testament entered as a land flowing with milk and honey, is now one of stones and thistles.

A moral society

All human communities have moral rules. Settled societies sometimes engrave their laws in stone, as did the Babylonian King Hammurabi 3800 years ago, or claim, as did the Jews, that God's finger inscribed the tablets of law. Is morality a purely human construct to be analysed by philosophers or, like so much else, are its foundations built on evolved traits that evolutionary biologists can help to untangle, providing useful insights?

The way in which chimpanzees share meat seems to be based on an inherited sense of justice that works to the advantage of each individual member of the species. Chimpanzees do not share fruits (except between mother and child), but fresh meat requires team work both to catch and to kill the other species, and meat rots soon after it is killed. A system where the ape that catches the meat shares it with those who took part in the hunt ensures cooperation in the next hunt, and by distributing what he cannot eat before the meat turns foul the successful chimpanzee enhances his status with his colleagues and rivals at no cost to himself. One way to gain support is to give meat to the most subordinate members of the troop.

Sharing is easy to explain, but what about empathy? Frans de Waal in his book *Good Natured* makes a strong case for the evolution of empathy among other primates. A rhesus monkey at the Wisconsin Primate Center was born with Down's syndrome. The young monkey was groomed and cared for by others in the troop in a kind and gentle way. Can one rhesus monkey trade places mentally with another? It is difficult to say, but apes do seem to have a brain big enough to see the world from another's perspective. Chimpanzees are distressed by hostility between members of the troop, and one individual may sometimes make a real effort to resolve conflicts between others. When animals that have been hostile to one another make up after a quarrel – sometimes they literally kiss one another – then the rest of the group may show signs of happiness.

Morality evolves because it aids individual survival. Male chimpanzees are in competition for access to females, but they still benefit if they resolve conflicts without too much physical aggression, because a cooperative group of males is better able to defend its territory against raiding males of another troop and better able to attack and kill individuals from a rival troop. But we are not chimpanzees, and while our morality may have the same roots, it is more complex and it has been honed by the environment of the hunter–gatherer. As noted, in hunter–gatherer societies there are important differentials in reproductive success, but food is shared, and status is not related to material goods or to public display. There is no money, no land ownership and no physical inheritance worth passing to the next generation, no chiefs and no serfs. Economic stratification of the type found throughout the modern world does not exist. Was it in such a world that human rules of justice and equity evolved?

Andrew Whiten from St Andrews University in Fife, Scotland, and others have suggested that over the millennia when we lived as hunter–gatherers we did indeed evolve behaviours to counter strong social hierarchies and to encourage the sharing of resources in an 'immediate return' economy. Bruce Charlton of the University of Newcastle upon Tyne has gone a step further and speculates that such an evolutionary predisposition could account for the human sense of natural justice and our sense of 'the inequity of inequality'. Much of public health policy, for example, is driven by a striving to reduce socioeconomic differentials in health. It seems to most of us intrinsically 'unfair' that the poor should have a higher mortality than the rich (something which is usually the case). Yet at the same time we establish hierarchies and respect and imitate the clan leaders of the past, or today's captains of industry. There is no reason why evolution should not give us contradictory predispositions if they help to optimize our behaviour in different environments. It follows that, even if we do think it unfair, as long as people use their wealth to improve their health, then differentials in death and illness are likely to persist in any economically stratified society. Attempts by communists to produce a non-economically stratified society not only failed but often produced a highly skewed distribution of resources, without the virtues of a free economy.

It seems plausible, then, that some parts of our moral systems are rooted in evolution, and in particular helped to adapt us to a hunter–gatherer way of life. Several things had to happen together for a moral system to evolve. Altruism can evolve in a social animal only if there is also reciprocity. For example, in the case of a fight for power in the social hierarchy, two individuals will each benefit if each is sure the other will come to his or her aid in a fight: literally, I will mind your back if you will mind mine. Mature females can help one another by sharing child care. The warlike predispositions of chimpanzees depend on team work and reciprocity. But evolution involves individuals, not groups, and it is based on competition between 'selfish genes'. We belong to a group because it is to our individual advantage. Altruism and reciprocity arise because in the end we benefit: there is no such thing as the evolution of a group as whole. Indeed, there is a perpetual pressure in any social animal for individuals to buck the system. The free-rider female who never minds another's child but has others care for her children would have an obvious reproductive advantage. The male chimpanzee who always ran away at the last moment from the inevitable dangers of group attack would be more likely to survive and therefore to pass his genes on to the next generation. For cooperation to work and altruism to survive, evolution has had to build in some counter-strategies based on benefits to the individual.

The cells that make up our bodies and form the astronomically complicated electrical networks of our brains are the result of millions of years of competition between selfish genes, modified by a dose of altruism that has probably been around for almost as long, mixed with a few, more recent, moral behaviours that serve to help us individually by making society more amenable. In 1997, a set of fossilized humanoid footprints were found on a piece of sand 60 miles (96 kilometres) north of modern Cape Town, in South Africa. They were dated to 117 000 years ago. Over that 117 000 years few or no changes have taken place in the human predisposition for sex, parenting, violence, language, music and desire to understand the world around us. What separates us from our forebears, who left those tracks in the sand, is a mindboggling set of opportunities, along with a global set of interlocking problems that our ancestors could never have envisaged – rapid population growth, economic development that is unsustainable in the long run, and competition between groups armed with weapons of mass destruction. Are we any better prepared than they would have been to solve these problems?

9 SEX AND POWER

'And even if [women] bear themselves weary – or ultimately bear themselves out – that does not hurt. Let them die. This is the purpose for which they exist.' Martin Luther, *The Estate of Marriage*, 1552

Suppose some dictator ordered all the males in a country to be killed on one particular day. Some women would be pregnant and half of their babies would be boys. As one man has the potential to father many children, in three or four generations society would be back to normal. If, however, that same dictator had ordered all the females to be killed, the society would have become extinct. The female who carries the pregnancy, breastfeeds and is the primary caregiver for the next generation is also the one who has the last word in setting evolutionary strategies. Women hold most of the biological chips, yet they are often ill treated. Women are battered, mutilated, sequestered and exploited. Why?

Male power

Male chimpanzees are larger than females and sometimes lose their temper with the females, but the females can generally escape their wrath, and bonobos have evolved a way in which females can pair up to prevent males overpowering them. Prolonged antagonism between the sexes or serious injury within a chimpanzee troop is rare. Human females, however, form strong sexual bonds with one male, and the road to monogamy for a previously promiscuous or polygynous species, where the male is larger than the female, faces some special problems. When the cold war that exists between the sexes turns into open conflict it is the woman who often loses.

Several aspects of evolution place women at a disadvantage when it comes to strife between the sexes. In addition to the greater physical strength and size of men, their need for assurance of paternity adds a second level of problems. The promiscuous chimpanzee can never 'know' who are his offspring, so paternity is not a major interest. Recent DNA studies of chimpanzees in the Côte d'Ivoire found that over half of the thirteen offspring of one troop were sired by chimpanzee males from another troop, and the females must have visited males in a neighbouring troop at the time of ovulation without their own troop's knowledge. Among species that establish harems, such as lions or gorillas, securing paternity becomes an overriding goal with a relatively straightforward solution: you fight off rival males. Among human beings, where the man commonly makes an investment in bringing up the next generation, the situation is more complex. Men are faced with the problem of establishing a monogamous (or polygynous) mating pattern, while embedded within a larger social group. In addition, men and women have a predisposition to have sex in private. Not surprisingly, sex outside the primary pair bond is both relatively easy and relatively common, and found in every society. Adultery by males and cuckoldry by females, however, are not symmetrical strategies. If we begin with a purely selfish interest in spreading our own genes, then adultery, where a man may father a child without necessarily making any long term investment in that child, differs from cuckoldry, where a woman conceives a child by another male but deceives the one to whom she is sexually bonded into a long term investment in that pregnancy. There are evolutionary reasons why it is part of the male reproductive agenda to try to assert his paternity, and to devise ways to avoid being made a cuckold. 'Upon the chastity of women all property in the world depends' wrote Dr Samuel Johnson, referring to English inheritance laws. Lord Kilbrandon, an English Law Lord, expressed it succinctly: 'Maternity is a matter of fact, paternity one of mere inference.' It is indeed a wise man who knows his own father. Finally, in most societies, the woman leaves the family into which she was born and joins the family of her sexual partner. In situations of conflict, the man's kin are likely to come to his support, while the women may have no-one to turn to. This happens, for example, in many marriages in contemporary India, where a young bride finds herself dominated by an older husband, his siblings and his parents.

In hunter–gatherer societies with few or no material goods and no land ownership, the relationship between men and women tends to be egalitarian. Men and women are mutually dependent for survival in a harsh desert environment. If violence occurs, the woman can move on: she does not depend solely on her mate for access to resources. Female virginity is not prized and among the San Bushmen divorce is merely a drifting apart in a relationship where affection has cooled. The Mbuti, who form the largest group of pygmy hunter–gatherers in Central Africa, have little division of labour according to sex, and leadership is minimal. Decision-making is by common consent, and all the food that is gathered by the women, or hunted by the men, is cooked communally and distributed in equal portions by the women. Fatherhood is associated with authority, but there is no great inequality between the sexes. In preliterate societies that engage in frequent warfare, however, as in the example of the Yanomamo, given in Chapter 8, then women are sometimes

The top primate

In some ways human sexual behaviour is more difficult to record than that of chimpanzees. We have sex in private and often in the dark. Royalty, film stars and famous politicians are a partial exception. They belong to groups with wealth and influence, and their lives are followed so closely by the public media that few sexual relationships go unnoticed – although there also is a risk of relationships being invented where none really exists.

Sex and a quest for power do indeed seem to go together. A biographer of Benito Mussolini wrote, 'All his life, like a stag in rutting season, he had a constant need to reassert his virility; and he rarely took time to remove his trousers or his shoes'. In the enforced equality of Communist China in the 1960s and 1970s, where everyone wore the same peasant pajamas and no one owned property, Chairman Mao Tse Tung still managed to be more equal than others sexually. According to Harrison Salisbury, 'Mao's quarters swarmed with young women', Mao enjoyed nude water ballets in his swimming pool and 'dancing partners' were at the ready wherever the Great Helmsman went.

Like the Gombe chimps, the sexual behaviour of the British royal family can be tracked over several generations. There is an interesting alternation of chastity and lasciviousness across generations and sometimes between brothers. Victoria and Albert had a passionate, monogamous marriage. As a bride, Victoria wrote to her Prime Minister, Lord Melbourne, about a 'most gratifying and bewildering night' and she confided in her private diary 'we did not sleep very much'. By contrast, Albert's brother had gonorrhoea, Victoria's uncle tried to rape his brother's girlfriend; and her father, Prince Edward, and all her uncles had numerous mistresses and illegitimate children. It was accepted for the times. Lord Melbourne answered Victoria's young idealistic claim that she could never marry a man who had loved another woman with the assertion that any man should be permitted at least one affair before marriage. Victoria's son, King Edward VII, had a number of deeply emotional and long-term relationships such as those with Lillie Langtry and Daisy Warwick, as well as many 'one night stands' when his equerries brought pretty women from the theatre or race course. It was difficult to say 'no' to a king. His beautiful deaf queen, Alexandra, was regally patient with Edward's 'pleasant little wickednesses' and even summoned his last mistress, the discrete but engaging Mrs Alice Keppel, to her husband's death bed. It has been suggested that Edward VII's eldest son, the Duke of Clarence, was Jack the Ripper, and although this is an example of prominent people attracting false and exaggerated tales, the fact that the idea could even be suggested is an insight into his dissolute life. Fortunately for the British monarchy, Clarence died of influenza at the age of 28. His brother, who inherited the throne as King George V, was chaste and naïve. Clarence had been engaged to Mary of Teck and when he died his bride-to-be was passed to his brother George – a practice found in some preliterate societies. It was an arranged marriage that worked, and George later wrote to his wife, Queen Mary:

> *When I asked you to marry me, I was very fond of you, but not very much in love with you, but I saw in*

treated brutally. Wife-beating and infanticide may occur if the paternity of a child is in doubt. Wives are often women captured during tribal wars.

In societies based on settled agriculture, where wealth is concentrated in land and property, then the inequality between the sexes may be heightened. At its most extreme, women may be treated as just one more of the man's chattels. One tendency is for wealthy men to sequester their wives from the rest of society. Women wore the veil when outside their homes in many Islamic communities, including Egypt and Turkey, until the early twentieth century, and the practice still persists today in many parts of the Middle East and Afghanistan. With the recent spread of Muslim fundamentalism, some women have gone back to wearing the *chuddar*, an all-enveloping black garment that completely encases all but the eyes of the woman, when out walking in the street. In Afghanistan in 1997, women were even excluded from hospital care, in order to segregate them from men. Among the Rajput of India, the greater a man's wealth, the more securely his women were locked away. The 'middle classes' kept their wives in walled gardens, while the upper classes locked them in rooms with tiny windows. The very richest women were kept imprisoned at the top of houses, with only slits of windows to the outside world. Under such conditions paternity was very rarely in question.

you the person I was capable of loving most deeply if you only returned that love ... I have tried to understand you and know you, and with the happy result that I know now that I do love *you darling girl with all my heart and I am simply* devoted *to you ...*

The British royal family continued to behave like a mediaeval extended family until very recently. Queen Victoria and Prince Albert determinedly married their children into the other royal houses of Europe. George V's eldest son, King Edward VIII was forbidden to marry the divorced Mrs Wallis Simpson and keep the throne. And the sister of Queen Elizabeth, Princess Margaret, was not allowed to marry Group Captain Townsend, her first love. The move towards a somewhat freer choice of marriage partner permitted to Queen Elizabeth's children has been less successful. Charles still partly belonged to an extended family system and a tradition of socially – but not constitutionally – acceptable polygyny, while the late Princess Diana seems to have come to marriage with a commoner's romantic view of monogamous marriage. Interestingly, Camilla Parker Bowles is a descendant of one of King Edward VII's romantic liaisons.

One television commentator described the Kennedy family, through four generations, 'as being about the horniest bunch that I have ever come across'. Joseph Kennedy, J. F. K.'s father, brought his mistress, film star Gloria Swanson, to meet his wife Rose. Both John and Robert Kennedy had many sexual liaisons and each was rumoured to have slept with Marilyn Monroe. President Kennedy's liaison is authenticated from a number of sources, including Marilyn's very public appearance at the president's forty-fifth birthday celebration in 1962, when she sang *Thanks for the Memories*. According to one White House staff member, 'Many of us felt her appearance at Madison Square Gardens would be like Marilyn making love to the President publicly after doing it in private all these months'. His wife, Jackie Kennedy, did not attend the party. Teddy Kennedy's political career almost ended at Chappaquiddick, and the 1991 accusations of rape against a young member of the Kennedy family at a party in Florida, even though unsubstantiated, reinforced the impression that wealth, power and sex often go together.

Other presidents may have been more discrete in their relationships, but Franklin D. Roosevelt is thought to have had a sexual relationship with Lucy Page (his wife Eleanor's secretary) and with 'Missy' LeHand (his own secretary). Dwight D. Eisenhower loved his wartime driver Kay Summersby – although it is suggested that he may have been incapable of physically consummating the relationship. And today, the Clinton sexual saga of claims and counter-claims continues to unfold.

Is the range of sexual partner change among the rich and famous greater than for 'the man in the street'? There is no way of knowing. What is certain is that human sexual behaviour is highly heterogeneous, varying across generations and between siblings.

Female power

If, as biology suggests, female strategies are critically important to reproductive success, then we need to look at the female side of the power equation a little more thoroughly. Among chimpanzees, research shows that females have their internal power structure, although it took thirty-five years of studying the Gombe chimpanzees for Jane Goodall and her colleagues to unravel the subtleties of female chimpanzee society. Male hierarchies are readily visible. The alpha or dominant male blusters and threatens his noisy way to primacy in the troop. He tears off branches to brandish and thumps the buttress roots of trees in unambiguous displays of power. He also – at least among *Pan troglodytes* – dominates the females, and the alpha male secures most mating opportunities. In the case of female chimpanzees, even the most assiduous observers were slow to detect a hierarchy, yet one exists. It is maintained by a system of 'pant-grunts', the chimpanzee equivalent of a nod and a wink. It is a noise that a more subordinate animal makes when she meets a more dominant female. As has been noted, female chimpanzees usually, although not always, leave the troop of their birth and enter a new troop at puberty. They tend to stay towards the centre of the area occupied by the troop, and they spend much feeding time either alone, or just with an infant.

The acknowledging pant-grunt may be low key, but it reveals a pattern of dominance that remains constant over many years. When the Goodall team correlated the dominance pattern with reproductive success they were in for a surprise. The more dominant the mother, the earlier her daughter became fertile, and the lower the rank of a mother, the higher the mortality of the young. Fifi, for example, a much photographed and televised dominant female at Gombe, has brought seven young to maturity, while some lower ranked chimpanzees have seen more than half their offspring die before age 5. Possibly the dominant females carve out the most prolific parts of the forest with access to the best fruit trees.

In the 1970s, one female Gombe chimpanzee named Pom began snatching and eating the babies of other chimpanzees in the troop. Initially, this stomach-churning behaviour was interpreted as a one-off pathology by a literally mentally unbalanced chimp. But the same behaviour has been observed at other sites and the infanticide usually involves high ranking chimpanzees killing the newborn infants of lower ranking animals. Could the evolutionary quest for reproductive success, which in female chimpanzees seems so subtle, sometimes turn to murder and cannibalism? In male gorillas, as we will see below, this certainly seems to happen.

The promiscuous mating pattern of chimpanzees seems to have permitted a female hierarchy to have evolved largely independently of any male hierarchy. The human polygynous/monogamous mating pattern necessarily links female status to her male sex partner, reinforcing male power, although not necessarily eliminating counter-strategies by females. As has been noted, the sex that makes the greatest investment in reproduction tends to be the more cautious in selecting mating partners. The greater coyness of women over sex, however, may be more complicated than it appears on the surface. On the one hand, it may be a partially inherited defence against the punishments males impose to secure paternity. On the other hand, there may be good reasons for some women to engage secretly in sex with more than one man at the same time. One way women might pre-empt the male drive for paternity is by deliberately soliciting a number of sexual partners. A sample of women belonging to the Ache hunter–gatherers in Paraguay reported that for each of their children they had an average of two partners. In certain cultural situations such a strategy may work, and among the Ache these 'godfathers' appear to contribute to the survival of the woman's children.

In those relatively few societies where inheritance passes through the female line, and which also tend to be technologically less complex, there is less concern for paternity. The Mehinaku women of Brazil are encouraged to engage in a variety of extramarital affairs and the men accept the notion of joint paternity. Revealingly, men in these societies often give a great deal of attention to their sister's offspring, who after all carry 25 per cent of their genes, and who may represent a more secure biological investment than the child of a sexual partner of uncertain paternity; a man can be certain that a niece or nephew will carry some of his genes, while if his wife cuckolds him the resulting child will not carry any of his genes. Among the ancient Picts in Scotland and in some African societies prior to European colonization, the right of kingship sometimes descended through the female or distaff line. Among the Lozi, the king's sister actually ruled half the kingdom.

Male infanticide

The poet Alfred, Lord Tennyson, born in the same year as Darwin, coined the phrase 'Nature, red in tooth and claw', and the concept of violent competition between animals has become hackneyed although still true. The idea of a similar competition between the two sexes of the same species is more recent and less part of everyday thinking. The ruthless nature of male behaviour is seen in several polygynous species, such as monkeys, chimpanzees and gorillas. Hanuman langurs ('Hanuman' is derived from the monkey god of Hindu mythology; 'langur' means long tailed) are slim, buff-coated monkeys with black faces and paws. They range over much of India and illustrate the competition between individuals of the same species as well as that between the two sexes that drives much of reproductive behaviour. The females are considerably smaller than the males and they remain in the troop of their birth for the twenty or so years that they live. Males leave their natal troop at puberty to join roving bachelors until they can fight their way to become the prime consort to a group of six to eight adult females. The behaviour of the two sexes towards new babies in the troop is fundamentally different. As soon as a baby is born, other females try to snatch it away from its natural mother, and growing infants are often taken up and cared for by other females. Sarah Hrdy, an anthropologist from the University of California at Davis, suggests that in this way females learn skills that will make them better mothers when their time comes. Interestingly, pregnant females snatch other monkeys' babies particularly often. From the natural mother's point of view, infant sharing may give her time to forage, and she often ignores her child's cries unless real danger arises, for example when a female from another troop tries to snatch a baby.

Males snatch infants only when attempting to kill them. Pregnancy in langurs lasts six and a half months and lactation up to twenty, so a new male might have to wait for two years before he could impregnate a female. If a new male succeeds in killing a suckling infant, the mother will be sexually receptive within days. Therefore a new male's interest is best served by murdering any suckling offspring of his predecessor. The female's interest is in the survival of her child; females will band together to resist the infanticidal attacks of males – although in the end the males, who are stronger, usually win. In Hrdy's careful observations in India she saw fourteen takeovers of groups of females by new males and in eleven of these a total of thirty-nine infants were killed. In 7000 hours of observing gorillas, Dian Fossey observed three cases of male infanticide and inferred the occurrence of three others. In Hrdy's words 'to the extent that infanticide is advantageous for males, and to the extent that it is a heritable disposition, a female may "choose" to breed with an infanticide so that her own sons will profit from killing another male's offspring. And herein lies the weakness in the combined female front'.

What happens when women with young children acquire a new husband or partner? Murder and infanticide are not only the most dramatic expressions of the struggle for power in sexual relationships, but they are single events, defined in blood, that rarely go unrecorded and so the statistics are easy to acquire. Wilson and Daly, whose analysis of homicide among children and adults we have already discussed, have also looked at patterns of infanticide in North America. They found that step-fathers were up to sixty times more likely than the biological father to kill a baby. Single parents are more likely to live in poverty, but step-parenting is spread across the economic spectrum. The tendency for a step-parent to commit infanticide is not linked to socioeconomic circumstances, but appears to be an expression of our biology. Most of the murders occur in the first two years of life, which fits with natural intervals of breastfeeding, when a suckling infant could have inhibited the ovulation of a man's new sexual partner. It seems that men, like gorillas, can be driven to kill the child conceived by their mate's prior lover. Sometimes, a woman will adopt her new lover's agenda and mothers have both battered and killed their own children under such circumstances. Obviously, for every man who assaults a step-child, or woman who assaults her existing children after making a new relationship with a man, there are huge numbers who behave as loving and committed parents. But a sixty-fold relative risk remains highly significant. We should use perspectives from evolutionary biology not to excuse the horror of killing a child, but to aid the quest to pre-empt child abuse: social workers, for example, should be particularly alert when a woman with a child under age 2 establishes a sexual relationship with someone other than the child's father.

Jan Vermeer, ***The Procuress***, **1656.** The oldest profession.

The double standard

As we have seen, the male focus on preventing cuckoldry, combined with his greater strength and the patrilineal structure of many societies, all help to put women at a disadvantage. Different cultures and different historical periods have expressed the resulting double standard in a variety of ways. The exploration of our biological predispositions does not tell us how to behave, but it helps to explain the ubiquity of the double standard. For example, as London and other British cities grew in the eighteenth and nineteenth century, huge numbers of women entered domestic service. In late eighteenth century London, one wife, Cecilia Thrale, wrote of her husband's liaison with the housemaid: 'It is the way, and all who understand genteel life think lightly of such matters.' Today, the same abuse of power happens on a yet vaster scale as tens of millions of young women pour into the exploding cities of the developing world looking for work. A study by the University of Nairobi found that many girls started to work as servants when they were as young as 6 or 7 years. Often they began by looking after other children, but within a few years they commonly ended up working long hours. Sexual abuse by the head of the house, his growing sons, relatives or visitors was common. The girl had no redress, and if pregnancy occurred she was likely to be expelled from the house. The same Nairobi study found that former housemaids were the commonest source of 12 to 15 year old prostitutes.

Women are also susceptible to male power in the more formal work place. 'Sexual harassment' is a new term for an age-old male abuse of women. In 1864, during the American Civil War, so many men left Washington for the front that the US Treasury had to hire seventy woman clerks. The young women complained and signed affidavits 'that they could only get their places, or hold them by yielding to the embraces' of their male supervisor. Many were said to be about 'to increase the population'. No action was taken.

Whereas in hunter-gatherer societies it was the men who hunted and the women who gathered, with the advent of subsistence agriculture it was the woman with a hoe who became the basic economic unit. The male, with little left to hunt, moved on to manipulate and control the economy. In North Africa, the Near East and Asia, where a man drives a plough pulled by domesticated animals and accumulates wealth to be handed on to his children, men often exert extreme control over women. A double standard of sexual morality is the rule rather than the exception in settled societies. While husbands jealously guard and protect their own wives, they often regard all other women as fair game. In Kenya, male adultery is accepted and almost expected, but if a wife should stray she may be left to fend for herself. An anthropological survey of 116 traditional societies found that in 43 per cent of them extramarital sex was accepted for men, but not for women. Only one in ten treated sexual affairs for men and women equally. The result of this double standard is that twice as many countries punish women for cuckoldry as punish men for adultery, and female punishments tend to be the more extreme. In France, a sentence of murder can be reduced to manslaughter on the plea of a *crime passionnel*. In the USA, even in the 1990s, women in the process of divorce and separation have been charged by vindictive husbands and unscrupulous lawyers with the crime of adultery. In 1990 a Wisconsin woman, Donna Carroll, was charged with breaking the state's adultery law.

Harlots, whores and hookers

A great many American prostitutes ('hookers') were sexually abused as children and, as adults, have become drug addicts as well. They have their own colourful vocabulary: vaginal intercourse is 'flat-backing', anal intercourse is 'up the dirt track' and oral stimulation (a 'blowjob') followed by vaginal intercourse is 'half and half'. When the walls of Jericho came tumbling down the only person who was not slaughtered by the victorious Israelites was Rahab (Joshua 2:1) – who had done all her tumbling earlier in a tiny bordello squeezed between the city walls. Not only did Joshua spare her life for sheltering his spies but he married her and she went on to become the ancestor of the prophets Jeremiah and Ezekiel.

Two thousand years earlier the Sumarians had had temple prostitutes. Later, every Babylonian woman, in Herodotus' words, had to go 'once in a lifetime and sit in the temple of Mylitta and give herself [as a prostitute] to a strange man'. The money earned in this unique custom went to the temple coffers. The Roman writer Horace described how the streetwalkers of the imperial city traded their services under the arches (or fornices) of the great public buildings – hence our word fornication.

Occasionally, members of the oldest profession made it to the top, as did the Empress Theodora who was placed in a brothel at age 12, married the emperor of Byzantium when she was 19, and was canonized after her death. Eleven hundred years later Nell Gwyn, with truth, could call herself the British King Charles II's 'Protestant whore'. But most prostitutes, throughout most of history, have been poor, providing a service for men for economic reward, not out of sexual desire.

In 1842 W. Tait published *Magdalenism* – the polite word for prostitution, since this was thought to have been Mary Magdalene's profession – describing prostitution in Edinburgh, Scotland, in the mid-nineteenth century. Most prostitutes were in their late teens and some were only 9 or 10. He noted 200 public brothels: first class catering to noblemen, merchants and military officers; second class for businessmen, clerks and theologians; and the third class for country folk, soldiers and sailors.

All contemporary big cities in the developing world have broadly similar arrangements. The medical journal *The Lancet* estimated that there were 6000 brothels and 60 000 prostitutes in London in 1857, and there are probably a similar number in the Cages in Bombay, India, today. In Dhaka, the capital of Muslim Bangladesh, a 1970s survey found that half the prostitutes came from landless families and some had literally been captured by armed men. All of them 'start as the property of some owner till the sales money is repaid. After that she becomes independent, working for some pimp.' One girl who was forced into prostitution told her parents that she was working in a hospital. When she was arrested and her profession became public the neighbours in her rural village forced her family to leave. The survey showed the girls' most frequent customers were students, followed by businessmen, and one in ten men were members of the police force.

She admitted to extramarital sex during a divorce case. Her husband also admitted to having an affair but was not charged. The case was eventually dropped on condition that Donna Carroll performed forty hours of community work.

In India, ancient beliefs and modern economics come together to exploit young girls. Some Indian temples still recruit Devadasi, or temple serving-maids and dancers. The parents are usually illiterate and always superstitious. If, for example, a crop fails, or the family wage-earner dies, the family may interpret this as a punishment by the god Yellema, and to acquire better luck in the future they may dedicate a daughter to the temple. The child, commonly when aged only 4 or 5, undergoes a marriage ritual with Yellema. Once dedicated to the god, she returns to her family, but can never marry. At puberty, the temple auctions her to the highest bidder to be his concubine, but she is often then resold and nine out of ten end up as prostitutes.

It can be painful to recognize how ruthless human beings can be in the pursuit of sex. For example, apes recognize and eat a vast range of leaves and fruits, and there is recent evidence that they may even take some for medicinal purposes. Human beings also have a fascination with the non-nutritive properties of plants, including the deadly addiction of tobacco leaves, coco leaves and fermented drinks, and this dependence on drugs can have a devastating effect on women. The pimps who manipulate their 'stables' of prostitutes on the streets or in the 'crack' houses of New York live in a world of violence, and are themselves despised by the rest of the community. Drugs, and most especially the extraordinarily addictive powers of crack cocaine, magnify and distort the struggle for power within sexual relationships to bizarre and horrible extremes. Female addicts will do anything for the drug, and the male supplier may exploit his power in sexual ways that are uniquely human in their depravity. Having physically and mentally abused the women who depend on him for drugs and external protection, there is only one more step he can take to assert his sexual dominance, and that is by sexually abusing the woman's children. Oral gonorrhoea has been diagnosed in six month old infants in crack houses.

Virginity

One way in which the male can guarantee his paternity is by insisting on female virginity at the time of marriage. In contemporary Lebanon or Pakistan, a girl who loses her virginity before marriage may be killed by a close male relative, a crime for which he is likely to receive only a light punishment from the civil courts. It is much more common for societies to

'Vyvod'

On the village street, between white-washed cottages, moved a strange procession, howling savagely. A crowd of people go along close together and slowly – it moves like a great wave, and before it goes a little horse ... In the front part of the wagon is a little naked woman, almost a girl, with hands bound by a rope. She holds herself sideways so strangely, her head, with its thick, twisted, fair hair, is held up and bent slightly backwards, the eyes are open and gaze somewhere into the distance with a dull, vacant look in which there is nothing human. Her whole body is covered with red and blue marks, round and long, the firm left breast is cut open, and from it trickles blood. And, in the wagon stands a portly peasant in a white shirt and black lambskin cap, under which, in the middle of his brow, hangs a strand of dark red hair. In one hand he holds the reins, in the other the whip, and methodically strikes it now on the back of the horse and now on the body of the little woman, who has already been cut about 'till she has lost all human form. The eyes of the red-haired peasant are bloodshot and glittering with savage triumph ... And, behind the wagon and the woman bound to it, rolls the crowd, shrieking, howling, whistling, laughing, yellow-mocking ... That is called vyvod *('execution'). Thus do the peasants punish their wives for adultery. I myself have seen it on the 15th July, 1891, in the village of Kandybouka in the Crimea.*

Maxim Gorki (cited in Ploss *et al.*, 1935)

punish the woman who bears an illegitimate child than the man who fathers it, and yet the woman has the double burden of having to rear the child and being socially ostracized. Nathaniel Hawthorne's book *The Scarlet Letter* and Mrs Gaskell's *Ruth* captured the emotions of those who were punished for premarital conception. The more pragmatic and pecuniary Scots instituted a system by which the Kirk (the Protestant Church in Scotland) demanded a hefty deposit from the couple on marriage, to be forfeited if a child was born within the ensuing nine months. Any attempt to conceal or dispose of the child was easily detected by the midwives, who looked to see whether any milk could be expressed from the woman's breasts. In seventeenth century New England, an unmarried woman was expected to name the child's father to the midwife during childbirth, as this was a moment when her life was in danger and she was not expected to lie. If an unmarried woman in Calvinist Scotland gave birth to an infant that died, she could be accused of its murder and might be executed. One wonders how many innocent women went to their deaths following an unavoidable stillbirth or cot-death.

Mid seventeenth century rural English Parish Records show that although 20 to 30 per cent of first conceptions occurred premaritally, most were legitimized by the marriage ceremony, so that only 1 in 200 births was out of wedlock. English parishes had an obligation to support a 'base child', and a Justice of the Peace could punish the mother if she was still unwed at childbirth, usually with a public whipping or, less commonly, by confinement in a house of correction. Punishments were often given on market day in order to attract maximum publicity. In 1621 Agnes Poole of Somerset was sentenced 'immediately after evening prayer to be whipped severely through the streets of the Parish until her body be bloodied'. Another unhappy woman received additional lashes because she stopped breastfeeding and the parish had to find the extra cost of a wet-nurse.

In Asia and the Middle East, and in at least one Jewish sect in the USA, there is a thriving industry where plastic surgeons attempt to recreate lost virginity by reconstructing the hymen – a task that is technically rather difficult. One shortcut is to draw a small quantity of blood prior to the wedding ceremony, treat it with heparin so that it does not clot, and put it in a small plastic sachet which the bride straps to her thigh prior to the wedding night. If she lost her virginity to her husband-to-be prior to the ceremony, then both could conspire to deceive parents and in-laws; if the man was the virgin and she the more experienced, then expressions of pain at the right moment whilst breaking the sachet could be expected to deceive her passionate and excited lover.

In a society stratified by wealth, where the few have financial and legal

The Oneida Community

John Humphrey Noyes, a nineteenth century American minister, interpreted Christian teaching on love and marriage in a radically new way. Marriage, he proclaimed, 'makes a man or woman unfit to practice the two central principles of Christianity, loving God and loving one's neighbour'. Therefore he put together the Oneida Community, which at its height involved about 200 people and survived as an economic unit for thirty years. They practised omnigamy where every man and woman, subject to their own free choice, could have intercourse with everyone else. If they fell in love, however, they had to confess the fault to the Community and break off the relationship. Noyes encouraged eugenic matings and a couple had to obtain permission from the elders to beget a child. To prevent unwanted pregnancies, the men had to practise coitus saxonicus or coitus obstructus. That is, at the moment of ejaculation the man (or his partner if she was strong enough) had to press on the perineum over the urethra to prevent ejaculation through the penis and force the semen back into the bladder. It is an ancient method of fertility control and was used in Saxony in mediaeval times – hence its name. However, Noyes believed it to be his own invention, just as have one or two twentieth century authors. Towards the end of his life Noyes insisted on sexually initiating every young woman and the Community fell to pieces.

control over the many, the feudal landlord or village headman may exercise sexual control by the practice of *jus primae noctis* or *droit de seigneur*, the right to deflower all the virgins in his domain. No doubt it is a custom more frequently imagined than experienced, though at least one Scottish king seems to have practised the right. It still exists, however, in parts of West Africa, such as Gabon. Unfortunately, the village headman has often accumulated a variety of sexually transmitted diseases during his long life, and he passes these on to the virgins with whom he has intercourse. Sexually transmitted diseases in turn can lead to pelvic inflammatory disease, blockage of the fallopian tubes, and hence lifelong infertility. Thirty–two per cent of Gabonese women suffer from primary infertility and are never able to conceive, a cruel price to have to pay for their unwilling precocious exposure to sex. The mean age at first intercourse in Gabon is 12 years.

Female genital mutilation

Ritual female genital mutilation is man's most cruel expression of his need to guarantee his paternity – at its most extreme it is a sort of perpetual virginity. It is estimated that over 80 million women in today's world have undergone some form of ritual mutilation. Unlike male circumcision, these rituals are designed to control, or in some cases totally eliminate, sexual pleasure for the woman. There are three types: in *sunna* the foreskin of the clitoris is removed, in *excision*, or clitorectomy, the whole clitoris is taken away, and in *pharaonic* the clitoris and labia majora and minora are cut away. These procedures may be done with a razor-blade, sharp knife or even a piece of broken glass, usually at or shortly before puberty. Female genital mutilation is practised in wide areas of East Africa and the Saudi-Arabian peninsula, and is virtually universal in certain tribes. Among the Pokot, who herd cattle and grow crops on the grasslands of northern Kenya, young women compete for male attention from an early age. They increase their perceived beauty by scarification and by adornment with coloured beads. Clitorectomy is performed at puberty, not in private as in many other tribes, but as a public ritual to which the girl submits with a considerable show of bravery. The ritual, disagreeable as it is, admits her to a sexual life of considerable vigour and variety prior to marriage, often to a man considerably older than herself. The strength of the desire to conform in all things to do with sex is illustrated by the fact that, in another East Africa tribe which also practises female circumcision, two women grew to maturity whose parents decided not to circumcise them – one of these women has committed suicide and the other has had a nervous breakdown.

Pharaonic circumcision, sometimes called infibulation, is limited largely to the Sudan. At some time in childhood, or shortly before puberty, the girl is held down, often by female relatives, while the traditional midwife excises the clitoris and the labia majora and minora, so that all the external genitalia are removed. The edges of the raw wound are then sewn together, sometimes with thorns or some other primitive form of suture, leaving only a small orifice for urine and menstrual fluid to escape. Swelling, or a badly performed operation, can lead to total retention of urine and menstrual fluid. If the operation is 'successful', the woman's perineum becomes a smooth mass of white scar tissue, not unlike a bald man's head, with a small orifice in the middle of it. Infibulation produces a living chastity belt, fashioned out of the woman's own flesh. Following marriage, intercourse is always painful, commonly difficult and sometimes impossible. In a recent survey of over 3000 infibulated women, nearly every one found sex painful and 84 per cent said they had never experienced an orgasm. The man, who may himself be sexually inexperienced, and too embarrassed to confess his inability to penetrate his bride, may have to resort to cutting the perineum open – there have been reports of acid being used to widen the hole. Continuous penile thrusting may produce a false vagina, or the couple may simply be forced, knowingly or unknowingly, into anal intercourse. If the woman becomes pregnant, birth poses an additional horror since the scar tissue often has to be cut in order to permit delivery to take place. The wounded area is then sewn up once again, almost always without any anaesthesia and often using the same primitive technology that characterized the initial ritual.

The World Health Organization and the International Planned Parenthood Federation have condemned this barbaric practice. A few educated families in contemporary Sudan are brave enough to break with the tradition of infibulation, or compromise by having the operation done under a local anaesthetic with some attempt made to disinfect the instruments. Such mutilation may seem tragic but remote from Western experience, but none the less it is still practised by some African immigrants to Europe, who continue to maintain their cultural traditions. In Britain, doctors have been outlawed from performing female circumcision for immigrants, although girls are still sometimes sent home on 'holiday' and return circumcised. Even Britain and the USA had their own indigenous female genital mutilation tradition in the nineteenth century, when clitorectomy was regarded as a 'cure' for epilepsy, sterility, insanity and masturbation. Isaac Baker-Brown, writing in the *Lancet* at that time, rationalized the procedure by stating that 'surgery shall come to the rescue to cure what morals should have prevented'. He described forty-eight different operations and founded a special hospital,

Female circumcision: six verbatim accounts

My aunt and the young Muslim doctor and his male assistant caught hold of me. The doctor explained that this was necessary for my future, to guarantee my marriage. They held me tight and I couldn't run away. The male assistant stretched my legs apart, and the doctor cut off the tip of my 'clitoris' with scissors.

Egypt Case Histories

I wondered what all that boiling water was for. Nobody said anything but by 6 a.m. our local barber had arrived; the elders in our house gathered. I was getting scared as I was only ten years old. My elderly aunt undressed me and blindfolded me with a scarf. I was then forcibly held down and my legs were pulled apart while the barber/surgeon did his work. I was screaming until I could scream no more and passed out.

Nigeria Case Histories

The night before the operation, the drums were beaten until late. Very early the next morning, two of my favourite aunts took me to the house of the excisor or operator, an old woman from the blacksmith caste. In Mali, the custom is that women from this caste do the operations of both clitoridectomy and infibulation. I did not know what excision really meant, though I had seen on several occasions a group of girls who were just excised walking along. It was not a beautiful sight. Their backs were bent and they looked like old women who could scarcely hold themselves up.

Once inside the house of the operator, I became terribly frightened, though I had been reassured that it would not hurt. It was very early in the morning, yet I perspired and my throat became all dry. I was told to lie down on a mat on the floor. Immediately, some big hands fastened themselves on my thin legs and opened them wide. I raised my head, but at once from both sides, two women held me down to the floor and immobilized my arms. Suddenly, I felt something being sprinkled on my genital area. Later, I learned this was sand, which is supposed to make excision easier. I was terrified. Suddenly, some fingers grabbed a part of my genital organs. I tried to escape but I could not move. A terrible searing pain pierced me through and through. The excisor cut the small lips and then the clitoris. I felt as if I was being torn to pieces. Then the operator put a mixture of herbs and butter on the wound to arrest the bleeding – I have never felt any pain as overwhelming as this.

Mali Case Histories

The tom became louder and so did the chanting. The Bundu mistress knelt before the girl … She held … a small knife with a steel blade, made locally. It had a long handle and a curved blade that was no bigger than a nail of a man … With the greatest care the Bundu mistress then cut off the labia minora and the skin surrounding the clitoris. Then the helpers took the legs of the girl and lifted them up towards her belly while the 'operating table' held her arms. Now the Bundu mistress cut out the entire clitoris and the soft parts of the vagina until her knife met firm tissue. The girl slowly recovered consciousness, sighed and then screamed from the pain. The girl then was … carried to the … Bundu mistress's hut, her legs were tightly bandaged to her thighs. She was laid down while the ceremony resumed with the next girl.

Sierra Leone Case Histories

My mother, sisters and wife have all had pharaonic circumcisions. So will my daughters. This has nothing to do with Islam but sometimes society governs people's lives. I would like not to circumcise my daughters but if I don't people will punish me in many ways and my wife and daughters will be the ones who suffer, too. People might talk about us for a long time to come, for example. Our relations with neighbours may go bad. Such things happen, and create problems. My wife is the one who makes the decision to circumcise our girls. I support her and we do it. My mother and sisters don't bother talking about it – they know it's going to happen. Public opinion supports pharaonic circumcision, I think, but personally I find sunna best. The Prophet Mohammed ordered it. We follow his teaching to remove the part of a woman which is sensitive to make her sexual needs more manageable.

Married man, 33, teacher, Khartoum, Sudan

Notes on deformations of the genital organs practised by the natives of Australia

The following notes on deformations of the male and female genital organs practised by the Aborigines of Australia may not be uninteresting to the Fellows of this Society. The information which I am about to communicate was collected and sent to the Anthropological Institute by Mr. B. H. Purcell, a gentleman who has, for the last 25 years, given great attention to the study of these natives amongst whom he resides.

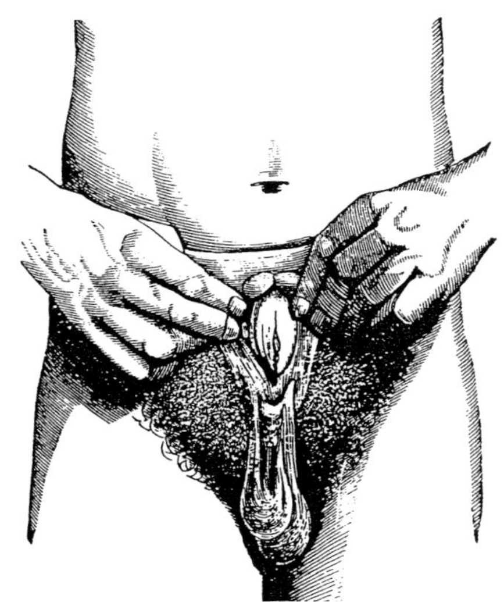

Circumcision – *This operation is practised all over Australia, except in Victoria and New South Wales, on boys at the age of eight years. The operation is performed by one man seizing the prepuce between his forefingers and thumbs and stretching it to the fullest extent, while the head man of the tribe transfixes it with a flint knife of lancet shape, sharpened on both sides and cuts it off with one circular sweep. After the bleeding has ceased the wound is dressed with the soft down of a duck or the eagle-hawk.*

The Myalgoordi have a somewhat different method of performing the operation. They divide the prepuce by four longitudinal incisions and then dissect each segment backwards 'to the butt of the penis,' removing each separately.

In the Northern Territory the prepuce is scored with a flint knife and is then dressed with irritating herbs so as to produce hypertrophy of the parts.

The operation is done for the purposes of cleanliness. The natives do not consider a person clean unless he has been circumcised, and a circumcising tribe will not eat food with one who is uncircumcised.

A Mika is a man upon whom an operation to produce artificial hypospadias [where the urethra opens on the underside of the penis] *has been practised for the purpose of preventing him from having any family. Three different operations are performed for this purpose.*

1st – On Corpus Christi Creek, Western Australia, the natives content themselves with making a small incision through the urethra immediately in front of the scrotum. Through this opening the semen is ejaculated during copulation, after the wound is healed.

2nd – On the Diamantina and Lower Georgiana the natives divide the urethra in front of the scrotum and again just below the glans penis, then cutting longitudinally along each side of the urethra dissect it out.

3rd – The most general plan of mutilation is that of which I show you a photograph. It is performed by placing a narrow piece of wood along the dorsum of the penis and drawing the loose skin tightly backwards over the wood. A flint knife is then inserted into the orifice and the urethra is laid open to the scrotum. Before the operation is performed the penis is beaten till it is benumbed. After the operation the penis is bandaged against the abdomen; should excessive inflammation of the wound occur during the healing process it is dressed with a kind of native clay or crushed eucalyptus leaves. The mortality after this operation is stated to be nil.

These operations are performed on youths at the age of 18 years, and only upon a certain number of them, namely, those who prove themselves indolent and the least useful members of their tribes.

J. G. Garson, M. D. *Medical Press Circular*, **108**, 189 (1894) (Read before the Medical Society of London, 5 Feb. 1894)

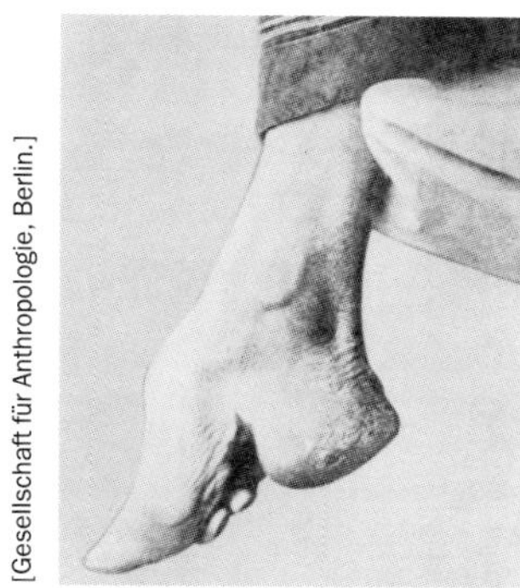
[Gesellschaft für Anthropologie, Berlin.]

The foot of a Chinese woman, following footbinding.

the London Surgical Home, to perform his mutilation. For little boys who masturbated, control was limited to sewing up their trouser pockets.

The footbinding of Chinese women, where the feet were broken and foreshortened to about half their true length, was another mutilation designed to control women, although unlike circumcision it was limited to the upper classes. Men argued that by altering a woman's gait, footbinding helped to tighten the vaginal muscles and thrust out the buttocks; and the procedure, by greatly reducing a woman's mobility, kept her a virtual captive of her lord and master. The woman became a 'desirable cripple' and only the wealthiest of men could afford to take such a cripple, unable to walk, as a bride, and so it was a way of advertising the male's status. Thus, in a perverted way, the pain and mutilation of footbinding increased the girl's chances in the marriage stakes. Her parents presumably connived in the practice from the time of her birth as they could see financial rewards in the future.

An educated nineteenth century Chinese woman wrote, 'First we bind our feet; second, our minds are bound; third, we are inferior and servants of our husbands'. The desire to conform sexually was so powerful that by the time of the Ming emperors a law was passed forbidding Mongols to bind the feet of their children. Since the Communist Revolution in 1949 footbinding has been outlawed and there are only a few women alive today whose feet were bound during childhood. In Taiwan, footbinding occurred in some regions and not in neighbouring ones. Arthur Wolf of Stanford University has studied changes in the birthrate in Taiwan and found that in footbinding villages it took longer for fertility to fall after World War II than in villages where footbinding was not practised, confirming the impact of the control of women.

Sometimes if we scrutinize contemporary society we may find some pale shadows of more extreme behaviours found elsewhere. Nearly all Western women, on some occasion or another, wear high-heeled or platform-soled shoes. And high heels do many of the things footbinding did, although in a softer, much more acceptable way: like footbinding, high heels accentuate the female gait, limit a woman's range of comfortable movement, and are associated with more injured tendons and broken ankles than flat shoes.

Another bizarre form of sexual exploitation of the wives of the wealthy was described by the English explorer John Hanning Speke. He was the first white man to enter Uganda in 1861, and he recorded how King Rumanika of the Karagwe constantly plied his wives with milk, sucked from a gourd with a straw, until they became like bloated seals, unable to stand, let alone to walk, and hence confined to the harem for life, to await his pleasure. Speke measured one wife as having a chest 4 foot 4 inches (132 cm) around and a thigh circumference of 2 foot 7 inches (79 cm). If young girls attempted to resist, they were forcibly fed while a man stood over them with a whip. Their obesity was both an advertisement of the king's wealth, and an assurance of his paternity.

Battered women

One million US women per year seek medical care as a result of physical assault by men, and one in five battered women in the USA have suffered at least ten attacks. Domestic violence in the USA causes more injuries than car accidents and street crime combined. Perhaps because our romantic ideals are so strong, much home assault goes unrecognized, or is treated by an emergency room doctor with a bandage and a tranquillizer.

In a study of slum living in the Philippines, Landa Jacano observed that families had an average of five major quarrels per month, with raucous shouting and wailing, hurling and breaking of objects; these sometimes ended with the wife running semi-naked into the *barrio*, a socially approved way of embarrassing her husband and forcing him to terminate the attack. As in apes, so in humans, adult violence is more likely if the male who does the

Male circumcision

In contrast to female circumcision, which seems to have arisen solely as a means by which men can increase their power over women, and which threatens a woman's very life, male circumcision may have developed for sound medical reasons, and could bring significant health benefits.

There are Egyptian wall carvings that depict the circumcision of young boys, and it may have been a wise precaution in a desert environment to prevent sand getting under the prepuce and setting up an inflammatory reaction. When Australian troops were sent to fight in the desert during World War II, many who were uncircumcised developed an acute inflammation of the glans penis (balanitis), and had to be circumcised. Perhaps the Jews merely inherited the practice of circumcision from the time of their bondage in Egypt.

Recent studies of the incidence of male circumcision and susceptibility to HIV infection throughout Africa have revealed some intriguing correlations; HIV infection rates are much lower amongst circumcised men, and circumcision is widely practised in desert areas but is virtually unknown in communities living in tropical rain forest. There is also some evidence to suggest that the incidence of other sexually transmitted diseases may be higher in uncircumcised men.

So it may all be related to the question of post-coital penile hygiene. In uncircumcised men, following sexual intercourse with an infected woman, bacteria or viruses may be trapped beneath the foreskin in a moist environment that enables them to survive and multiply, eventually to enter the penile orifice and thence infect the individual. In circumcised men, the organisms would be more easily washed or brushed off the glans penis in the dried secretions.

So male circumcision may not be the unkindest cut of all, and could even be a wise precaution at a time when sexually transmitted diseases are becoming rampant.

battering, or the female victim, were themselves violently treated as children. There is also a sexual bias in our attitudes to domestic violence which, like infanticide, is shocking but possibly deep-seated. When a psychologist from Michigan State University staged fights to be witnessed by unsuspecting passers-by, he found that men usually went to try to split up a simulated quarrel between other men, or to separate two fighting women, but no man ever interfered when another man appeared to be beating up a woman.

Economic deprivation nearly always puts women at a disadvantage. An ancient Chinese poet once wrote,

How sad it is to be a woman
Nothing is held so cheap

Confucius said in his *Admonitions to Women*, 'Obey heaven and follow fate.' Women often have to deal not only with the aggression of their husbands, but also with the hostility of their in-laws. For millennia, women in traditional societies such as China or India have grown up under the yoke of their fathers, being passed to the control of their husbands at around the age of puberty, only to end their lives as the servants of their sons. Divorce is a disgrace, and suicide the only refuge for the desperate. In the rare cases where a woman does have legal control of her property, it is all too easily taken away from an illiterate teenaged wife by her older, scheming in-laws. Although one in six marriages in Bangladesh ends in divorce, only one woman in fifty claims the few rights to which she is entitled after a marriage break-up. Women in the developing world continue to be exploited as mere breeding stock and beasts of burden: they make up half of the population, and do two-thirds of the physical labour, yet they receive only one-tenth of the world's gross income, and control only one-hundredth of its property. In Central Africa, for example, women may spend four hours a day merely fetching water and firewood.

In 1994 Lorena Bobbitt attracted considerable publicity in the USA when she cut off her husband's penis with a knife, following a long history of physical and mental abuse in her marriage. It is a revenge as old as the knife, and in Thailand approximately 100 such episodes have been reported in the past decade. One wife of a philandering man fed the severed organ to the ducks, and the phrase 'I'll feed you to the ducks' is widely understood. A surgeon at Siriraj Hospital in Bangkok has reattached thirty penises.

Wife burning

The most extreme expression of male control over women was 'suttee', the Hindu tradition where a wife was expected to leap onto her husband's funeral pyre, sacrificing her life, to die beside his corpse. When the Greeks under Alexander the Great fought their way into India they commented on the custom of suttee. A widow who immolated herself on her husband's funeral pyre could expect 350 000 years of happily married life in heaven. Both wives and concubines died: even a cat that fell onto its master's cremation pyre was interpreted as a display of feline loyalty. No doubt there were wives whose belief in an afterlife was strong enough to sustain them in their moment of sacrifice, and stories abound of widows who gave themselves eagerly to the flames. Most widows did not die of their own free will. Sometimes a deep pit was dug in which to build the funeral pyre so that if the wife changed her mind she could not flee the flames; in Bengal the widow's feet were tied to a post driven into the ground in the middle of the funeral pyre. The Islamic rulers of the Hindu population tried to stop this practice, and when the British came the governor-general, Lord William Bentinck, had it outlawed. The last official case of suttee was when Maharaja Sarup Singh died in 1861 – but it was a slave girl and not his wife who was burnt. In 1987 in the north Indian state of Rajasthan, 18 year old Roop Kanwar threw herself on her husband's funeral pyre. It is said she was cajoled to jump into the flames by frenzied villagers, and that when she tried to escape purified butter was thrown on the fire to increase the flames. An expensive shrine has been built deifying her memory – although in 1996 the government also began legal proceedings against thirty-nine people for abetting the suicide. Historically there has never been a human society where men were expected to commit suicide after the death of their wives.

Wife burning is also sometimes a tragic end to disputes over dowries. Asha was 14 years old when she was married. Her father makes a living making garden fences and trellises and he spent his life savings (about US $500) on her wedding. Her in-laws sent her back to beg for more food and money. They began kicking and torturing her. She was pregnant when they set her on fire. Asha lived long enough in hospital to deliver a stillborn boy and to accuse her father-in-law of murder. Six hundred and ninety women were burnt to death in New Delhi in 1990 alone, but only one in fifty of those accused of bride-burning ever go to jail. It is easy to label the death as suicide or a cooking accident – after all these really do happen as well.

'Chaste to the last...'

In ancient Rome, six virgin priestesses tended the sacred fire in the Temple of Vesta in the Forum. The ritual dates back to the beginning of Rome, although the present remains date from a rebuilding of the circular temple in AD 191. Christianity took over from the Vestal Virgins the rite of lighting Easter candles with a spark struck from flint and steel. The Virgins enjoyed the best real estate in the city and front seats in the Colosseum, but they were whipped by the *pontifex maximus* if they let the flame in the temple go out, and if they lost their virginity before their thirty year term was up they were buried alive. Plutarch describes such an execution,

> *The unfortunate guilty woman is carried on a funeral car, to which she is bound with straps of leather, through the Forum, the Vicus Longus and Alta Semla as far as Porta Collins. The crowd opens in silence to let the funeral procession pass: not a word is heard, not a single lament. Silent tears fall from the eyes of every spectator. Finally the procession reaches a point near the opening of the crypt, the ladder is removed, the opening closed with a huge stone and a large quantity of earth is heaped over it so as to conceal all traces of the tragic site.*

Cornelia, the Head of the Vestal Virgins, was falsely accused of incest by the Emperor Domitian. According to Pliny,

> *Cornelia implored Vesta and all the other gods, frequently calling out, 'How can Caesar think me polluted? While I have carried out the sacred rites, he has conquered and triumphed!...' As she was carried down into the underground cell, her gown caught on in some obstruction. She tried to free it, and the executioner offered her his hand. But she turned her face away: chaste to the last, she refused his polluting touch on her pure and spotless body.*

The harem

As groups of hunter–gatherer nomads turned into settled societies, increasing wealth was concentrated in the hands of a few men, such as kings or tribal rulers. These men sometimes replaced the practice of having several wives at one time with the keeping of many women in a harem, as in the case of King Solomon in the Old Testament, the Mogul rulers of India, some Roman emperors, Turkish sultans and the emperors of China. A distinction was usually drawn between their numerous concubines and a few official wives. The Chinese emperors of the T'ang Dynasty had their harems organized by a secretariat of elderly ladies, who kept the most meticulous records of when and with whom the emperor had intercourse. Some harems were managed with all the finesse of a stud farm: early in this century, the Nizam of Hyderabad's concubines were delivered of four of his children in the space of eight days. In the Chinese imperial harem the date of menstruation, the day and hour of successful sexual unions and first sign of pregnancies in the concubines were all recorded. In some cases every woman who slept with the emperor was indelibly tattooed with cinnamon.

The Ottomans, who ruled Turkey and vast areas of the Middle East from 1288 until the monarchy was abolished in 1922, developed the harem in a bizarre way which, by an ironical twist, eventually shifted the power back to women. At the beginning of the Ottoman Empire women were the unveiled companions of their warrior husbands; as the empire became more wealthy they changed from being partners into luxury items, and eventually into mere sexual objects. The abundance of female slaves as a result of ever expanding wars led to what historian Edmund Taylor has called 'erotic inflation'. The number of available women became so large that the sultan ceased to distinguish between queens and concubines. Women competed, literally to the death, to bring forth the next heir to the throne. Towards the end of the Ottoman Empire the concubine who regularly shared the sultan's bed sometimes spent as much time watching for her potential assassins as pandering to his sexual pleasures. Every woman wished to become pregnant and in turn to prevent her rivals from giving birth. When a harem woman thought she was pregnant, she kept it a secret for as long as possible. The children who were born were subject to frequent 'accidents'. For example, of the thirty or so children that Abdul Medjid fathered, half died in infancy.

The larger the harem, the greater the potentate's drive for exclusive sexual access. The Ottoman harem was guarded by both black and white eunuchs, who presented no threat to their lord and master's paternity. The senior amongst them was called 'the Guardian of the Gates of Felicity', and others were given such poetic titles as 'Chief Nightingale Keeper'. There were castrated cooks, guards, and men whose tongues had been cut out, all herded together in a gossip-ridden, plot-filled community alternating between sycophancy and murder. While the despot wallowed in sexual excesses, the running of the empire was delegated to foreign-born vizier-slaves and its defence to armies of mercenaries.

The sultanship was originally passed on from brother to brother, but from 1389 onwards the procedure was changed and simplified by executing all the brothers of the reigning Sultan so the title passed to one of his sons. This had the effect of enhancing competition between the women of the harem to produce the next heir. Eventually the system which had begun as one in which one man exerted virtually total power over women, changed to one in which many competing women controlled a weak and isolated man.

Until the collapse of the Chinese monarchy in 1912, many eunuchs were employed in the Forbidden City in Beijing. Sun Yaoting, the last of the imperial eunuchs, died aged 93 in 1997. Those who had been castrated kept their dried penis and testicles in a box, so they could be buried with them ready for any subsequent resurrection. Sun Yaoting's box was confiscated by communist Red Guards and he is reported to have said, wistfully, before his death, 'When I die I will come back as a cat or a dog.' In 1933, F. Wagenseil, an enterprising German anthropologist, carried out a detailed clinical examination of thirty-one imperial eunuchs. He was amazed to find that almost all of them had no signs of a penis or scrotum, just a small orifice through which they passed urine. Some reported having had had their penis and scrotum simply cut off with scissors. Others had had the penis and scrotum strangulated with a silk tie so that the organs became necrotic and fell off – farmers still castrate young lambs with a tight elastic band applied around the neck of the scrotum. But most unfortunate of all were those men of Korean origin who had had their external genitalia smeared with human faeces before a pack of hungry dogs was turned loose on them. It seems that in matters sexual, man's inhumanity to man knows no bounds.

The struggle for equality

The struggle for equality by women was beautifully satirized 2400 years ago by the Greek writer Aristophanes in his play *Lysistrata*. The women of Athens become increasingly frustrated by the drain on resources as a result of their menfolk's constant warfare with neighbouring states. The women decide to mount a counter-attack, and their first move, significantly, is to seize control of the Athenian treasury, thereby gaining control of the economy. They then give the *coup de grâce* by withholding their sexual favours from the men until they cease fighting, rapidly bringing the men to their knees. But it is only in the past 100 years that anything like a genuine revolution in the status of women has occurred. Undoubtedly, inequalities still exist, but legally, economically and socially great strides have been made in the status of women in many modern industrialized societies.

It is revealing to read some of the early feminist literature, like Mary Wollstonecraft's *Vindication of the Rights of Woman*, written in 1792. She was one of the first to mount a reasoned attack against the prevailing view of Church and State that women were implicitly inferior to men, the weaker vessel, created for the greater glorification and pleasure of men. In those days, marriage for a woman marked her civil death; she lost her freedom, her name, her identity as an individual, and many of her legal rights. Since Mary Wollstonecraft had given birth to a child out of wedlock by a man who then deserted her, and then chose to live in sin with a leading radical of the day, only to die in childbirth at the age of 37, her unconventional lifestyle did not endear her to the British establishment. Walpole dismissed her as 'a hyaena in petticoats'. But by today's standards, her feminism seems tame indeed; she could even be accused of being a 'male chauvinist', since she accepted as fact 'that, from the constitution of their bodies, men seemed to be designed by Providence to attain a greater degree of virtue'. She did not dare, or maybe did not even think, to press for equality between men and women. Over 100 years were to elapse before women in England were able to sue their husbands for divorce on the grounds of adultery, or have the right to vote.

Of all the countries in the world today, Sweden has perhaps struggled hardest to achieve sexual equality. Since the end of the 1960s, laws promoting sexual equality in the work force have been passed. Marriage is no longer considered a prerequisite for having children, and it is now common for a man and a woman to live together and have one or more children before getting married. Following childbirth, there is a statutory entitlement to twelve months' paid leave of absence for either parent. Divorce is made easy, and is increasingly common. And yet, in spite of all this, there is still a major difference between the sexes in the choice of subjects in school or university, or careers pursued.

Perhaps the noble and necessary struggle for equality between the sexes is most likely to be won when the differences between the sexes are also recognized. Men are likely to continue to pursue military careers and women to predominate in the caregiving professions, to cite but one example. A maternal instinct may be constitutionally very different from a paternal one, and hence seek very different modes of expression, but society needs to ensure that one sex is not regarded more highly than the other or rewarded disproportionately.

The battle between the sexes

Biological insights into human behaviour, particularly our sexual behaviour, are often unpopular or misunderstood. For example, the idea that men may have a polygynous sexual agenda built into them, and that there are demonstrable behavioural differences between the two sexes are unpopular conclusions for feminist theories built on a political as opposed to a biological foundation. The fact that a significant number of women do indeed attempt to cuckold their regular sexual partners demonstrates that male strategies to secure paternity are important: patriarchy is not an end in itself, but it has evolved to help to ensure male reproductive success. Genetic studies from Switzerland, Britain and the USA show that between 1 and 30 per cent of children are not the children of the woman's husband, or regular sexual partner. The lower the status of the man, the more likely his wife is to make him a cuckold. There are some data suggesting that women in a long term sexual relationship will dress more provocatively near to the time of ovulation, and when in the presence of men other than their partners, than do women without stable relationships.

Evolution proceeds by a blind, groping, fumbling process of trial and error that eventually favours certain inherited characteristics influencing the survival of our offspring. We have inherited a behavioural legacy from the lifestyle of our hunter–gatherer ancestors, which continues to mould much of our behaviour. Men are more driven by the immediate, short term gratification of sexual intercourse, although they often love and invest in the children they father. Women have evolved to be driven by a broader range of strategies for producing surviving offspring, networking with one another, and with a special ability to juggle the many demands of raising a family. Just as the differing reproductive agendas of men and women will persist into the foreseeable future, so will the male drive to enforce paternity, and with it the possibility of sexual inequality, exploitation of women and violence both physical and mental.

There can be no doubt that, from a biological point of view, women make more investment in reproduction than do men. Modern technology gives both men and women reproductive choices. For the first time in history it is possible to decide when to have a child and when not to have a child. Should not society, through its laws and its education, give women choices over their own fertility, and protect women and children from male violence? Should not an interdependent, technically complex society offer women medical care during their pregnancy, and provide them with time away from paid employment to breastfeed and nurture their children?

Fortunately, our powers of free will and rational thought can help us to overcome the self-seeking interests of our selfish genes. We have been able to move away from the biological competition between individuals and can attempt to enforce altruism within our species. Thus, nearly all societies restrain men from, and condemn them for, killing infants fathered by a previous male. We are capable of remarkable acts of altruism. We can love our neighbours as ourselves, or lay down our lives for a friend. Perhaps the ultimate act of altruism is to adopt another's child, and lavish upon it all the care and affection one would give to one's own son or daughter. In evolutionary terms, our selfish genes may be a driving force, but we have also acquired the capacity to hold the reins, and give that drive a new direction.

10 DYING FOR LOVE

'And I looked, and behold a pale horse; and his name that sat on him was Death, and hell followed with him.'
Revelation 6:8

All forms of life are in competition. Every buttercup, jellyfish, or human being is in a continual battle against a myriad insects, viruses, bacterial and fungal pests, and each parasite in turn is struggling against its host's defences. As human beings, we are entirely dependent on other animals and plants for our growth and survival. By the same token, we are also attractive fodder for other creatures, from the half dozen people eaten by sharks or tigers in the world each year, to the tens of millions who die from attacks by infectious diseases caused by bacteria or viruses. Evolution is a continual life and death competition between millions of different species containing different genetic information. The battle between destructive parasites and their unwilling hosts may well have been a major factor in the evolution of sex itself. In turn, the wet warmth of sexual intercourse has become an easy route for some infections to spread from host to host.

Parasites and people

We have used our brains to devise vaccines and develop antibiotics, but the life and death evolutionary struggle continues between our genetic code and that of the viruses, bacteria and protozoans that cause malaria, influenza, cholera, AIDS, tuberculosis, rabies and innumerable other diseases. Moreover, the march of civilization, with burgeoning human numbers and changing lifestyles, is creating new opportunities for diseases to step up their attacks, as the spread of the human immunodeficiency virus (HIV) that causes AIDS illustrates. HIV already infects over twenty million people, and an estimated 16 000 new infections occur every day. AIDS is virtually certain to have killed 40 million people by the opening decades of the twenty-first century – more than died as civilians and combatants in the horrors of World War II. HIV has enormous destructive potential partly because it is a new disease. It would take many, many generations for human beings to evolve successful defences against HIV. Currently, the tiny fragment of genetic information in

[Hulton Getty Picture Collection Limited.]

Christopher Columbus' return. Martín Alonso Pinzón, the captain of the Pinta (the first of Columbus' three ships to make landfall in the New World and the vessel illustrated above right) is said to have died from syphilis shortly after returning home from the Caribbean in March 1493. Some of the crew enlisted with Gonzalo Fernández de Córdoba, who joined forces with King Charles VIII, of France in mounting the siege of Naples.

Fray Ramon, who chronicled Columbus' voyages, mentions the 'sores that we call the French sickness' that were described in the folk mythology of the Caribbean islanders. The disease was recorded in parts of Italy from 1494 onwards and was widespread in Europe by 1498. A physician, Ruiz Diaz de Isla, treated some of Columbus' crew, giving an unusually accurate description of syphilis, including the observation that intercurrent malaria would arrest the progress of the disease – a shrewd observation that was used in therapy until the discovery of penicillin. Whether or not syphilis really was the first export from the New World, it certainly hit fifteenth century Europe with exceeding virulence.

this new virus has the edge on the 6 feet (2 metres) of DNA, three billion nucleotides and the hundred thousand or so genes in the human genome.

New plagues

Parasites and their hosts have been evolving together for well over a billion years, and there has never been a moment in the evolution of multicellular animals when we have not had to deal with a load of viruses, bacteria and protozoa. But as we become more numerous and our lifestyle changes so we lay ourselves open to new plagues. When farming communities reached a critical size in the Middle East and China, 5000 to 10 000 years ago, people found themselves exposed to a whole new set of infections: influenza (from pigs), bubonic plague (from rats), measles (from cattle or dogs), and smallpox (from cows). Although we can no longer identify many of the diseases, ancient history is replete with examples of plagues that decimated the first settled communities. The Old Testament describes how when the Assyrian King Sennacherib besieged Jerusalem, 'the angel of the Lord went forth, and smote in the camp of the Assyrians a hundred and fourscore and five thousand: and when they arose early in the morning, behold they were all dead corpses' (Isaiah 37:36). As the Roman Empire established trading contacts with Asia, so new plagues entered Europe. Devastating epidemics occurred in AD165 and again in AD 251, and in the latter case 5000 people per day died in Rome. The sixteenth century voyages of discovery took European parasites around the world and, in return, brought syphilis back to Europe. The conquistadores brought new diseases to the previously uninfected peoples of Central America and when Hernando Cortés reached Mexico City in 1519, smallpox had raced ahead of his troops and Montezuma's army was already dying. In this century, measles and other common Western diseases have killed a large percentage of previously isolated, preliterate societies such as the Amazonian Indians.

Usually a disease that jumps from one species to another is much more serious for a new host than one that has been around for a long time. For example, if the seemingly innocuous human cold sore virus infects a monkey it may kill it. The Ebola virus that kills 70 per cent of the people it infects within a few hours, causing haemorrhage from the mouth and other bodily orifices, probably comes from infected fruit bats which are eaten by chimpanzees, who die, and whose fresh corpses are then eaten by humans. Whether or not Ebola harms the bats is uncertain.

Why diseases spread

Some parasites, such as the influenza virus, evolve unusually rapidly. In the USA today, influenza kills as many as 20 000 people per year, usually children, the elderly or those with some other disease. The influenza virus mutates frequently and changes the special molecules it uses to stick to the respiratory tract of the host, often outstripping the ability of the human immune system to make protective antibodies. In addition, some strains of influenza virus have evolved a way to pick up genetic information from influenza viruses that attack other species, such as pigs or ducks. Some recent human influenza epidemics probably began when pigs ate duck faeces in farms in China or South-East Asia. In this case, intensive agriculture provided a mixing vessel for new and potentially lethal strains of influenza.

The plague, or Black Death, was another disease resulting from changes in human behaviour. It is primarily an infection of burrowing rodents, such as the marmot, but occasionally it spreads to rats. When the rats die of the infection then their fleas pass it to other animals. The plague spread to human

Patient Zero: 'I've got cancer, I'm going to die and so are you.'

In 1979, long before AIDS was understood, Gaetan Dugas developed a Kaposi's tumour on his face. Dugas had been adopted at birth by a French Canadian couple. In the 1970s he joined Air Canada as a flight steward. He was a trendy dresser, handsome, self-centred, hedonistic and vain. He flew to San Francisco to march in the Gay Freedom Day parades, flew to New York to join gay parties on Fire Island, and he flew back and forth to Paris as part of his work. 'I'm the prettiest one,' he would say on entering a gay party. Between 1970 and 1980, by his own reckoning, Gaetan Dugas had about 250 different sexual partners each year.

In 1980 and 1981 epidemiologists from the US Centers for Disease Control (CDC) in Atlanta began seeing more and more cases among gay men of Kaposi's sarcoma and of *Pneumocytstis carinii* pneumonia (PCP). One of these epidemiologists, Don Francis, realized that the cause might be a previously unknown virus. Don's colleagues at the CDC, Mary Guinan, Bill Darrow and others, began to explore sexual networks among the gay community. Of the first 248 gay men diagnosed with AIDS in the USA, 40 had had sex with Dugas, or with someone who had had sex with him.

In 1982 Dugas moved permanently to San Francisco, at a time when the gay bath-houses were doing a booming business. Gaetan would have sex with another man, turn up the lights in the cubicle, show his partner the recurrent Kaposi's tumours and say, 'I've got cancer, I'm going to die and so are you.' As insight into AIDS as a sexually transmitted disease grew, he was told to stop visiting the bath-houses. 'I've got it, they can get it too' was his answer. No social pressure or legal restraint existed to quarantine Gaetan. Attempts to close the bath-houses were branded as homophobic, and left-wing liberals sided with hard-nosed entrepreneurs to keep them open. To the fury of other flight attendants, Gaetan went back to work for Air Canada – he wanted to keep his access to free holiday travel. He survived several bouts of PCP and lived until March 1984. Approximately 4000 gay men in America had by then developed AIDS, and soon after Gaetan's death Bill Darrow published a paper on the sexual spread of AIDS in the *Journal of American Medicine*. Gaetan Dugas was referred to as 'Patient Zero', but went unnamed.

Most people with HIV infection want to protect others. A few do not, and they are exceedingly dangerous. In 1996 and 1997, in the USA a street-wise petty thief named Nushawn J. Williams infected eleven women. One was only 13 years old.

beings only when people lived in incredibly filthy, overcrowded conditions with large populations of rats, as occurred in the big cities of the ancient world and of preindustrial Europe. Traders brought the plague to Europe in the fifth century AD, and again in October AD 1347, when a ship from the Orient sailed to Sicily, its crew already dying from the scourge. By 1351, twenty to thirty million were dead, out of an estimated total European population at that time of seventy-five million.

When a disease kills its host, or the host generates protective antibodies to defend itself, then the infective agent rapidly runs out of new opportunities for infection. Therefore, for a disease to maintain itself it needs a certain minimum pool of people who can catch the disease and then pass it on to others. For example, a person with measles is infectious for only a few days before he or she manufactures antibodies to block the disease (or dies). Calculations show that it requires a minimum of 7000 susceptible individuals to prevent the virus running out of possible hosts. As immunity lasts a long time, the pool of susceptible individuals is composed primarily of children who have not had measles and therefore lack protective antibodies. In order to have about 7000 susceptible children, you need a total population of about 300 000 to 400 000. As we saw in Chapter 8, populations of this size did not arise until after settled farming began. Our hunter–gatherer ancestors certainly could have had scabies or tapeworms but not measles or plague. Today, the whole world is virtually one common pool of potential hosts for new infections, and the jet airliner has brought everyone within a day's journey of one another, giving the term 'airborne disease' a new meaning. Paradoxically, things which are at the very heart of civilized living can sometimes make new plagues more likely.

Why sex?

At first sight, the histrionics of sex seem to make it unnecessary to ask 'Why have sex at all?' Yet it is a profound biological problem. Finding a mate of the same species but opposite sex takes time, energy, and is often dangerous. It takes additional effort to protect, feed and train the next generation until it is able to reproduce itself. If evolution really is a process of ruthless competition, then why have sex? The end result of sexual reproduction is that an individual contributes only half of her or his genes to the next generation, and winds up with a 50 per cent chance of not even replicating their own sex. At first glance, cost-effective, predictable, rapid, vegetable, asexual reproduction, or cloning, seems a much preferable way of passing on the thread of life with the greatest self-interest.

Asexual reproduction does indeed have many advantages and enables an animal, plant or parasite to exploit its environment rapidly. But it also leaves it vulnerable to unexpected changes. Asexual reproduction is like sunbathing – fine so long as the sun shines. Should the environment alter, then the asexual population may be doomed unless it can reshuffle its genes and reach a new solution to the new problems it now faces. Parasites usually multiply rapidly and bacteria, as a result of their microscopic size, can double their numbers in less than an hour. By contrast, multicellular animals such as ourselves can take decades to reproduce themselves. If one bacterium, for example, develops resistance to an antibiotic, it can rapidly outbreed and replace the bacteria that were sensitive to the antibiotic. The struggle between animals and their diseases is fought out on an evolutionary playing field slanted in favour of bacteria and other parasites. We have two primary ways of restoring the balance. One is the development of the immune system and the other is sexual reproduction. The immune system consists of billions of cells (lymphocytes), which are able to make a vast array of different antibodies. When a new parasite invades the body, a group of lymphocytes already programmed to make blocking antibodies is stimulated and multiplies rapidly.

Sex, by mixing parental genes at the time of fertilization, gives an organism much more genetic variety than occurs by the processes of asexual reproduction on which most bacteria depend. Maternal and paternal genes are rearranged every time the chromosome number is halved to form a new sperm or egg. William Hamilton of Oxford University argues that the recombination of large blocks of DNA, characteristic of sexual reproduction, diversifies the genetic structure of the offspring more rapidly than blind mutation could have done. If a new disease strikes there are likely to be a few individuals able to resist it. For example, in 1950 the myxomatosis virus was introduced into the rabbit population of Australia. In the first year 99.8 per cent of infected animals died, but slowly a genetically more resistant population emerged. Even though fewer than 1 per cent of the rabbits carried genes that resisted the virus, these animals multiplied and today only 25 per cent of rabbits infected with myxomatosis die. Research is showing that, although HIV ends up killing well over 95 per cent of those infected, there is a very small group of people lucky enough to carry genetic information enabling them to resist infection. It will take hundreds of generations, however, for people lucky enough to have a natural resistance to HIV to replace the huge numbers of susceptible indivduals who will die.

[The National Gallery, London.]

***Marriage à la Mode*, William Hogarth, 1743.** Hogarth's painting depicts the libertine Viscount Squanderfield consulting a venereologist. The pillbox in his crutch suggests that he has a venereal disease. Whilst he seems cheerfully unconcerned about his infection, his weeping young mistress, whom everybody ignores, dabs a tear from her cheek. The dress and deportment of the venereologist says it all – squalor and deference, mixed with arrogance and cunning. His female assistant is marked with syphilitic spots, and is clearly depicted as his procuress. The skull is marked with syphilitic erosions. The narwhal's tusk affixed to the skeleton-filled cabinet is a presumed aphrodisiac, and other phallic symbols abound.

Sexually transmitted diseases

The fluids that transmit life may also carry death. In both sexual intercourse and venereal infection an alien speck of life makes its way deep inside the body and gives rise to many changes. Sexually transmitted diseases (STDs) range from the fungus infection known as thrush, which can be tiresome but never causes irreparable damage, to hepatitis B that can kill after a long delay, and to the lethal HIV. Many STDs, such as gonorrhoea or chlamydia, are much more damaging to women than to men. Men tend to suffer mild symptoms, such as pain on passing urine, that alert them to seek treatment, while women may not notice anything is wrong. Women are more likely to catch an STD from an infected man than vice versa, because any infected material remains as a pool in the vagina for many hours, while nothing comparable happens to the man. STDs may cause little long term permanent damage in men, but in women the fallopian tubes can become blocked, causing life-long infertility. On top of this biological asymmetry, in many traditional societies failure to conceive is usually blamed on the woman and may lead to the break up of a marriage, even though the husband has often given her the infection that caused her infertility, or is himself infertile. The Kikuyu of Kenya, however, permit a childless woman to test her own fertility by having intercourse with one or more men who belong to her husband's close-knit social group, created when he was circumcised with a number of other boys at puberty.

In the modern world, more and more young people are beginning to have sex before marriage, sometimes beginning intercourse in their early teens. In the USA, 50 per cent of adolescents report having had more than one sexual partner, and one in ten has six or more. Nor surprisingly, half of all cases of STD occur in men and women under age 25, and in the USA alone there are 2.5 million new STD infections per year among teenagers. Gonorrhoea, or 'the clap', is increasing more rapidly in young girls than in young men. Chlamydia is a less well known sexual disease and tends to cause less severe symptoms than gonorrhoea, but it can easily lead to irreversible damage to the fallopian tubes and life-long infertility. In the 1970s, an epidemic of genital herpes made the headlines. Once caught, the herpes virus stays for life, multiplying in host cells as they themselves divide. Periodically, when cell and virus get out of step, painful blisters occur. No cure is known. Less publicized, but more dangerous, is the human papilloma virus, which passes almost unnoticed when infection first occurs. In women, however, the papilloma virus is associated with a greatly increased risk of cancer of the neck of the womb. Cervical cancer kills 5000 women a year in the USA. In Latin America it is sixteen times more common in women whose husbands

[Wellcome Institute Library, London.]

Syphilis strikes Europe. The first illustration of a syphilitic was in a woodcut attributed to Albrecht Dürer, 1496. The affected individual is depicted for German readers as a foppish Frenchman. The zodiacal sign about his head refers to the presumed origin of the disease from the conjunction of five planets in the year 1484 in the sign of the Scorpion, which ruled the genitalia.

have had multiple sexual partners than in those whose husbands report that they are monogamous; this emphasizes the man's role in detonating this venereal time bomb in his wife. Fortunately, cervical cancer is easily curable if diagnosed early by microscopic examination of cells scraped off the neck of the womb – a test first described by George Papanicolaou and Herbert Traut in 1941.

STDs are cumulative over time: the older you are the more likely you are to have met an STD, and possibly still to carry the infection. Women commonly have sex with men who are some years older. For example, 70 per cent of girls in the United Kingdom have their first sex with an older man, and he can be the bridge carrying the infection to them. All forms of STD can be greatly reduced if men use condoms, and gonorrhoea and chlamydia can be reduced if women use spermicides. Anything which makes it more difficult for a pathogen to pass from one partner to the other during sexual intercourse can have an important impact in slowing the spread of STDs. Even a partial interruption of transmission sets up a beneficial spiral of events: first, the individual's own risk of acquiring the disease is reduced; and, secondly, because everyone is a little less likely to catch the disease, so they are also less likely to meet an infected person if they do engage in risky sexual behaviour.

'A most presumptuous pox'

Syphilis is a bacterial infection. When Christopher Columbus' crew arrived back in Lisbon on 3 March 1493, they brought a new, virulent strain of the disease back from the New World. It was called the Great Pox, to distinguish it from smallpox, and it was quickly recognized as being transmitted by sexual intercourse – hence the name *syphilis*, from the Greek for 'companion of love'.

The disease that struck Europe in the 1490s was more severe and killed more rapidly than syphilis does today. It was called 'a most presumptuous pox', and victims suffered from pustules that were 'dark green and the sight thereof was more grievous unto the patient than the pain itself; and yet the pain was as though they had lain in the fire'. As in the developing countries today, poverty then drove many women into prostitution, and syphilis spread rapidly across Europe. It appeared in Naples in 1494 amongst the mercenary troops hired by the French King Charles VIII to besiege that city. So great was the impact of syphilis that the siege was lifted. As the mercenaries returned to their countries of origin, however, they spread the infection all over Europe. By 1498 syphilis had reached Asia, and by 1505 Japan. The British King Henry VIII had many symptoms of the later stages of syphilis.

The cleanest army in the world?

In the 1930s the US Surgeon-General claimed that one in ten adult Americans had syphilis. It was probably an exaggeration, but it is known that about 60 000 babies were born annually suffering from the disease, and all forms of sexually transmitted disease were common before the introduction of penicillin in 1943. The USA made heroic efforts to have 'the cleanest Army in the World' in France in World War I, and any soldier who had had sex with a local girl was required to report to a chemical prophylaxis centre within three hours. Here he had to sit on a special stool to have his genitals washed and the penile urethra flushed out with a mercury-based antiseptic. Both the British and American armies issued condoms to all men going on leave. Nevertheless, almost seven million days of active service were lost as a result of venereal disease, and a total of 383 706 soldiers were diagnosed with syphilis, gonorrhoea or chancroid between April 1917 and December 1919. In September 1919 a yearly admission rate of 766.55 per 1000 was reported. After 1918 venereal diseases became socially more visible. In 1935 Connecticut became the first state to pass a law requiring a blood test for syphilis before marriage. In a legislative double standard, but perhaps also recognizing contemporary social norms, some states required only the groom to be examined. Many of these laws remain in force in the USA today.

With the passage of time, syphilis has become a slower burning, although still potentially lethal, disease. Today, venereal syphilis begins as a painless ulcer (called a chancre) on the genitals, followed in three to six months by more general symptoms, such as fever. Untreated, it can result in damage to the brain, heart and great blood vessels. Winston Churchill's father, Randolph, died of syphilis. Henrik Ibsen's late nineteenth century play *Ghosts* deals with a promiscuous husband who passes syphilis to his son congenitally.

In 1909, the German microbiologist and immunologist Nobel laureate Paul Ehrlich introduced Salvarsan, a drug based on arsenic that worked better against syphilis than anything used previously. In 1943, John Mahoney introduced penicillin for the treatment of syphilis, and infections in US army recruits fell from 45 per 1000 at the beginning of World War II to only 2 per 1000 in 1956. Ehrlich called Salvarsan a 'magic bullet', because it poisoned the syphilis bacterium before it killed the person. The proliferation of 'magic bullet' antibiotics has probably been the greatest triumph of twentieth century medicine. But new antibiotics must be developed all the time as bacteria often become resistant to those in use. Revealingly, penicillin, the first true antibiotic, was discovered by Sir Alexander Fleming and used to treat casualties during World War II. He did not invent a new compound but isolated a chemical that fungi had evolved over hundreds of millions of years in competition with bacteria. In this case, a battle for survival between other species was turned to human advantage.

AIDS

AIDS (acquired immune deficiency syndrome) has a combination of attributes that no science fiction writer would have dared to invent. It is incurable, and almost universally lethal. For a decade or more the person carrying the virus can be symptom-free but infectious. HIV does not kill directly: people with HIV die from a miserable and painful collection of bacterial and fungal diseases that flourish as the virus attacks the person's immune system. HIV cannot be caught by drinking from contaminated cups, by shaking hands or from toilet seats; it does not persist for a long time in the bedclothes like smallpox, and it is not carried from person to person by mosquito bites like malaria. Indeed, HIV is so fragile, that it can survive only in 'bodily fluids' that are warm and contain an essential mixture of salts and proteins. Blood, semen, vaginal secretions and breast milk provide this safe environment.

AIDS was first identified in 1981, when Michael Gottlieb treated four cases of an unusual lung disease called *Pneumocystis carinii* pneumonia (or PCP) in San Francisco. All were previously fit young men and all were homosexuals. They were the first of hundreds of thousands of Americans who were to die of AIDS. AIDS, like the rabbit myxomatosis virus when it first appeared, seems to have the potential to kill well over 95 per cent of those infected. In 1984 Luc Montagnier in Paris isolated the virus (HIV) that causes AIDS.

The good news about AIDS is that it is mainly sexually transmitted. At a global level, nearly all AIDS is spread by sexual encounters. If HIV behaved like its cousin the common cold virus and could be caught by coughing and sneezing, instead of being transmitted merely in bodily fluids, then it might have infected most of the human race by now. The bad news is that often we do not know who is carrying the virus. Sex is a powerul urge, and people take risks, even when they know they are infectious, or they suspect their partner carries the virus. Sometimes, as in the case of sex workers, individuals have no choice about with whom they have sex. Anal intercourse transmits the virus more effectively than vaginal because the cells lining the rectum are more

The Burk Family, 1985. Patrick Burk, the father of the family, was a haemophiliac, who had unknowingly become infected with HIV from contaminated blood clotting-factors. He has since died of AIDS. He was having unprotected vaginal intercourse with his wife, Lauren, who also became infected with HIV. She became pregnant and bore him a son, Dwight, who acquired the infection from his mother either before, during or after birth. Dwight died of AIDS soon after this photograph was taken, and Lauren some years later. Nicole, their elder child, survives as an AIDS orphan.

[Lynn Johnson / Aurora and Quanta Productions, Inc.]

easily damaged than those lining the vagina and this permits easier transfer of the virus. In addition to sex, HIV can be transmitted by a contaminated blood transfusion, by people using intravenous drugs (who sometimes share needles), and it can pass across the placenta from an infected mother to her fetus or be transmitted by breastfeeding.

A virus is a tiny package of genetic material, even smaller than a bacterium. In order to multiply a virus must hijack the biochemical factory of a living cell. The coat that protects the genetic material of HIV, for example, is made partly from the membrane of the cell it infects. It is as if the Ford Motor Company smuggled their blueprint into General Motors and the General Motors factory started turning out Ford motor cars. An oddity of HIV is that it uses a genetic code based on ribonucleic acid (RNA) to carry information in the infected cell, instead of the more usual DNA. A special enzyme, called reverse transcriptase, ensures that the RNA message is translated into the host cell's DNA.

Like the polio virus, which is highly selective and damages only cells in the spinal cord, HIV attacks one variety of white blood cell, but one that happens to be crucially important in the body's natural defences against infection. Metaphorically, HIV commits its crime by killing the policemen, in this case the immune cells that protect against infections. Death may come from the pneumonia caused by the unusual bacterium *Pneumocystis carinii* mentioned earlier, or it may be from tuberculosis, as happens to many people who are infected with HIV in Africa, or from other bacterial or parasitic infections. The four gay men in San Francisco whom Dr Gottlieb first treated for *Pneumocystis carinii* pneumonia in 1981 were no different from other people in being exposed to the *Pneumocystis* bacterium – what made them vulnerable was that they were unable to deal with an infection which the rest of us often meet, but which our immune systems keep in check.

Like genital herpes, HIV once caught, is yours for life. Like rabies, once infection has occurred it is almost invariably lethal, although while rabies kills in a few days the HIV virus has a long silent latent period between infection and the first manifestations of the disease. On average, 50 per cent of those who are infected begin to show symptoms of AIDS or ARC (AIDS-related complex) eight to ten years after the first infection. During the whole of this time the individual with HIV has the potential to infect other people. From a public health perspective, AIDS kills too slowly. The longer the victim feels well and behaves normally, and the more successful therapies are at ameliorating the symptoms of the disease, the greater the risk that an infected individual will pass the virus on to others. This is not a reason for not trying every affordable and rational treatment, but it underscores the role of prevention in this disease of paradoxes.

The AIDS virus is difficult to transmit, even during sexual intercourse, and some discordant couples, where one partner has the infection and the other does not, have had unprotected sexual intercourse about a thousand times without passing the virus. But the presence of other STDs, such as gonorrhoea, greatly increases the risk of acquiring or transmitting AIDS. This is because such diseases damage the genital epithelium, making it easier for HIV to reach the blood stream. In the West, clusters of heterosexual HIV infection occur as a result of infection from drug users or bisexual men, but a self-sustaining heterosexual epidemic has not occurred. In parts of the developing world, where the average number of sexual partners may be greater, where access to condoms is more limited than in the West, and where STDs commonly go untreated, then the heterosexual spread of HIV has the capacity to produce a devastating, self-sustaining epidemic. In Thailand, by 1991, one in thirty young men aged 20 to 22 carried the virus, and in one provincial city,

Stigmatization

On 22 September 1497 the Town Council of Edinburgh held an emergency meeting to discuss the sudden appearance of a 'new contagious Distemper, supposed to be venereal, called the Grandgore.' It had arrived in Edinburgh in the aftermath of the raising of the siege of Naples in 1495, and this disease, later to be called syphilis, was spread all over Europe by the disbanded mercenary army of King Charles VIII of France.

The Scots decided that in order to prevent the spread of this dreaded new disease, all infected individuals were to be banished to the Island of Inchcolme in the Firth of Forth, which is a pretty bare, barren, inhospitable island. Anyone who was subsequently found to be infected and still at large in the city 'Salle be brynt on the cheik with the marking irne that thai may be kennit in tym to cum.' So stigmatization because of sexually transmitted disease has a very long history. But at least with syphilis there were outward and visible signs that a person was infected, and this made it possible to contain the spread. From a public health point of view it is far more difficult to deal with HIV, where for many years an individual may remain asymptomatic but infectious to others. Screening is not a viable option, particularly when there is no cure on offer.

AIDS.
Prevention is the only cure we've got.

[Australia's *Grim Reaper* advertising campaign, 1987.]

The grim reaper. This Australian advertisement conveyed the correct message, that prevention is the only cure, but the alarmist approach did more to scare than to educate.

the rate was one in ten. (Thailand, however, is one of the few places where a concerted effort to reduce the rate of new infections by promoting condoms and making 'condom-only' brothels is paying dividends.) In the Republic of South Africa, one in ten pregnant women now carries HIV, and in the province of KwaZulu it is one in five. In parts of Malawi levels of infection are even higher.

HIV has the ability to evolve more rapidly than any other known organism and this is one reason why a vaccine has been so difficult to develop. Smallpox, in contrast, was eradicated because it is a highly stable virus and one kind of vaccine blocked all infections, whether the individual lived in Sweden or Somalia. In addition, the symptoms of smallpox followed within a few days of infection and during the short time the individual was infectious their body was covered with an instantly recognizable set of blisters: therefore, those at risk could be quarantined or vaccinated – with or without their consent. As noted, most of the people spreading HIV around the world do not even know they have the disease. Even if an effective vaccine is eventually developed, HIV will never be eradicated. If the AIDS epidemic is to be brought under control, it will be through prevention.

The politics of AIDS

Plagues terrify. They bring out the worst in people. When the Black Death spread across the Middle East and Europe in the fourteenth century the

Muslims blamed it on the Christians and the Christians blamed the Jews. In Strasbourg, 2000 Jews were burned alive on a large scaffold erected in their own cemetery.

Medical scientists now know how every individual molecule fits together to make the AIDS virus. The nature and the course of the infection in adults and children is fully understood. The real problem in preventing AIDS lies not in the laboratory, but in the bedroom and in the council chamber. If we are scientifically honest, then outside one or two highly circumscribed areas, the billions of dollars spent on HIV prevention have achieved relatively little. The spread of AIDS is the biggest public health failure of the twentieth century.

As the AIDS epidemic has spread across the globe, governments, without exception, failed to take action as early as they should have done. Even some medical agencies supplying treatments to haemophiliacs delayed taking needed action until it was too late. People, it seems, will count coffins, but they are not prepared to be convinced by scientific predictions.

Given the pattern of HIV spread, it is self-evident that AIDS will almost always appear first in intravenous drug users, prostitutes, and gay men. If HIV infection can be retarded in these groups then human lives will be saved and the downstream spread of the epidemic into the general population will be slowed. But in the real world of politics, it is always easier to put resources into 'innocent' groups, such as people who acquire HIV through contaminated blood transfusions, than it is to improve the health of prostitutes. The Global Programme on AIDS set up by the World Health Organization in the 1980s spent more money on testing blood for transfusions than on treating STDs in prostitutes or buying condoms, although the latter strategies could have had a greater impact on the epidemic.

The US government under President Reagan obstructed action early in the epidemic, when most lives might have been saved. Almost twenty years later the US Congress still opposes the distribution of clean needles to drug addicts, even though other countries have shown the efficiacy of such a policy. The Vatican continues to teach that men with the AIDS virus in their semen should not use condoms. In 1990, at a conference, a priest from the Institute of the Family in Rome was asked what should a married haemophiliac man do if he had acquired the AIDS virus from treatment for his blood clotting disorder. The reply was that the man should abstain from sexual intercourse with his wife, but if the abstinence was threatening the integrity of the marriage, then he should have intercourse – but without a condom. In other words, it is preferable to kill your wife with AIDS, than to re-examine a teaching based on an interpretation of 'natural law' made by the Early Fathers of the Church 1500 years ago.

By particular misfortune, AIDS entered the gay commuity in the USA at almost the exact moment that homosexual men had begun to establish their own lifestyle. In cities such as San Francsico, a large population of gay men came out of the closet. The frequency of homosexual intercourse and rate of change of partners rose rapidly, particularly with the spread of the bath-house culture. Some gay men reported having more than a hundred different sexual partners in a year. Biologically, the gay community in North America (and to a lesser but very real extent in the rest of the developed world) became a single interconnected sexual network. HIV spread rapidly, and between 1981 and 1997 in San Francisco alone 25 000 cases of AIDS were reported and 17 000 died. In contrast, over the same interval, in the same population there were only 300 cases of HIV infection as a result of heterosexual infection.

Infected people are much more vocal than those who are merely at risk of infection: 'I know I am going to die unless something is done' is a much

Arise Sir Condom!

Fable has it that Dr Condom was a physician to King Charles II of Britain, knighted – an appropriate term – for his inventive contribution to monarchical welfare. Sadly, there is no evidence that a Dr Condom ever existed, and anyhow contraceptive sheaths were first described a century earlier by the Italian physician Fallopio, who also gave his name to the fallopian tubes that carry the eggs from the ovary to the uterus. It is possible that the word is a corruption of the Latin *quondam* or *condus*. In 1705, the Duke of Argyll obtained from London 'a certain instrument called a quondam, which occasioned the debauching of a great number of Ladies of quality, and other young gentlewomen'.

The oldest extant condoms were recently discovered by archaeologists in a midden in Dudley Castle, dating, interestingly, from the time of Charles II; they were made out of animal intestine.

The oldest – and to this date only – genuine written reference to a royal use of condoms comes from the Royal Archives in a letter of 26 April 1749 from Colonel Joseph Yorke, the Secretary to the British Embassy in Paris, and concerns the amorous ways of King Louis XV of France:

> *I had a Commission given me about the same time, which diverted me much, and I confess putting all the Circumstances together, I almost suspect they are destined for the service of the closet, in case such apprehensions should prevail again: The commission was, to procure from England, as it is not a manufacture of this Country, 300 or more, of those preventive machines, made use of by the Gallant tho' prudent young Gentlemen of this age; I was desired for fear of search or seizure as a Counterband, to have them directed for H.M.C.M., and I expect them with great impatience, tho' my merchant was startled at the quantity, and begg'd a few days extraordinary to provide them; I am almost tempted to ask an exclusive privilege for the importing of them into France, and think it would be a very genteel way of raising a fortune. I ask pardon for troubling your Royal Highness with so ridiculous a story, tho' upon my honour I don't think I am much out in my conjecture; the person that gave me the Commission is the King's Maître d'Hotel.*

stronger motivation than 'There is a low possibility I may get this infection in two years' time.' The result is that there is now a range of expensive and difficult-to-use drugs which ameliorate the symptoms of full-blown AIDS, but much less research has been completed on a chemical method which women could use to protect themselves against HIV infection. There are millions of women in developed and in developing countries who suspect their sexual partner may be putting them at risk of HIV infection, but who are not in a position to negotiate the use of a condom. Spermicidal chemicals kill HIV in the test tube, but in high doses they can also cause vaginal irritation, which could increase, rather than slow, HIV transmission. Clearly careful research is needed, but in comparison with work on new therapies it is relatively easy and simple to conduct research into cheap virucides that could be used in developing countries. Yet after fifteen years of waiting little has been done.

Of course, therapies deserve study, and anything that makes a horrible disease less painful is welcome. In the 1990s many new drugs against the AIDS virus have been developed. Some block the replication of the virus by supplying inappropriate building blocks for the genetic code, while others inhibit the enzyme that copies the viral RNA into the DNA of the infected cell. Modern treatments can reduced HIV to undetectable levels in the blood, but such therapies often cost over US $10000 per year, they have serious side effects, and in the end the virus is always likely to mutate, escape the therapy and kill the patient.

The harsh fact remains that the human propensity to deny many aspects of human sexuality and to place the cart of treatment in front of the horse of prevention has allowed the AIDS epidemic to spread more rapidly than it needed to do. No single country acted as early as it should have done. Early in the epidemic, the San Francisco gay community failed to close the bathhouses, even though it was clear they were a major site for spreading infections.

Where did AIDS come from?

Louis Pasteur demonstrated that spontaneous generation never happens. HIV, like all other living things, must have evolved from a very closely related infectious agent carried by some other mammalian species. It should be remembered, though, that the original species may have hosted the AIDS virus for so long that it may now show few or no symptoms of the disease. Several hundred laboratory chimpanzees have been deliberately infected with HIV, both by injection and by placing infected material against the cervix, as would occur in sexual intercourse. Infected animals developed antibodies, and the virus seems to live on in the same way it does in human beings yet, with one exception, all the infected chimpanzees have remained healthy. Could HIV have come from chimpanzees? An HIV-like virus has been isolated from wild chimpanzees in Gabon, and it will infect human cells in the laboratory. The African vervet monkey harbours a simian immunodeficiency virus (SIV) that produces a lethal AIDS-like disease when injected into Asian rhesus monkeys. HIV-2, the human virus strain of the AIDS virus that is found in parts of West Africa, has been isolated from sooty mangabey monkeys from that area.

Whatever the animal origin of HIV, how was it spread? Most probably the virus was transmitted during hunting. Apes and monkeys are still killed for their meat, and there has been a long, sad history of capturing primates for zoological parks, circuses or laboratory experiments. It is common to kill adult females in order to capture their infants. Obviously, there are many opportunities when a wounded animal might bite its tormentors, or when a hunter skinning a dead animal might cut himself with his knife, thus infecting himself with the virus.

Perhaps there were a number of past occasions when HIV jumped from its host to human beings. The victim would probably have lived for a decade or so before dying from a disease such as tuberculosis, which would never have been traced back to an injury from a wild animal. Such an infected individual could have passed HIV on to one or more sexual partners, and perhaps a child or two was infected by its mother during pregnancy and died in infancy, but a self-sustaining epidemic would not have occurred: the spark jumped but there was not the tinder to be ignited.

The current AIDS epidemic probably occurred because of the dramatic social changes that have swept Africa and the rest of the world in the second half of the twentieth century. People have become more mobile. Perhaps the African hunter who got infected bought a bicycle to visit his girlfriend in another village, and she lived on a truck route frequented by long-distance lorry drivers hauling felled timber to the coast, and had other boyfriends beside the hunter. One of them was offered money for sex by a foreign visitor. Twenty-four hours later that person was half way around the world in San Francisco. We shall never know the details. One way or another, the critical mass of infected individuals grew much larger than in the past, and the human tinder caught fire. The recent increase in Africa's population, the migration of young men to big cities to look for work, the weakening of tribal traditions, the movement of single women to urban areas where they may strike up a series of sexual relationships or be driven by poverty into frank prostitution, the rape of the rain forests by multinational corporations eager for cheap timber, and the invention of the jumbo-jet could all have contributed.

Stopping AIDS

In theory, the necessary knowledge already exists to halt all further spread of AIDS today. Unlike cholera, HIV is not transmitted in dirty water; unlike influenza, it is not coughed and sneezed about the place; unlike malaria, there is no insect vector. The spread of the virus is determined purely by human behaviour: people decide to have unprotected sex, or to risk using drugs. It follows that there are three ways to try to interrupt the pandemic: to educate people about the nature of the disease and about ways in which the virus is spread (and ways in which it is not spread); to provide easy access to condoms and to clean needles and syringes; and to treat all other sexually transmitted diseases, which are an important factor in the acquisition and transmission of HIV. Some pilot projects to slow the spread of AIDS have succeeded. It has been shown, for example in Cameroon, that prostitutes will protect themselves against sexual diseases if given knowledge and opportunity. In Nairobi the cost of averting one HIV infection through educating sex workers and providing condoms is as low as US $10. Even in a poor country, the cost to society of caring for someone dying from AIDS is often several hundred dollars. When condoms have been made accessible in small stores and appropriately priced, as in the Democratic Republic of Congo, use has risen rapidly. In a

The condom – an Italian invention

It was syphilis that led the Italian anatomist Gabriel Fallopio to develop the condom. In 1564, in his book on syphilis, *De Morbo Gallico* (The French Disease), he says the following:

> *As often as a man has intercourse, he should (if possible) wash the genitals, or wipe them with a cloth; afterward he should use a small linen cloth made to fit the glans, and draw forward the prepuce over the glans; if he can do so, it is well to moisten it with saliva or with a lotion; however, it does not matter ... I tried the experiment on eleven hundred men, and I call immortal God to witness that not one of them was infected.*

We have never thought of using a condom for *post-coital* prevention of sexually transmitted diseases, and although it would only protect the man and not the woman, perhaps we should develop Fallopio's ideas further. A suitably medicated cap placed over the glans after intercourse might be the ideal way of delivering bactericidal or virucidal drugs to the site at which organisms are most likely to enter the male reproductive tract, namely the urethral opening.

disease that is increasing exponentially, it should be self-evident that the sooner education and services are made available to those at highest risk, the greater will be the impact. Unfortunately, such interventions are still perceived as being controversial in many quarters, and even those implementing programmes sometimes have little sense of scale. As a result, HIV continues to race around the globe at a terrifying pace.

Whatever way we look at AIDS, it is going to be much more expensive than is currently acknowledged. In particular, the cost of inaction in the preventive field today will be immeasurably more expensive in lives lost and economic opportunities foregone tomorrow. Looked at globally, the AIDS pandemic is only just beginning. There are 50 000 orphans whose parents have died from AIDS in one province of Tanzania, and there may be as many as ten million AIDS orphans in the whole of Africa. Once AIDS becomes manifest, then if no treatment is given the individual usually dies from concurrent infections within a year. AIDS is now the commonest cause of adult death in several parts of Africa, such as Uganda, Malawi and the Côte d'Ivoire, and the annual death toll worldwide is approaching two million. Even in the USA, by the early 1990s more Americans had died from AIDS than were killed fighting in the Vietnamese war.

The spread of HIV in India rocketed upwards during the 1990s. There may be over 100 000 prostitutes in Bombay (now Mumbai), and most already have at least one bacterial STD and many two. It has been obvious since the early 1980s that these unhappy women would become heavily infected with HIV once the virus reached India, but prevention was begun too late and too little was done. By the end of the 1990s sex workers all over India had become heavily infected with the AIDS virus and the potential for further spread is mind boggling. By the early years of the new millennium more people may carry the virus in India than have been infected in the whole of the rest of the world since AIDS was first recognized.

HIV can cross the placenta and infect the fetus directly, the baby may become infected at birth by contact with the mother's blood, or it may acquire the infection from her breast milk. As many as 30 per cent of infants born to HIV-positive mothers will be infected in this way. The drug AZT has recently been shown to be very effective in reducing the risk of an HIV-infected woman passing the virus to her fetus, but it is so expensive that it is beyond the reach of most people in the developing countries. And if women in these countries were to abandon breastfeeding from fear of HIV transmission, the powdered milk would kill more babies than the HIV would have done. So vertical transmission in developing countries will remain a fact of life – or death – since nearly all infected children will be dead before the age of 5.

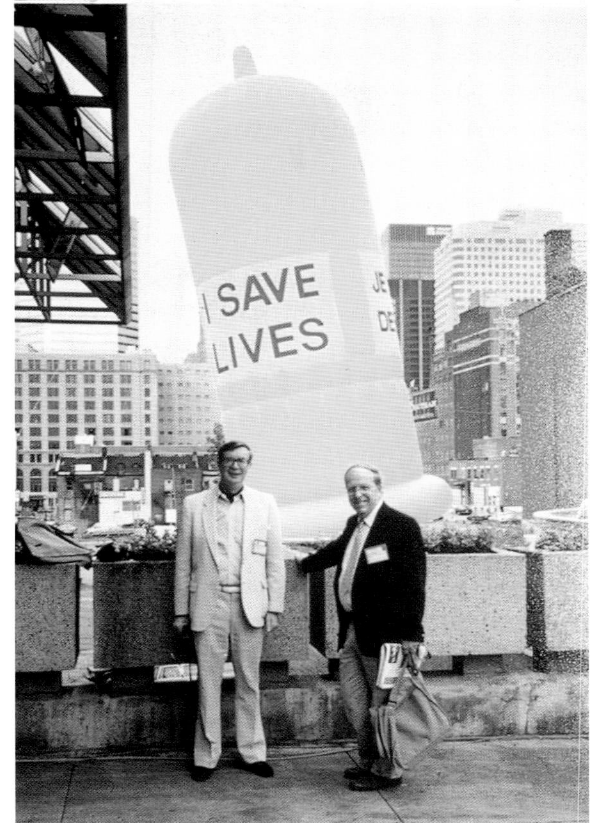

The world's largest condom. The authors beside their 2180 cubic metre (77 000 cubic foot), nipple-ended, non-lubricated hot air balloon at the 1989 Montreal AIDS conference. This condom, 6 metres across and 9 metres high (20 feet by 30 feet) was made to draw attention to this life-saving device. It is the only condom licensed to carry a passenger, but was banned from flying at the International Hot Air Balloon festival in Albuquerque, New Mexico, on the grounds that it was obscene.

Intellectually, we can ponder the paradox that sex may have evolved partly as the multicellular organism's answer to the rapid reproduction and genetic change found in bacteria and viruses, and that sex and mortality itself appear to be inextricably linked. We may with some truth say that even life itself is a fatal sexually transmitted disease. But, at a more immediate level, AIDS reminds us that our dominion over the rest of Nature is not as secure as we once thought. AIDS has jolted us into remembering that evolutionary competition has not come to an end. It was not an accident, but a consequence of rapid cultural change and the explosion in human numbers that made possible the spread of HIV: it was a plague waiting to happen. And there is no reason to believe that AIDS is the last assault of its type. With the rising human population, global travel and new techniques – from intensive farming to germ warfare research – the potential for new diseases rises. The conquest of disease is a battle that is never over.

11 SEX AND MORTALITY

'Only in the world I fill up a place which may be better supplied when I have made it empty.'
William Shakespeare, *As You Like It*, Act 1, Scene 2

[M.B. Renfree.]

Disposable male? *Antechinus stuartii*, a marsupial shrew, lives in the forests of eastern Australia.

The tiny marsupial shrew (*Antechinus stuartii*) lives in eastern Australia. With the approach of the mating season in the spring, the males, driven by their rising testosterone levels, become increasingly aggressive towards one another and stake out territories in the forest. The females come into oestrus and all the matings take place in a two week rutting period. The males become scrawny, bald and battle-scarred, and the increased amount of stress hormone produced by their adrenal glands depresses their immune systems, so they succumb to opportunistic infections and parasites, rather like people with AIDS. As a result, there is a cataclysmic male die-off, and every male in the population perishes before the females have had a chance to produce new male replacements when they give birth to their litters one month after mating. The survival of the species therefore hangs by the thread of those as-yet-unborn male fetuses, who will become sires of the next brood a year later. If young males are castrated before the rut and released back into the wild, they can survive for another year or two, as do the females. This is a dramatic demonstration of the poisonous effects of testosterone; no sex, no death!

A similar situation exists with domestic cats, where castrates live longer than intact toms, and it has been most dramatically illustrated in wild Soay sheep on the island of St Kilda, off the west coast of Scotland; Soay rams castrated at birth live many years longer than their intact male counterparts. The message is stark and simple. Once the male has completed his task of siring the next generation he is superfluous, and becomes an unwelcome competitor for females and their young when food becomes scarce. How sensible to use his testosterone to bring about his premature demise.

No sex, no death is central to the myth of the Garden of Eden. Adam and Eve ate of the fruit of the tree of knowledge, became sexual beings and were expelled from Paradise: 'for dust thou art and unto dust shalt thou return' (Genesis 3:19). Can biological observations 'explain' death more fully than theological speculation?

The highly stressed human male executive with his ulcers and coronary diseases may be telling the same story as little *Antechinus*. Over 50000 men

[National Gallery of Canada, Ottawa.]

***Eve, the Serpent and Death*, Hans Baldung, *ca.* 1510–15.** In the myth of Adam and Eve, God denies the first couple eternal life as a punishment for their wilfulness. Christ also recognized the intuitive link between sex and death: 'The children of this world marry, and are given in marriage: but they which shall be accounted worthy to obtain that world, and the resurrection from the dead, neither marry, nor are given in marriage: neither can they die any more' (Luke 20: 34–6). Saint Paul closed the theological circle: 'as in Adam all die, even so in Christ shall all be made alive.' (1 Corinthians 15: 22).

aged from 50 to 64 die from heart attacks in the USA each year, but only one-third as many women of the same age succumb to the came cause. Could it also be that among men castration would increase the expectation of life?

At first sight it might seem improbable that a population of men would be available for study who had had their testicles removed early in life. Tragically, in the early decades of this century, more than twenty states of the USA passed laws compelling sterilization and in some cases even castration of men institutionalized for mental illness, or who had committed certain crimes such as rape. In 1969 Drs Hamilton and Mestler followed up a group of these men and discovered that castrated men, on average, live 13.6 years longer than men with testicles. Men who had been admitted to institutions with a variety of problems and have remained there all their lives are not representative of the normal population, but Hamilton and Mestler gathered data on more than 1000 castrated and non-castrated men from the same set of hospitals for the mentally retarded in the state of Kansas. The difference in survival is the largest of any known intervention. Smoking a pack or more of cigarettes a day, for example, reduces an individual's expectation of life by 4.9 years – a significant amount – but nothing compared with the extra life castration brings. Men who are castrated before puberty live even longer than those who are castrated later in life. Not only may life seem longer to the eunuch – it is longer!

Males, then, may die at a higher rate than females because they are partially redundant, but why should females die? Why not just go on reproducing generation after generation of young? All sexually reproducing animals have a finite lifespan. By contrast, bacteria and protozoa, which divide into identical cells, can continue to multiply for as long as the environment allows and enjoy potential genetic immortality. The melding and shuffling of chromosomes during the production of eggs and sperm ensures that every child of sexual intercourse is a unique individual: he or she is also condemned to mortality. Sexual animals with their alternating generations of eggs plus sperm and multicellular bodies, achieve genetic immortality only through total biological equality with an individual of the same species but opposite sex and the necessarily limited lifespan of the multicellular body: Faust should not have been called upon to forfeit his soul to achieve immortality, but to acquire his sexuality.

Animal cells, including those of human beings, can be kept alive in glass dishes or small bottles containing special growth medium. When groups of cells, including fragments of human tissue, are cultured in this way they will live for many generations. But in 1961 Leonard Hayflick discovered that most of the cell lines that are perpetuated *in vitro* cease to grow and divide after a specific number of cell divisions, just as appears to be the case in the whole animal. A small proportion of cells in tissue culture, however, change their behaviour. They become undifferentiated and cancer-like and will continue to multiply for as long as they are kept at body temperature and supplied with external nutrients. Immortality can be restored to the cells that make up our bodies but only at the expense of the specialized functions that are the foundation of multicellular life.

Male castration

> *The fact is that animals, if they be subjected to a modification in minute organs, are liable to immense modifications in their general configuration. This phenomenon may be observed in the case of gelded animals: only a minute organ of the animal is mutilated, and the creature passes from male to the female form. We may infer, then, that if in the primary configuration of the embryo an infinitesimally minute but essential organ sustains a change of magnitude one way or the other, the animal will in one case turn to male and in the other to female; and also that, if the said organ be obliterated altogether, the animal will be of neither one sex nor the other.*

Thus wrote Aristotle in his *History of Animals*, over 2000 years ago. The origins of male castration are lost in the mists of antiquity, and already by Aristotle's time it was a common practice in man and animals, used as a way of modifying sexual behaviour. It was not simply the inviting scrotal position of the testes that led to their removal, because Aristotle also describes the routine castration of cockerels, whose intra-abdominal testes had to be destroyed by means of hot irons thrust into the abdominal cavity.

> *Birds are castrated at the rump at the part where the two sexes unite in copulation. If you burn this twice or thrice with hot irons, then if the bird be full grown, his crest grows sallow, he ceases to crow, and forgoes sexual passion; but if you cauterise the bird when young, none of these male attributes or propensities will come to him as he grows up.*

In the Byzantine era, male castration was a necessary pre-requisite for a career in politics, since it rendered you incorruptible by sexual temptation. And as we are told in the Bible (Matthew 19:12), 'There be eunuchs, which have made themselves eunuchs for the Kingdom of Heaven's sake.' In eighteenth century Russia, a peasant named Kondraty Selivanov took this biblical statement literally, and after castrating himself, founded a religious sect that eventually numbered 300 000 emasculates. Selivanov's portrait reveals a man with a wispy beard and a fine head of hair – baldness is a sign of circulating testosterone and you never see a bald eunuch. Selivanov's castrated followers revered him as the son of the virgin Empress Elizabeth, having been conceived by the Holy Ghost!

Research is coming tantalizingly close to understanding the molecular basis of cell mortality. Each chromosome in a cell is capped with a special region called the telomere. Elizabeth Blackburn of the University of California, San Francisco, has shown that the telomere consists of simple DNA codes that are repeated up to seventy times. The same code is found from yeast cells to human cells and it is laid down by a unique enzyme which is a mixture of a protein and RNA. Such an enzyme is found both in the stem cells that give rise to sperm and eggs, and it is found in bacteria which can multiply indefinitely, but not in normal body, or somatic cells. In the mortal cells of our bodies, every time the cell divides, the telomere is shortened and the fuse on the end of life also grows shorter. Cancer cells, however, contain the enzyme that repairs the telomeres, permitting uncontrolled cell growth. What will this specialized area of cell and molecular biology lead to? Will it just be an interesting observation, will it provide new ways of treating cancer, or might it uncover the molecular key to human longevity?

The castration of women

In contrast to the castration of men, which antedates the beginning of historical record, the castration of women is both much more difficult to perform and much more recent in origin. The first recorded operation took place in the sixteenth century. Regnier de Graaf tells us of a farmer, infuriated by his daughter's perpetual flirting, 'who tied her up in a suitable manner and castrated her; he happened to be skilled in castrating female pigs; his daughter consequently forgot her lustful passion and thence forward attended sedulously to her domestic duties and nothing else.' Wilhelm Magnus tells a similar story of a mare gelder in Mainz, Germany.

The great surgeon, Sir Percival Pott of St Bartholomew's Hospital, London, famous to generations of medical students as the origin of the eponymous leg fracture, recorded in 1775 how he had occasion to operate on a young girl of 23 whose ovaries were protruding through a hernia in the abdominal cavity. Following removal of the ovaries, he reported that her breasts shrank markedly in size and she never menstruated again. Although this was the first accurate description of the consequences of ovariectomy in a woman, and the first clue to the fact that menstruation is under ovarian control, his observation passed unnoticed by the medical community.

The person who really alerted medical interest in the castration of women and its consequences was a young French doctor, Roberts. He was on a mission to India, and on his way from Delhi to Bombay came across a group of dancing girls, or *hidjras*, who on clinical examination, proved to have poorly developed breasts and did not menstruate. Although he could find no surgical scars and the women denied having been castrated, he became convinced that they must have been forcibly ovariectomized. He returned to France and reported his findings in a public lecture in 1843. Public and medical opinion in Europe was incensed at the idea that Eastern despots were castrating women to serve their licentious propensities.

Even the record of the USA is by no means unblemished. In the nineteenth century, Dr Robert Battey of Athens, Georgia, developed and advocated bilateral ovariectomy as a cure for hysteria in young girls – it became known as Battey's operation, and enjoyed a brief but terrifying popularity. By 1906 it was estimated that 150 000 women had been castrated. Although the practice did not spill over into Europe, Battey was elected into Honorary Fellowship of the Edinburgh Obstetrical Society for his contributions to gynaecology.

The ageing process

Twenty-two centuries ago, Aristotle said, 'the causes of the length and brevity of life call for investigation'. The investigation is still going on. In general, the busy mouse 'wears out' faster than the racehorse, but there is more than body size influencing longevity. Human beings live longer than whales, but tortoises can live longer than we do. Probably, the pace of reproduction and the investment we make in each individual offspring are important factors, in addition to body size.

Possibly there are biochemical changes that slowly degrade cell function. Oxygen is normally restricted to certain cell compartments, but free radicals or highly reactive oxygen atoms may leak out and slowly poison the cell. Excess sugars may form sticky bonds with proteins, rather like the caramelization of burnt sugar. While there is still debate over what exactly is happening (for example, do antioxidants such as beta-carotene counter damage caused by free radicals?), it is known that reduced calorie intake during youth can cause an extension of lifespan. Young rats given 30 per cent fewer calories live 30 per cent longer. Insurance company data show that those who live longest tended to be underweight in their twenties and to gain weight slowly in middle age.

The physical and mental performance of both sexes climbs slowly in the teens to peak in the twenties, thirties, and then declines little by little in the forties, fifties and sixties. Top physical performance for games such as tennis, comes in the twenties. Mathematicians and musicians such as Newton, Einstein and Mozart often also make their greatest mental contributions in the third decade of life. However, biologists often excel in their thirties and forties, and politicians in their fifties and sixties. The US Constitution requires an individual to be 25 years old before standing for election to Congress and at least 35 to run for president. Writers and artists of all kinds often have carried their creativity well into their eighth or ninth decade – or have been carried into longevity by it. Picasso, Matisse, George O'Keefe and Michelangelo come to mind, among painters and sculptors, along with Rebecca West, playwrights George Bernard Shaw and Marc Connolly, architect Frank Lloyd Wright, choreographer Martha Graham and pianist Artur Rubinstein. Nevertheless, Yehudi Menuhin might be the first to admit that he did not play the violin quite as well at 82 as he did at 15.

The average expectation of life in the USA has risen from 45 years in 1900 to 73 for men and 79 for women in 1996. Advances in hygiene and medical care have extended the average rather than the maximum length of human life. The greatest increases in the expectation of life have come largely from reduced infant and childhood mortality as a result of the conquest of infectious diseases, rather than from the conquest of cancer, heart disease or other aspects of ageing. Certainly more people are surviving into old age, and today there are a remarkable 36000 people aged 100 years or older in the USA.

Jeanne Calment (21 February 1875 – 4 August 1997). Madame Calment lived longer than any other human being – 122 years. As a teenager, she met Vincent Van Gogh in her birth place, Arles; 'very ugly, ungracious, impolite, sick' she called him. She married in 1896 and her husband was too old to fight in World War I. Her grandson predeceased her by thirty-seven years. She rode her bicycle until she was 100, broke two bones in a fall at the age of 115 and only gave up smoking when she was 117. She became increasingly frail after age 110 and had to move into a nursing home, and for two or three years before her death she became almost totally deaf. She had a feisty attitude to life, characteristic of people who live a long time: 'I only have one wrinkle', she once said, 'and I am sitting on it.'

Cases of what appear to be rapid premature ageing occasionally begin in childhood, but it is not certain whether the process is really comparable to ageing in an old person. Diabetes appears to accelerate the appearance of arthritis, cataracts and atherosclerosis – all attributes of ageing. Exotic attempts to increase lifespan by such ruses such as adding vitamin E to the diet or transplanting thymus cells have not been demonstrated to work. Experiments have been published purporting to show an effect on longevity of these and other compounds, but the real explanation is merely that animals eat less when dosed with these odd substances and therefore lose weight. Then, like other underweight animals, they live a little longer. Unlike the intriguing work of molecular biologists on telomeres, the search for some Methuselah pill to take every day in order to live longer seems likely to remain unfulfilled. Whatever way we look at it, for the present, life is a terminal condition.

Curiously, while vitamin production and other efforts to slow ageing are a multibillion dollar industry, the one thing that most unambiguously and dramatically accelerates ageing and shortens life expectation, namely smoking, has proved difficult to control. Some limitation of advertising is occurring in developed countries, but growing tobacco continues to be subsidized by the US government and the European Common Market. 'Tobaccosis', as Rei Ravenholt, a distinguished epidemiologist, has called it, has become the leading killer in much of the developed world. Columbus observed the smoking of tobacco on the island of Cuba in 1492 and Queen Elizabeth I 'was as familiar with a tobacco pipe as with her sceptre'. Tobacco was sniffed and chewed, but the rolled paper cigarette was only perfected in 1884. Cigarette consumption has multiplied 100 times in the twentieth century. Almost half a million people die from smoking-related diseases each year in the USA. In contrast, about 30000 people a year die from other addictions, such as crack cocaine or heroin. Globally, a hundred million people will die in this century from tobacco-related illness, a number roughly equal to the global toll of death from international warfare over the same interval. Indeed, if as seems likely, the supply of free cigarettes to US troops in World War II led to 10 per cent of men becoming addicted, then by now more men will have died as a result of smoking than were killed in combat.

The menopause

Aristotle wrote,

> *the menstrual discharge ceases in most women about their fortieth year; but with those in whom it goes on longer it lasts even to the fiftieth, and women of that age have been known to bear children. But beyond that age there is no case on record.*

The menopause is reproductive death several decades before ordinary cell (somatic) death. Even allowing for the fact that women may live longer today than did our hunter–gatherer ancestors, undoubtedly many women always lived well beyond the menopause. What is it, and why did it evolve?

For most animals, life after reproduction is invisible to evolution. Individuals can no longer compete in the battle of survival of the fittest, once they have passed on their genes to the next generation. But among female primates, where caring for the next generation is more prolonged, the mother may still be contributing to her own reproductive fitness for some time after the birth of her last child. For chimpanzees, who teach their young the tricks of survival and rules of social behaviour, parental survival beyond weaning is increasingly important.

In a way, the menopause is a biological recognition of the increasing importance of cultural evolution. The immediate cause of the human menopause is that the ovary runs out of its supply of eggs, and so the monthly cycle of hormone changes causing menstruation no longer needs to take place: fertility ends with a full stop not a period. The menopause, like so much else, depends solely on the hormones that circulate – or do not circulate. The gradual decline of fertility that occurs in women during their forties has its shadow, but not a complete parallel, in other primates.

Parturition is probably more difficult for human beings than for any other mammal. The risk of death in childbirth rises rapidly, and women over 40 years have five times the death rate of women in their twenties. If women did go on having children in their fifties most might end up dying as a result of pregnancy or delivery. Even today if a woman dies in Bangladesh there is a 98 per cent chance that her infant will succumb also. Have we evolved a menopause to ensure that women live to bring up the children they have rather than die whilst trying to have more? Another possible biological pressure to evolve a discrete menopause may be related to the increasing risk of congenital abnormalities that occurs with rising maternal age. Unlike the man, who makes new sperm all the time, the eggs in a woman's ovary have been 'frozen' in the last phase of chromosomal rearrangement since she was a fetus in her mother's womb. Perhaps for this reason congenital anomalies become more common with increasing maternal age, and a 40 year old, for example, has a one in forty risk of having a baby with Down's syndrome.

The menopause, then, may protect the woman against the dangers of childbirth, the risks of congenitally abnormal children, secure her role as successful parent of her youngest children until they themselves are independent, and provide her group with essential wisdom and information about the world in which they live. But perhaps we can learn most about the human menopause by looking at those other big-brained mammals, the whales and dolphins. Toshio Kasuya and Helene Marsh studied pilot whales killed off Japan and found no female pregnant over the age of 36 and none with functioning ovaries over age 40. Yet several females in any school were 'post-menopausal' and the oldest was 63 years old. Some female sperm whales also seem to live long after the age of childbearing. Remarkably, some female pilot whales were still breastfeeding up to fourteen years after their last delivery. Do these old female pilot whales provide continuity of information for the school? (Pilot whales dive to as much as 2000 feet (about 600 metres) and a long term memory of the ocean floor may be important.) Do they breastfeed their last-born child until it becomes adult, or do they wet-nurse the children of other females in the school?

There is no such thing as a male menopause. Men go on making sperm and secreting testosterone from puberty until death, albeit with some slowing in production in later life. The differing reproductive responses to ageing in men and women once again reflect the much smaller investment made by men in reproduction, so it is always to a man's evolutionary advantage to leave open the possibility of fathering a child, even though his chances of finding a fertile mate may be reduced and he is unlikely to see his child pass puberty. The menopause is another testimony to Nature's dual standard for the two sexes.

In contemporary Papua New Guinea, 50 per cent of women have had their menopause by the age of 43.6 years, but since mediaeval times and in most of the rest of the world, the average age when women stop menstruating is 50. Women who have never had children have an earlier menopause than those that have children and, for reasons not understood, mothers of twins enter the menopause about a year earlier than other women. Women who smoke, on average, have a menopause two years earlier than those who do not.

The most comprehensive study of the physical symptoms of the menopause comes from the Dutch town of Ede, where menopausal women have been intensively monitored since 1967 by the late Pieter van Keep, Anna Oldenhave and others. The menopause itself can be defined only retrospectively and it is usually considered to have occurred when six months have elapsed without a spontaneous period. However, signs of an impending climacteric are often apparent a decade beforehand and in Ede a quarter of women were having irregular periods by their early forties.

About half of all women sail through the menopause with few complaints, while the other half may have a miserable time of variable duration and intensity. The commonest problems are hot flushes (and their accompaniment night sweats) and episodes of irritability or depression, sometimes with fits of crying and general loss of self-confidence. In the Dutch study half of all women experienced hot flushes. The drying and thinning of the vagina associated with lack of oestrogen may make intercourse painful and also predisposes women to urinary incontinence, particularly when they laugh or strain; 15 per cent of menopausal women suffer from some degree of incontinence, although by no means all of them seek medical advice. Despite the apparent disadvantages of the menopause, 60 per cent of women in Ede said they were pleased to be finished with their periods.

While medical science, at least at its present level of knowledge, is unable to halt the ageing process, it can do a great deal to improve the quality of life for the aged. The ability to replace the oestrogen which is lost when the ovaries cease to release eggs at the menopause is particularly interesting, and more and more women are turning to hormone replacement therapy (HRT). Medical fashion and cultural expectation, however, lead to wide variations in the use of HRT, from 60 per cent of German women to only one in ten of Japanese. For some, the benefits of HRT are dramatic and immediate: the hot flushes are cured, the night sweats disappear, intercourse is no longer difficult, and the woman has a greater confidence in herself. The unseen advantages may be even greater. A study of 2000 women from Oklahoma, California, North Carolina and Iowa found that those using oestrogens over age 40 suffered fewer deaths than those who did not. There is a reduction in the risk of fractures, stroke and other types of cardiovascular disease. Oestrogens have an important effect on the skeleton, and without them calcium is lost from the bones. When an older individual breaks a hip they have an up to 20 per cent greater chance of death in the year that follows, due to inactivity.

The use of oestrogen by itself, while advantageous in many ways, stimulates the cells lining the uterus (the endometrium) and increases the risk of endometrial cancer. For those women who have an intact uterus the trick is also to take the hormone progesterone for part of each month. This leads to shedding of the uterine lining, removing the risk of cancer but subjecting the woman to light bleeding. In theory, women could use HRT for decades, but most women choose to stop after some years.

Expectations

How people view ageing and the menopause is influenced by their cultural expectations. In a monogamous society, sex is likely to continue after the menopause. By contrast, in West Africa a woman is embarrassed by pregnancy once she becomes a grandmother, as it is evidence that she is still having sex. Nevertheless, the passion of sex and vitality can continue into later life. Sex expert Alex Comfort has said that sex after middle age is like riding a bicycle. There are three reasons why you don't do it so often or stop altogether: you have less strength, you think you look ridiculous or you haven't got a bicycle!

Different societies interpret the physical changes associated with the menopause in different ways. Geoffrey Chaucer's contemporary, John Gowar, wrote in the *Mirror of Man*,

More than all of them I despise
The old woman who is flirtatious
When her breasts are withered.

Shakespeare alternated between a vision of an older woman as someone not far removed from a witch ('an old trot with ne'er a tooth in head, though she have as many diseases as two and fifty horses' – *The Taming of the Shrew*, Act I, Scene II) to a person of worth and wisdom, like the nurse in *Romeo and Juliet*. In the eighteenth and nineteenth centuries older women were expected to withdraw into a world of quiet dignity. Victorian spinsters received the courtesy title of 'Mrs' when they reached the menopause. In Dickens' novels old women have little individuality or self-worth: Miss Maidstone in *David Copperfield* is a symbol of harshness, and Miss Havisham in *Great Expectations* is a symbol of decay, her body and personality having crumbled in a cobweb-filled, claustrophobic room where the clock has stopped at the moment she was abandoned by her fiancé on her wedding day. Today, we no longer expect the menopausal woman to wear dark colours and fade from social view like a poorly developed photograph exposed to the sunlight of youth, but perhaps we still overemphasize the vitality of women in their teens and twenties.

In India today, a Hindu widow is supposed to remain unmarried, even if she is in her teens or twenties. In Indonesia, half the women aged 50 to 54 are widows or live apart from their husbands. So many widows are driven into prostitution in Ghana that they have formed a trade association called the Ghanaian Widows' Association. Among the Tiwi aborigines of Australia, where, as we have seen, women are 'betrothed' even before they are conceived, a woman of 40 to 50 is likely to have survived several husbands and to be the oldest wife of a younger man. Just as the Tiwi assumed that sexual intercourse causes puberty, so they concluded that the stopping of intercourse caused the menopause. As sexual activity wanes, however, the older woman's power increases: 'She can sit all day in camp and send other wives out hunting.'

Among some of the hill tribes of northern Thailand, the menopause is an occasion for celebration. A feast is held and many ducks and other animals are eaten. In a symbolic sense the woman attains the status of a man and can take part in male rituals, such as planting the first rice seedlings. According to a Christian missionary, on the night of the feast, a saying goes round the village that the other couples 'should not spin thread or get their arms and legs in a tangle', the former being a traditionally female task and the latter a pleasant euphemism for sexual intercourse. The woman's own children are supposed to abstain from intercourse for several months after the ceremony.

Cancer

An individual's risk of developing cancers becomes greater with age, but for three important reproductive cancers – of the ovary, uterus and breast – the rate of increase in these cancers slows at the menopause. At the same time, these three cancers are becoming more common overall, particularly in developed countries. Breast cancer now occurs in one in eleven US women and kills one in eighteen. It has become more common in every industrialized nation and with every passing decade of the twentieth century. The mutilating disfigurement of mastectomy for breast cancer is universally feared. A great deal of effort has been put into promoting self-examination of the breast and regular mammography to detect breast cancer early. These efforts are worthwhile, but there is no escaping the fact that treatment is often disappointing. Remarkably little thought has been given to prevention. It is here that an evolutionary perspective has most to offer.

The genes that control our reproductive function were selected to fit the life circumstances of preliterate hunter–gatherer societies, not today's postindustrial world. One factor that has changed is lack of exercise, and in a study of 8000 college alumni Rose Frisch of Harvard University has shown that athletic women have half the breast cancer risk of non-athletes. Another

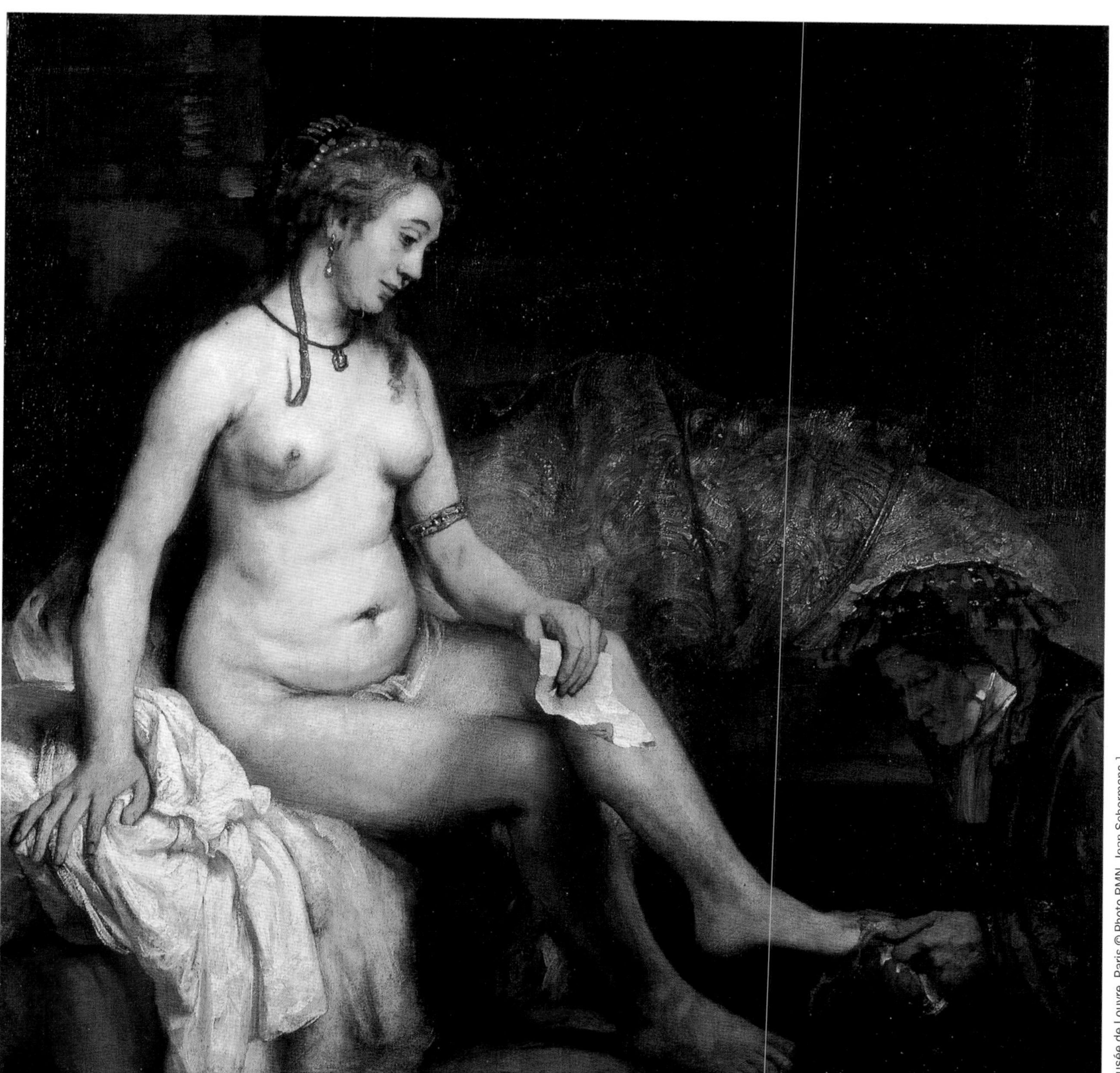

***Bathsheba at her Bath*, Rembrandt, 1654.** The Bible tells us how King David looked down from the roof of his palace and spied Bathsheba taking her ritual bath after menstruation, and in the words of the Old Testament, 'the woman was very beautiful to look upon' (2 Samuel, 11:2). Like any top primate, 'he took her ... and he lay with her'. Later King David contrived to have Bathsheba's legitimate husband killed in a battle.

Rembrandt's picture captures the melancholy look on Bathsheba's face as she holds King David's letter, but it also captures something else – an ever-so-slight shadow under her left breast. It has been suggested that the model, Hendrickje Stoffels, had an early cancer of the breast, and that Rembrandt was such a remarkable artist that he captured the puckering of the skin and slight fullness of the breast characteristic of breast cancer, perhaps without even knowing she had cancer. Stoffels was 28 when the picture was painted and she was pregnant with Rembrandt's child. He was 48 and had been a widower for some years and, although the couple never married, their love affair was tender and lasted until she died in 1663. The comparatively late age of child-bearing and her death nine years later after a long illness would fit with the diagnosis of breast cancer.

HeLa immortalized

Henrietta Lacks died of cancer on 4 October 1951. She was under 30 when the cervical cancer was first diagnosed. She had a very vascular form of tumour and it killed her in less than a year. However, when she was first admitted to Johns Hopkins Hospital in Baltimore, a tiny piece of tissue was taken and given to Dr George Gey who tried to grow the cells in tissue culture. After many similar efforts had failed, Henrietta Lacks' tumour took hold – it grew so rapidly and so well that daughter colonies of cells were passed to laboratories all over the world where they live on today as HeLa (a contraction of the patient's name) cells. The genes in Henrietta Lack's cervical cells have given rise to a greater mass of tissue since she died than they ever gave rise to in her life. The cancer cell that kills is potentially immortal, while the healthy body cell has a limited span of life.

factor is diet. A US woman receives 40 per cent of her calorie intake as fat, twice as much as a contemporary Japanese woman, whose intake is probably nearer that of our Stone Age ancestors. Breast cancer is five times commoner in the West than in Japan: is diet a factor? There is also a well documented relationship between reproductive cancers and patterns of child bearing. Studies show that breast, ovarian and endometrial cancer are more common in women who have an early puberty, a late menopause, who postpone child bearing, and who do not breastfeed their babies, or do so briefly. These are all changes in reproductive patterns associated with a modern way of life. On average, US women with college degrees postpone child bearing until they are over 26 years old, perhaps a decade and half after they went through puberty. Only 7 per cent of US women will breastfeed their babies for twelve months or longer. By contrast, women in modern hunter–gatherer societies have their first birth in the later teens or early twenties (only a few years after they first menstruate) and they will have four to eight children, each of which may be breastfed for three to four years, two to three of which are associated with the suppression of ovulation. Our Stone Age ancestors (or a contemporary woman in the Highlands of Papua New Guinea) may have had an average of fifty menstrual cycles in a lifetime, while a modern woman has about 450 – nine times as many. Breast cancer is 120 times as common in a Western woman today as in a hunter–gatherer. It seems that incessant ovulation and the accompanying hormonal turmoil is abnormal and highly dangerous.

The risk of developing ovarian cancer appears to be directly proportional to the number of times a woman sheds an egg. Tubal ligation, or voluntary surgical sterilization, also apparently reduces a woman's risk of developing ovarian cancer. Is some carcinogen carried along the fallopian tubes from the uterus to the ovaries every time a woman menstruates? Numerous menstrual cycles also increase the risk of uterine cancer, although it is also notable that obese women are at higher risk of this particular malignancy, probably because fatty tissue is a source of oestrogen and high oestrogen levels stimulate cell division in the lining of the uterus. Women using the contraceptive pill have a quiescent uterus and ovulation is inhibited and, exactly as might be expected, oral contraceptives reduce the risk of both uterine and ovarian cancer. Use of the pill for five years approximately halves a woman's risk of ovarian cancer and the protection persists for ten to fifteen years after taking the last tablet. While the media trumpeted the adverse cardiovascular side-effects of the original high dose oral contraceptives, relatively few women know of this protection against cancer – and even some physicians do not understand the true nature of this discovery. Indeed, among women under 35 the protection against cancer outweighs the proven adverse risks of the pill. Oral contraceptives are the Philosopher's Stone, and by taking the contraceptive young women on average actually live very slightly longer than non-users. From a biological perspective, for the modern woman, using oral contraceptives is less unnatural than not using them.

Epidemiological studies in the USA and one in China suggest that breastfeeding a baby significantly reduces a woman's risk of breast cancer later in life. Perhaps the most interesting data are the study from Hong Kong of women who trade in small boats paddling among the crowded junks. They propel their tiny craft with a single oar and, if they are right handed, the handle covers the right breast, so they feed their babies from the uncovered left breast. If breast cancer develops then it is usually in the breast that has not been suckled. But supposing we extrapolate from this finding and state, as appears to be true, that replacing breastfeeding by bottle-feeding increases the risk of breast cancer in adult women. In any other area, the identification of such a 'new carcinogen' would lead to a great outpouring of media and political concern. Legislation would be passed compelling manufacturers to prevent any trace of the product from coming into contact with human beings. But few laws have been passed that ensure that women have the legal right to be with their babies early in lactation, and no lawyers, however litigious, have ever thought of suing a manufacturer of milk formula for causing breast cancer.

'Age, I do abhor thee'

Manipulating the reproductive organs is not the same as turning back the clock of ageing. The limitations and discomforts of old age remain. They are unpleasant but, as Maurice Chevalier quipped, 'I prefer old age to the alternative'. A survey by Age Concern of Great Britain found four out of five adults can visualize situations where they would not wish to go on living in old age, particularly if constant pain, crippling disease or senility supervene. People fear loss of independence and poor health more than lack of money. In Shakespeare's words, 'Age, I do abhor thee, youth, I do adore thee.'

Evolution acts only upon that part of our life that influences reproduction. For example, there is no way biology could evolve genes to make death from causes such as cancer less painful. During terminal illness, some cancers invade bones or damage nerves, causing prolonged pain which has no functional significance, and merely makes the end of life more miserable. Such pain lies totally outside any evolutionary influence. Understanding nature does not mean we have to follow it, and fortunately over the last 100 years the relief of terminal pain has become a valid and modestly successful part of

'a small operation would be necessary...'

In August 1810, the novelist Fanny Burney felt a small pain in her breast. Her husband M. D'Arblay persuaded her to see Antoine Dubois the foremost gynaecologist in Paris and *accoucheur* to the Empress. He recommended that 'a small operation would be necessary to avert evil consequences' and enlisted the help of Baron Larrey, a surgeon who had attended the wounded at the battle of Waterloo, amputating 200 limbs in one day. Fanny's doctors had decided on a mastectomy, in an age before anaesthesia. The tradition was not to tell the patient when the operation would be performed. In fact, Fanny was in high anxiety for three weeks. In the early nineteenth century, operations were done at home. Fanny wrote to her sister Esther that 'the sight of the immense quantity of bandages, compresses, sponges, lint made me quite sick – I walked backwards & forwards till I quieted all emotion, & became, by degrees nearly stupid – torpid, without sentiment or consciousness.' She was given some wine. Dubois, Larrey, a surgical assistant, and four men who would hold her down on the bed, entered her room. Her face was covered with a sheet and the surgical team communicated by signs. After a terrible silence, Larrey began to operate.

> *when the dreadful steel was plunged into the breast – cutting through veins - arteries – flesh – nerves – I needed no injunctions not to restrain my cries. I began a scream that lasted unintermittingly during the whole time of the incision – & I almost marvel that it rings not in my ears still! So excruciating was the agony. When the wound was made, & the instruments withdrawn, the pain seemed undiminished, for the air that suddenly rushed into those delicate parts felt like a mass of minute but sharp & forked poniards, that were tearing the edges of the wound – but when again I felt the instrument – describing a curve – cutting against the grain, if I may so say, while the flesh resisted in a manner so forcible as to oppose & tire the hand of the operator, who was forced to change from the right to the left – then indeed, I thought I must have expired. I attempted no more to open my Eyes, – they felt as if hermetically shut, & so firmly closed that the Eyelids seemed indented into the Cheek. The instrument this second time withdrawn, I concluded the operation over – Oh no! presently the terrible cutting was renewed – and worse than ever, to separate the bottom, the foundation of this dreadful gland from the parts to which it adhered – Again all description would be baffled – yet again all was not over, – and Dr Larry rested his own hand, & Oh Heaven! – I then felt the Knife racking against the breast bone – scraping it! – This performed, while I yet remained in utterly speechless torture, I heard the Voice of Mr. Larry, – (all others guarded a dead silence) in tone nearly tragic, desire everyone present to pronounce if anything more remounted to be done; The general voice was Yes, – but the finger of Mr. Dubois – which literally felt elevated over the wound, though I saw nothing, & though he touched nothing, so indescribably sensitive was the spot – pointed to some further requisition – & again began scraping! – and, after this, Dr. Moreau thought he discerned a peccant attom – and still, & still, M. Dubois demanded attom after attom – My dearest Esther, not for days, not for Weeks, but for Months I could not speak of this terrible business without nearly again going though it! I could not think of it with impunity! I was sick, I was disordered by a single question – even now, 9 months after it is over, I have a head ache from going on with the account! & this miserable account, which I began 3 Months ago, at least, I dare not revise, nor read, the recollections so painful.*
>
> J. Hemlow (ed.), *The Journals and Letters of Fanny Burney* (Madame D'Arblay), Vol VI *France 1803–1812*, 1975

By 1811, both nitrous oxide (laughing gas) and ether were known to put people to sleep, but it was another fifty years before they were used routinely as anaesthetics in operations. Fanny recovered from the operation and lived for another thirty years.

medical care. The fact that evolution has left the last few years of life to a ragged decay also means that this may be the area where the medical arts can most genuinely improve on Nature.

Perhaps it is not surprising that we seem to have some control over when we die: our death can be accelerated or retarded by the way we live. The familiar phrase of 'having something to live for' is born out by statistics. Married men have a lower death rate than unmarried men and fewest deaths are found among those with children. Using data from over 90 000 deaths in Finland, Taako Kaprio and his collegues showed that the death of one spouse is more likely than would occur by chance to be followed by that of the other shortly afterwards. The effect is more marked in men than women, but the risk lasts for a shorter time in men and is abolished by remarriage, while in women remarriage does not have a similar beneficial effect on mortality. In 1973, Phillips and Feldman used mortality statistics to suggest that famous people were least likely to die in the months prior to their birthdays, while the unknown were most likely to die at this time. They postulated that, the more famous you are, the more likely you will want to join in celebrating your birthday and you do not want to miss the occasion. For those who live alone, instead of being something to look forward to, birthdays can be a dreary reminder of one's own mortality. Four of the signatories to the American Declaration of Independence, including Thomas Jefferson, died on or soon after 4 July, and presumably looked forward to the anniversary with the same anticipation that they would their birthdays. But how do our emotions shift the time of death? Post mortems show that cardiovascular deaths increase in the groups at risk for premature death due to loneliness. Perhaps grief also impairs the immune system, as deaths due to infection and cancer increase after bereavement. Whatever the process, it is a forceful reminder of the primate's need for companionship: Shakespeare was right in *Macbeth* when he wrote:

Give sorrow words: the grief that does not speak
Whispers the o'er fraught heart, and bids it break.

Turning life on or off

While we cannot necessarily get more years out of life, we can use our technology and social policy to get more life out of the years that we have. Currently, we do not always make the optimum decisions. Our society is not as generous as it could be in helping the aged live at home. Meals-on-wheels, or a handle to prevent slipping in the bath, can work wonders but may be difficult to obtain; yet we may spend half a lifetime's savings keeping a person alive for three more months with intensive hospital care. As there is no consensus about the meaning of death in modern society, physicians are often poorly trained in this area. The doctor may see death as evidence of his or her failure and, like other onlookers, not want to face reality. To communicate with a dying person, physical contact is most important; it is essential to touch, to hold, to embrace, but these things are the antithesis of how physicians are taught to relate to their patients.

Nothing can prepare people for surviving the death of a loved one. It is incomprehensible that someone who meant so much will not return: for the bereaved, everything they see, touch, hear or smell, screams a message about the one who died. Day and night take on new meanings. Life-long habits in sleeping or grooming are suddenly suspended. If the loved one died in the operating theatre or in some high technology setting, then death itself can be even more difficult to believe. The corpse should be seen and perhaps embraced. The modern physician needs to learn from previous generations, who were less likely to succeed in saving life but more experienced in offering comfort to those grieving. A study by the Edinburgh Medical Group found that doctors could be the worst people in the community to deal with death: the police were seen as the best, since they are matter-of-fact and do not avoid the issue.

Our multicellular body can survive only so long as we can bring oxygen and nutrients to, and remove waste materials from, each cell. Death is the failure of one or more organs, such as the kidneys, that maintain the environment the brain requires to function. The numerous, complex, message-carrying nerve cells are especially vulnerable and brain death takes place within a few minutes after the heart stops. There are accounts of near-death experiences in which the sick person sees a bright light or a shutter rising, and sometimes reports considerable tranquillity. These changes are merely the way the brain reacts to near fatal lack of oxygen.

As brain death always puts an end to breathing, until recently the cessation of the circulation provided a universal and practical definition of death. But what about when the brain is only half dead, or a machine keeps the lungs ventilated? We now have technologies that can keep people half alive for increasingly long intervals. The functions of the gut can be replaced by intravenous feeding, the kidney by dialysis, the burden of respiration eased with a tracheostomy, and a machine (or a dead donor's heart) can be substituted for our own, at least temporarily. Eight out of ten Americans now die in hospital. The USA is estimated to spend a billion dollars per day on hospital

Chang and Eng – united in life and death

Identical twinning can occur as late as 14 to 16 days after fertilization, when two primitive streaks (see p.123) develop in the inner cell mass of one egg; in the case of conjoined twins, the two primitive streaks are incompletely separated. Conjoined twins are called 'Siamese' twins after Chang and Eng, who were born in Thailand (Siam) in 1811 and who were joined together by a thick band of flesh and cartilage at their chests. A normal vaginal delivery was only made possible because they were twisted through 180° and came out head to tail. The king of Siam considered them a bad omen and thought of having them put to death, but relented. Chang was the more dominant and orchestrated the children's movements. Their father died when they were eight, and a Scottish merchant persuaded their mother to release them for a tour of the USA and Britain.

They left Siam at the age of 18, appearing initially in theatres and at exhibitions, and eventually under contract for the great American circus showman, Phineas T. Barnum. The twins were examined by medical authorities in Europe and the USA and, though it was found that they shared no vital organs, no one would accept the responsibility for separating them surgically. Today this could have been accomplished easily.

By the age of 28, Chang and Eng had amassed a substantial fortune, and sought respite from their life of constant travel and display as freaks. They became naturalized United States citizens, taking Bunker as their last name. They settled as farmers near Mount Airy, North Carolina, and married the English sisters Sarah and Adelaide Yates. The wedding took place only after a great deal of community opposition and threats of violence, and some ministers refused to marry them on the grounds that it was bigamy. But they insisted that, although conjoined and identical, they were two separate people. Eventually the hostility subsided into amicable acceptance, and the ribaldry about the joint sex lives of the two couples wore itself out. Together, Chang and Eng fathered 22 children.

[Hulton Getty.]

The twins were extremely good-natured despite their imprisoned togetherness. They learned English readily and were uncommonly literate and sophisticated. In their business dealings, they bargained hard and well. They were slave owners, and the Civil War saw them almost bankrupted. They had a long-standing arrangement of spending half the week at Chang's house and the other half at Eng's. In 1871 Chang's health began to fail and as his bouts of illness became more severe and frequent, their personal relationship deteriorated. Eng became obsessed with the fear that if Chang died he must die too – although their family physician, Dr Hollingsworth, promised that if either twin appeared to be near death, he would operate in an effort to save the other.

In January 1874, Chang developed pneumonia. One night, Eng awakened from a deep sleep with a start: he listened for Chang's laboured breathing, and there was none. Eng called out frantically. The first to arrive at the twins' bedside was one of Eng's sons. The boy went around the bed to look, and said quietly, 'Uncle Chang is dead, Father.'

Dr Hollingsworth was summoned, but he was some distance away in the town. While awaiting his arrival, Eng's family sought desperately to help him. After his initial terror, he became peaceful, but complained of severe pains in his limbs. 'I am very bad off,' he told his wife Sarah. They massaged his arms and legs and tried to keep him warm. His strength waned. He said faintly, 'May God have mercy on my soul,' and lost consciousness. He died just two hours after being told his twin was dead. What did he die of?

The photograph shows Eng (*left*) and Chang (*right*) when they were about 60 years old.

care of the terminally ill, many of whom may not even know where they are. If all our organs, including our brain, are decaying, how much support should be given? The fact that we can support bodily functions artificially obliges us to devise new ways of ethically turning off our new-fangled machines when the brain is dead or the sheer cumulative burden of discomfort and lack of independence makes life no longer worth living. In the case of dementia, modern medicine often tries to maintain life, however dismal. But perhaps we should learn from an older generation that called pneumonia an old person's friend, and think carefully before treating every illness in an old and demented person aggressively.

Most industrialized nations spend 7 or 8 per cent of their Gross National Product on health, but the USA spends a remarkable 13 per cent, and unless something is done about the current rate of growth, the whole of the US economy could be devoted to health care in the next fifty years! In Western democracies old people are beginning to wield a social and political power that evolution would never have granted them. In Europe, the proportion of the population over 65 will climb from one in eight today to one in five in the

A life worse then death

In 1995, Jean-Domenique Bauby was 43 years old and editor in chief of the French magazine *Elle*. He suffered a catastrophic brain haemorrhage that left his brain alert, but which paralysed him from head to toe. An alert nurse noticed he could blink one eye. He wrote of his experiences in one of the most extraordinary books ever written entitled *The Diving Bell and the Butterfly*. An assistant would read out the letters of the alphabet in the order of their use, E S A R I etc., and Bauby would blink when the one he needed was reached. Painfully, letter by letter, he spelt out his book. The diving bell symbolized his 'locked-in syndrome' and the butterfly his unfettered mind.

On Father's Day his two young children visit:

Want to play hangman? asks Théophile, and I ache to tell him that I have enough on my plate playing quadriplegic. But my communication system disqualifies repartee: the keenest rapier grows dull and flat when it takes several minutes to thrust it home. By the time you strike, even you no longer understand what seemed so witty when you started to dictate it, letter by letter. So the rule is to avoid impulsive sallies. It deprives conversation of its sparkle, all those gems you bat back and forth like a ball – and I count this forced lack of humor one of the great drawbacks of my condition.

But we can certainly play hangman, the national preteen sport. I guess a letter, then another, then stumble on the third. My heart is not in the game. his face is two feet from mine, my son Théophile sits patiently waiting – and I, his father, have lost the simple right to ruffle his bristly hair, clasp his downy neck, hug his small, lithe, warm body tight against me. There are no words to express it. My condition is monstrous, iniquitous, revolting, horrible. Suddenly I can take no more. Tears well and my throat emits a hoarse rattle that startles Théophile. Don't be scared, little man. I love you. Still engrossed in the game, he moves in for kill. Two more letters: he has won and I have lost. On the corner of the page he completes his drawing of the gallows, the rope, and the condemned man.

J.-D. Bauby, *The Diving Bell and the Butterfly*, 1997

Jean-Dominique Bauby died two days after the publication of his book.

year 2025. If health care is not a blank cheque, how do we decide who gets it? Should health care be allotted by social worth? But who will decide who is most worthy? Should a 25 year old mother have access to an artificial kidney before a 24 year old bachelor without a family? If one heart is available for transplantation, do we withhold it from the person who injured their heart by smoking and give it to the one whose heart was damaged by a virus? Do we leave medical care to the free market? A sick person is not in a position to bargain, and those who are paid to give treatment are not necessarily the best gatekeepers of the expensive care they dispense: health care cannot be allotted by the laws of supply and demand, like the cost of a loaf of bread.

So where do we go from here? Perhaps we can build a concensus that physicians have an obligation to relieve suffering, but society as a whole must bear some of the costs. Life and health are universal and positive goods, but there is no requirement to extend life under all circumstances: decisions about dying can and should respect the autonomy and wishes of the individual concerned. A pioneer scheme in the state of Oregon lists those diseases that it is worth the health care system attempting to cure while encouraging humane, symptomatic care for those whose illnesses are terminal. Sooner or later all societies will have to face decisions of this type. The Oregon framework will not take the anguish or responsibility out of an individual's decisions, but it may enable them to keep faith with those of our species who are dying, and extend love and dignity to the terminally ill, as we ourselves would wish. In many countries it is possible to write a living will to define one's treatment in death – the one certain event in life.

Life after death?

At some point in our evolution as sentient animals we realized the inevitability of death. Other animals with big brains – whales, elephants, chimpanzees – show distress when one of their number dies, try to revive sick adults, and in the case of elephants, chimpanzees and some monkeys a grieving mother will carry a dead offspring around for a number of days. The bewilderment is understandable and felt by anyone who grieves for someone close to them. Death is a curious finale, apparently without a purpose. It is incomprehensible. How can the vividness of life end as a slowly rotting corpse? Charles Darwin's religious beliefs suffered their greatest setback when his favourite daughter, Ann, died. We are all puzzled by the attribute, or essence, that seems to leave the body when the heart stops beating. Our sense of humour is sometimes our only defence – how commonly jokes mock death!

In the words of Sir Walter Scott,

And come he slow, or come he fast,
It is but Death who comes at last.

As an intensely social animal our brains are filled with millions of memories of those with whom we interact, and when the death of a loved one occurs all our past experience tells us they should return. The grief we feel when a loved one dies, and which we seem to share with other big-brained animals, can be explained as the process that repairs the shredded threads of memory and expectation torn apart by the loss. We would not be very interesting animals if we recorded a death in the same dispassionate way that we fill in our tax forms. But the fact remains, it is sometimes much easier to believe in ghosts, or in assertions about eternal life made by some religious creed, than it is to accept that the brain has stopped working and the person is dead and can never, and will never, wake up again. An imagined afterlife is understandable and often reassuring. Survival after death is the engine that powers all of the world's religions, from primitive animism or the fundamentalism of the Texan Baptist, to the complexity of Hindu and Buddhist reincarnation.

Not surprisingly, death has accumulated a larger body of myths and superstitions than any other link in the chain of life. Some seem remote and odd to us today but were powerful and real at the time. When Howard Carter opened Tutankhamen's tomb in 1922 it looked like a royal garage sale, but this jumble of priceless objects had been sealed away for over 3200 years as a result of an all-pervading belief in life after death. The ancient Egyptians reconciled birth and death with ubiquitous collections of goods, elegant rituals, boisterous processions and an extraordinary investment in the physical preservation of the corpse. The pharaoh was divine, linking earth and heaven, just as the pyramids on the desert margins of the Nile seemed to rise to pierce the sky. The three great pyramids of Giza seem to have been a representation of Orion's Belt, thereby bringing heaven to Earth. The land of Egypt was reborn each year with the annual flooding of the Nile. The gods gave humankind food, and humankind gave the Earth's bounty back to the gods, before redistributing it back to society. The awesome Egyptian temples with their graceful carvings and busy hieroglyphs were processional ways for the gods' images, and the administrative centre for an economy without money: they were the Vatican, Whitehall, Pentagon and Fort Knox rolled into one. We continue to ritualize death, and in the USA the contemporary corpse is as thoroughly injected, carefully made up, pickled, trussed, trimmed and dressed as any pharaoh. At the University of Minneapolis you can get a

Suttee

Behind this furnace stood an erection of bamboo in the form of a bridge, of the same width as the square of masonry, about forty feet long and sixteen to eighteen feet high; steps of bamboo led up to it in the rear. In the centre there is a small house, affording a last resting place for the victim, in which she waits until the ceremonies for her husband are finished and his body has begun to burn. The side of the bamboo scaffold nearest the fire is protected by a wall of wet banana stems. Upon the bridge lies a plank smeared with oil, which is pushed out a little over the fire as soon as the time for the leap draws near. There is a door at the end of the bridge that is not removed until the last minute. The victim sits in the house on the bridge, accompanied by a female priest and her relatives … Then she makes her toilet; her hair especially is combed, the mirror used, and her garments newly arranged; in short she arrays herself exactly as she would for a feast. Her dress is white, her breasts are covered with a white scarf; she wears no ornaments and, after the preparations to which she has been subjected, her hair at the last moment hangs loose. When the corpse of the prince was almost consumed, the three wives got ready; they glanced one towards another to convince themselves that all was prepared; but this was not a glance of fear, but of impatience, and it seemed to express a wish that they might leap at the same moment. Then the door was opened and the plank smeared with oil pushed out, each took her place on the plank, made three reverences by joining her hands above her head, and one of the bystanders placed a dove upon her head. When the dove flies away the soul is considered to escape. They immediately leaped down. There was no cry in leaping, no cry from the fire; they must have suffocated at once … During the whole time from the burning of the prince till the leap of the victims, the air resounded with the clangour of numerous bands of music; small cannon were discharged … There was not one of the 50,000 Balinese present who did not show a merry face; no one was filled with repugnance and disgust except a few Europeans whose only desire was to see the end of such barbarities.

From 'An account of the Island of Bali', *Journal of the Royal Asiatic Society*, **IX**, 1877. Quoted in Miguel Covarrubias, *Island of Bali*, 1937, reprinted 1977

Bachelor's degree in Mortuary Science, and the US funeral industry claims the country has more embalmers than fire stations.

No-one on Earth, even among the bizarre and extreme range of do-it-yourself religious beliefs found in some parts of the Western world, now believes in the vision of life after death that sustained the Ancient Egyptians for 3000 years. Yet many more people still try to escape the reality of death than are willing to accept it. Scientific objectivity may steal the warm cloak of comfort that the idea of life after death provides, but honesty in the face of the inevitable is the best policy. Many stories told about the afterlife hold as much terror as succour. The second century theologian Tertullian promised that the Christians would look down from Paradise and watch their tormentors suffer in hell. The Aztecs of Mexico sacrificed tens of thousands of men by tearing their living hearts out with an obsidian knife to 'feed' the sun. Once captured, the sacrificial victims usually acquiesced in their murder, as the fate of a man's soul depended not on how he lived, but on how he died. Those who died in battle or on the altar had an equal opportunity of going to heaven. The victim's flesh was eaten by priests and nobles, so they could partake of the sacred nature of the sacrifice. When individuals from our cultural tradition die bravely, sustained by a belief that they will enter heaven, we call them martyrs: if they belong to alien culture we call them fanatics. An Islamic fundamentalist youth who hijacks an aeroplane understands that he or she may die in the attempt, but has an unquestionable belief in the afterlife, and may seek a martyr's death in the television colosseum of today's world.

Once the concept of an afterlife is established, it follows that believers in the particular road to heaven will feel driven to ensure that everyone else follows the same path that they have discovered. To the true believer, how we arrive at eternal life is often more important than Earthly freedoms: religions founded by martyrs often turn, in a few generations, into armies of torturers. The thirteenth century Cathars, or Albigensians, were a Christian sect from southern France who held that the soul was an essence that fled from an unclean vessel at death. (The word heretic comes from the heretication or sacrament that Cathar priests administered to a dying person.) They often behaved with virtue in a cruel and undisciplined age, but their particular road to heaven was perceived to be an error by the rest of the Church. In 1209 Pope Innocent III ordered a crusade against the Albigensians. The Holy Inquisition invited every scoundrel in Europe to rob, rape and burn the Cathar heretics. So important was the orthodox road to heaven that for the next 400 years there was hardly a market place in continental Europe that was not rent with the screams of someone being burnt alive for attempting to enter the afterlife through some non-approved door. Meanwhile, Islam was fighting its way around the world converting vast cohorts of people to the path laid out by the Prophet.

A belief in a soul has been pervasive and often absolute throughout most of history and, one must suppose, prehistory. The third century philosopher Origen taught that souls existed before the bodies that housed them, and even the stars had rational souls. To the Hindu, the soul is destined for perpetual reincarnation. Buddhism has a view of the world that in one way is closer to the Darwinian: 'The cause of death is not disease but birth'. Buddha taught that each generation was linked to the preceding one by an evolving bundle of attributes or karma, passed from one generation to another on the long road to perfection, a sort of spiritual counterpart of DNA. In another sense Buddhism is the reverse of evolution, a vision of moral evolution against a background of biological stasis: 'birth is suffering, decay is suffering, disease is suffering, death is suffering.' Five centuries before Christ, Prince Gautama, or Buddha the Enlightened One, looked towards a spiritual exploration of an inner world, not outward to a discovery of the external world through science.

Until the nineteenth century, the biologist looked for the hand of God in Nature, and the theologian read Aristotle as well as Saint Augustine. Leonardo da Vinci drew a cross-section of the human skull with meridians showing where to find the soul. It was argued that the brain distilled an essence into the ventricles or cavities within it, which was passed to the pituitary gland at the base of the brain. (When we sneeze and say 'bless you' it is a relic of the fact that the mucus from the nose was thought to represent the distillate from the ventricles of the brain.) René Descartes, philosopher, scientist and inventor of coordinate geometry, chose to locate the soul in the pineal gland. Today we know the pineal acts as an hourglass of time, secreting melatonin, the hormone measuring darkness, the days and the seasons. Alas, modern anatomy and physiology still have not found a place in which to house a human soul.

Sex and death are linked in many religions. Buddha began to seek religious enlightenment after first seeing suffering, poverty and death outside his father's palace: 'He returned to the palace, deeply pondering, and, that night, while his pleasure girls lay sleeping in unbecoming postures at his feet, he revolted from sensual pleasures, and at the same time the flame of compassion awoke within him.' For a Muslim, sex is an obligation and becomes part of the afterlife. It is said that upon arriving in heaven a man will not even blink for the first forty years as his vision will be so overwhelmed by the beauty of the virgins confronting him. For the Hindu, the existence of an afterlife was so certain that wives of rich men were burnt on their dead husband's funeral pyre so they might remain together in the hereafter.

For the Christian, sex is redundant after death and at worst a sin before. Sinful sex and putrifying death were linked. Popular mediaeval preachers often juxtaposed the two in vivid metaphors. One, Jacques de Vitry, told of the monk who fell violently but secretly in love with a woman, so much so he even dreamt of her when she died. Desperate, he opened her grave and embraced the corpse: 'He filled his nostrils with that putrifying flesh and the stench henceforth cured him of all concupiscence.'

Saint Augustine's teachings brought new problems. Was the Virgin Mary 'conceived in inequity and sin' as the tenth century theologian Saint Anselm maintained, or was she immaculately conceived without the sin of intercourse and uncontaminated by desire? In 1854 Pius IX ended a millennium of passionate debate by proclaiming the dogma of the Immaculate Conception. Did the Virgin's freedom from sex also free her from the grave's decay? In 1858 Bernadette Soubiroux, an illiterate French teenager, had a vision in a grotto at Lourdes where Mary said, 'I am the

Immaculate Conception'. In 1950 Pope Pius XII promulgated the encyclical *Munificentissimus Deus* confirming the Assumption of the Virgin Mary who 'was taken up body and soul into the glory of Heaven'.

Darwin's grand vision

Darwin closes *The Origin of Species* with a lyrical description of evolution:

> *It is interesting to contemplate a tangled bank, clothed with many plants of many kinds, with birds singing on the bushes, with various insects flitting about, and with worms crawling through the damp earth, and to reflect that these elaborately constructed forms, so different from each other, and dependent upon each other in so complex a manner, have all been produced by laws acting around us. These laws, taken in the largest sense, being Growth with Reproduction; Inheritance which is almost implied by reproduction; Variability from the indirect and direct action of conditions of life, and from use and disuse: a Ratio of Increase so high as to lead to a Struggle for Life, and as a consequence to Natural Selection, entailing Divergence of Character and the Extinction of less-improved forms. Thus, from the war of nature, from famine and death, the most exalted object which we are capable of conceiving, namely, the production of the higher animals, directly follows. There is grandeur in this view of life, with its several powers, having been originally breathed by the Creator into a few forms or into one; and that, whilst this planet has gone cycling on according to the fixed law of gravity, from so simple a beginning endless forms most beautiful and most wonderful have been, and are being evolved.*

The idea of a Creator who breathed life into some original form seems to have been a statement Darwin agonized over. He realized the revolutionary nature of his book and may have decided it was just impossible to challenge Victorian Christianity directly. Elsewhere Darwin speculated about life evolving from inorganic precursors in the way most present-day biologists now believe occurred.

The soul, as well as the creation of life, has also been pushed aside by patient scientific observation. Artistotle's Nutritive Soul has been replaced by molecular messengers in the embryo, his Sensitive Soul, by electrical messengers in neurones, and the Rational or Divine Soul by alternating generations of free-living gametes and sexual beings formed from the fusion of those sperm and eggs. Darwin's 'grand vision' of life and death continues to divide science from religion, in the same way as did his assertion that human beings are descended from the apes. The understanding of evolution, and the discoveries made by microscopists and molecular biologists, define a slowly changing system in which fertilization and death are individual links in a continuous biological chain of immense antiquity and vast future potential.

Scientific medicine has been astonishingly successful in bringing our average expectation of life closer to our potential biological lifespan and in taking away much of the pain that sometimes accompanies death. But we are not able, like the Sleeping Beauty, to put the human body into a deep sleep for a long interval or, like Frankenstein, create new life from a corpse. Each unique generation of human beings can and must learn from its parents, but would our lives benefit if our progenitors were with us for longer? We might be interested to meet our great, great, great grandparents, and be wiser if we could learn more about their world, but there is a limit to the useful time generations can overlap. In the end, we have to sort out our current problems with only our unique mixture of genes, assisted by whatever experiences come our way. We need the right balance of love, wisdom and information from those who have gone before us. Yet by the same token, the plain fact is that, like our parents and our grandparents before us, the effort to pass on our genes and the relevant body of information we enjoy must be packed into a few decades – a vibrant moment at the end of a thread of life extending back over billions of years of evolution.

Modern reproductive technology challenges conventional thinking but does not alter the basic equations of birth and death. It is already theoretically possible to give birth to a clone of one's self (see p. 126). The fact that viable sperm can be recovered from the testes after death raises new ethical dilemmas about a widow's right to conceive her dead husband's child. We live in a changing world that needs the variation evolution supplies as a result of sexual reproduction. Today, Napoleon's genes might lose every battle he fought; deep-frozen Paul McCartney clones would carry the same innate musical talent as their twin but they would be children of another age and it would be unlikely that their music would hit the Top 10 charts in the year 2063.

Like any animal that is the product of sexual reproduction, we enjoy one brief life, a somatic expression of the information given to each cell in our body from the unique pattern created at fertilization. The body can no more exist after death than we did before conception. Like the picture that fades when the television is turned off, when we die we stop illuminating our tiny patch of the world. The life of our soma begins dangerously and ends soberly, but both our entry and our exit have been partially released from superstition.

Cloning: escape from death?

When Ian Wilmut and his colleagues in Roslin, Scotland, announced in the pages of the journal *Nature* in February 1997 that they had been able to take the nucleus from a sheep mammary cell growing in tissue culture, fuse it to an unfertilized sheep egg whose nucleus had been removed, and produce a normal liveborn lamb, subsequently named Dolly in honor of Dolly Parton, the public response was overwhelming. Admiration of the scientific achievement was overtaken by paranoia, stemming from fear of the unknown. What if people attempted to clone humans, like Dr Mengele in the film *Boys from Brazil*? There were presidential demands that human cloning should be banned forthwith, and the publicity-seeking Dr Dick Seed (*sic*) in the USA, who announced his intention to give it a try, only inflamed the debate. Entirely overlooked was the fact that Nature has been successfully cloning humans by embryo splitting since time began; not only are Siamese twins such as Chang and Eng natural clones, but so too are all identical (monovular or monozygotic) twins, which occur with a frequency of four pairs per 1000 births in all human races. There are even occasional reports of identical triplets, quadruplets or quintuplets – the Dionne quins of Canada (see p. 124) are a famous example. All are produced from a single, fertilized egg, and are genetically identical to one another. But whereas Dolly was produced experimentally, by the very inefficient process of nuclear fusion (it took over 270 attempts to produce her), identical twins, triplets, etc. are produced naturally, by embryo fission.

What is so exciting about the cloning of Dolly is that it has demonstrated that, under the right conditions, a differentiated cell in the adult can be made to de-differentiate and become totipotent, to give rise to a completely new individual. One of the intriguing questions this research raises is Dolly's age. Was she truly 'born again', brand-new from the moment of conception, or was she already as old as the somatic cell whose nucleus gave rise to her? If the former, Dolly should have the lifespan of any other sheep; if the latter, then she may die prematurely. Dolly's lifespan will tell us much about the biology of ageing. Is the inevitability of death due to an accumulation of deleterious mutations in the DNA? If so, cloning an adult individual may not provide us with the longed-for escape from death. Only time will tell. In the meantime Dolly produced a normal lamb early in 1998. She is not alone, as Ryuzo Yanagimachi and his colleagues in Hawaii have now successfully cloned large numbers of mice.

The transmission of the genetic and cultural information between generations is indeed rather like a runner in a relay race passing the baton on to the next athlete. After handing over the baton we may run a few more paces to slow down, but biologically it is pointless to go on running for the sake of running. Biology has given life a rhythm and a purpose. Most people wish, like other animals, to pass on their seed to another generation and we are all part of the rich cultural transmission of information that distinguishes us from other primates. It is our participation in our culture, drawing from it and giving to it, that adds meaning to our lives beyond reproduction. Perhaps evolution did not do too bad a job in fixing the lifespan of *Homo sapiens* to be about 25 000 days, a little over three score years and ten.

12 TOO MANY PEOPLE

'You will recollect that Franklin Roosevelt in a speech on 6th January 1941 said: "In the future days, which we seek to make secure, we look forward to a world founded upon four essential freedoms. The first is freedom of speech and expression. The second is freedom of every person to worship God in his own way. The third is freedom from want. The fourth, freedom from fear." And I would suggest that it is time to consider a fifth freedom – freedom from the tyranny of excessive fertility.' Sir Dugald Baird, *British Medical Journal*, 1965

Evolution has cast us in the role of the slowest breeding mammal on Earth. We are the last to reach sexual maturity, we have the least chance of becoming pregnant at any given ovulation, and we have one of the longest natural intervals between births. Fertility in women declines in their late thirties and early forties and, to make sure females do not bear children too late in life, we have evolved a clear-cut menopause. Yet, in spite of our low natural fertility, reproduction has been the engine driving evolution. Every 110 hours ($4^1/_2$ days) there are one million more births than deaths on this planet. Can we exercise a voluntary control of our fertility, or will we revert to the starvation, disease and unrestrained aggression that are the bloody marks of biological competition? Whether we can reverse our biology and bring our numbers into equilibrium may decide our long term future as a species.

Family size is falling in many parts of the world. The peak growth in global population – the excess of births over deaths each year – occurred sometime in the 1990s. The fall in fertility is welcome and it is largely a testimony to the success of family planning programmes launched in the 1960s and 70s. Unfortunately, it does not herald the end of what, with justice, has been called the population explosion. Although there has been a very slight decline in the number of births, the number of young people entering the fertile years is at an all time high. Demographic growth still has great momentum, especially in countries such as Pakistan that were slow off the mark in offering family planning choices to their citizens. On any biological scale the changes taking place in human numbers are unprecedented. Unless everything possible is done to help people to have the smaller families they want, then the twenty-first century could still face some cataclysmic problems as the result of unbridled human population growth.

Natural and unnatural fertility

Kelly Stewart has studied mountain gorillas living in the Virunga volcanoes of Rwanda and Zaïre (now the Democratic Republic of Congo). Over years

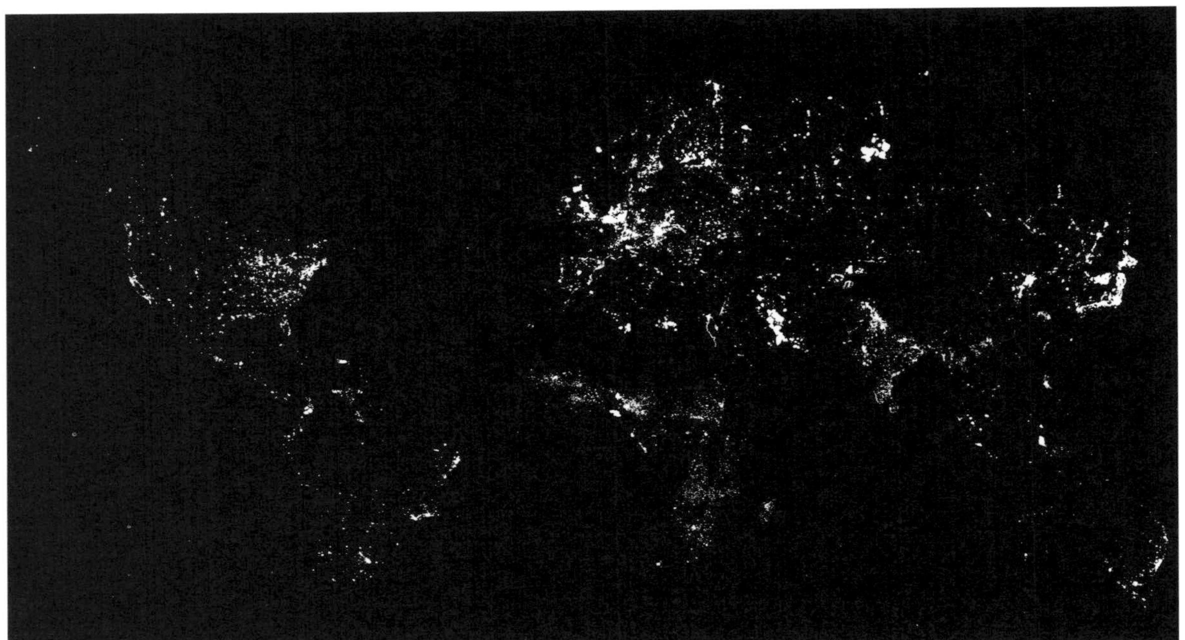

[W. F. Sullivan III.]

The Earth at night, 1974–1984. A composite photograph from US Air Force weather satellites, depicting human energy consumption around the world. Amongst the most prominent lights are the flares of the oil wells in the Persian Gulf (*centre right*), and in Siberia (*top right*). The great cities of Europe are easily identified, and the coast of Spain and Portugal is etched by lights from holiday villas. The North African oil wells are evident, and the thread-like line of the Nile. The blackness of the Sahara Desert is girdled to the south by fires as the edges of the rain forest are destroyed. Northern India and Pakistan are revealed by the lights of New Delhi, Lahore and Allahabad, whereas poverty dims the lights of the millions living in Calcutta to the East. Beijing is the beacon of China, whereas the whole of Japan is ablaze with light – all ultimately derived from oil imported from the Persian Gulf. Even the Sea of Japan is alight, reflecting the powerful arc lights of Japan's squid fishing fleet. Australia reveals the barrenness of its Red Centre, with lights confined to the eastern seaboard. The great cities of North America are clearly visible, whereas Mexico City, for all its millions, is barely visible. South America reveals the location of Bogota, Recife, São Paulo, Rio and Buenos Aries. The Amazon Basin and Brazil are suspiciously black – had the photograph been taken at another time of year, we would have seen the flickering fires of burning rain forest, as in sub-Saharan Africa.

But this snapshot of human activities is also notable for some of its other omissions. Indonesia, the fourth most populous country in the world, can be identified by a flare from the oil wells on Sulawesi, and a pinpoint of light that is all we can see of the ten million people living in the capital, Jakarta. If all developing countries started using energy at the rate of the developed countries, how long would it be before fossil fuel reserves were exhausted, and all the lights extinguished?

The Worship of Venus (*detail*), Titian, 1519. Population growth gains its momentum from the large number of children already born who have yet to reach reproductive age.

[Prado, Madrid / Bridgeman Art Library.]

of patient observation she has documented how gorillas, exactly like preliterate human societies, breastfeed their infants for an average of forty-six months, and ovulation is suppressed for eighteen months to two years. Even the details of breastfeeding are similar, with frequent short bouts of suckling lasting two to three minutes taking place at least twice an hour. But ironically, gorillas are on the verge of extinction, and for every gorilla alive today there are between 500 000 and one million people crowding the planet. The San Bushmen of the Kalahari Desert are contemporary hunter–gatherers, who still migrate long distances and live in a harsh desert environment. When food is scarce a breastfeeding woman may actually lose weight as she pours energy into her child. Among the San the average woman has fewer than five children, with just over four years between each birth, and until recently half of the children could be expected to die before they themselves could reproduce.

The large families of the Victorian age and of the present developing world are a recent and, it is to be hoped, temporary aberration that arose when patterns of breastfeeding changed but effective contraception was not available. The Hutterites are a religious minority in USA and Canada who have rejected many aspects of the modern world, including contraception, while adopting other modern technologies, such as bottle-feeding and modern paediatric medicine. If a Hutterite woman marries at age 20, she can expect, on average, to have twelve to thirteen children before the menopause, more than twice as many as a San woman would have. The Hutterites demonstrate in an extreme way the changes that have given rise to the contemporary explosion in human numbers: namely, early puberty, an erosion of the contraceptive effects of breastfeeding, fewer infant deaths and increased child survival thanks to improved medical care, and a failure to adopt modern contraceptives.

Population growth is a form of compound interest which can bring dramatic changes in relatively short order. The rate of population growth among the San is equivalent to doubling their numbers every 300 years. Usually, over such a long interval some famine or plague normally increases the death rate and over the centuries the San population was in equilibrium

Thomas Robert Malthus

Thomas Robert Malthus published his famous *Essay on the Principle of Population as it Affects the Future Improvement of Society* in June 1798. The first edition was anonymous, although he added his name to all subsequent editions.

Malthus was only 32 at the time of its publication, leading a comfortable bachelor's existence in Jesus College, Cambridge, where he was studying Mathematics and Theology. His *Essay* was primarily aimed at rebutting the unbridled optimism of his contemporaries who, inspired by the French Revolution, saw humankind progressing ever upwards to a world of universal abundance, peace and prosperity, where all would be equal in health, wealth and happiness. Although the world's population was only about one billion in Malthus' day, he could already see that there must be limits to its growth. He concluded that human populations, if left unchecked, would double every 25 years, whereas the ability of the Earth to provide subsistence for this growing population would only increase arithmetically. Thus he reasoned that there must be 'a strong and constantly operating check on population from the difficulty of subsistence'. The key question was to determine the nature of this check.

Initially he envisaged a 'preventive check' of late marriage – he himself did not marry until 38, and had only three children – and a 'positive check' from high levels of infant and childhood mortality. To this he added certain 'vicious customs with respect to women', presumably a euphemism for abortion, and 'great cities, unwholesome manufacturers, luxury, pestilence and war' – in short, a catalogue of misery and vice. The word 'Malthusian' has been associated with this gloomy prospect ever since, but his forebodings have an increasingly prophetic ring of truth about them.

The one thing that Malthus completely failed to foresee was the importance of contraception as a way of holding human population growth in check. Indeed, he condemned contraception within marriage as 'unnatural promiscuous concubinage'.

Malthus died in 1834, and is buried in Bath Abbey. It would be difficult to think of any book, before or since, that has aroused such deeply conflicting reactions, from the highest praise ('Malthus's *Essay* is a work of youthful genius', John Maynard Keynes) to the most violent condemnation ('Mr Malthus is cast in his action against God Almighty', Robert Southey). Friedrich Engels referred to Malthus' 'vile, infamous theory, this hideous blasphemy against nature and mankind'. Malthus' obituary notice in *The Times* consisted of one sentence: 'We see with regret the announcement of the death of Mr. Malthus, the eminent writer – a man whose private virtues were not, and could not be, disputed by those who were most hostile to his views on political economy'.

The public reaction against Malthus was a foretaste of things to come, and it epitomizes today's reluctance of Church and State to take a rational stand on the control of human population growth, thereby condemning the less fortunate in this world to a life of starvation, misery and pestilence, as Malthus predicted.

with the environment. In contemporary Angola, just a few hundred miles north of where the San used to roam the plains of Africa, the average woman now has 7.2 babies by the time she reaches the menopause and the population doubles every 22 years.

The population explosion

Ten thousand years ago there were no more than ten million people in the world. By the time of Christ, human numbers had risen to perhaps 300 million. We did not pass the one billion mark until about AD1800, but had reached two billion by 1930, three billion by 1960, four billion by the early 1970s and over six billion by the turn of the century. Such is the nature of exponential growth. Population growth has great momentum and, like a supertanker under way, it cannot be stopped suddenly. Given the current global population and taking into account changing patterns of fertility, it is projected that human numbers will grow to between nine and fifteen billion in the next century. The world has coped remarkably well with a doubling of human numbers over the past forty years, and this has given many economists and politicians a sense of invulnerability. But, from a biological perspective the next doubling of human numbers, which on current projections will take place in another forty-seven years, is exceedingly threatening. There were 255 million people in the whole of Africa in 1960. By the year 2000 there will be 780 million, and the population will be set to double in another twenty-six years. Even if the number of children per family in Africa falls to 2 by the year 2030 (something that is unlikely unless policies related to family planning change rapidly), the continent will end up with 1.4 billion people. If reaching replacement levels of fertility is delayed until 2065, then the population of Africa will grow to 4.45 billion before stabilizing – or more people than there were in the whole world in 1970. Even if all the remaining African tropical forests are cut down and the land used for productive agriculture, this would be an unsustainable population. The population of India grows by a staggering one million additional people every twenty-one days, and in one year increases by a number equal to the combined populations of Norway, Sweden and Finland. Six hundred million people now live in the shanty towns of the developing world, and that number will double early in the twenty-first century. Such vast numbers overshadow and distort everything else that is happening, or will happen, in politics, economics, and the pursuit of human happiness.

Small animals, such as rats and shrews, are short lived and have evolved a 'boom and bust' approach to reproduction. They multiply rapidly as a

The uncertain future of our world

In 1996, the United Nations Population Division published its Global Population Assessments and Projections. Optimists will no doubt take comfort from the fact that the rate of population growth continues to decline in many developing countries, whilst most developed countries now have extremely low rates of growth. But pessimists will be quick to point out that between 1990 and 1995 we have witnessed the greatest increase in world population in history, and this population will continue to grow for many decades to come. If every country averages 2.1 children per family by 2050 then global population will reach 9.4 billion in that year, as compared to 5.7 billion in 1995. However, to reach 2.1 children poor countries will need a great deal of help from developed nations. If the affluent developed countries continue to shirk their responsibilities and fail to provide family planning assistance to developing countries, we will not be able to satisfy even their existing unmet demand for contraception, and the global population could well exceed eleven billion by 2050. It is a sad fact that some major donors, like the USA, have already failed to honor their pledges for increased international family planning assistance made at the World Population Conference in Cairo in 1994.

These global projections of population growth are bad enough, but the devil lies in the detail. The population explosion yet to come will be almost exclusively confined to developing countries, who are least able to cope with its consequences. The 1950 populations of developing countries will almost quintuple by 2050, with the addition of more than 6.8 billion people. This is unlike anything that the world has ever witnessed before; no country in Europe ever experienced such massive population growth rates even at the peak of their population growth in the eighteenth and nineteenth centuries.

By far the highest rate of growth between 1995 and 2050 will occur in sub-Saharan Africa, AIDS notwithstanding, where it is expected to be 184 per cent. If this becomes a reality, it can result only in a disaster. Nigeria is destined to become one of the population giants of the future; in 1950, its population was only about 33 million but, by 1995, it had already become 112 million, and by 2050 it is expected to reach almost 339 million. With its ethnic and religious divisions, and a fragile and corrupt political system will it be able to avoid dissolving into anarchy?

The greatest number of people will be added to the world between 1995 and 2050 in Asia, which is expected to contribute a further two billion, a 145 per cent increase. By 2050, India will have become the most populous nation on Earth, adding a further 604 million people to its current 1995 population of 929 million. It will have out-grown China, which will add only (!) another 296 million to its current 1995 population of 1.22 billion. Indonesia, the sleeping giant of Asia, will grow from 197 million to 318 million by 2050.

Even in the developed world there will be some spectacular changes. The population of the USA will increase from 267 million in 1995 to 348 million in 2050, a bad example to the rest of the world, making it the fourth most populous nation, certainly the most 'effluent', and hence the greatest threat to the world's environment and its dwindling natural resources. In contrast, the populations of Japan, Germany and Italy will decline significantly, whilst France and the UK will remain relatively unchanged at around 58 million apiece.

An interesting way of summarizing this bewildering mass of statistical information is to list the ten most populous nations in 1995, and to see the major changes that will have taken place by 2050. How might that change our natures? There's the question. The only certainty is that our world faces a very uncertain future. We have the knowledge and the means to hold human population growth in check, but we lack the corporate social and political wisdom to act on it.

Population numbers (in thousands) of the ten most populous nations in the world in 1995, and in 2050

Nation	1995	Nation	2050
China	1220000	India	1533000
India	929000	China	1516000
USA	267000	Pakistan	357000
Indonesia	197000	USA	348000
Brazil	159000	Nigeria	339000
Russian Federation	148000	Indonesia	318000
Pakistan	136000	Brazil	243000
Japan	125000	Bangladesh	218000
Bangladesh	118000	Ethiopia	213000
Nigeria	112000	Iran	170000

Source UN Population Estimates and Projections, medium variant 1996.

result of early puberty, short gestations, large litter sizes and short birth intervals, and so they can exploit their environment to the limit. Come a poor season or a harsh winter, they die in large numbers. The lemmings are a well known extreme example of this strategy. Larger mammals, with longer lifespans, either breed continuously but space their pregnancies by a feedback mechanism dependent on lactation, or like sheep or deer breed once a year. Occasionally, natural regulatory mechanisms break down and disaster follows. In 1944 twenty-nine reindeer were introduced to St Matthew Island in the North Pacific. The island had lush vegetation and was without predators (apart from foxes) and the deer multiplied rapidly. Their numbers built up to around 6000 by 1965, but by this time there was evidence of habitat destruction and the animals were in poor bodily condition. That year, the winter was particularly severe, and most animals died of starvation and exposure, leaving a mere forty-two survivors. Nine billion people in the twenty-first century will stretch the ability of the planet to provide food and absorb pollutants to the limit. Somewhere on the road to very much higher numbers, human populations might collapse into death on an unprecedented scale, leaving much of the global environment ruined.

The first significant increase in human numbers took place with the transition from hunting and gathering to settled agriculture. People began to live at much higher densities, and as we saw in Chapter 10 they were exposed to new diseases. There is some evidence that they were shorter in stature and perhaps not quite as healthy as they had been as hunter–gatherers. A second and much greater increase in human numbers began in nineteenth century Europe and North America. An improved diet, feeding-bottles, cow's milk and the early weaning of babies increased fertility, while more stable political conditions, a better water supply, and simple advances in public health and hygiene brought down death rates. For the first and probably the last time in the history of the industrialized nations, a large family became the norm. It took the West a long time and much pain to bring the birth rate into equilibrium with the falling death rate. The will might have been there, but the means were not available. Thus the population of Britain multiplied over three times in the nineteenth century, and Europe exported millions to the Americas, Australasia and parts of Africa. Here they virtually destroyed any remaining indigenous hunter–gatherer communities, overwhelmed many of the urban agricultural societies they found, and set about converting others to their own religious beliefs.

In Europe and North America the birth rate began to fall in the late nineteenth century. Individuals struggled to control their fertility with coitus interruptus, a few poor quality and under-the-counter contraceptives and illegal abortion. Only in the second half of the twentieth century did access to modern forms of contraception, voluntary sterilization and safe abortion become widespread. But as soon as these methods appeared, birth rates plummeted. Today the average woman in Europe or North America has two children or fewer, and in Catholic Spain and Italy the average is only 1.2 children each. In every country where several methods of family planning are available, backed up by safe abortion, family size is approaching or already below replacement levels.

In the past thirty years a remarkable and paradoxical change has occurred in Western attitudes towards global population growth. In the 1960s and 70s there was widespread awareness of the 'population explosion', and rich nations developed the political will to promote family planning programmes around the world. Today, when the human population has

Population and the Peruvian environment

Shyness and confusion about sex affects technology, politics and policy setting. At the 1993 Earth Summit in Rio issues of population were completely omitted from a United Nations review of the environment.

No sensible person doubts that Western consumption, both directly and indirectly, threatens huge parts of the environment. But population growth also has a direct and indirect impact. Warren Hern is a physician who has been visiting the Shipibo Indians of the Peruvian Amazon for a generation. He records the following:

> *Twenty or thirty years ago, the traveler camping on the Ucayali found difficulty sleeping on the beaches at night because of the constant noise of fish and their predators such as alligators (actually white caimans). Now, the traveller's sleep is not disturbed by the fish, since these are few in most places. Sleep is disturbed by the whine of the fishermen's outboard motors.*
>
> *Pucallpa, which had a population of around 2,500 in the early 1940s, reached some 25,000 in the early 1960s, and its population now is thought to be in the neighborhood of 250,000. That is a hundredfold growth in thirty years.*
>
> *In 1983, during canoe trips through the canal between Lake Yarinococha to its outlet onto the Ucayali a few kilometers downstream from Pucallpa, I would always identify between fifty and sixty species of birds, with multiple observations of each species. The canal was lined by canopy forest in most places. The forest is gone now and I seldom identify more than a few individuals of four or five species. The banks of the canal are lined by settlers and farms.*
>
> *The area around Yarinococha, which was occupied principally by canopy rain forest in 1964, now looks like Oklahoma. It comprises cattle ranches and scrub vegetation. The bush area between Pucallpa and Yarinacocha that contained seasonally flooded forest and swamps in 1964 is now filled with causeways, roads, and houses. The Shipibo living around Pucallpa can no longer derive most of their subsistence from fishing in Yarinacocha. They buy their fish in the market.*

The Shipibo had a number of traditional practices including polygyny that helped to reduce fertility, but now they have the highest fertility of any known human group.

Dr Hern provides abortions in the USA, and he has been forced to wear a flack jacket as the result of threats from extremists. Would the Shipibo have been happier and their culture more intact today if the law had also permitted abortions in Peru?

indeed doubled, when family planning programmes have been demonstrably successful in many places, and when there is impeccable evidence that hundreds of millions of people want smaller families, the threat of continued rapid population growth has been pushed off the public agenda. Funding to extend family planning choices to poor people is collapsing.

Economic and ecological implications

The contemporary growth in the population of developing countries is even more rapid than that which overtook the Western world a century ago. It is taking place from a much larger population base and it lacks the safety valve of emigration that the West used in the nineteenth century. The gap between rich and poor, both at a global level and within societies, grows larger each year. The Gross National Product of the USA, with its 250 million inhabitants, is greater than that of all the lesser developed countries with their total of four billion inhabitants. Half the population of India live on less than US $10 per person per month. In 1960, Japan and Brazil had comparable per capita incomes and economic growth rates. Over the following generation, Japan had a much lower birth rate than Brazil, which is one important reason why today the average Japanese is eight times as wealthy as the average Brazilian.

Often we ask the wrong question. When will we run out of food? What will rising carbon dioxide levels do to the atmosphere? Each single item may have a plausible technical solution, but the real problem is: can we deal with every ecological problem our increasingly interconnected, economically driven world will throw up? We do not ask where a balloon will burst after it is inflated, but when – and we flinch in anticipation. It is the same with the impact of human numbers and technology on the fragile, already overstretched biosphere – the immeasurably complex interrelated web of living things and of water and air at the surface of the Earth.

The implicit belief of many people that man's ingenuity and technology will always keep pace with rapid population growth may prove to be cruelly disillusioning. We cannot flee to outer space. We have never even put ten people into orbit on the same day, whereas to hold global numbers in check we would have to put nearly a quarter of a million people into space every day. Even if the moon had an atmosphere we could breathe and water to make it fertile, at current rates of human growth, the moon would fill to the present density of population on Earth in less than a decade.

In the end, of course, if the birth rate is not brought down by voluntary means, then inevitably death rates must rise. The scale of death due to famine and disease needed to balance current population growth rates would be a catastrophe of unimaginable magnitude. If an atomic weapon as destructive as the bomb dropped on Hiroshima had been dropped every day since 6 August 1945 it would not have halted human population growth (although the possibility of a nuclear winter and the radiation aftereffects do indeed give atomic weapons the potential of destroying civilization as we know it). The horrors of World War II are thought to have killed, directly and indirectly, thirty million combatants and civilians. Deaths from AIDS over the first ten years of the twenty-first century will represent only about four months' aggregate population growth over the decade.

The problems of population growth are going to have to be solved on this planet, and largely within the countries with the worst problems. We are going to need some genuine technological miracles and a much improved availability of family planning choices. We will need to grow more food. Great progress has been made in recent decades. The Indonesian rice harvest doubled in the past fourteen years and the Mexican grain output quadrupled in thirty-five years. But will yields go on rising? The institution of a free market economy could increase grain output from the once bountiful plains of the Ukraine, but the rise of a new dictator in a country like Nigeria could undermine food output there. Politics may be difficult to predict, but we can be pretty sure there is no good agricultural land left to bring into cultivation, and our intensive agricultural systems consume a great deal of energy – itself a finite resource. In the USA, a quarter of all irrigated land is using underground water reserves more rapidly than they are naturally replenished. In the Punjab, which supplies much of the grain for India and Pakistan, water tables are falling. Today 550 million people are short of water, and in 2025 that number will grow to three billion. In Madagascar, grain production has declined by one-fifth since the 1970s, due to the inappropriate use of former forest lands. The 'green revolution' selected wheat and rice that put more energy into producing seeds than stalks, but there is little margin of improvement left in this area. In addition, planting huge areas with virtually genetically identical crops gives bumper yields today but risks vulnerability from disease tomorrow. India can feed itself but, if one new blight appears, India could go hungry. Many parts of the oceans are grossly overfished, and for the first time in history the global catch of fish in 1989 was less than that of the year before. Modern fishing boats use half-mile-long drift nets (about 1 kilometre) that catch up to 400 tons of fish at a time. Coral reefs are destroyed with dynamite and fish poisons. In 1981 to 1985 the worldwide felling of the rain forest amounted to 7.4 million acres (3 million hectares) annually; ten years later the destruction was estimated to have reached 26.7 million acres (11 million hectares) per year. The annual loss of the

'The flesh of your mother sticks between my teeth'

Over millions of years, odd plants and animals arrived on remote Pacific islands, on driftwood or blown by storms. Lush forests, giant flightless birds and tortoises evolved and marine mammals and oceanic birds nested on predator-free shores. About 2000 years ago, the Polynesians with their large canoes and skilled navigators began to populate these same islands. Rapidly, many species became extinct, such as the moas of New Zealand and the giant goose of Hawaii.

Polynesian settlers first reached Easter Island, over 1000 miles (1600 kilometres) from anywhere, about 1500 years ago. They found a paradise of tall trees, huge nesting colonies of tame birds, good soil and seas rich with seals and porpoises. When the first Europeans discovered the island on Easter Sunday in 1722 they found a treeless wasteland, with a few rats and chickens, 2000 ill-fed people, half a dozen leaky canoes and 200 huge, improbable, stone statues that have fascinated visitors ever since.

The history of the island's plant life has been reconstructed by studying pollen grains trapped in sediments, and bones from middens tell archaeologists what people ate and allow some estimate of the island's fluctuating population. The society that built the statues reached its zenith between AD 1200 and 1500. Statues over 30 feet (9 metres) tall and weighing over 80 tons were hauled great distances on wooden rollers. Whatever they meant to the tribes who made them, the statues are evidence of a well-organized and technically developed society. Among other things they built sea-going canoes and harpooned dolphins for meat. But their population outstripped their resources.

The forests were destroyed, there was no wood to move statues or build canoes to hunt porpoises, the land became degraded, the birds were exterminated and the rats (stowaways on big canoes) joined the islanders in destroying the capacity of the land to support the people. Instead of 10 000 to 20 000, the population fell to about 2000. Easter Island was caught in the demographic trap. People had nowhere to emigrate to, no help could reach them from outside, and they starved and fought one another.

The planet Earth is an island in an ocean of space. There is no one out there to help us, and we have nowhere else to go. Even if the Moon were fertile, had an atmosphere that would support life and we had the rockets and the fuel to travel there, we would fill it to capacity in ten years.

Altruism flees with diminishing resources. The last stage of the insupportable population explosion in Easter Island seems to have been most painful of all. Human bones started to appear in the middens. The oral memory of this cannibalism still lives on in a present-day term of abuse: 'The flesh of your mother sticks between my teeth.'

Amazonian rain forest is equivalent to cutting and burning all the vegetation over a parcel of land the size of Austria. In 1997, over one million acres (0.4 million hectares) of rain forest in South-East Asia were burning at the same time, bringing a choking smog to cities such as Singapore hundreds of miles away. The world has never seen such loss of biodiversity in so short a time. Never before has one species of animal changed the face of the planet – and the damage is likely to accelerate over the next generation.

There can be no doubt that each person living in a rich country, such as Japan or the USA, damages the environment much more than one individual from a poor country, such as Tanzania or the Philippines. However, most reasonable people wish those in underprivileged nations to enjoy some semblance of wealth. The next century will have to accommodate increasing numbers of people, many of whom will be increasingly rich. An idea of the changes that have already occurred in the twentieth century can be gained from a single remarkable statistic: the world now produces and consumes in fifteen days what it took one full year of economic activity to achieve in 1900.

The discovery of new oil reserves is not keeping pace with rising demand. A 1998 estimate by petroleum industry consultants Colin Campbell and Jean Laherrère predicts the global production of conventional oil will peak and then begin to decline as soon as the first decade of the twenty-first century. By 1991, the USA was spending $50 billion a year importing oil. Oil can be made from coal and tar shales, but only by burning fuel to process the shales, pouring out vast quantities of carbon dioxide and adding to global

A tale of two countries

The impact that improving access to family planning has on the birth rate is powerfully illustrated by the experience of Pakistan and Bangladesh. Originally they were two parts of the same Muslim nation, except Pakistan was slightly richer and more urbanized, while Bangladesh is one of the world's poorest countries, where three-quarters of the women are illiterate and one-fifth of all children die before they reach puberty. By conventional thinking, if family size were to fall in either country, it should be in Pakistan first. In 1975, in both nations, women bore on average seven children and fewer than 10 per cent of couples used contraception. In Pakistan little realistic effort was made to make family planning accessible, while in Bangladesh the government and non-governmental organizations worked to make it easier for women to control family size. Condoms and pills were sold in 100 000 little shops and kiosks, and there was one government clinic or contraceptive outlet for every 500 people, compared with one for 3500 in Pakistan. Unlike Pakistan, Bangladesh made menstrual regulation (or very early abortion) available and 12 000 people were trained to use the simple equipment needed to complete this procedure. By 1997, women in Bangladesh had an average of 3.6 children, and 45 per cent were using some form of contraception, while in Pakistan family size remained stuck at 5.6 and fewer than one in five were using contraception. Even more remarkable, contemporary couples in Bangladesh want to have only three children and young brides under the age of 20 say they only want 2.5 children – which is close to biological replacement level. The key to these changes has been to make available a wide range of family planning services.

Fertility declines rapidly only when there is a choice of several reversible contraceptives, access to voluntary sterilization and some effort to provide safe abortions. Even though much remains to be done, Bangladesh has started to tackle all these problems.

When serious family planning efforts began in Bangladesh in about 1980 the population was 92 million, compared with 85 million for Pakistan. As a result of the greater access to family planning in Bangladesh, by the year 2025 Pakistan will have 50 million more people than Bangladesh (233 million vs. 180 million). It is difficult to think of any happy ending to the demographic problems Pakistan has created for itself. But even the more modest growth in Bangladesh will bring stark problems, as Bangladesh is the same size as the state of North Carolina and has few resources other than mud, water, and very many people. Today, the density of population in Bangladesh is equivalent to that of squeezing every person now alive in the whole of the world into the USA. Will the rest of the world learn from Bangladesh?

weather change through accelerating the greenhouse effect. The industralized world can reduce energy consumption by using more efficient technologies, but China and other newly developed nations are rapidly increasing their energy use. By the year 2025 global energy use will have risen between two- and eight-fold. From the point of view of food production and energy use the world's growing population is trying to run up the down escalator. A 1993 meeting of the world's scientific academies, including the British Royal Society and the American Academy of Sciences, concluded, 'Science and technology may not be able to prevent the irreversible degradation of the natural environment and continued poverty for much of the world'.

Barriers to birth control

The poignant thing about our present crisis in human numbers is that much of it could have been prevented. The people who are contributing most to the population explosion are sometimes those who want additional children least. The problem that faces us is not technical, but political and religious. Global population is not so much a problem looking for a solution, as a solution looking for resources.

Perhaps the key to understanding our predicament lies in our inherent sexual modesty, which leads us to cover up our genitals by day and copulate in private at night. It is a set of behaviours that seem to be related to the evolution of a strong sexual bond between parents, but this bashfulness also makes it extremely difficult to adopt an open, rational approach to reproduction and its control. As a result, we know which film star drives a Porsche, but not which one might have used a condom; and we know which president's wife shops at Nieman Marcus or Harrods, but we do not know which one might have had an abortion. Society has raised barriers to contraception, while exploiting our sexual proclivities in other ways. We advertise everything from air travel to soft drinks by association with sex, but we draw the line at advertising the contraceptives that individuals and society need for responsible reproduction and to control sexually transmitted diseases.

We try to wrap up discussion of sexuality and conceal family planning services from social view. We put cigarettes into vending machines, but leave birth control pills on prescription. We have eliminated smallpox by vaccinating millions of people throughout the world, often without informed consent. We go slow on offering voluntary sterilization in a country such as Bangladesh, where millions of people want it, because we have not devised a way of ensuring the best possible quality of service.

The Church and contraception

The Early Fathers of the Christian Church failed to grasp that sex was the basis of adult love, and instead equated it with Original Sin. By claiming that sexual intercourse was licit only if it was associated with the possibility of procreation, they categorized women as dogs, where copulation does indeed coincide with ovulation and sex is limited to procreation. Saint Clement of Alexandria, who lived in about AD 180, forbade sexual intercourse during menstruation, if the woman was pregnant, after the menopause, or if the wife was infertile. A century after Clement, the theologian Origen took literally Christ's enigmatic words, 'For... there be eunuchs, which have made themselves eunuchs for the Kingdom of Heaven's sake' (Matthew 19:12) and castrated himself. Over the centuries, theologians contrived to proscribe sex on Fridays (the day Christ died), on Thursdays (the day He was arrested), on Saturdays (in honour of the Virgin Mary), on Sundays (in memory of the Resurrection) and on Mondays (in memory of the Departed). Even Tuesdays and Wednesdays were forbidden during the forty days of Lent. Other priests argued that intercourse could take place only with the woman positioned on her back, and the more devout fashioned a heavy garment with a small hole in it so that the minimum of bodily contact took place during intercourse. Sex was literally an undercover operation. The Church condemnation of contraception reached its apogee in the fifteenth and sixteenth centuries. Article 133 of the German emperor's penal code of 1532 prescribed death for the use of contraception or abortion of an animate fetus: men were to be beheaded and women drowned.

Our Judeo-Christian tradition has been persistently, and sometimes violently anti-woman. Women, it was assumed, kept the faith less. Such extremes of ignorance and superstition might have disappeared with the passing of the mediaeval world, if it were not for the towering influence of two great theologians: Saint Augustine, who lived in the declining years of the Roman Empire, and Saint Thomas Aquinas, who lived in thirteenth century Italy. Saint Augustine taught that, as a result of Adam's disobedience to God in eating the apple, Nature was deranged and he interpreted sex as the Original Sin. The only moral justification he could see for intercourse was to conceive a baby: 'That which cannot be done without lust, must be done in such a way that it is not done for lust.' Aquinas wrote, 'in carnal intercourse, more than at any other time, man becomes like the beasts, on account of the vehement delight which he takes therein... before sin [*referring to Adam and Eve*] there would have been no such intercourse of man and woman.' These teachings were challenged in the nineteenth century by atheists, in the first half of the twentieth century by Protestants and in the 1960s by most senior

Catholic theologians. But the Vatican always resisted change. With the introduction of the contraceptive pill in the 1960s, Catholics in Europe and America began to use contraceptives as did the rest of the population. Pope John XXIII set up a six-man commission to review teaching on birth control. Cardinal Ottaviani and other conservatives in the Vatican tried to pack the Pontifical Commission with their own supporters, but still the majority came down in favour of family planning, leaving decisions over contraception to the conscience of the individual. Overruling his own Commission, Pope Paul VI published the encyclical letter *Humanae Vitae* (Of Human Life) on 29 July 1968. In essence, it upheld the teaching of Augustine and Aquinas:

> *The direct interruption of the generative process already begun and, above all, direct abortion, even for therapeutic reasons, are to be absolutely excluded as lawful means of controlling the birth of children. Equally to be condemned, as the Magisterium of the Church has affirmed on various occasions, is direct sterilization, whether of the man or of the woman, whether permanent or temporary. Similarly excluded is any action, which either before, at the moment of, or after sexual intercourse, is specifically intended to prevent procreation – whether as an end or a means.*

From an evolutionary perspective, *Humanae Vitae* is not only slightly off target, it is the reversal of the truth. To affirm that love can be separated from procreation is to strike at the heart of the family and at the bond between parents. In 1633, when the Church clashed with science and forced Galileo Galilei to recant his teaching that the Earth went round the sun, it made a grave and embarrassing mistake (which it did not set fully set right until 1992), but the majority of humankind did not suffer. *Humanae Vitae* was different: it brought great suffering to women and families around the world, and gravely set back public ability to assist family planning.

As noted, the first group to challenge the Christian condemnation of family planning were nineteenth century, agnostic, free-thinkers in Britain. Francis Place, who at the age of 19 married a girl two years younger than himself and eventually fathered fifteen children, was the first person to use the printed word to promote contraception. John Stuart Mill, the philosopher, who wrote the famous *On the Subjection of Women*, also advocated birth control, as did Robert Dale Owen, the social reformer. These ideas spread to the USA with the publication by the physician Charles Knowlton in 1832 of a slim volume called *The Fruits of Philosophy: or The Private Companion of Young Married People*. This book, which described vaginal douching as a method of family planning, was reprinted in the 1870s by two courageous British free-thinkers, Charles Bradlaugh and Annie Besant. They were sentenced to imprisonment and a heavy fine for publishing a work 'likely to deprave public morals', but were later acquitted. The trial attracted great publicity, and sales rose from 1000 copies a year to 100 000 in three months. Within a short time there was a measurable decline in the British birth rate.

But the battle for reproductive freedom was only just beginning. In the 1870s the USA became increasingly conservative. Anthony Comstock lobbied Congress to pass the notorious 1863 Act for the Suppression of Trade in and the Circulation of Obscene Literature and Articles of Immoral Use. As head of the New York Society for the Suppression of Vice he claimed to have personally arrested 3873 people. Asked why he classified contraceptives with pornography, Comstock replied, 'If you open the door to anything, the filth will pour in and degradation of youth will follow'. Margaret Sanger, the US family planning pioneer, challenged the Comstock laws by opening her first family planning clinic in New York in 1916 and was promptly arrested. In Britain there was no law against providing family planning choices, but when Marie Stopes opened the 'first birth control clinic in the British Empire' in 1921, she met hostility from both the Church and the medical profession. Between the two world wars, the book *Ideal Marriage* by the Dutch gynaecologist Theodor van de Velde was placed on the Vatican's Index of Prohibited Books. Some members of the German Catholic hierarchy were so obsessed with perceived sexual immorality that they welcomed Adolf Hitler's stand against 'the plague of obscene literature'. *Ideal Marriage* was banned by the Church and then burnt by the Nazis.

Science retarded

Today there is a large, unambiguous, easy-to-measure desire for smaller families spreading across the globe. The World Fertility and later surveys, begun as an idea put forward by Rei Ravenholt of the US Agency of International Development in the 1970s, demonstrate that between 50 and 80 per cent of women in Asia and Latin America, who already have three or more children, want no more. In Peru, the average woman has nearly seven children, but says she only wants four. Given the means to control their fertility, enough people make rational and predictable choices to bring the birth rate crashing down. If all unwanted pregnancies could be prevented immediately, global population would stabilize at about seven to eight billion. Unfortunately, both the scientific underpinning of contraceptive development and the freedom to disseminate contraception and safe abortion have been held back by political, medical and religious conservatism. In Ireland in 1991 it was still against the law to sell a condom, except through a registered outlet, rather in the way that dangerous drugs are dispensed to addicts.

While it was Christian sailors who first circumnavigated the globe, Christian philosophers who founded modern science, and Christian yeomen and burghers who put together modern economic capitalism, Christian attitudes to reproduction and its control were an unmitigated disaster. Until 1959, the US National Institutes of Health were explicitly forbidden to support research on contraception. In the World Health Organization, hostility from the Vatican State prohibited the development of a Human Reproduction Programme for the promotion of contraceptive research until 1972. Consequently, there was a gap of more than a generation between the development of the first antibiotics and the first oral contraceptives. Research

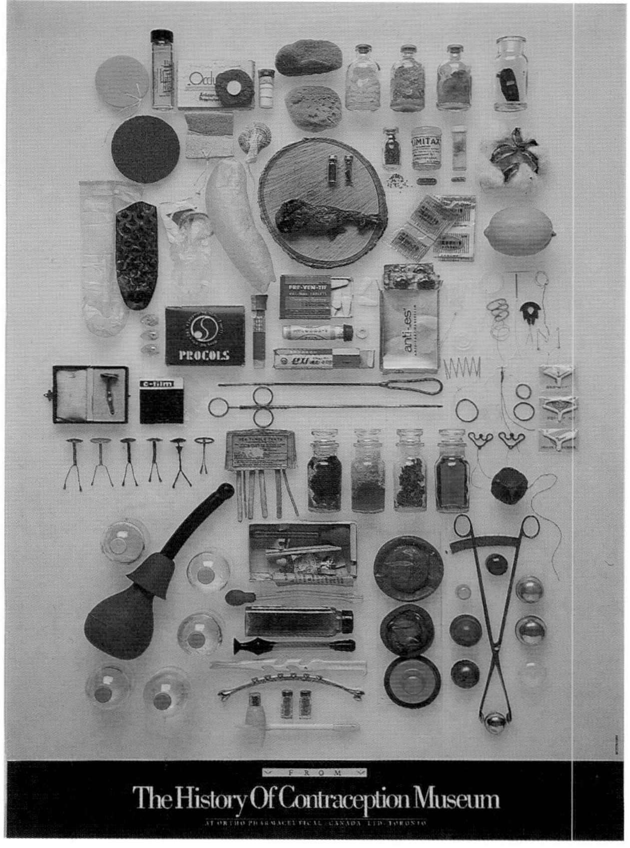

A cornucopia of contraceptives, ancient and modern. Some of the items on display in the History of Contraception Museum at Ortho-McNeil Inc., Don Mills, Ontario, Canada.

[Janssen-Ortho Inc.]

that could and should have taken place earlier was blocked. The biological possibility of using hormones for oral contraception was well described by an Austrian physiologist, Ludwig Haberlandt, in the 1920s. Oral contraceptives were brought to fruition only in the late 1950s, when the redoubtable Margaret Sanger persuaded the Jewish physiologist Gregory Pincus at the Worcester Foundation in Shrewsbury, Massachusetts, and the Roman Catholic obstetrician John Rock in Boston, to undertake needed research. It is symptomatic of the problems that have bedevilled family planning that even at the time the contraceptive pill was invented contraceptives were still illegal in the state of Massachusetts. For this reason, much of the early work on the method had to be conducted in Puerto Rico.

Plants, people and pills

From the seventh century BC, the Greek colonists of Cyrene in Libya exported a plant called silphium all over the Mediterranean. The plant graced the city's coins. A related plant, asafetida, is used to give Worcestershire sauce its distinctive flavour. Silphium was probably a partially effective oral contraceptive, and is mentioned by the Greek physician Dioscorides. (Contemporary research demonstrates that asafetida can block implantation in rats.) Indeed, silphium was so popular that by the first century after Christ it was harvested to extinction. One of Aristophanes' characters recalls, 'Don't you remember when a stalk of silphium was sold so cheap?'

Today's oral contraceptives also depended on a plant for their development. As soon as the hormonal control of the menstrual cycle and pregnancy was unravelled in the first half of the twentieth century, the theoretical possibility of a hormonal contraceptive became apparent. In 1921, the Austrian physiologist Ludwig Haberlandt wrote, 'It needs no amplification; of all methods available, hormonal sterilization based on biological principles, if it could be applied unobjectionably in the human, is an ideal method for practical medicine and its future tasks of birth control.' But it was only in the 1950s that two remarkable ladies – Margaret Sanger, the American family planning pioneer, and Katherine McCormick, the American philanthropist – joined forces to cajole medical scientists into developing a practical oral contraceptive. Both women were in their seventies. They urged Gregory Pincus, a Jewish reproductive biologist, and Min-Chueh Chang, a Chinese reproductive biologist trained in Cambridge, England, both of whom were working at the Worcester Foundation in Shrewsbury, Massachusetts, to collaborate with John Rock, a distinguished Roman Catholic gynaecologist in Boston, Massachusetts, to do the development work.

But however ingenious the science, oral contraceptives would have been impractical without a cheap source of orally active synthetic hormones. This part of the jigsaw was provided by one of the most colourful of all the people who gave the world the contraceptive pill – Russel E. Marker. The son of an impoverished share cropper, a brilliant chemist (Marker devised the octane rating used on petrol pumps), he was also stubborn and impetuous. He walked out of university before finishing his Ph.D. When he was told he could not work on plant sources of hormones by Rockefeller University he resigned. When he suspected that the Mexican wild yam might prove a chemical source for sterol precursors he went to Mexico with a shovel and dug up yams. By 1943 he had a few jam jars full of synthetic progesterone – worth at the time a staggering quarter of a million dollars. Marker considered he was duped out of the profits he deserved by the pharmaceutical industry, gave up chemistry and became a recluse in Mexico. He hardly knew about, and certainly never intended, the oral contraceptive revolution he had helped to bring about.

Family planning arrives late

Contraceptives were not legal throughout the USA until the Supreme Court ruling *Griswald v. Connecticut* in 1965. The simple fact that global population is almost bound to reach 10 billion before we can achieve equilibrium is a result of the momentum built in to current population growth. Approximately half the population living in the developing countries today are below the age of marriage, and even if family size falls exceedingly rapidly the numbers will still continue to grow. The destructive force of population momentum is seen most vividly in China. When the notorious one-child family policy was launched in the late 1970s, the population was over 900 million. As a result of rapid population growth in the preceeding decades, there were so many more young people entering their fertile years that, even with family planning and a one-child policy, the population had grown to 1.24 billion by 1997. In other words, in a generation China had to house, educate, feed and provide jobs for as many extra people as currently live in the USA. The USA and China are the same size geographically, but the USA is more richly endowed in natural resources and incomparably richer in its industrial base.

Nobody in China likes the one-child policy. It is difficult for party leaders to enforce, distasteful for doctors, and painful for families. Physical coercion has been reported and there is no doubt that some women have been forced to have an abortion they did not want. But in historical perspective, the real tragedy of China is that choices are being taken away today because they were not offered earlier. Today, Chinese women are pressed into having sterilizations and abortions they do not want because their mothers were forbidden voluntary sterilization and abortions they did want – and if those choices had been available, then today's population momentum would not have been built up. It was the stubbornness of Mao Tse Tung and the Communist leadership, who refused to introduce family planning when it could have been offered in a voluntary way in the 1960s that has led to the no-choice situation of the 1980s and 1990s. Other developing countries – Mexico, Egypt, Pakistan – have very little time to act before falling into the same demographic trap.

Fortunately, voluntary family planning programmes, realistically put in place, work exceedingly well. The fall in family size that is occurring around the world is very largely a consequence of the improved access to family planning achieved in the past three or four decades. Access includes making contraceptive choices available to the poor either free or at appropriately subsidized rates. The problem is that rich nations often lack the political will to help poor nations to improve family planning services quickly enough. If we fall even further behind the unmet need for family planning than we are at present, then the global population will end up many billions higher than it need be. The time it will take to bring the human population into balance will overlap with the generations that must begin the incredibly difficult task of establishing a biologically sustainable economy – one where fossil fuels no longer change the atmosphere, where waste products are recycled, where as many trees are planted as are cut down, and where we take no more out of the environment than we can return to it. The difficulty of making the transition from our present energy-intensive economic systems to a biologically sustainable set of industrial processes and transport systems will depend in large part on how many people there are, and how rich they are. How rich they are drives their level of consumption. It is hard to persuade people to consume less. Americans do not want smaller cars, Europeans wish to continue to enjoy holidays in the sun, and middle class Indians want more refrigerators. It is actually easier to deal with how many people there are because many people all over the world want smaller families. While making family planning more available will not solve all our problems, it is essential if they are to be solved.

Problems of human population growth are distressing, not only because of their fearful implications, but because, unlike human aggression or the

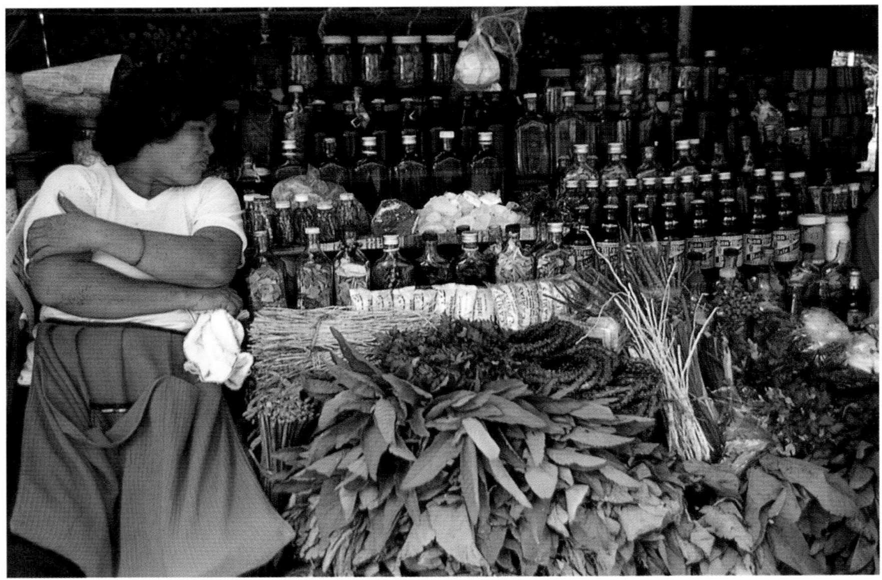

[Joe Cantrell.]

Inducing menstruation. All over the world, women trying to control their fertility attempt to bring on a delayed period. Possibly the remedies being sold here by a herbalist in the Philippines do not work. However, early spontaneous abortions are common enough, so that some women will go on to recommend the product to others in the belief that it had the required action. These vendors in Manila are particularly interesting because their stalls are attached to the busiest and most beloved Catholic church in the city; traditional remedies and religion are culturally interwoven and, when you ask them how to take the herbs, they say, 'Use them three times a day, in memory of the Father, Son and Holy Ghost'.

control of nuclear weapons, we already have the means to restore natural patterns of fertility. We could have held human population at lower levels if we had chosen to make family planning services available earlier. We were designed to be a slow breeding animal and it is not as difficult as some people think to bring births and deaths into balance. Once people have the means to control their fertility they go on having sex, but there is no empirical evidence that people want any specific number of children. With the exception of a brief post-war baby boom, every generation in the USA for the last century and a half has had fewer children per family than its predecessors. In 1997, the average Japanese woman was having 1.5 children in her fertile lifetime, and the average German 1.3. Although it would be rash to project people's behaviour that far ahead, it does seem as if there is nothing magical about a two-child family.

Successful family planning

In South Korea in 1960, the average woman had six children, the population grew by 2.9 per cent per year, and the economy by less than 2 per cent – more slowly than the population. A realistic family planning programme was put in place where sterilization was subsidized, contraceptive pills were made available without prescription and the abortion law was reformed. Today the average woman has only 1.6 children and in thirty years the per capita income has jumped from US $82 a year to almost US $10000. The South Korean economic miracle would not have taken place without family planning and safe abortion. Other countries could have seen similar fertility declines if they had been similarly straightforward about family planning. In 1960 the Philippines were richer than South Korea, but the Church obstructed access to the fertility regulation choices people needed, and today South Koreans are eleven-fold richer per head than the Filippinos. If the Philippines had taken the South Korean road, then by the year 2050 their population would have stabilized at seventy-four million – a large number, but perhaps compatable with widespread social and economic progress. As it is, their population in 2050 is projected to reach 127 million and it will still be growing.

The provision of family planning services is not going to overcome a corrupt government (the Philippines suffered under the Marcos government for many years), but falling fertility can be a welcome short-cut to economic development. Without it, social progress becomes like a sand castle before the tide. The Philippines can never catch up with South Korea in the foreseeable future. Some economists have pointed out that the real cost of raw materials continues to fall, and that more people means more hands to work and more

Intra-uterine contraceptive devices. IUDs have had a stormy clinical and political history. First described in 1868, their use was well established by the Polish obstetrician Richard Richter in 1909. Grafenberg in Germany and Ota in Japan developed metal devices in the 1930s and 40s and both were arrested by their fascist governments. In 1962, Jack Lippes of Buffalo introduced easy-to-use, flexible plastic devices, and in the 1970s Jaime Zipper in Chile discovered that the addition of copper reduces failure and side effects.

No one quite knows how IUDs work; they certainly prevent fertilization, but they may also sometimes act by bringing about the destruction of the fertilized blastocyst.

Most IUDs do cause heavier menstrual flow and they increase the risk of pelvic infection, so they are a bad choice for young women with more than one partner – or whose partner has more than one partner – but can be excellent for older, married women. IUDs have an uneven reputation because they can be badly designed, or can be used by people in a silly way. In 1970, Hugh Davies of Baltimore devised the Dalkon Shield, which because of its large surface area was associated with an unacceptably high incidence of infection, and lawsuits eventually led to the bankruptcy of the manufacturer, A.H. Robbins. In parts of Europe, such as France, IUDs remain widely used, and in China they are the commonest method of birth control. Recently a new hormone-releasing IUD called Levo Nova or Mirena has started to come on the market in Europe. Not only does it drastically reduce the volume of blood lost at menstruation (making it also an ideal medical alternative to hysterectomy for women with heavy periods as they approach the menopause), but it also has the lowest failure rate of any known contraceptive, reduces the incidence of pelvic infections, and remains effective for up to seven years. Many see it as the ideal contraceptive of the future for women.

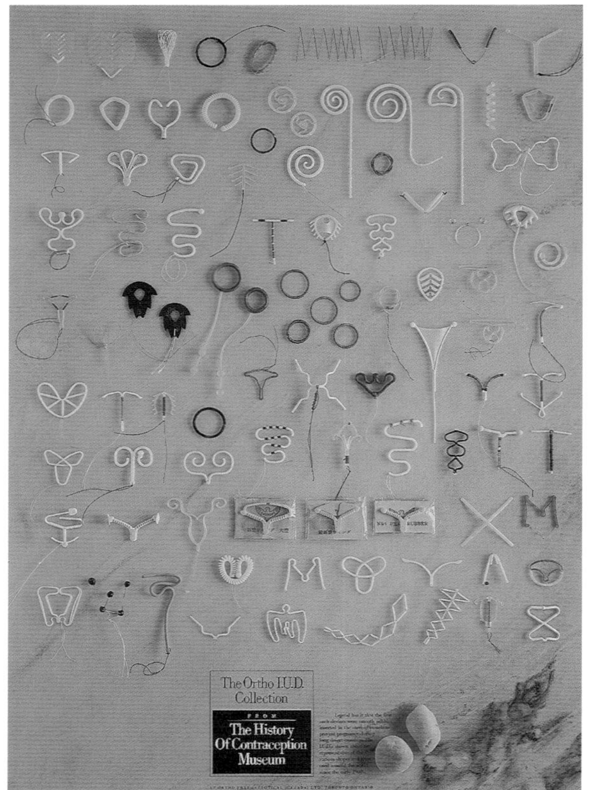

[Janssen-Ortho Inc.]

brains to solve problems, so we need not worry about population growth. Unfortunately, the pavement dwellers of Calcutta are not going to win Nobel prizes, or even get the opportunity to find enough to eat. Those who are lucky enough to be employed have to support many dependents, and there is little or nothing left over for saving and investment. As a consequence, such countries are unable to accumulate the wealth necessary to create the infrastructure of schools, roads, health services, housing and sanitation to keep

[Mary Evans Picture Library.]

The Operation, **Thomas Rowlandson.** Thomas Rowlandson (1757–1827) was the greatest British caricaturist of the eighteenth century. He lampooned the royal family, the Church and politicians and he produced risqué prints that he sold for sixpence each to a bawdy public. (When an edition of Rowlandson's works was seized by the British Customs in 1977, it was pointed out that the prints came from the Queen's collection in Windsor Castle – 'If the paintings are good enough for Her Majesty, they are good enough for her subjects', quipped the defence lawyer.) His print of an abortion shows obvious familiarity with the procedure, and horror in the faces of the three women sharing a bowl of soup – presumably prostitutes in a brothel. The doctor is probably using the metal enema syringe not for vacuum aspiration, which was invented later in the century, but to inject soapy water between the placenta and the uterine wall – a method still used in many parts of the world to induce abortion.

pace with the ever-increasing population. Family planning is not an alternative to improvements in other areas, but it is a catalyst to change. In Thailand, for example, a study found that more children of rural families with only one or two children attend secondary school, compared with children from larger families, even when other factors such as income or parental education were taken into account. As more girls go to school throughout the developing world, the status of women will improve.

Abortion

People typically turn to cure before prevention, and abortion is a key variable in fertility decline. It is something individuals want – often to the point of putting their lives on the line to get it – but society commonly denies its existence. It is an unpalatable but consistent empirical truth that abortion rates usually rise as family size begins to fall and no country has achieved a two-child family without the use of abortion. Abortion challenges the male need to prove paternity and to have power over women, as we explored in Chapter 9. Many women do not like to recognize that they may have an unwanted pregnancy one day, but statistics show that, on average, every woman on the planet will have one abortion before she reaches the menopause (obviously some women will have many abortions and others none, but the frequency of abortion cannot be gainsaid).

Publicly we find it extraordinarily difficult to deal with this most private of decisions. Yet abortion solves mistakes. In the all important decision about becoming a parent, a five minute operation can put the Humpty Dumpty of life's affairs back together again: it reverses time's arrow. Surveys show that a small number of people believe abortion is murder. Another group believe a woman has an unfettered right to do anything she wishes with the embryo in her womb. Many people do not like abortion, but make exceptions for 'hard' cases. In 1983, in a free and secret ballot, the people of Ireland voted by two to one to amend Article 8 of their Constitution, to include the words: 'the state acknowledges the right to life of an unborn child, with due regard to the equal right of the life of the mother.' At the end of 1991 a 14 year old girl became pregnant following rape by her best friend's father. A Dublin court injunction, interpreting the Constitution, prevented the girl from having an abortion in London. Ireland was plunged into a political and religious crisis. Two-thirds of the population, including many who had voted for the original amendment, were sympathetic to the girl's tragic plight. Eventually, the government paid the costs of an appeal and the girl's freedom to travel outside Ireland was upheld.

An estimated fifty million women obtain abortions each year. Unsafe techniques include poisons (such as ergot or quinine), physical trauma to the abdomen, or the insertion of foreign bodies into the uterus. In Bangladesh a tree root is used and in Latin America a rubber urinary catheter is often pushed through the cervix. Subsequent tetanus, other infections, kidney failure and haemorrhage can cause serious illness or death. By contrast, vacuum aspiration abortion can be performed with a hand-held US $20 plastic syringe and a flexible plastic cannula, no bigger than a drinking straw. The equipment can be sterilized and reused hundreds of times, and it can be done safely and cheaply in virtually any part of the world. Early abortion has a mortality of fewer than 1 in 100 000 procedures. It is ten-fold safer than childbirth or tonsillectomy in the same community.

Legislation has little or no effect on abortion numbers. In 1966 the dictator Nicolae Ceauşescu reversed a previously liberal abortion law in Romania. Nine months later the birth rate doubled. But then it began to fall back to its previously low level – and the maternal mortality began to rise as illegal abortion networks were established. Abortionists were imprisoned. Women in factories were examined and questioned about their periods. Yet abortions continued to rise and the birth rate went on falling. Over 13 000 women are estimated to have died during this dictatorship of fertility. Orphanages filled with abandoned children. In December 1989 Ceauşescu was overthrown. Within 48 hours the new government liberalized the abortion law. In the first year of the liberal law over one million abortions were done in hospitals and polyclinics – but the birth rate hardly changed,

Massage abortion (*opposite*). From Burma, through Thailand, the Philippines and down to Indonesia, traditional midwives know how to perform massage abortion. A village woman with an unintended pregnancy lies on the split bamboo floor of her home while the midwife reaches with her fingers behind the pubic bone to steady the uterus. Then she applies pressure with her hands, her elbows, and if that fails with her bare feet, stamping on the woman's abdomen, until bleeding into the vagina begins. Sometimes she will use the pestle that village women have to grind corn. If the procedure becomes unendurably painful she will withdraw to return a few days later. If successful, she is paid with a chicken, or given some other small gift. In urban areas, payment is more likely to be in cash. When asked by the interviewer how many massage abortions she had performed, the midwife in this picture said in a deadpan voice, 'One a day for ten years.'

[Joe Cantrell.]

evidence of the rate of illegal operations that had taken place under the most Draconian set of penalties.

On average, Romanian women have five or more abortions in a lifetime. Every second US woman, on average, has at least one abortion before she reaches the menopause, while in the Netherlands only one in six women has an abortion during the whole of her reproductive life. These differences reflect the effect of different levels of contraceptive use. In Romania modern contraceptives are not available and in the USA services are uneven and expensive. In the Netherlands it is expected that safe abortion should be available, but only to be used as a last resort. There is a commitment to good family planning, a high use of oral contraceptives, access to morning-after pills and the choice of voluntary sterilization.

A global choice

Wherever several methods of contraception have been made available, backed up by access to safe abortion, family size has plummeted. Technically, such choices could be made universally available: appropriate technologies exist, and women and men would certainly use the services. It costs US $5 to US $20 per year to provide contraceptive choices, but there are hundreds of millions of people for whom even this much is too expensive. At the beginning of the 1990s, less than 2 per cent of foreign aid (about one billion US dollars a year) was spent on family planning, and much of that was poorly used. Few developed nations give as much as 1 per cent of their gross domestic wealth to overseas assistance, so the rich nations are spending much less than one part in 10 000 of their wealth to help international family planning. The 1994 International Conference on Population and Development, held in Cairo, made an eloquent appeal for a broad range of reproductive health services and spelt out many ways in which the status of women might be improved. Unfortunately, neither developed nor developing countries have been willing to come up with money to pay for these services. It would cost Western taxpayers less than a penny a day to provide universal access to

In one minute

By the end of the century we will share our fragile planet with over 6 000 000 000 other human beings. But to most of us a billion is not very different from a million: indeed, the British and Americans differ over whether one billion is a thousand million (USA) or a million million (UK). Either way it is an unimaginably large number, and perhaps it is easier to visualize smaller numbers. What happens in the world every minute?

70 000 000 000 000 000 000 sperm are manufactured by the human race

1 000 000 human eggs are ovulated

60 000 men ejaculate

500 women conceive

200 fertilized eggs are lost through natural wastage

40 abortions are deliberately induced

260 births occur – 225 of them in developing countries, 8 in the USA (population 261 million), 8 in Egypt (population 51 million), and 1 in England (population 49 million)

1 woman dies from pregnancy, childbirth or abortion

21 infants under one year of age die, mostly of malnutrition

100 adults die of disease or old age

2 US teenagers get pregnant

50 acres (20 hectares) of tropical rain forest are destroyed

4500 tons of oil are consumed

1 000 000 dollars are spent by the nations of the world on armies and armament

family planning and set the world on course for a stable population of about ten billion or less. With that number of people – and a great deal of luck and good will – the world might just squeeze by and move to a biologically sustainable economy, without irreversibly damaging huge portions of the biosphere.

A human right

Family planning is a democratic enterprise. The freedom to determine our family size, like the other great human freedoms, is one that experience shows is used responsibly by individuals. The aggregate of individual decisions concerning fertility regulation can be as good as, or sometimes better than, a declared national policy. Democracy and demography have the same linguistic root, and for many people the right of access to contraception may be even more important than the right of access to the ballot box.

Family planning is most likely to assume its rightful role in the world when its advantages are clearly seen, information about it is accurately given and its colourful but destructively controversial history is understood. Even if our planet had no limits to the numbers of people it could accommodate, even if there were no issues of unemployment, no risk of sexually transmitted diseases and no fear of AIDS, there would still be the same imperative to offer couples the right to plan their families. Contraception heals the wounds modern living inflicts on natural patterns of human reproduction. Children born too close together and too soon or too late in the mother's life are at greater risk of death and ill health. Badly timed pregnancies also endanger the mother's health and, as we saw in Chapter 11, lifelong patterns of child-bearing are related to cancer later in life.

In the first chapter of Genesis God commanded the first man and woman to 'Be fruitful and multiply, and replenish the earth and subdue it' (Genesis 1:28). Global population at that time is recorded as two. We can no longer afford to allow past attitudes to block access to contraception, sterilization and abortion. Such attitudes have already wasted a key generation in the fertility transition. If we miss even one more decade of opportunity we may put an intolerable strain on the interconnected web of life that has evolved on this planet for thousands of millions of years – and on which we are totally dependent for food, habitation and much of the joy of living. Our future and that of life on Earth is at stake.

13 THE ANIMAL WITHIN US

'Science has always defeated religious dogma point by point when the two have conflicted ... The essence of humanity's spiritual dilemma is that we evolved genetically to accept one truth and discovered another.'
E. O. Wilson, *Consilience: The Unity of Knowledge*, 1998

Evolutionary biology cannot tell us how to behave in the modern world, but it can provide valuable insights into why we behave in certain ways. Both sexes are essential for the survival of our species, but women are the rate-limiting resource in reproduction and men compete for access to women. Often men seek to control women. We are intensely social creatures and also

Where Do We Come From? What Are We? Where Are We Going? **Paul Gauguin, 1897.** Gauguin struggled with these questions, painted them into a work of art, ingested poison, vomited, and lived.

highly sexed. We learn from our parents and from those around us, and from an early age we monitor our kin and those close to us. We identify with the group we were born into, and commonly show antagonism to any out-group. At the same time we are unambiguously a single species, as there are no two races on earth – however different their faces, their skin colour or their physique – who cannot get together and have children.

In this book we have tried to look for consistent patterns of behaviour, found across many cultures, that probably represent the inherited predispositions that evolution has given us in the areas of mating, parenting, social behaviour and relationships between groups. Most of these predispositions are highly flexible, and the plasticity that is built into so much of human behaviour means that the same predisposition may express itself in a many different ways. As we saw in Chapter 7, an Ayoreo mother in Paraguay who kills her newborn baby may still be maximizing her life-long reproductive

[Tompkins Collection, Museum of Fine Arts, Boston]

potential and can also be an exceptionally loving and indulgent parent. Culture is not something to be explained in terms of itself, but it is an elaborate structure, partly sculpted by the behaviours evolution has bequeathed us. The problem that faces us in today's fast-changing world is that we must accommodate to many things for which evolution never prepared us. We are living beyond our genetic inheritance, in an artificial environment of which we have no prior evolutionary experience; we are hunter–gatherer women and men lost in a concrete jungle; we are spear-throwing warriors with fingers on the nuclear button.

Human beings have always asked where we came from and how we got here. Darwin's 'dangerous idea' of biological evolution was a fundamental reformulation of everything humans had believed since the dawn of history. Instead of expressing a static moral order in which humans were part of a divine plan, evolution asserts that all living creatures are the product of immensely slow changes brought about by inherited variations and reproductive competition between individuals. Can we use such insights to cease doing some things evolution predisposes us to do, such as making war on our neighbours? Can we now choose to go in a direction in which brute evolution would never have taken us? It is useful to begin by asking why our behaviour is seemingly so complex and so subtle.

Why have a big brain?

We might like to think our big brains evolved so that we could carve totem poles, knap flints, bridge rivers, or use plant genetics to bring about the green revolution. But it is a mixture of hubris and our bashfulness over sex that causes us to think these might be the reasons. In reality evolution judges biological success by the number of our progeny. If our selfish genes have created an immensely complex multicellular body merely to give eggs and sperm the maximum chance of meeting and surviving to the next generation, then we need to understand that the evolution of the most prodigious part of that body, the brain, might also be explained by sexual competition.

There are plenty of animals that do very well with small brains. Rats live everywhere we do, some species of dinosaur survived for millions of years, and pigeons can find their way home better than most people. So why have a big brain? Elephants, apes (including ourselves), whales and dolphins all have big brains. The most complex, organized and integrated information system we know about in the whole universe is the brain of a sperm whale, weighing 35 lbs (16 kilograms), or more than ten times the weight of a human brain. Clearly, there must be a general relationship between body size and brain size, but even taking this into account big-brained animals are always intelligent creatures. Ultimately it may have been the cunning strategies and coalitions with friends and relatives needed to secure the best mate (and without the danger of too much physical violence) that required most brainpower.

If sexual selection played a role in the expansion of our brains, how exactly did it work? Darwin was interested in the extravagant tails of male birds of paradise. He proposed that female choice promoted the evolution of certain male attributes. In 1979 an Israeli, Amotz Zahavi, at the University of Tel Aviv, took this idea one step further, and pointed out that if males evolved false advertisements of sexual attractiveness, females would evolve counter-strategies to detect cheating. Therefore, argued Zahavi, perhaps some of the more flamboyant aspects of sexual dimorphism, such as the 8 to 10 foot (2.5 to 3 metres) wide antlers of the now extinct Irish bull elk, were indeed actual handicaps. If we take a verbal short-cut to summarize a blind, unconscious evolutionary process, then the message such a handicap signals to a discerning female is: 'I must be an outstandingly fit and strong potential mate for the

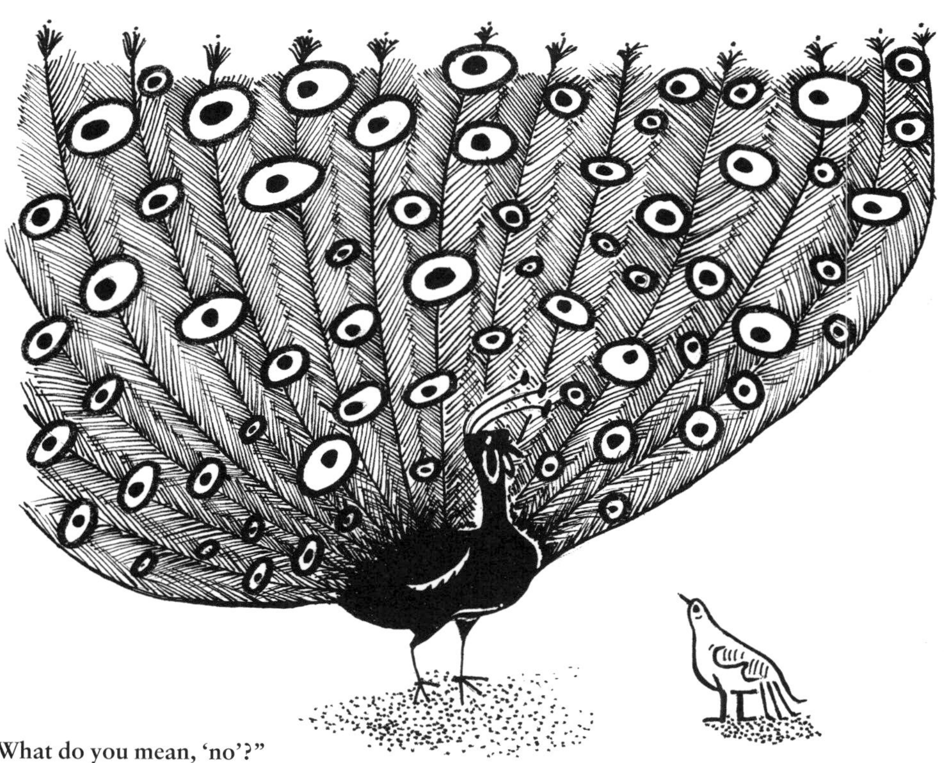

"What do you mean, 'no'?"

[Source unknown.]

very reason that I can afford to carry these ridiculous things on my head!' Whether the explanation is correct or not, it seems plausible that females would select mates who were sexually attractive to other females, because if they had a son that child would inherit such attractiveness and, in turn, leave most progeny in the next generation. In this way, sexual selection becomes a runaway process, and, for example, the peacock's tail becomes enormous for the simple reason that peahens like a male with a big tail. Geoffrey Miller has suggested that the human brain, like the tail of the peacock or the antlers of the elk, became bigger and bigger because both sexes selected partners with bigger brains. As noted in Chapter 4, contemporary brides and grooms tend to seek out partners of similar intelligence.

There is no reason why more than one evolutionary pressure should not have driven the increase in hominid brain size. There seems, for example, to be a relationship between length of life and brain size, and perhaps a bigger brain better prepares a creature to survive the seasons of want which all long-lived creatures face sooner or later. We also need a big brain for language, whether language evolved as a social glue to replace grooming or for some other reason. What is certain from the fossil record is that the hominid brain expanded particularly rapidly between 600 000 and 100 000 years ago.

Even if sexual competition was the main force driving the evolution of all this 'computing power', the exploding human brain proved to be of immense benefit in areas far outside reproduction. Instead of being a handicap, like the beautiful but clumsy tails of male birds of paradise, a large brain proved immeasurably useful. The human brain is perhaps the most remarkable product of evolution. It is an immensely complex mixture of analytical capacity and memory that expresses many different adaptations that have evolved over hundreds or thousands of generations to promote the survival of our genes. There is no single survival mechanism, but an interlocking series of behaviours directed towards specific ends. As Donald Symons wrote:

> *No mechanism could possibly serve the general function of promoting gene survival because there is simply no general, universal way of doing so. What works in one species may not work in another; what works in the infant may not work in the adult; what works in the female may not work in the male; what works in a given species at a given time may not work at another time; what works in solving one kind of biological problem may not work in solving another. And in every case, 'what works' is determined in the crucible of evolutionary times.*

As our brain evolved, so our capacity to trap prey, store food, and record events through speech and writing improved. Evolution has also given us a body that helped us to use our intelligence in secondary ways. Dolphins, whales and elephants do not have hands to enable their big brains to make and manipulate very complex tools. (A trunk is nowhere near as useful as two hands.) It is this combination of a big brain and clever hands that has produced our technology.

Culture and politics

Our big brains have given us a unique ability to augment the slow, undirected workings of the evolutionary rule-book by something better: rapid cultural change. DNA is the immortal umbilical cord of genetic information tying the generations together. Humanity's triumph over death is the persistence of cultural information accumulated over time. After delivery, the mother is linked to her baby through the nipple and it is during the natural interval of breastfeeding that our brains balloon to their final size. As a youngster grows it is also fed the sounds specific to its parent's language. Ultimately, the thread of knowledge that we help to transmit from the past into the future is woven by all members of our species: our individual contribution is tiny, yet essential. Language, settled living, population growth and the division of labour made civilization possible.

From a biological perspective we might judge a civilization by its ability to meet the physical and behavioural needs of the next generation. By that criterion modern civilization faces some serious problems. As US and European societies have become richer, they have invested relatively less in education and child care. One problem arises from the nature of money. We have been able to devise a universally acceptable symbol to equate the price of this book, eating a hamburger, teaching someone Serbo-Croat, shampooing hair, or buying the contraceptive pill, but bringing up the next generation is not normally given a price tag.

As we saw in Chapter 7, individual self-interest is slowly skewing public policy away from investing in the next generation. In 1960 the US Federal budget allotted twice as much per capita to children as it did to the aged: in 1990 children under 18, received on average $4200 in education and other benefits, while citizens over 65 enjoyed an average of $11 000 a year. The 12 per cent of the US population over retirement age now receive 54 per cent of social service spending. In a way, we have been hoist with our biological petard. Evolution depends on ruthless competition, even though altruism is also woven into our genes. Politicians are driven by the desire to please adults, who vote, rather than the needs of children, who do not. It is a post-Darwinian world, where an appropriate investment is no longer made in the next generation.

Social changes are pulling the rivets from many different parts of family and social living. In Britain, prior to the industrial revolution, exceptionally few people lived alone: in a study by Cambridge historian Peter Laslett, only 1 per cent of English households surveyed between 1574 and 1821 consisted of an individual living alone without a spouse, children or kin of some sort. Today, large numbers of people live alone and whole families are atomized by change. Divorce is increasingly common and one-quarter of US families are now headed by single mothers, whose opportunities for earning are limited.

We use our unique mobility not to tie the generations together, but to separate them. Parents may end up commuting long distances and only meeting for a few weary hours at the end of the day, when the children's needs get short shrift. Children are mesmerized by television from an early age, and by the time a US child leaves school she or he has spent more time in front of a television set than behind a classroom desk. A survey by the Center for Media and Public Affairs counted 2605 acts of violence on one representative day (7 April 1994) on television channels in Washington, DC. Leonard Eron of the University of Michigan has found that boys who watched a great deal of violent television when they were sampled at age 8, were more likely to be convicted of violent crimes by age 30. As adults they were also more likely to punish their own children harshly and to abuse their wives. It is difficult to exclude the effect of other social variables, and not all studies show such an effect but everything we know about the primate family suggests that exposure to violence as a child may make the problem of adult violence worse.

Religion

As the pace of change in everyday life accelerates, people sometimes escape into a belief in the supernatural. Gallup Polls have found that 29 per cent of US citizens believe in astrology, nearly a quarter in reincarnation, and over one-third in the literal truth of the Bible. A study of adolescents in Scotland found that 30 per cent of 10 to 15 year olds and half of 11 year olds felt God 'helped them'.

Formal religion can provide needed support for sexual partners in bringing up their children, and extended succour to the young or the sick. There are a number of scientific, epidemiological studies demonstrating that individuals and families with clear religious beliefs are measurably more healthy than others. Hypertension is lower among Sephardic Jews (of Spanish

[Ognissanti, Florence / The Bridgeman Art Library.]

Saint Augustine in his Study, Sandro Botticelli (detail of fresco, n.d.)

Saint Augustine was born in North Africa in AD 354, as the Roman Empire was collapsing under Barbarian assaults. He studied in Carthage and Babylon, and before he was converted to Christianity and baptized in 387, he had lived with a woman by whom he had one child. His book *Confessions of a Sinner* gives a graphic account of his stormy youth. 'Bodily desire, like a morass, and adolescent sex welling up within me exuded mists which clouded over and obscured my heart, so that I could not extinguish the clear light of true love from the murk of lust. Love and lust together seethed within me. In my tender youth they swept me away over the precipice of my body's appetites and plunged me in the whirlpool of sin.'

As a Christian, he was to become one of the most influential theologians of all time. He taught that, as a result of Adam's disobedience to God in eating the apple Eve offered him, Nature was deranged. Augustine was distraught because his sexual reflexes remained intact in spite of his conscious desire to suppress them: his tumescent penis constantly put him to shame. In his own words 'because of this, these members are rightly called *pudenda* (parts of shame) because they excite themselves just as they like, in opposition to the mind which is their master, as if they were their own masters.' He had unknowingly stumbled upon the power of the autonomic nervous system, but he interpreted this 'diabolical excitement of the genitals', so hideously out of control, as visual proof of our inability to control our sexuality, and hence of Original Sin. He saw the fact that woman was formed merely out of one of Adam's ribs as proof that she was 'the weaker part of the human couple', man's helper, but also his temptress, who through her sexual attractions could lead him to disaster. Augustine argued that the only justification for sex was to conceive a baby: 'That which cannot be done without lust, must be done in such a way that it is not done for lust.' His teaching remains the foundation of today's condemnation of contraception by the Vatican. (Augustine also condemned the rhythm method, although in the twentieth century the Church abandoned this logic.)

Augustine lived in a world where justice had become totally corrupt, and a person accused of a crime was found guilty or acquitted according to the size of the bribe (Latin *gracia*) they could give to the Roman judge. The bribe was actually paid over by a patron (Latin *patroni*). Augustine seems to have carried these ideas over into his theology. He saw man as utterly helpless and totally dependent on God's Grace, or *gracia*, although patron saints could intercede for you. Saint Augustine engaged in a long theological debate with a contemporary British monk called Pelagius who believed man could exercise free will, and he attacked Augustine's concept of *gracia* and *patroni*, with their capricious and unjust connotations. Although many people followed Pelagius, Augustine succeeded in branding him a heretic. (Heretic comes from the Greek word for 'free choice'.)

Augustine's prohibitions on contraception continue to cast a dark shadow around the world. In 1997, for example, Cardinal Sin of the Philippines, building on Augustine's condemnation of contraception, described condoms as 'only fit for animals'.

Oliver Cromwell unknowingly provided the perfect riposte to Saint Augustine's view on Original Sin in his famous letter to the General Assembly of the Church of Scotland on 3 August 1650:

> *'I beseech you, in the bowels of Christ, think it possible you may be mistaken.'*

or Portuguese descent), Zen Buddhists, Baptist clergy, and Benedictine monks than in control groups. The higher a man rises in the Mormon priesthood the lower is his risk of developing cancer. Unfortunately, the stability that religion provides is difficult to separate from the danger that ancient myths will end up stunting contemporary judgement.

The wonderful advantage of cultural information over genetic is that it is so much easier to change and update. The limitations of cultural information are that it has to be imposed on the genetic background of a hunter–gatherer ape, and we pick it up as we go along, until it becomes part of our mental furniture. In practice, it can be very difficult to reprogramme cultural information once we have acquired it. In the case of sexual behaviour, the very fact that sex can be shaped by culture into so many different forms, based on the biological directives we have inherited, also makes us anxious about behaving 'correctly'. Religion often attempts to provide the missing assurance, but it can also be used as a whip and scourge. It is intriguing to see how almost all religions have chosen to prohibit at least one aspect of sexuality that is regarded as perfectly normal by other religions. Perhaps religious prohibition of certain normal and healthy appetites engenders a feeling of inadequacy and humility in us, and thus reinforces our adherence to a particular belief. Contrast the ancient Egyptian religion that believed that the world began with a wholesome, divine masturbation, with that of Saint Thomas Aquinas who condemned masturbation as a 'sin against nature', and therefore as worse than a sin against another person, such as adultery or rape.

In several important areas, religion and biology come to different conclusions about the use of technology. It is religious groups who lead the lobby against access to contraception and the choice of abortion. The number of unintended pregnancies and induced abortions in the world would be much smaller if Pope Paul VI had jumped the other way when he wrote the encyclical *Humanae Vitae* in 1968, and endorsed contraceptive use as his own Commission on the subject recommended.

Perhaps the sensible thing, when manipulating reproduction or sustaining the dying, is to try to create a reasonable framework where those closest to the situation can discuss problems in all their complexities. It is not easy to weigh the quality of life in the balance of human judgement, but it is not impossible either. In particular, we need to avoid legislating rights that Nature never intended and humankind cannot implement. Given the right set of circumstances, nearly all pregnant women will choose to use technology to detect a serious abnormality early in pregnancy, so they can seek an induced abortion where a natural one has failed to occur. Nearly everyone has come to welcome the use of our intelligence to relieve the pain often associated with

Some men by belief, or a quirk of life, never engage in sexual intercourse. The fifth century Saint Simeon Stylites lived on top of a 60 foot (18 metre) pillar for thirty years. His biographer records how some cynic hired a prostitute to test his chastity but Simeon lit a candle and held his finger in the flame and 'when it burnt and scorched he felt it not, for the lust that was upon him'. It is not clear whether this episode took place on top of the pillar, but it is said that when morning came he had resisted seduction but lost all his fingers. Saint Jerome, who was one of the most learned of the Early Fathers of the Church wrote of his experience as a hermit.

Saint Hilarion was a contemporary of Jerome and also a hermit whose dreams, as illustrated in this nineteenth century painting, were filled with visions of gourmet meals and seductive maidens.

The interesting thing is not that these things happen but that any religion expects a mature person with testosterone in their veins not to try to mate. In 1976, at age 42, and still a virgin, Eamonn Casey, Roman Catholic bishop of Galway, Ireland, fell in love with Annie, young enough to be his daughter. He acknowledged and partially supported his child Peter, but with great suffering to both parents the story was kept secret for 17 years. Sometimes the urge to mate is driven to focus on the celibate's own sex. As a young man, Peter Ball fell in love with a young woman, but he was persuaded by his spiritual adviser that his vocation was to be an Anglican monk. He rose to be Bishop of Gloucester and associated with Margaret Thatcher and Prince Charles. Like a latter day Hilarion, Bishop Ball slept on a horsehair pallet, and rose at 4.30 a.m. to pray for one and a half hours on his knees. In 1993, tragedy struck and he admitted gross indecency with a aspirant monk aged 17 and resigned his bishopric.

For rare individuals, celibacy does indeed concentrate the mind. Isaac Newton was the child of illiterate parents and his father died before he was born on Christmas Day 1642. According to his mother he would have fitted into a 'quart pot' and only her intense love and undivided attention can have kept him alive at all. Yet by age 3 his mother remarried and virtually abandoned him. He grew into an obsessive, absentminded, guilt-ridden genius who invented calculus at age 22 and gave science the equations that sent men to the moon 400 years later. By his own account he never had intercourse – or as he put it 'violated chastity' – with either sex in his 85 years of life. Newton was afraid of close human relationships and focused his energies on intellectual problems, keeping them, as he said, 'constantly before me' until he solved them.

Descartes, Gibbon, Hobbes, Pascal, Swift, Mendel and Spinoza were also solitary figures who made great contributions to philosophy and science. It seems that rare individuals, while failing to pass their genes to others, can be unusually fertile in creating ideas – unless those ideas relate to sex itself, when they can be extraordinarily restrictive. Saint Jerome wrote:

> *It is disgusting to love another man's wife at all, or one's own too much. A wise man ought to love his wife with judgement, not passion. Let a man's love govern his voluptuous impulses, and not rush into intercourse – he who too ardently loves his own wife is an adulterer.*

The Temptation of St Hilarion, Dominique Loius Papety, 1843–4

[Wallace Collection, London / The Bridgeman Art Library.]

dying, but there is no imperative to keep 'alive' a body that houses an irretrievably damaged, non-functioning brain.

Serendipitous accidents

The end result of evolution often gives a strong impression of design, but over thousands of millions of years of slow change, there has never been any forward planning. Thus, for example, the hand is a combination of bones, muscles, nerves, tendons and skin that the best engineer would find difficulty in improving. But the human birth canal and spine are flawed designs. The limitations of the birth canal were noted in Chapter 6, and anyone who has had back pain knows that the mutations that turned a quadruped into a bipedal animal leave something to be desired.

Yet the lack of purposeful design may offer a life-saving escape from some of the problems posed by contemporary living. We can guess from the undirected nature of evolution that our predispositions are likely to focus on immediate causes, not the underlying drives that we now know shape long term evolution. Animals, for example, have a drive to copulate, but not necessarily to fill the empty uterus. Given the way the reproductive system has evolved, the drive for sexual intercourse works perfectly well in propagating the species. Any cat in season is focused entirely on finding a tom with whom to mate. We can be virtually certain that, whatever neuronal circuits the cat's genes have strung together in the animal's brain to produce this behaviour, it does not perceive itself as seeking to be pregnant. A cat's mating behaviour probably evolved independently of the instinct to lick and feed the kittens that arrived as a consequence of mating. Many people want children, and some will go to great pain and expense to have a child of their own, or will find joy and fulfilment in adopting a child, but there is no empirical evidence of what might be called a *kinderstat* – an internal drive to have a specific number of children. If they did have an inherited drive to have large families, then it would be difficult to explain how people in Nigeria have an average of six children, but those in Spain only 1.3. It would be impossible to explain why the generation of fertile women who lived in South Korea in the 1960s had six children, while their direct descendants living in the same country thirty years later average fewer than two offspring.

It may well be to our advantage that evolution is a series of improvisations, and that our predispositions are not always tightly linked – at least in our daily thoughts – to promoting the survival of our genes. By evolving the drive for sex, evolution achieved the ultimate in reproduction; yet we may not be thinking about reproduction when we are having sex, and indeed we may fear such an outcome of the sexual act. The superficial nature of our drives also offers us an escape from their worst consequences: if *Homo sapiens* had been born with a predisposition to have six children, rather than a drive for sex combined with a predisposition to love children, then global population would never stop exploding. Can we envisage a modern society, given our predisposition for sex, that would vote to seriously curtail sexual activity for normal adults? In short, by trying to understand the evolutionary origins of our behavioural predispositions we can identify opportunities that permit us to behave in counter-evolutionary ways that in turn promote stability and sustainability in the modern world.

Perhaps the most serendipitous separation of actual behaviours from their ultimate evolutionary goals is in the area of kin recognition. Human beings, like other social species, will often favour their genetic kin, as we saw in Chapter 2 in relation to the Mormons. Family groups, especially brothers, can create formidable alliances. The Carthaginan general Hannibal, 2200 years ago, and Saddam Hussein, the present leader of Iraq, both made their brothers and close relatives part of a warrior clique. The first controlled flight of an aeroplane in 1909 was made possible by the combined effort of brothers Orville and Wilbur Wright. But for every pair of genetic relatives their are many more examples of unrelated couples who have proved equally creative: Sir Arthur Sullivan and W. S. Gilbert, in the nineteenth century and Richard Rodgers and Oscar Hammerstein in the twentieth were wonderful writers and composers; Dave Packard and Bill Hewlett built a multi-billion dollar business in a lifetime; and Francis Crick and James Watson worked like brothers to unravel the structure of DNA, even though they came from different sides of the Atlantic. Among other species, non-relatives (unless of the opposite sex and directly involved in reproduction) rarely cooperate as closely.

Close cooperation between genetically unrelated individuals may be facilitated by the fact that kin recognition among human beings appears to be based on proximity, not genetic relationships. Children identify as kin any other child with whom they spend long intervals at an early age. As Shepher showed in studies of Israeli children brought up in kibbutzim, adults never select someone they knew as a child as a marriage partner, even though most of them had no genetic links whatsoever with other children in the kibbutzim. Just as the sex drive led to pregnancy in a hunter–gatherer society, so kin recognition based on proximity also worked effectively for most of human history, when our species lived in small bands and nearly everybody a child met when growing up was likely to be a brother, sister, cousin or other relative. Evolution could have selected an alternative mechanism, as for example one based on the ability to smell or taste our kin – this is not as implausible as it sounds, and it is the biological basis for kin recognition among some species of amphibians. If we had all our present attributes, but a different system of kin recognition, then modern society might not work in anything like the same way. Our ability to form bonds of close friendship with non-kin in school, in the same coffee shop, or office postroom is probably facilitated by the fact that we are able to confuse daily contact with someone with genetic relatedness. This confusion may also be a key to understanding modern warfare.

Warfare among the chimpanzee *Pan troglodytes* consists of a group of related males going outside their normal territory, surprising and out numbering individuals from an unrelated troop and killing them. Such lethal fighting within the same species gives the victorious troop access to the resources of the defeated group. From a biological perspective such fighting only 'makes sense' if those engaged in the fighting are genetically related, and therefore they and their kin stand to benefit from any increase in resources resulting from risking their lives: in evolution you never risk your life for someone other than kin. Human wars are often also over resources, and expectation of booty certainly drove pirates to attack and may have driven many other armies. However, most young men risking their lives in the firing line of a modern war are not thinking about king and country, about access to resources or about permitting more of their genes to survive to the next generation. When the bullets are flying, it is loyalty to the rest of the platoon, and perhaps revenge for some prior incident, that keeps men fighting. Army basic training, along with the experience of the battlefield itself, seems to create a sense of kinship, even where no genetic relationship exists.

Until very recently, nearly all societies contrived to reinforce the human predisposition to avoid killing individual members of their 'in-group', while exterminating alien 'out-groups' with bloodthirsty thoroughness. It is a distinction chimpanzees might well understand. All State religions, from that of the Aztecs to the Church of England, in some way or another, have blessed warriors, while still condemning murders. Indeed, the Old Testament appears to summarize our biological predispositions rather accurately, combining the Sixth Commandment, 'Thou shalt not kill,' with almost continuous warfare. Until very recently, warfare commonly achieved the biological goal of destroying the enemy and appropriating his resources. Hitler's concept of *lebensraum* (living space) in World War II would have seemed perfectly natural to practically any military leader prior to the twentieth century.

Some religions advocate pacifism, but it is not a teaching that has been able to overcome our species' propensity for warfare. The new, and in some ways hopeful, development of the twentieth century has not been in pacifism but in a rejection of warfare as a way of appropriating resources. There has also been a weakening of the social structures that made for loyal groups of fighting men, along with the maturation of alternative ways to channel the predisposition of young men to beat up their neighbours.

In World War II, the Allies demanded unconditional surrender, but then turned biology inside out by behaving with remarkable benevolence. The Marshall Plan provided the foundation for a democratic Germany, and aid was poured into Japan. Instead of appropriating the enemy's resources, the victors built up the defeated and turned them into powerful trading partners. Since the middle of this century, the international community has taken to stopping wars well short of their ultimate goal of destroying the enemy. The Six Day War, fought between Arabs and Israelis, was stopped by outside pressure, and the defeated Arabs remained inside the new frontiers of Israel. The fact that wars are less likely to achieve their biological purpose of creating *lebensraum* is encouraging.

One of the things a populous, settled society permits is new outlets for our inherited predispositions. The Greeks established the Olympic Games in 776 BC. Revealingly, as the Games drew near, a Sacred Truce was declared and honored. Athletes and spectators from all over the Greek mainland and islands – who were often at war with one another – attended the Games in peace. The competitors were young men who at any other time would have formed the backbone of the army. Women (and slaves) were excluded from the Games. Although built around individual achievement, each competitor carried the honour and cheers of his home town. Eventually, even the Romans were admitted to the Olympic Sanctuary, and the Games were only discontinued by order of the Christian Emperor Theodosius in AD 393.

Instead of happening every four years in one place, and encouraging individual achievement, team sports have become part of daily living and virtually every city in every developed country has a team towards whom it feels a loyalty. Organized sports allow for competition within a framework of fairness. The British wrote the first formal rules for football in 1744. Rugby football was invented at Rugby School in 1823. In the USA, baseball was codified in 1845 and the first intercollegiate American football game was played in 1869. The Olympic Games were revived in 1896 under the leadership of the French Baron Pierre de Coubertin. Team sports are played primarily by young men in the prime of physical fitness. More men than women crowd into football and baseball stands, or watch games on television. When wives and girlfriends take an interest, it is as much to support the man they love, as to support the team he loves. Team sports are territorial in nature, promoting the 'in-group'/'out-group' feeling that is so characteristic of human warfare. There is joy when the home team beats the away team, and despair when they lose. As, on average, defeats and victories are equal in number, Richard Wrangham has suggested that perhaps there is something in us that makes the pleasure of victory correspondingly greater than the pain of defeat. The hooliganism that occasionally accompanies sports matches is displayed exclusively by young men. In short, team sports share some of the behaviours associated with chimpanzee and human warfare, and they could be described as a form of masturbation to alleviate military desires.

Whatever the combinations of causes, improbable as it may seem, in relation to the size of the global population the twentieth century may prove to have been the most pacific in history. It hardly seems the time to be optimistic about the future of warfare, but warfare in *Pan troglodytes* and in preliterate human societies appears to be an ongoing process. Actual fights may be relatively far apart but peace never really reigns. So if we think of the twentieth century as a whole and take into account the relatively long intervals of peace and calculate death rates on the total population, then it does appear that bows and arrows and even bare fists can kill a higher proportion of the population than submarines, bombers, tanks and atomic bombs.

Honest messages

In a search for status and for mates, human beings learn to dissemble. From the age of 3 or 4 we develop the skill to lie and to detect lies – and, alone among all the animals, we learn to blush. The better we are at detecting lies, the better we necessarily become at lying. Imagine a population of honest individuals, all harmoniously sharing information and cooperating with great efficiency in the exploitation of resources. Now imagine that a lying machiavellian individual is born, who continually outwits and exploits his or her honest neighbours, eventually acquiring a disproportionate share of the available resources. The machiavellian offspring do well and multiply rapidly. As long as the population consists mainly of honest individuals, the machiavellians enjoy an advantage. But what happens when, after several generations, the honest individuals have been almost totally replaced by machiavellians? Now practically everyone is lying and cheating, and a mutation that was of initial benefit is rapidly proving to be a disadvantage. The few remaining honest individuals find themselves living in a very different world, and they now have an advantage accessing resources and begin to leave more offspring. In biological terms, an evolutionarily stable situation will arise when there is some sort of balance between machiavellians and honest folk. It may look at first glance as if evolution designed a benefit for the group, but in reality the evolutionarily stable situation has always served individual self-interest. An even more interesting and subtle evolutionarily stable situation would be where each individual inherited both a mixture of machiavellian and honest mutations. Honesty sprinkled with deceit might well benefit an individual's selfish genes, and perhaps corresponds most closely with the real world.

For honesty to work it must be visible and testable. Animals communicate in many ways. A message that is costly to give is more likely to be trusted than one that costs little or nothing to give. Grooming, as we have seen, may owe part of its widespread use to the fact that it requires an investment in time. The exchange of food can be used to make a statement about honesty – giving someone food is costly. But why did evolution choose sex as the basis of a bond between certain primates, including humans?

Sexual intercourse exposes each partner's vulnerability. Hyaenas have evolved a greeting ceremony where an animal returning to the pack after a brief absence places either their penis or greatly enlarged clitoris between the bone crushing, sharp teeth of their companions who make up the pack. Human and bonobo homosexual and heterosexual bonding is not quite as spine-chilling, but nevertheless it involves (literally) exposing one's self to another person. The external genitalia are easily hurt. The whole act of sex exposes each partner to disappointment, ridicule, or criticism. It is a costly enterprise and therefore a behaviour suitable for building honest bonds.

Civilization has added to our biological predisposition two novel systems that enhance honesty: the law and scientific method. The legal system brings specialist training and formal tests of honesty. It uses society's power to arrest the potential liar, and then asks other adults to judge the honesty of that person's claim not to have committed the putative crime. The scientific method is based on the most rigorous test of the honesty of other people's claims. It requires that if you wish to join the scientific community then you must specify all the antecedents of any idea or discovery, and then tell everything in sufficient detail that a reasonable person could repeat whatever has been done, in order to see for themselves whether they achieve the same result. The activity under scrutiny may be, for example, an experiment in a test tube, a prediction about the orbits of stars that will never be visited, or the theory of natural selection. We believe in evolution because there is nothing in the natural world whose structure and function cannot be explained by evolutionary processes, even though the changes taking place may have been spread over millions of years. In some ways, not being able to dissemble runs counter to our innate predispositions, but scientific method is a simple idea that more than anything is civilizing the world at an accelerating pace.

Insight

The idea that evolutionary biology can help not only to explain human behaviour, but also to suggest solutions to some of society's most intractable problems still surprises many people. Yet behaviour, like anatomy, has manifestly been shaped by evolution: all races, for example, have a common set of facial expressions for friendship, disgust, fear and surprise, and even a blind person smiles. Primatologist Alison Jolly of Rockefeller University has observed, 'the physiologists or anthropologists who claim humans have no innate behaviour, or imagine innate behaviour as somehow derived from conscious awareness, probably haven't had a baby'. She was referring to the irresistible urge to push in the second stage of delivery, once the neck of the womb is fully stretched open, a process that is identical in humans and other apes.

While recognizing the genetic predispositions underlying many behaviours, it is still true that there are extremely few human behaviours that are not modified by our surroundings. Facial expression may be an exception, but for most complex and important behaviours evolution seems to have determined that what is coded in our genes should be as open ended as possible. It is essential that our predispositions should be easily moulded by our upbringing to fit into any one of a thousand discrete environments. Each society builds a different structure on the same biological foundations. To further complicate matters we are compelled to look at our neighbours only through the windows of our own social house.

A newborn child is not a blank sheet of emotional and behavioural paper. In anthropologist Laura Betzig's words, 'The question it seems to us, that should be asked at this time is not whether evolution has shaped our behaviour but how.' One way to begin to tease out biological from social factors is to look for aspects of human behaviour that are consistent across cultural and historical frontiers. Thus, there is no country where more women are in prison than men, suggesting men are predisposed to be more aggressive than women. We saw in Chapter 2 how male/male homicide is almost forty times more common than female/female. The number of women arrested as a percentage of total arrests varies from 2 in Brunei to 10 in the Netherlands and South Korea to 20 in New Zealand and the West Indies. These are powerful statistics and they tally with biological hypotheses. Men are more competitive and risk taking because women are the rate-limiting resource in reproduction. Women, for their part, make intuitive, more carefully balanced decisions about how much effort to invest in their children, yet when driven to the wall by poverty, as were the widows of eighteenth century Ostfriesland, loving mothers will act with the same harshness as any other animal.

Biology can help to explain our entrances and our exits, our altruism and our competitiveness, our sexuality and the way we put our families together. We can begin to understand why different physical investments in reproduction have led women and men to expect different things from marriage, and what causes conflicts between children and parents. We can answer the riddle of why the living world is so filled with pain and suffering, and we need no longer propitiate non-existent gods by sacrificing the lives of our children, as did the ancient Carthaginians, or tearing the hearts out of our neighbours, as did the Aztecs. Evolution judges us solely by the number of genes we contribute to the next generation, and whether it hurts to break a bone or die of cancer is beyond the ken of natural selection: there is nothing in Nature's constitution about the pursuit of happiness, only a drive to contribute the maximum number of offspring to the next generation.

A biological understanding can tell us why our bodies must die to make room for the next roll of the genetic dice, but an insight does not necessarily make it any easier for the individual to adjust to our body's mortality. The fact that we have insight into the inevitability of death is a somber thought: the fact that we stand on the shoulders of others in our cultural evolution challenges us to leave the world a better place for our progeny to enjoy in future generations.

Our bodies and brains are put together by virtually the same genes that our ancestors inherited 100 000 years ago, and probably our Ice Age repertoire of behaviour has changed little. We evolved to live in small bands who survived by gathering vegetables (something women did slightly better than men) and hunting animals (something men did slightly better than women). The picture is more complex than a troop of chimpanzees, but not unrecognizably different. People and chimpanzees cooperate to achieve certain tasks and males band together to defeat and kill rival troops. Males, in particular, make shifting coalitions to gain power, if need be by biding their time before unseating a rival. Young women and young chimpanzees usually leave the troop of their birth and nearly always mate with males with whom they did not associate as children. Both species originally spaced their pregnancies by long intervals of breastfeeding. Unless things go terribly wrong, both species invest years of devoted love in bringing up the few children they produce.

The *hoka hoka*

The adolescent female sits watching the older one. When the older female wants hoka-hoka *and has seen the adolescent is waiting, she lies on her back and spreads open her thighs. The adolescent quickly approaches and they embrace. Lying face to face, like humans in the missionary position, the two females have quick, excited sex. Their hip movements are fast and side to side, and they bring the most sensitive sexual organs – their clitorises – together. Bonobo clitorises appear large (compared to those of humans or any other apes) and are shifted ventrally compared to chimpanzees ... to allow pleasurable* hoka-hoka *– which typically ends with mutual clutching limbs, muscular contractions, and a tense, still moment. It looks like orgasm.*

R. Wrangham and D. Peterson, *Demonic Males, Apes and the Origins of Human Violence*, 1996

The female touch

This book has emphasized that women and men have different reproductive agendas. Sarah Hrdy, writing about langur monkeys, commented,

> *the demands of reproduction have led to the evolution of two quite different creatures, two sexes caught in the bounds of irreconcilable conflicts. In only a few areas will the self interests of consorts overlap.*

But she could have been writing about the human species. Much of our civilization has ended up giving men more and more advantage in the 'irreconcilable conflict'. We have described many situations where men, who are stronger and innately more aggressive, use their strength to dominate women. Men and women have different needs, different perceptions and even slightly different brains. Can females manipulate and alter the male agenda?

Among *Pan troglodytes*, the species of chimpanzee that Jane Goodall began to study in Tanzania in 1968, the males are always dominant and often give the females a tough time. The females are smaller and an individual female leaves the troop in which she has grown up to enter another troop at puberty, when she is particularly vulnerable to male battering. She is relatively inexperienced, may not be fully grown and has no friends. For the already established females she is a potential competitor, and they treat her warily, as any group of older women might treat the arrival of a nubile teenager.

Between 1975 and 1991 the Japanese primatologist Takayoshi Kano studied bonobo chimpanzees in Wamba in Zaïre (now the Democratic Republic of Congo). As we saw in Chapter 2, bonobos use sex to reduce tension in the troop. Mutual masturbation between females establishes a pair bond, and in Richard Wrangham's words 'They certainly give every appearance of enjoying sex enormously.' When a female migrates at puberty to join a strange troop, the first thing she does is to establish a same-sex relationship with an established female in the group with lots of *hoka-hokas* (sexual intercourse). Males also engage in same-sex activity but they do not seem as intense as the female partnerships. Both sexes also remain strongly heterosexual, but a pair of females who have sex together also bond as friends, and they will come to one another's support in any crisis, and although female bonobos are slimmer and more lightly built than the males, two females in a partnership are more than a match for a single male. Bonobos are the only mammal where the social structure is built around related males, but females are the dominant sex and, for example, two sexually bonded females can take food from a larger male.

Male and female bonobos fight among themselves and many males carry injuries that may have resulted from fights within the troop. (In one troop there are three adult males without testicles and it is possible this is the result of assaults by rivals.) Observations are limited and primatologists still have much to learn about bonobos, but to date bonobos have not been observed to fight the sort of bloody wars characteristic of *Pan troglodytes* and our own species. Richard Wrangham and Dale Peterson in their book *Demonic Males* described how a Japanese primatologist, Genichi Idani, studying bonobos in Zaïre, was witness to some of the most remarkable and revealing observations ever made on our fellow primates. Over about two months and on about thirty occasions in 1986, two groups of bonobos met at a site where sugar has been provided to encourage the chimpanzees out of the jungle.

> *A few minutes later Idani saw the two parties emerge from either side of the clearing and move slowly toward the sugar cane, looking at each other. Idani recognized the individuals of one party as members of E-group; the others were from P-group. Gradually, individuals from the two parties sat down within a few yards of each other, continuing to call, not fighting but not mingling either. It was a standoff, with two parties separated by a sort of demilitarized zone. And then, after thirty minutes of this strange truce, a P-group female crossed the neutral ground and had a* hoka-hoka *with a female from the other community. What followed was unprecedented for ape watchers. For the next two hours the parties fed and rested together almost as if they were members of a single community, with only the mature males of the two groups still quietly retaining their old social boundaries.*

It should not be inferred that we could, or should, use sex in the same way. The bonobo solution is unique to bonobos. The lesson for human beings is that three related primates, namely ourselves, bononos and chimpanzees, have evolved very different solutions to male aggression. What we should do, taking into account the fact that men are innately more aggressive than women and that wars are primarily a male activity, is perhaps to contrive ways of appointing many more women to political office. Women network better than men, they are more interested than men in finding solutions rather than losing face, and they are more empathic.

The deciding moment

Cultural evolution has overtaken that of biology. We are now so numerous and our activities are so far reaching that we are changing the face of the planet more rapidly than living things can adapt. By an accident of evolution, at this moment, we have become stewards of future life on Earth. As individuals, we must accommodate to unprecedented changes in the physical and social world around us. As members of larger communities, we must attempt to direct an ever-accelerating series of changes so as to secure our own survival and, if possible, ensure the betterment of the world around us.

We are at what may prove to be the deciding moment in history, not just for our species but also for all other living things. The increase in global economic activity each year is greater than the annual economic production of the world a century ago. In the first half of this century we learnt how to hunt whales to extinction, in the second half we have perfected a technology to empty the sea of smaller fry. Roads and chain saws are eliminating 99 acres (40 hectares) of tropical rainforest a minute. Global agriculture destroys twenty-four billion tons of top soil a year but it has to feed approximately ninety million more people each year. By the year 2050 the average person in the developing world will have to be fed from a block of land only 36 yards (33 metres) square. The litany of ozone holes, desertification, acid rain, global warming, the *Exxon Valdez* and Chernobyl is long and does not need extending, but it all adds up to one species being able to irreversibly damage huge swathes of its environment, and therefore ultimately to mortally wound itself – and other living things.

Our descendants may look back at the generation spanning the threshold to the third millennium as not necessarily the cleverest, most artistic or most brutal, but as the generation when primate evolution was tested most intensely. Our story is not a blip in recent history, but possibly the last act of a drama involving all living things. As the energy of the Big Bang has been dissipated over the last fourteen billion years and entropy has made an ever enlarging universe more and more chaotic, so on one rocky fragment left over from stellar evolution the opposite change has occurred, and something of increasingly improbable complexity has arisen. The heavier elements were forged from the fundamental particles crushed and twisted in suns and supernovae explosions, and condensed into molecules. Eventually, these molecules formed proteins, DNA and the other building blocks of living things from which the Blind Watchmaker has assembled cells. For some types of cell, being part of a multicellular plant or animal increased the opportunity to pass on genetic information. Our bodies are complex survival machines for an unbroken chain of genetic information stretching back over almost 4000 million years of competition and evolution.

In the hierarchy of improbable complexity, sexual reproduction was an important step, made all the more singular by the fact that biologists are still not entirely confident they can fully explain its pervasive popularity. Another was the evolution of the nervous system. At some point, the frenzy of electrochemical signals became so complex that self-consciousness arose; it is certainly also present in monkeys, probably in dogs and possibly in crocodiles. Although it represents a new level of doing things, however, it remains so mysterious that we still have no way of defining exactly when so momentous a step occurs in our own progress from an egg implanted in our mother's uterus to being a wilful toddler. Perhaps, like the chasm between childhood innocence and the hormone-driven sexuality of puberty, we know when we or others stand at either side of the line, but cannot really say when we are crossing it.

In a handful of species – the dolphins, whales, elephants and apes – evolution has fashioned a set of big brains, partly, it would seem, so we can outwit fellow members of our own species in the race to couple sexually and to pass our selfish genes on to the next generation. The human brain has 100 billion nerve cells, many making tens of thousands of connections with other neurones. And as behaviours became increasingly complex, it even became part of our self-interest to evolve love, kindness and altruism. While Christian theologians look for explanations of a Fall from Grace and of Original Sin, scientists, understanding biological competition, have to dig deeply for explanations of altruism. But explanations do exist. In the complex and subtle world of animal and most especially human behaviour, we may never know exactly how a particular trait evolved, or which of several plausible scenarios is the one our ancestors actually followed, but there is virtually nothing in Nature that evolution cannot explain – and some things only evolution can explain. For example, our evolution from fishes explains why we have a particular concentration of salts in our blood and why the nerve supplying our larynx dips down into our chests and arches around the aorta before returning to supply the vocal cords.

Evolution is a set of compromises and blind adjustments to new problems. Our big brain took so many years to programme and practise its skills that it became in the female's interest to evolve new behaviours to try to secure one male's monogamous interest – a strategy that half worked and half failed to unite the viviparous, lactating female, who must invest so much in each child, and the opportunistic male. So wide is the gulf between the sexual agendas of the two sexes that we are astonished and overwhelmed when love breaks in.

Slowly, and at great pain and cost, an ape that walked on two legs, had small teeth, four fingers and an opposable thumb, and an enormous brain, evolved in an environment that rewarded dexterity and memory, developed language, tools and culture, thus pulling us away from our more hairy, knuckle-walking cousins. We ended up an odd, contradictory creature, with a head so big our parents must cradle it on their shoulders when they move us in the first six months of life. As adults we develop pendulous breasts, a moderately large penis, a high forehead and a larynx so high in our throats that we are almost the only animal that can choke to death when eating. Over tens of thousands of years the hunter–gatherers, our ancestors, slowly developed new technologies, until about 11 000 years ago roving bands of people began to settle in villages and small towns. The agricultural revolution had begun, and with it an explosion of population occurred making possible in settled communities the division of labour which drives contemporary society. Darwinian evolution is incapable of looking ahead, and we can be certain that, whatever end-point our past evolution has now reached, it did not prepare us for the civilization we have serendipitously created.

We cannot escape our animal origins. The ancient dichotomy between human and animal, like that between spirit and body, no longer applies. The further we travel on the road of 'civilization', the greater the need to understand where we came from. One of our problems is that we think locally and respond to the suffering of those around us, but all too easily lose a sense of scale about the world as a whole. Our cultural inheritance, like our genetic inheritance, is transmitted by behaviours rooted in sexuality. It is parents, bonded by sexual intercourse, who teach the next generation how to live. There is closeness between intellectual and sexual intercourse: Eve ate of the 'tree of the knowledge of good and evil'. The Hebrew words *da at* meaning knowledge also have overtones of sex, as do the English verbs 'to know' and 'to penetrate'.

Adam and Eve were expelled from their Garden of Eden. Present-day men and women could destroy their Eden while still living in it. Can we develop the insight to manage the biosphere intelligently? Can we think through and respond to the combined effects of our accelerating economy and burgeoning human numbers?

The thread of cultural information must be broken, reassorted and reassembled by each generation. But, alas, cultures sometimes congeal into superstitions and dogma, which prevent us updating and adjusting the thread of cultural information. Sentient individuals often ask key questions, but commonly come up with wrong answers. Where the answers are difficult to find the human brain tends to make them up: we abhor an intellectual vacuum. Myths which began for lack of knowledge, crystallize into rituals and heavenly commandments: 'Thou shalt', or more commonly 'Thou shalt not'. Such creeds and codes remove the need, or indeed the freedom, to think and to make choices and they make us prisoners of our own belief systems. They stymie the rational development of moral decision-making and all too easily decompose into hypocrisy.

For most of our life on Earth, human beings lived in a cage built from superstition and with bars of ignorance denying us access to the world of knowledge and understanding outside. Over the last century a few of those bars were cut away and in the past several decades most of the rest have been weakened. But like a primate in the zoo that has become accustomed to, and even dependent on, its captivity, we have yet to make up our minds to walk out of our open cage. Unfortunately, unlike the monkey in a cage, there is no one outside to feed us or clean up the mess we make – we must push aside the bars of superstition if we are to survive.

And what of Adam and Eve in the twenty-first century? Let us strive to give all women, not just the fortunate few, equality of opportunity with men, but with the freedom to do things differently from men, reflecting their very different biological agenda. This could produce a new sound, never heard before, that would echo around the world – the sound of men's and women's hands clapping together as they celebrate the differences that ultimately make them essential to one another for the perpetuation of our species and for the fulfilment of our brief lives on this planet.

BIBLIOGRAPHY

1 Beginnings

Barnes, J. (ed.) (1984). *The Complete Works of Aristotle*, vol. 1, *History of Animals, Generation of Animals*. Princeton: Princeton University Press.

Darwin, C. (1859). *The Origin of Species by Means of Natural Selection, or the Preservation of Favoured Races in the Struggle for Life*. London: John Murray.

Darwin, C. (1871). *The Descent of Man and Selection in Relation to Sex*. London: John Murray.

Dawkins, R. (1976). *The Selfish Gene*. Oxford: Oxford University Press.

Dawkins, R. (1986). *The Blind Watchmaker*. Harlow, Essex: Longman Scientific and Technical.

Diamond, J. M. (1991). *The Rise and Fall of the Third Chimpanzee*. London: Random Century Group Ltd.

Fossey, D. (1983). *Gorillas in the Mist*. Boston: Houghton Mifflin.

Freeman, D. (1983). *Margaret Mead and Samoa: the Making and Unmaking of an Anthropological Myth*. Cambridge, MA: Harvard University Press.

Galdikas, B. M. F. (1995). *Reflections of Eden: My Life with the Orangutans of Borneo*. London: Victor Gollancz.

Goodall, J. (1986). *The Chimpanzees of Gombe: Patterns of Behavior*. Cambridge, MA: Belknap Press.

Hamburg, D. A. and McCown, E. R. (1979). *The Great Apes*. Menlo Park, CA: Benjamin/Cummins.

Harvey, W. (1651). *Exercitationes de Generatione Animalium*. London.

Harvey, W. (1653). *Anatomical Exercitations, Concerning the Generation of Living Creatures*. London: J. Young for O. Pulleyn.

Jocelyn, H. D. and Setchell, B. P. (1972). *Regnier De Graaf on The Human Reproductive Organs: An Annotated Translation of Tractatus de Virorum Organis Generationi Inservientibus (1668) and De Mulierum Organis Generationi Inservientibus Tractatus Novus (1672)*. Journal of Reproduction and Fertility Supplement, 17. Oxford: Blackwell.

Jolly, A. (1985). *The Evolution of Primate Behavior*. New York: Macmillan.

Jones, S., Martin, R. and Pilbeam, D. (eds.) (1992). *The Cambridge Encyclopedia of Human Evolution*. Cambridge: Cambridge University Press.

Kano, T. (1992). *The Last Ape. Pygmy Chimpanzee Behavior and Ecology*. Stanford: Stanford University Press.

Malthus, T. R. (1798). *An Essay on the Principle of Population*. Reprinted in Penguin Books 1982. Harmondsworth: Penguin.

Mead, M. (1928). *Coming of Age in Samoa: a Psychological Study of Primitive Youth for Western Civilization*. New York: William Morrow.

Mittwoch, U. (1981). Whistling maids and crowing hens – hermaphroditism in folklore and biology. *Perspectives in Biology and Medicine*, **24**, 595–606.

Pagels, E. (1988). *Adam, Eve, and the Serpent*. London: Weidenfeld and Nicholson.

Paley, W. (1828). *Natural Theology*. Oxford: J. Vincent.

Savage, T. S. and Wyman, J. (1847). Notice of the external characters and habits of *Troglodytes gorilla*, a new species of orang from the Gaboon River. *Boston Journal of Natural History*, **5**, 28-43.

Short, R. V. (1977). The discovery of the ovaries. In *The Ovary*, 2nd edn, vol. 1, ed. Lord Zuckerman and B. J. Weir, pp. 1–39. London: Academic Press.

Short, R. V. (1979). Harvey's conception: 'De generatione animalium', 1651. In *Developments in Cardiovascular Medicine*, ed. C. J. Dickinson and J. Marks. pp. 353–63. Lancaster: MTP Press Ltd.

Short, R. V. and Weir, B. J. (eds.) (1980). *The Great Apes of Africa*. Journal of Reproduction and Fertility, Supplement, **28**. Cambridge: The Journals of Reproduction and Fertility Ltd.

Strier, K. (1992). *Faces in the Forest: The Endangered Muriqui Monkeys of Brazil*. Oxford: Oxford University Press.

Tanner, N. M. (1981). *On Becoming Human*. Cambridge: Cambridge University Press.

Whitteridge, G. (1981). *Disputations Touching the Generation of Animals by William Harvey*. Translated with introduction and notes. Oxford: Blackwell.

Wilson, E. O. (1978). *On Human Nature*. Cambridge, MA: Harvard University Press.

Wilson, E. O. (1992). *The Diversity of Life*. Cambridge, MA: Harvard University Press.

Wrangham, R., McGrew, W. C., de Waal, F. B. M. and Heltne, P. (1994). *Chimpanzee Cultures*. Cambridge, MA: Harvard University Press.

2 The Polygynous Primate

Alexander, R. O., Hoogland, J. L., Howard, R. D., Noonan, K. M. and Sherman, P. W. (1979). Sexual dimorphisms and breeding systems in pinnifeds, ungulates, primates and humans. In *Evolutionary Biology and Human Social Behavior: An Anthropological Perspective*, ed. N. A. Chagnon and W. Irons, pp. 402–35. North Sciturate MA: Duxbury Press.

Barnes, J. (ed.) (1984). *The Complete Works of Aristotle*, vol. 1, *History of Animals, Generation of Animals*. Princeton: Princeton University Press.

Bartell, G. D. (1971). *Group Sex. A Scientist's Eyewitness Report on the American Way of Swinging*. New York: Wyden.

Betzig, L. L. (1982). Despotism and differential reproduction: a cross-cultural correlation of conflict asymmetry, hierarchy and degree of polygyny. *Ethology and Sociobiology*, 3, 209–21.

Betzig, L. L. (1986). *Despotism and Differential Reproduction: A Darwinian View of History*. New York: Aldine Publishing Company.

Daly, M. and Wilson, M. (1978). *Sex, Evolution and Behavior*. North Sciturate, MA: Duxbury Press.

Daly, M. and Wilson, M. (1988). *Homicide*. New York: Aldine de Gruyer.

Darwin, C. (1871). *The Descent of Man and Selection in Relation to Sex*. London: John Murray.

de Waal, F. (1989). *Peacemaking among Primates*, Cambridge, MA: Harvard University Press.

de Waal, F. and Lanting, F. (1997). *Bonobo: The Forgotten Ape*. Berkeley: University of California Press.

Diamond, J. M. (1991). *The Rise and Fall of the Third Chimpanzee*. London: Random Century Group Ltd.

Dixson, A. F. (1987). Observations on the evolution of the genitalia and copulatory behaviour in male primates. *Journal of Zoology*, **213**, 423–43.

Fay, R. E., Turner, C. F., Klassen, A. D. and Gagnon, J. H. (1989). Prevalence and patterns of same-gender contact among men. *Science*, **243**, 338–47.

Ford, C. S. and Beach, F.A. (1952). *Patterns of Sexual Behaviour*. London: Eyre and Spottiswoode.

Goodall, J. (1986). *The Chimpanzees of Gombe: Patterns of Behavior*. Cambridge, MA: Belknap Press.

Glickman, S. E. (1995). The spotted hyaena from Aristotle to the Lion King: reputation is everything. *Social Research*, **62**, 503–37.

Hagood, W. O. (1996). *Presidential Sex: From the Founding Fathers to Bill Clinton*. Secancus, NJ: Carol Publishing Group.

Hrdy, S. B. (1997). Raising Darwin's consciousness: female sexuality and the prehominid origin of patriarchy. *Human Nature*, **8**, 1–49.

Jones, S., Martin, R. and Pilbeam, D. (eds.) (1992). *The Cambridge Encyclopedia of Human Evolution*. Cambridge: Cambridge University Press.

Leonowens, A. H. (1870). *The English Governess at the Siamese Court: Being Reflections of Six Years in the Royal Palace at Bangkok*. London: Trubner & Co.

Mulvihill, D. J., Tumin, M. M. and Curtis, L. A. (1969). *Crimes of Violence*, vol. 11. Pittsburgh: University of Pittsburgh Press.

Norris, K. S. and Pryor, K. (1991). *Dolphin Societies and Puzzles*. Berkeley: University of California Press.

Poole, J. H. (1994). Sex differences in the behaviour of African elephants. In *The Differences between the Sexes*, ed. R. V. Short and E. Balaban, pp. 331–46. Cambridge: Cambridge University Press.

Ridley, M. (1993). *The Red Queen: Sex and the Evolution of Human Nature*. New York: Penguin Books.

Schmacher, A. (1982). On the significance of stature in human society. *Journal of Human Evolution*, **11**, 697–701.

Schonfeld, W. A. (1943). Primary and secondary sexual characteristics. Study of their development in males from birth through maturity, with biometric study of penis and testes. *American Journal of Diseases of Childhood*, **65**, 535–49.

Short, R. V. (1979). Sexual selection and its component parts, somatic and genital selection, as illustrated by man and the great apes. *Advances in the Study of Behavior*, **9**, 131–58.

Short, R. V. (1997). The testis: the witness of the mating system, the site of mutation and the engine of desire. *Acta Paediatrica*, Supplement, **422**, 3–7.

Symons, D. (1979). *The Evolution of Human Sexuality*. Oxford: Oxford University Press.

Tripp, C. A. (1987). *The Homosexual Matrix*. New York: Meridian.

Wilson, E. O. (1978). *On Human Nature*. Cambridge, MA: Harvard University Press.

Zuckerman, S. (1932). *The Social Life of Monkeys and Apes*. London: Kegan Paul, Trench, Trubner &Co. Ltd.

3 Sex and Gender

Berghe, V. den (1980). Royal incest and inclusive fitness. *American Ethologist*, **7**, 300–17.

Boone, J. L. (1988). Parental investment, social subordination and population processes amongst 15th and 16th century Portuguese nobility. In *Human Reproductive Behaviour*. ed. L. Betzig, M. Borgerhoff Mulder and P. Turke. pp. 201–19. Cambridge: Cambridge University Press.

Clutton-Brock, T. H. (1989). Female transfer and inbreeding avoidance. *Nature*, **337**, 70–1.

Clutton-Brock, T. H., Guinness, F. E. and Albon, S. D. (1982). *Red Deer: Behavior and Ecology of Two Sexes*. Chicago: Chicago University Press.

Diamond, J. M. (1991). *The Rise and Fall of the Third Chimpanzee*. London: Random Century Group Ltd.

Fisher, R. A. (1930). *The Genetical Theory of Natural Selection*. Oxford: Clarendon Press.

Foucault, M. (1980). *Herculine Barbin. Being the Recently Discovered Memoirs of a Nineteenth Century French Hermaphrodite*. New York: Parthenon Books.

Gomendio, M., Clutton-Brock, T. H., Albon, S. D., Guinness, F. E. and Simpson, M.J. (1990). Mammalian sex ratios and variation in costs of rearing sons and daughters. *Nature*, **343**, 261–3.

Hewlett, B. S. (1988). Sexual selection and parental investment among Aka pygmies. In *Human Reproductive Behaviour: A Darwinian Perspective*, ed. L. Betzig, M. Borgerhoff Mulder and P. Turke, pp. 263-76. Cambridge: Cambridge University Press.

Hill, K. and Hurtado, A. M. (1996). *Ache Life History: The Ecology and Demography of a Foraging People*. New York: Aldine de Gruyter.

Hrdy, S. B. (1996). Raising Darwin's consciousness: female sexuality and the prehominid origins of patriarchy. *Human Nature*, **8**, 1–49.

Hughes, R. (1986). *The Fatal Shore. The Epic of Australia's Founding*. New York: Alfred A. Knopf.

Lloyd, E. (1993). Pre-theoretical assumptions in evolutionary explanations of female sexuality. *Philosophical Studies*, **69**, 201–15.

Michael, R. T. ,Gagnon, J. H., Laumann, B. O. and Kolata, G. (1994). *Sex in America: A Definitive Survey*. New York: Little Brown and Co.

Moir, A. and Jessel, D. (1989). *Brain Sex: The Real Difference between Men and Women*. London: Michael Joseph.

Reinisch, J. M., Rosenblum, L. A. and Sanders, S. A. (eds.) (1987). *Masculinity/ Femininity*. New York: Oxford University Press.

Rowse, A. L. (1977). *Homosexuals in History: A Study of Ambivalence in Society, Literature and the Arts*. London: Macmillan.

Shepher, J. (1971). Mate selection among second generation kibbutz adolescents and adults: incest avoidance and negative imprinting. *Archives of Sexual Behavior*, **1**, 293–307

Short, R. V. (1994). Why sex? In *The Differences Between the Sexes*, ed. R. V. Short and E. Balaban. pp. 3–22. Cambridge: Cambridge University Press.

Stirling, P. (1989). *So Different*. Sydney: Simon and Schuster.

Symons, D. (1979). *The Evolution of Human Sexuality*. Oxford: Oxford University Press.

Tannen, D. (1990). *You Just Don't Understand. Women and Men in Conversation*. London: Virago.

Tiger, L. and Shepher, J. (1997). *Women in the Kibbutz*. London: Penguin Books.

Voland, E. (1988). Differential infant and child mortality in evolutionary perspective: data from late 17th to 19th century Ostfriesland, Germany. In *Human Reproductive Behaviour*, ed. L. Betzig, M. Borgerhoff Mulder and P. Turke, pp. 253–61. Cambridge: Cambridge University Press.

Wellings, K., Field, J., Johnson, A. M. and Wadsworth, J. (1994). *Sexual Behaviour in Britain*. London: Penguin Books.

Wistrand, B. (1981). *Swedish Women on the Move*. Stockholm: The Swedish Institute.

Zahavi, A. (1975). Mate selection – selection for a handicap. *Journal of Theoretical Biology*, **53**, 205–14.

4 Love and Marriage

Abbie, A. A. (1976). *The Original Australians*. Adelaide: Rigby.

Alexander, R. D. and Noonan, K. M. (1979). Concealment of ovulation, parental care, and human social evolution. In *Evolutionary Biology and Human Social Behavior: An Anthropological Perspective*, ed. N. A. Chagnon and W. Irons, pp. 402–35. North Sciturate, MA: Duxbury Press.

Betzig, L. L. (1986). *Despotism and Differential Reproduction: a Darwinian View of History*. Hawthorne, N. Y.: Aldine.

Betzig, L., Mulder, M. B. and Turke, P. (eds.) (1988). *Human Reproductive Behaviour: A Darwinian Perspective*. Cambridge: Cambridge University Press.

Binford, L. (1991). *Cultural Diversity Among Aboriginals of Coastal Virginia and North Carolina*. New York: Garland.

Gilbran, K. (1997). *The Prophet*. London: Random House.

Goodale, J. C. (1971). *Tiwi Wives: A Study of the Women of Melville Island, North Australia*. Seattle: University of Washington Press.

Johnson, C. N. (1988). Dispersal and the sex ratio at birth in primates. *Science*, **332**, 276–8.

Jones, S., Martin, R. and Pilbeam, D. (eds.) (1992). *The Cambridge Encyclopedia of Human Evolution*. Cambridge: Cambridge University Press.

Leonowens, A. H. (1870). *The English Governess at the Siamese Court: Being Reflections of Six Years in the Royal Palace at Bangkok*. London: Trubner & Co.

Malinowski, B. (1929). *The Sexual Life of Savages*. London: Routledge and Kegan Paul.

Perkin, J. (1993). *Victorian Women*. London: John Murray.

Ploss, H. H.,Bartels, M. and Bartles, P. (1935). *Woman: An Historical Gynaecological and Anthropological Compendium*, ed. J. Dingwall . London: William Heinemann (Medical Books) Ltd.

Potts, M. (1988). The nature of love. In *Stress and Reproduction*, ed. K. E. Sheppard, J. H. Boublik and J. W. Funder, pp. 103–14. New York: Raven Press.

Short, R. V. (1976). The evolution of human reproduction. *Proceedings of the Royal Society of London*, Series B, **195**, 3–24.

Shostak, M. (1981). *Nisa: The Life and Words of a !Kung Woman*. Cambridge, MA: Harvard University Press.

Stone, L. (1977). *The Family, Sex and Marriage in England, 1500–1800*. London: Harper & Row.

Symons, D. (1979). *The Evolution of Human Sexuality*. Oxford: Oxford University Press.

Udry, R. and Eckland, B. K. (1984). Benefits of being attractive: differential payoffs for men and women. *Psychological Reports*, **54**, 4–56.

Wrangham, R. W. (1993). The evolution of sexuality in chimpanzees and bonobos. *Human Nature*, **4**, 47–79.

5 Sex and Pregnancy

Bachrach, C. A. and Mann, M. C. (1988). Sexual activity among U.S. women of reproductive age. *American Journal of Public Health*, **78**, 320–1.

Barnes, J. (ed.) (1984). *The Complete Works of Aristotle*, vol. 1, *Generation of Animals*. *Princeton*, NJ: Princeton University Press.

Bondeson, J. and Molenkamp, A. (1996). The Countess Margaret of Henneberg and her 365 children. *Journal of the Royal Society of Medicine*, **89**, 711–16.

Ellis, B. J. and Symons, D. (1990). Sex differences in sexual fantasy: an evolutionary psychological approach. *Journal of Sex Research*, **27**, 527–55.

Ford, N. M. (1988). *When Did I Begin?* Cambridge: Cambridge University Press.

Greene, G. (1976). *Lord Rochester's Monkey*. London: Futura Publications.

Haig, D. (1997). Genetic conflicts in human biology. *Quarterly Review of Biology*, **68**, 495–532.

Hariton, E. B. and Singer, J. L. (1974). Women's fantasies during sexual intercurse: normative and theoretical implications. *Journal of Counseling and Clinical Psychology*, **42**, 312–22.

Hertig, A. T., Rock, J. and Adams, E. C. (1956). A description of 34 human ova within the first 17 days of development. *American Journal of Anatomy*, **98**, 435–93.

Hunter, W. (1774). *The Anatomy of the Human Gravid Uterus Exhibited in Figures*. Birmingham.

Kaufman, M. H. and Jaffe, S. M. (1994). Historical review: an early caesarean operation (1800) performed by John and Charles Bell. *Journal of the Royal Society of Medicine*, **39**, 69–74.

Kinsey, A. C., Pomeroy, W. B. and Martin, C. E. (1948). *Sexual Behavior in the Human Male*. Philadelphia: W. B. Saunders and Co.

Love, B. B. (1992). *Encyclopaedia of Unusual Sexual Practices*. Fort Lee, NJ: Barricade Books.

Luker, K. (1984). *Abortion and the Politics of Motherhood*. Berkeley: University of California Press.

MacArthur, J. W. (1938). Genetics of quintuplets. 1. Diagnosis of the Dionne quintuplets as a monozygotic set. *Journal of Heredity*, **29**, 323–9.

Michael, R. T., Gagnon, J. H., Laumann, E. O. and Kolata, G. (1994). *Sex in America: A Definitive Study*. New York: Little Brown and Company.

Pereira, M. E. (1983). Abortion following the immigration of an adult male baboon (*Papio cynocephalus*). *American Journal of Primatology*, **4**, 93–8.

Rooks, J. P. (1997). *Midwifery and Childbirth in America*. Philadelphia: Temple University Press.

Singer, C. (1955). The scientific views and visions of Saint Hildegard (1098–1180). In *Studies in the History of Method of Science*, ed. C. Singer, pp. 1–55. London: William Dawson and Sons Ltd.

Steptoe, P. C. and Edwards, R. G. (1978). Birth after the reimplantation of a human embryo. *Lancet*, **ii**, 366.

Symons, D. (1979). *The Evolution of Human Sexuality*. Oxford: Oxford University Press.

Wellings, K., Field, J., Johnson, A. M. and Wadsworth, J. (1994). *Sexual Behaviour in Britain*. London: Penguin Books.

6 Birth and Breastfeeding

Armstrong, S. (1990). Labour of death. *New Scientist*, 31 March, 50–5.

Consensus Statement (1988). Breastfeeding as a family planning method. *Lancet*, **ii**, 1204–5.

Fildes, V. A. (1986). *Breasts, Bottles and Babies. A History of Infant Feeding*. Edinburgh: Edinburgh University Press.

Fildes, V. (1988). *Wet Nursing. A History from Antiquity to the Present*. Oxford: Blackwell.

Forbes, T. R. (1950). Witch's milk and witch's marks. *Yale Journal of Biology and Medicine*, **22**, 219–25.

Fortney, J. A., Susanti, I., Gadall, S., Saleh, S., Rogers, S. M. and Potts, M. (1986). Reproductive mortality in two developing countries. *American Journal of Public Health*, **76**, 134–8.

Graham, H. (1950). In *Eternal Eve*, pp. 334–43. London: Heinemann.

Howell, N. (1979). *Demography of the Dobe !Kung*. New York: Academic Press.

Hunter, J. (1861). *Essays and Observations on Natural History, Anatomy, Physiology, Psychology and Geology*, vol. 1, pp. 239–9. London: John van Voorst.

Mbaruku, G. and Bergstrom, S. (1995). Reducing maternal mortality in Kigoma, Tanzania. *Health Policy and Planning*, **10**, 71–5.

Meltzer, D. (1981). *Birth: An Anthology of Ancient Texts, Songs, Prayers and Stories*. San Francisco: North Point Press.

Ploss, H. H.,Bartels, M. and Bartles, P. (1935). *Woman: An Historical Gynaecological and Anthropological Compendium*, ed. J. Dingwall . London: William Heinemann (Medical Books) Ltd.

Short, R. V. (1992). Breastfeeding, fertility and population growth. In *Nutrition and Population Links: Breastfeeding, Family Planning and Child Health*. United Nations Subcommittee on

Nutrition Discussion Paper 11, pp. 33–46. Geneva: World Health Organization.
Short, R. V. (1994). What the breast does for the baby, and what the baby does for the breast. *Australian and New Zealand Journal of Obstetrics and Gynaecology*, **34**, 262–4.
Stewart, D. B. (1984). The pelvis as a passageway. Evolution and adaptations. *British Journal of Obstetrics and Gynaecology*, 91, 611–17.
Stewart, K. J. (1988). Suckling and lactational anoestrus in wild gorillas (*Gorilla gorilla*). *Journal of Reproduction and Fertility*, 83, 627–34.
Thapa, S., Short, R. V. and Potts, M. (1988). Breast feeding, birth spacing and child survival. *Nature*, 335, 679–82.
Verkuyl, D. A. A. (1988). Oral conception. Impregnation via the proximal gastrointestinal tract in a patient with an aplastic vagina. Case report. *British Journal of Obstetrics and Gynaecology*, **95**, 933–4.
Warner, M. (1976). *Alone of All her Sex. The Myth and Cult of the Virgin Mary*. London: Weidenfeld and Nicholson.
Wollstonecraft, M. (1792). *Vindication of the Rights of Woman*. Reprinted in Penguin Classics 1985. London: Penguin.
Wood, J. W. (1994). *The Dynamics of Human Reproduction: Biology, Biometry, Demography*. New York: Aldine de Gruyter.
Yalom, M. (1997). *A History of the Breast*. New York: Alfred Knopf.

7 Growing Up

Barker, D. J. P. (1994). *Mothers, Babies and Disease in Later Life*. London: British Medical Journal publishing group.
Burgos, P. E. and McCarthy, L. M. (1984). Ayoreo infanticide: a case study. In *Infanticide: Comparative and Evolutionary Perspectives*, ed. G. Hausfater and S. B. Hrdy, pp. 520–30. New York: Aldine de Gruyter.
Campbell, K. L. and Wood, J. W. (eds.) (1994). *Human Reproductive Ecology*. Annals of the New York Academy of Science, **709**.
Daly, M. and Wilson, M. (1988). *Homicide*. New York: Aldine de Gruyter.
Daw, S. F. (1970). Age of puberty in Leipzig, 1727–49, as indicated by voice breaking in J. S. Bach's choir members. *Human Biology*, **42**, 87–9.
de Waal, F. and Johanowicz, D. L. (1993). Modification of reconciliation behavior through social experience: an experiment with macaque species. *Child Development*, **64**, 897–908.
Flinn, M. (1988). Parent-offspring interactions in a Caribbean village: daughter guarding. In *Human Reproductive Behaviour: A Darwinian Perspective*, ed. L. Betzig, M. Borgerhoff Mulder and P. Turke, pp. 189–201. Cambridge: Cambridge University Press.
Frisch, R. E., Wyshak, G. and Vincent, L. (1980). Delayed menarche and amenorrhea in ballet dancers. *New England Journal of Medicine*, **303**, 17–19.
Garner, D. M., Garfinkel, P. E., Schwartz, D. and Tompson, M. (1980). Cultural expectations of thinness in women. *Psychological Reports*, **47**, 483–91.
Goodall, J. (1986). *The Chimpanzees of Gombe: Patterns of Behavior*. Cambridge, MA: Belknap Press.
Halpern, C. T., Udry, J. R., Campbell, B., Suchindran, C. and Mason, G. A. (1994). Testosterone and religiosity as predictors of sexual attitudes and activity in adolescent males. A biosocial model. *Journal of Biosocial Science*, **26**, 217–34.
Harlow, H. F. (1962). The heterosexual affectional system in monkeys. *American Psychologist*, **17**, 1–9.
Harlow, H. F., Harlow, D. K., Dodsworth, R. O. and Arling, G. L. (1966). Maternal behavior of rhesus monkeys deprived of mothering and peer associations in infancy. *Proceedings of the American Philosophical Society*, **110**, 58–66.
Humphries, S. (1988). *The Secret World of Sex: The British Experience 1900–1950*. London: Sidgewick and Jackson.
Kirkland, G. (1986). *Dancing on My Grave: An Autobiography by Gelsey Kirkland with Greg Laurence*. Garden City, NY: Doubleday.
Kubicka, L., Matejcek, Z., David, H. P., Dytrych, Z., Miller, W. B. and Roth, J. (1995). Children from unwanted pregnancies in Prague, Czeck Republic, revisited at age 30. *Acta Psychiatrica Scandinavica*, **91**, 361–9.

Kukl, P. K., Andruski, J. E., Christovich, I. A., Christovich, L. A., Kozhevinkova, E. V., Ryskina, V. L., Stolyasova, E. I., Sundberg, U. and Lacerda, F. (1997). Cross-language analysis of phonetic units in language addressed infants. *Science*, 277, 684–6.

Macintyre, S. (1992). The effects of family position on status and health. *Social Science and Medicine*, 35, 453–64.

Maclean, C. (1977). *The Wolf Children*. London: Allen Lane.

Malcolm, L. A. (1970). *Growth and Development in New Guinea – A Study of the Bundi People of the Madang District*. Monograph Series No. 1, Institute of Human Biology, Madang. Chipping Norton, NSW: Surrey Beatty & Sons.

Pinker, S. (1994). *The Language Instinct*. New York: W. Morrow and Co.

Resnick, M. O., Bearman, P. S., Blum, R. W., Bauman, K. E., Hawrris, K. M., Jones, J., Tabor, J., Beurking, T., Sieving, R. E., Shaw, M., Ireland, M., Earing, L. H. and Udry, J. R. (1997). Protecting adolescents from harm: findings from the National Study of Adolescent Health. *New England Journal of Medicine*, 278, 823-32.

Richardson, D. W. and Short, R. V. (1978). The time of onset of sperm production in boys. *Journal of Biosocial Science*, Supplement 5, 15–25.

Salk, L., Lippsitt, L. P., Sturner, W. O., Reilly, B. M. and Levat, R. H. (1985). Relationship of maternal and perinatal conditions to eventual suicide. *The Lancet*, i, 624–7.

Schwartz, G. and Rosenblum, L. A. (1982). Primate infancy problems and developmental strategies. In *Handbooks of Developmental Psychology*, ed. B. B. Wolman, G. Stricker, S. J. Ellman, P. Keith-Spiegel and D. S. Palermo, pp. 63–75. Upper Saddle River, NJ: Prentice Hall.

Shade, A. R. (1983). Gynecologic and obstetric problems in the female dancer. *Clinics in Sports Medicine*, 2, 515–23.

Shostak, M. (1981). *Nisa: The Life and Words of a !Kung Woman*. Cambridge, MA.: Harvard University Press.

Snow, C. E. and Ferguson, C. A. (eds.) (1977). *Talking to Children: Language Input and Acquisition*. Cambridge: Cambridge University Press.

Suomi, S. J. (1986). Behavioural aspects of successful reproduction in primates. In *Primates: The Road to Self-sustaining Populations*, ed. K. Benirschke, pp. 331–40. New York: Springer-Verlag.

Trivers, R. L. (1994). Parent–offspring conflict. *American Zoologist*, 14, 249–64.

8 The Civilization of Sex

Blake, J. A. (1978). Death by hand grenade: altruistic suicide in combat. *Suicide and Life-Threatening Behaviour*, 8, 46–59.

Brain, C. K. and Sillen, A. (1988). Evidence from the Swartkrans cave for the earliest use of fire. *Nature*, 336, 464–6.

Chagnon, N. A. (1983). *Yanomamo: The Fierce People*. New York: Holt, Rinehart and Wilson.

Chagnon, N. A. and Burgos, P. (1979). Kin selection and conflict: an analysis of a Yanomamo axe fight. In *Evolutionary Biology and Human Social Behavior: An Anthropological Perspective*, ed. N. A. Chagnon and W. Irons, pp. 213–37. North Sciturate: Duxbury Press.

Charlton, B. G. (1997). The inequality of inequality. Egalitarian instincts and evolutionary psychology. *Journal of Health Psychology*, 2, 413–25.

de Waal, F. (1996). *Good Natured: The Origins of Right and Wrong in Humans and Other Animals*. Cambridge, MA: Harvard University Press.

Diamond, J. (1997). *Guns, Germs and Steel: The Fates of Human Societies*. London: Random House.

Dunbar, R. I. M. (1991). Functional significance of social grooming in primates. *Folia Primatologica*, 57, 121-31.

Dunbar, R. I. M. (1996). *Gossip, Grooming and the Evolution of Language*. Cambridge, MA: Harvard University Press.

Dye, T. and Steadman, D. W. (1990). Polynesian ancestors and their animal world. *American Scientist*, 78, 207–15.

Eaton, S. B. and Konner, M. (1985). Paleolithic nutrition. *New England Journal of Medicine*, 312, 283–9.

Flannery, T. F. (1994). *The Future Eaters: An Ecological History of the Australian Lands and People*. Sydney: Reed Books.

Hachiya, M. (1946). *Hiroshima Diary: The Journal of a Japanese Physician August 6 – September 30, 1945*. Chapel Hill, NC: University of North Carolina Press.

Hersey, J. (1946). *Hiroshima*. New York: Alfred A. Knopf.

Holper, J. J., (1996). Kin term usage in *The Federalist*: Evolutionary foundations of public rhetoric. *Politics and the Life Sciences*, **15**, 265–72.

Manson, J. H. and Wrangham, R. D. (1991). Intergroup aggression in chimpanzees and humans. *Current Anthropology*, **32**, 369–90.

Martin, P. S. (1973). The discovery of America: the first Americans may have swept the Western Hemisphere and decimated its fauna in 1000 years. *Science*, **179**, 969–74.

O'Connell, R. L. (1995). *The Ride of the Second Horseman: The Birth and Death of a War*. Oxford: Oxford University Press.

Read, K. E. (1966). *The High Valley*. New York: Charles Scribner's Sons.

Sherry, M. S. (1987). *The Rise of American Airpower: The Creation of Armageddon*. Princeton, NJ: Yale University Press.

Stewart, K. M. (1947). Mohave warfare. Reprinted in *The Californian Indians: A Source Book*, ed. R. F. Heizer and M. A. Whipple, 1962, pp. 369–82. Berkeley: University of California Press.

Terraine, J. (1985). *Right of the Line: the Royal Air Force in the European War 1939–45*. London: Hodder and Stoughton.

van der Post, L. and Taylor, J. (1984). *Testament to the Bushmen*. New York: Viking Penguin.

Whiten, A. and Byrne, R. W. (1988). *Machiavellian Intelligence: Social Expertise and the Evolution of Intellect in Monkeys, Apes and Humans*. Oxford: Clarendon.

Wrangham, R.W. (1993). The evolution of sexuality in chimpanzees and bonobos. *Human Nature*, **4**, 47–79.

Wrangham, R. and Peterson, D. (1996). *Demonic Males: Apes and the Origins of Human Violence*. Boston, MA: Houghton Mifflin.

9 Sex and Power

Ariès, P. and Béjin, A. (1985). *Western Sexuality: Practice and Precept in Past and Present Times*. Oxford: Blackwell.

Barker-Benfield, G. J. (1976). *The Horrors of the Half-Known Life: Male Attitudes Toward Women and Sexuality in Nineteenth-Century America*. New York: Harper and Row.

Brodie, F. (1986). *The Devil Drives. A Life of Sir Richard Burton*. London: Eland.

Daly, M. and Wilson, M. (1988). *Homicide*. New York: Aldine de Gruyter.

Flandrin, J. -L. (1979). *Families in Former Times: Kinship, Household and Sexuality*. Cambridge: Cambridge University Press.

Fleming, J. B. (1960). Clitoridectomy – the disastrous downfall of Isaac Baker Brown FRCS (1867). *Journal of Obstetrics and Gynaecology of the British Empire*, **67**, 1017–34.

Goodall, J. (1986). *The Chimpanzees of Gombe: Patterns of Behavior*. Cambridge, MA: Belknap Press.

Graham, H. (1950). *Eternal Eve*. London: Heinemann.

Gulik, R. H. (1974). *Sexual Life in Ancient China: A Preliminary Survey of Chinese Sex and Society from ca. 1500 B.C. till 1644 A.D.* Leiden: Brill.

Harris, S. (1950). *Woman's Surgeon: The Life Story of J. Marion Sims*. New York: Macmillan.

Hrdy, S. B. (1997). Raising Darwin's consciousness. Female sexuality and the prehominid origins of patriarchy. *Human Nature*, **8**, 1–49.

Hyam, R. (1990). *Empire and Sexuality: The British Experience*. Manchester: Manchester University Press.

Jocano, F. L. (1975). *Slum as a Way of Life. A Study of Coping Behavior in an Urban Environment*. Quezon City: University of the Phillippines Press.

McLaren, A. (1984). *Reproductive Rituals: The Perception of Fertility in England from the Sixteenth Century to the Nineteenth Century*. London: Methuen.

Mitchison, R. and Leneman, L. (1989). *Sexuality and Social Control: Scotland, 1660–1780*. Oxford: Blackwell.

Pearsall, R. (1969). *The Worm in the Bud: The World of Victorian Sexuality.* London: Weidenfeld and Nicholson.

Ploss, H. H.,Bartels, M. and Bartles, P. (1935). *Woman: An Historical Gynaecological and Anthropological Compendium*, ed. J. Dingwall . London: William Heinemann (Medical Books) Ltd.

Quaife, G. R. (1979). *Wanton Wenches and Wayward Wives: Peasants and Illicit Sex in Early Seventeenth Century England.* London: Croom Helm.

Stone, L. (1977). *The Family, Sex and Marriage in England, 1500–1800*. London: Weidenfeld and Nicholson.

Wagenseil, F. (1933). Chinesische Eunuchen. *Zeitschrift für Morphologie und Anthropologie*, 32.

Wollstonecraft, M. (1792). *Vindication of the Rights of Woman*. Reprinted in Penguin Classics 1985. London: Penguin.

10 Dying for Love

Brandt, A. M. (1985). *No Magic Bullet: A Social History of Venereal Disease in the United States since 1880*. New York: Oxford University Press.

Crosby, A. (1969). The early history of syphilis. *American Anthropologist*, 71, 218–27.

Davenport-Hines, R. (1990). *Sex, Death and Punishment: Attitudes to Sex and Sexuality in Britain since the Renaissance*. London: Collins.

Hamilton, W. D. and Zuk, M. (1982). Heritable true fitness and bright birds: a role for parasites. *Science*, **218**, 384–7.

Hayflick, L. and Moorehead, P. S. (1961). The serial cultivation of human diploid cell strains. *Experimental Cell Research*, **25**, 585–621.

Hines, N. E. (1963). *Medical History of Contraception.* New York: Gamut.

Kaprio, J., Koskenvuo, M. and Rita, H. (1987). Mortality and bereavement: a prospective study of 95 647 bereaved persons. *American Journal of Public Health*, 77, 283–7.

Kassler, W. J., Wasserheit, J. N. and Cates, W. (1995). Sexually transmitted diseases. In *Health Promotion and Disease Prevention in Clinical Practice*, pp. 273–90. Baltimore: Williams and Wilkins.

Letter from Mr Macky, Professor of History, to Mr MacLaurin, Professor of Mathematics in the University of Edinburgh, and by him communicated to the President of the Royal Society, being an extract from the books of the Town Council of Edinburgh, relating to a disease these, supposed to be venereal, in the year 1497. *Philosophical Transactions of the Royal Society*, 1743, **42**, 420–1.

Mann, J. (general ed.) (1992). AIDS *in the World, the Global* AIDS *Policy Coalition*. London: Harvard University Press.

Mann, J. M. and Tarantola, D. J. M. (1998). HIV 1998: the global picture. *Scientific American*, July 1998, 62–3.

Marsh, H. and Kasua T. (1991). An overview of the changes in the role of the female pilot whale with age. In *Dolphin Societies: Discoveries and Puzzles*, ed. K. Pryor and K. S. Norris. Berkeley: University of California Press.

McNeill, W. H. (1976). *Plagues and Peoples*. New York: Doubleday.

Shilts, R. (1987). *And the Band Played On: Politics, People and the* AIDS *Epidemic*. New York: St Martin's Press.

11 Sex and Mortality

Allman, M. M., McLaughlin, T. and Hakeen, A. (1993). Brain weight and life-span in primate species. *Proceedings of the National Academy of Sciences*, **90**, 118–22.

Barnes, J. (ed.) (1984). *The Complete works of Aristotle. History of Animals*, Book IX. Princeton, NJ: Princeton University Press.

Bernstein, H., Byerly, H. C., Hopf, F. A. and Michod, R. E. (1985). Genetic damage, mutation, and the evolution of sex. *Science*, **229**, 1277–81.

Braithwaite, P. A. and Shugg, D. (1983). Rembrandt's Bathsheba: The Dark Shadow of the Left Breast. *Annals of the Royal College of Surgeons of England*, **65**, 337–8.

Burger, H. G. (1999). Endocrinology of the menopause and hormone replacement therapy. In *The Oxford Textbook of Endocrinology,* eds. J. P. Walsh, H. Teede and H. G. Burger. Oxford: Oxford University Press. (In press).

Buschsbaum, H. J. (1984). *The Menopause.* New York: Springer Verlag.

Call, P. (1979). *Vasily L. Kelsiev: An Encounter between the Russian Revolutionaries and the Old Believers.* Belmont, MA: Nordland.

Darwin, C. (1871). *The Descent of Man and Selection in Relation to Sex.* London: John Murray.

Dawson, J. (1986). Easeful death. *British Medical Journal,* **293**, 1187–8.

de Moulin, D. (1983). *A Short History of Breast Cancer.* The Hague: Martinus Nijhoff.

Eaton, S. B., Pike, M. C., Short, R. V., Lee, N. C., Trussell, J., Hatcher, R. A., Wood, J. W., Worthman, C. M., Blurton-Jones, N., Konner, M. J., Hill, K. and Bailey, R. (1994). Women's reproductive cancers in evolutionary context. *Quarterly Review of Biology,* **69**, 353–67.

Greer, G. (1991). *The Change: Women, Ageing and the Menopause.* London: Hamish Hamilton.

Hamilton, J. B. and Mestler, G. E. (1969). Mortality and survival: comparison of eunuchs with intact men and women in a mentally retarded population. *Journal of Gerontology,* **24**, 395–411.

Hemlow, J. (1975). *The Journals and Letters of Fanny Burney (Madame D'Arblay).* Oxford: Clarendon Press.

Hunter, K. (1964). *Duet for a Lifetime: The Story of the Original Siamese Twins, Chang and Eng Bunker.* London: Michael Joseph.

Jewell, P. A. (1997). Survival and behaviour of castrated Soay sheep (*Ovis aries*) in a feral island population on Hirta, St. Kilda, Scotland. *Journal of Zoology,* **243**, 623–36.

Ladurie, E. L. (1980). *Montaillou: Cathars and Catholics.* London: Penguin.

Lee, A. K. and Cockburn, A. (1985). *Evolutionary Ecology of Marsupials.* Cambridge: Cambridge University Press.

Melico, M. M. (1983). Castrati singers and the lost "cords". *Bulletin of the New York Academy of Medicine,* **59**, 744–64.

McAvoy, B. R. (1986). Death after bereavement. *British Medical Journal,* **293**, 835–6.

Peschel, E. R. and Peschel, R. E. (1987). Medical insights into the castrati in opera. *American Scientist,* **75**, 578–83.

Potts, M. (1994). Grief has to be. *Lancet,* **343**, 279.

Renfree, M. B. (1992), Diapausing dilemmas, sexual stress and mating madness in marsupials. In *Stress and Reproduction,* eds. K. E. Sheppard, J. H. Baublik and J. W. Funder, Serono Symposium **86**, pp. 347–60. New York: Raven Press.

Scitovsky, A. A. (1984). The high cost of dying. What do the data show? *Health and Society,* **62**, 591–607.

van der Maas, P. J., van Delden, J. J. M., Pijnenborg, L. and Looman, C. W. N. (1991). Euthanasia and other medical decisions concerning the end of life. *Lancet,* **338**, 669–70.

Wakayama, T., Perry, A. C. F., Zuccotti, M., Johnson, K. R. and Yanagimachi, R. (1998). Full-term development of mice from enucleated oocytes injected with cumulus cell nuclei. *Nature,* **394**, 369–74.

Wallace, D. C. (1997). Mitochondrial DNA in aging and disease. *Scientific American,* **277**, 40–59.

World Health Organization (1996). *Research on the Menopause in the 1990s.* WHO Technical Report **866**. Geneva: WHO.

Wilmut, I., Schnieke, A. E., McWhir, J., Kind, A. J. and Campbell, K. H. S. (1997). Viable offspring derived from fetal and adult mammalian cells. *Nature,* **385**, 810–13.

12 Too Many People

Asbell, B. (1995). *The Pill: A Biography of the Drug that Changed the World.* New York: Random House.

Baird, D. (1965). A fifth freedom? *British Medical Journal,* **ii**, 1141–8.

Bernstein, C. and Politi, M. (1996). *His Holiness: John Paul II and the Hidden History of our Time.* New York: Doubleday.

Besant, A. (1878) *The Law of Population: Its Consequences and its Bearing upon Human Conduct and Morals.* London: Freethought Publishing Company.

Brown, H. and Leech, M. (1927). *Anthony Constock: Roundsman of the Lord.* New York: Albert and Charles Boni.

Brown, S. S. and Eisenberg, L. (1995). *The Best Intentions.* Washington, DC: National Academy Press.

Campbell, C. and Laherrère (1998). The end of cheap oil. *Scientific American,* **278**, 78–83.

Djerassi, C. (1979). *The Politics of Contraception.* New York: W. W. Norton.

Donaldson, P. J. (1990). *Nature Against US: the United States and the World Population Crisis, 1965–1980.* Chapel Hill: University of North Carolina Press.

Graham-Smith, F. (ed.) (1994). *Population: The Complex Reality.* London: The Royal Society.

Hardin, G. (1993). *Living within Limits: Ecology, Economics and Population Taboos.* New York: Oxford University Press.

Himes, N. E. (1936). *Medical History of Contraception.* Reprinted 1963. New York: Gamut Press.

Howell, N. (1979). *Demography of the Dobe !Kung.* New York: Academic Press.

Kaiser, R.B. (1985). *The Encyclical that Never Was: The Story of the Commission on Population, Family and Birth, 1964–66.* London: Sheed and Ward.

Knowlton, C. (1876). *Fruits of Philosophy; or, The Private Companion of Young Married People.* London: Freethought Publishing Company.

Kulczycki, A., Potts, M. and Rosenfield, A. (1996). Abortion and fertility regulation. *Lancet,* **347**, 1663–8.

Lassonde, L. (1997). *Coping with the Population Challenges.* London: Earthscan Publications.

Malthus, T. R. (1798). *An Essay on the Principle of Population.* Reprinted in Penguin Books, 1982. London: Penguin.

Moffett, G. D. (1994). *Critical Masses: The Global Population Challenge.* New York: Penguin Books.

Myers, N. (1994). Collision course. *Science and Public Affairs,* Spring, pp. 1–4.

Myers, N. (1995). Environmental unknowns. *Science,* **269**, 358–61.

Noonan, J. (1965). *Contraception: A History of its Treatment by the Catholic Theologies and Canonists.* Cambridge, MA: Harvard University Press.

Place, F. (1822). *Illustrations and Proofs of the Principle of Population, Including an Examination of the Proposed Remedies of Mr Malthus, and a Reply to Mr Godwin and Others.* London.

Pope Paul VI. (1968). *Humanae Vitae: Encyclical Letter on the Right Ordering of the Procreation of Children.* London: Catholic Truth Society.

Poole, J. (1993). *The Harm We Do: A Catholic Doctor Confronts Church, Moral and Medical Teaching.* Mystic, CT: Twenty-Third Publications.

Potts, M. (1997). Sex and the birth rate. *Population and Development Review,* **23**, 1–39.

Quaife, G. R. (1979). *Wanton Wenches and Wayward Wives: Peasants and Illicit Sex in Early Seventeenth Century England.* London: Croom Helm.

Reagan, L. J. (1997). *When Abortion was a Crime: Women, Medicine and the Law in the United States, 1867–1973.* Berkeley: University of California Press.

Riddle, J.M. (1997). *Eve's Herbs: A History of Contraception and Abortion in the West.* Cambridge, MA: Harvard University Press.

Rock, J. (1968). *The Time has Come: A Catholic Doctor's Proposals to End the Battle over Birth Control.* New York: Longmans.

Sanger, M. (1931). *My Fight for Birth Control.* New York: Farrar and Rinehart.

Shelton, J. R., Jacobstein, R. and Angle, M. (1992). Medical barriers to access to family planning. *Lancet,* **340**, 1334–5.

Sheps, M. C. (1965). An analysis of reprodutive patterns in an American isolate. *Population Studies,* **21**, 65–80.

Short, R. V. (1976). The evolution of human reproduction. *Proceedings of the Royal Society of London,* Series B, **195**, 3–24.

Stewart, K. J., Harcourt, A. H. and Watts, D. P. (1988). Determinants of fertility in wild gorillas and other primates. In *Natural Human Fertility: Social and Biological Determinants*, ed. P. Diggory, M. Potts and S. Tepper, pp. 22–36. London: Macmillan.

Stopes, M. C. (1923). *Contraception (Birth Control): Its Theory, History and Practice. A Manual for the Medical and Legal Professions*. London: John Bale, Sons, and Danielsson.

Wrigley, E. A. (1969). *Population and History*. London: Weidenfeld and Nicholson.

13 The Animal Within Us

Augustine, St (1961). Confessions of a sinner. In *The Conquest of New Spain*, ed. R. S. Pine-Coffin, p. 38. London: Penguin.

Barklow, J. H., Cosmides, L. and Tooby, J. (eds.) (1992). *The Adapted Mind*. New York: Oxford University Press.

Boswell, J. (1988). *The Kindness of Strangers: The Abandonment of Children in Western Europe from Late Antiquity to the Renaissance*. New York: Parthenon.

Charlton, B. G. (1996). What is the ultimate cause of socio-economic inequalities in health? An explanation in terms of evolutionary psychology. *Journal of the Royal Society of Medicine*, **89**, 3–18.

Crawford, M. and Marsh, D. (1989). *Nutrition and Evolution*. New Canaan, CT: Keats Publishing.

de Waal, F. (1989). *Peacemaking among Primates*. Cambridge, MA: Harvard University Press.

Diamond, J. (1997). *Guns, Germs and Steel: The Fates of Human Societies*. London: Jonathan Cape.

Dunbar, R. I. M. (1991). Coevolution of neocortex size, group size and language in humans. *Behavioural and Brain Sciences*, **16**, 681–735.

Erdal, D. and Whiten, A. (1995). On human egalitarianism: an evolutionary product of machiavellian status escalation. *Current Anthropology* **35**, 287–93.

Eve, R. A. and Dunn, D. (1990). Evidence of pseudoscientific beliefs among high school biology and life science teachers. *The American Biology Teacher*, **52**, 10–21.

Hamilton, W. D. (1964). The genetical evolution of social behavior. *Journal of Theoretical Biology*, **31**, 1–52.

Hamilton, W. D. (1972). Altruism and related phenomena in social insects. *Annual Review of Ecological Systematics*, **3**, 193–232.

Idani, G. (1991). Cases of inter-group encounters in pygmy chimpanzees at Wamba, Zaire. In *Primatology Today: Proceedings of the XII Congress of the International Primatology Society*, ed. A. Ehara, pp. 235–8. Amsterdam: Elsevier.

Jolly, A. (1985). *The Evolution of Primate Behavior*. New York: Macmillan.

Kano, T. (1992). *The Last Ape. Pigmy Chimpanzee Behavior and Ecology*. Stanford: Stanford University Press.

Miller, G. (1996). Sexual selection in human evolution: review and prospects. In *Evolution and Human Behavior: Ideas, Issues and Applications*, ed. C. Crawford and D. Krebs, New York: Lawrence Erlbaum.

Owens, I. P. F. and Short R. V. (1995). Hormonal basis of sexual dimorphism in birds: implications for new theories of sexual selection. *Trends in Ecology and Evolution*, **10**, 44–7.

Pope Paul VI (1968). *Humanae Vitae: Encyclical Letter on the Right Ordering of the Procreation of Children*. London: Catholic Truth Society.

Pusey, A., Williams, J. and Goodall, J. (1997). The influence of dominance rank on the reproductive success of female chimpanzees. *Science*, **277**, 828–31.

Smith, J. M. and Parker, G. A. (1976). The logic of asymmetric contests. *Animal Behaviour*, **24**, 159–75.

Symons, D. (1979). *The Evolution of Human Sexuality*. Oxford: Oxford University Press.

Wills, C. (1993). *The Runaway Brain: The evolution of human uniqueness*. London: Harper Collins.

Wrangham, R. and Peterson, D. (1996). *Demonic Males: Apes and the Origins of Human Violence*. London: Bloomsbury.

Zahavi, A. (1975). Mate selection – selection for a handicap. *Journal of Theoretical Biology*, **53**, 205–14.

INDEX

Page numbers in *italics* refer to illustrations or their captions